Gender and German Cinema

Gender and German Cinema

Feminist Interventions

VOLUME II:
GERMAN FILM HISTORY/GERMAN HISTORY ON FILM

edited by

Sandra Frieden

Richard W. McCormick

Vibeke R. Petersen

Laurie Melissa Vogelsang

BERG

Providence / Oxford

Published in 1993 by
Berg Publishers, Inc.
Editorial offices:
221 Waterman Street, Providence, RI 02906, U.S.A.
150 Cowley Road, Oxford OX4 1JJ, UK

A CIP catalogue record for this book is available from the British Library.

Library of Congress Cataloging-in-Publication Data

Gender and German cinema : feminist interventions / edited by Sandra Frieden ... [et al.].
p. cm.
Filmography: v. 1, p. ; v. 2, p.
Includes bibliographical references and indexes.
Contents: v. 1. Gender and representation in new German cinema — v. 2. German film history/German history on film.
ISBN 0–85496–947–0 (cloth; v. 1) — ISBN 0–85496–243–3 (pbk.; v. 1). — ISBN 0–85496–323–5 (cloth; v. 2). — ISBN 0–85496–324–3 (pbk.; v. 2)
1. Motion pictures—Germany—History. 2. Women in motion pictures. 3. Feminism and motion pictures—Germany.
I. Frieden, Sandra G.
PN1993.5,G3G357 1993
791.43'652042—dc20 92–25618
CIP

Cover photo: Ossi Oswalda as Ossi and Hermann Thimig as Lancelot in Ernst Lubitsch's *The Doll* (1920). Photo courtesy of Museum of Modern Art/Film Stills Archive.

Printed in the United States by Edwards Brothers, Ann Arbor, MI.

Contents

Contents of Volume I: Gender and Representation in New German Cinema

Acknowledgments

The editors would like to thank Helke Sander, Valie Export, Gabriele Weinberger, Renate Möhrmann, and Joyce Rheuban for their kind help in providing and/or obtaining photos for this volume. For computer help, we thank Bill Barthelmy, Karen Storz, and Leo Duroche. Angelika Rauch and Peter Mühle also provided much help in their functions as Research Assistants at the University of Minnesota, as did Thomas Stratmann and Tanya Reifenrath at the University of Houston. For moral support "when the details got too petty," we thank Karl Schaefer and Joan Clarkson; and for their tolerance, Blake, Cary and Kelly Frieden. Isa and Susana McCormick provided playful distraction. Robert Riddell, John Lowney, Ellen Maly, and Marion Berghahn at Berg Publishers were wonderfully supportive editors. The organization Women in German gave us the momentum to follow through on our original idea (and introduced us to each other), and we thank everyone who encouraged us.

We dedicate these volumes to the memory of Sydna (Bunny) Weiss and Sigrid Brauner, both of whom shared our joy in this project.

Foreword

Gender . . .

> "Until we understand the assumptions in which we are drenched we cannot know ourselves."
>
> — Adrienne Rich, *On Lies, Secrets and Silence* (New York: W.W. Norton, 1979), 35.

Our experience of the world, we understand Rich to say, coheres as an immersion and a surfacing. Our assumptions lie about us – some buoyant, others held in suspension, still others massive and unwieldy, submerged in the silence that Rich would have us interrupt. Nothing is superfluous here, nothing innocent. The assumptions in which we are drenched are not just idle conjectures, suggestive speculations, working hypotheses. Nor are they the ideas, objects, and people we only take for granted. In a more secret and profound way, these assumptions work to appropriate, to seize, to dispossess us of our own presence. Saturated with the collective dogmas of our histories, we see ourselves and the world only through the murky perspective of how-things-have-always-been-and-are-supposed-to-be; contradictions are lost in the undertow. Surfacing, then, to follow this metaphor, means getting (at least) our heads above water. We need to see the contradictions of our own experience: they validate our uniqueness even as they intensify our fear of drowning. Indeed, the point is not to get out of the water, but to learn to swim.

Our experience of the world, then, is cast in contradictions. Once we surface, we begin to refract our assumptions through the filter of our own experience (instead of the other way around), seeking a reconciliation and a coherence that do not obliterate contradictions, but rather illuminate them from many sides. The particular interest of these two volumes is to refract the history of German cinema, with all its contradictions, through the specific category "gender."

Why "gender"? Gender shapes our experience of the world – not exclusively, but profoundly, not uniformly, but persistently. With our birth into a gendered society, our perceptions of self and of others are defined within contexts of "masculine" and "feminine." While the socialization process assures that we all learn the meanings of strength and sensitivity, of dominance and dependency, of coercion and nurturance, this same process contorts us to impossible posturings of gender-appropriate behaviors. Human energy is thus harnessed in the service of gendered proprieties, from voice inflection to choice of profession. Gendered ways of being and gendered ways of seeing are imprinted to a depth we have only begun to explore.

Feminism, as both philosophy and politics, informs and reforms by exposing the contradictions and the consequences of gendered socialization. As a philosophy, feminism understands that societies ascribe to women *and* men supposedly "natural" characteristics – characteristics, in fact, to which societies subject their members from birth. It does not quite go without saying that most societies, at great cost to both women and men, assign inequitable importance and power to men, based on such characteristics. As a politics, feminism gives voice to the contradictions, works to question and change the value systems that perpetuate and cherish those traits understood as "masculine" over those understood as "feminine." Feminism, then, is quite meaningfully a *body* of thought aimed at change.

The products and the processes of cinematic production provide an illustrated study of gendered socialization. Feminists (among others, to be sure) see in film analysis the opportunity for a graphic accounting of existing social structures: not merely in historical representations of values and experience, but as the workings of contradictions and associations revealed in content, internal structure, and layers of social relations. Film, predominantly representational, provides illustrated social self-perceptions – social narratives of development cast to the judgments taught by culture. We can study cinematic reception as a cultural artifact: how a contextualized image elicits desired responses based on shared historical and cinematic-communicative experiences. Insofar as cinema depends on substantial financial resources, we may study the "rules" of its production and distribution in a given society – why some films (and some filmmakers) are highly visible, while others are in effect suppressed. Insofar as cinema is national and historical, we can study its function within a given society to (re-)produce or question the values and archetypes, the idols and idylls of the producing culture. Indeed, such studies of cinema's functioning within society have brought feminist cine-analysts to question the very forms and modes of cinematic communication, and in particular to investigate those cinematic issues which relate to cultural self-understanding and to feminism's project of change: what can cinema teach us about ourselves and about the processes, assumptions, contradictions, and limits of our socialization? How does cinema function within the experience of the individual and within society to perpetuate the status quo or to question it? Can film and the study of it be agents of social change?

Feminism(s)

Our mention of feminism is not coincidental. The category of "gender" is used here neither to disguise, nor to efface a feminist agenda. It is our goal in the two volumes of *Gender and German Cinema* to "intervene" in German film criticism by presenting a number of feminist discussions of German films – just as German feminist filmmakers have attempted to intervene in the course of German film history since the 1960s. This project arose from our frustration with publications that for the most part ignored films by women directors and feminist approaches to German film. At this point, Patrice Petro's excellent *Joyless Streets: Women and Melodramatic Representation in Weimar Germany*[1] is just about the only book-length analysis of German cinema that is explicity feminist. Our volume includes discussions of German films from a number of historical periods, and it presents a variety of ways that feminism deals with German films. Feminist film criticism, like feminism in general, is by no means monolithic; a number of theoretical approaches have been developed and applied in examining issues of gender. Some of the essays in these two volumes analyze cinematic technique, production, distribution, and reception; some debate the politics of representation – of women, of female sexuality, and of history in general. There are psychoanalytically based investiga-

1. Patrice Petro, *Joyless Streets: Women and Melodramatic Representation in Weimar Germany* (Princeton: Princeton Univ. Press, 1989). As we go to press, we are also happy to see another such publication: *Women and New German Cinema* by Julia Knight (London: Verso, 1992).

tions of visual pleasure in the cinema, there are sociohistorical studies, and essays which draw on both approaches (as well as others). German films from a number of periods in the long history of German film production are discussed: from *The Doll* (1919) to the 1980s, from films made in the Weimar Republic and the Third Reich to films of both post-war German states. Films by both female and male directors are examined.

There is admittedly a strong emphasis here on films by women and on the representation of women in films by directors of either sex. If we are examining the ideological construction of gender in film and society, why the almost exclusive focus on the construction of the "feminine" gender? Our reasons are primarily pragmatic: once again, work by feminist filmmakers and feminist critics concerned with the cinematic representation of women has for too long been ignored, especially with regard to German cinema. In addition, it is precisely such feminist work that initiated the broader project of investigating the dynamics of gender in the culture at large. "Men's studies," for instance, is obviously modeled after women's studies, and the more serious (and honest) adherents of such studies acknowledge the debt to feminism. The construction of masculinity is certainly related to the construction of feminity; indeed, they support the same dominant ideology. We welcome more work unmasking the social and psychic construction of the myths of masculinity. Nonetheless, as oppressive as such myths may often be – to men as well as women – one should not forget the obvious asymmetry in power relations between the two genders. Patriarchal societies do place burdens on men, too (especially men whose class, ethnicity, or sexual orientation is devalued by those societies), but it is clear that the burdens placed on women are almost always greater (by definition: in patriarchal societies, women are valued less than men).

Monique Wittig has asserted that only the female gender is "marked," that the male gender is conflated with the universal in patriarchal discourse, and the female is limited therefore to a particular "sex" (and thus with sexuality in general). It is thus only logical that a critical investigation of the female "gender" in particular would expose the contradictions of the ideological system called "gender."[2] There is, however, much theoretical

2. See for example Judith Butler's discussion of Wittig in *Gender Trouble: Feminism and the Subversion of Identity* (New York: Routledge, 1990), 18–21, etc.

debate around the category "gender." Constance Penley, in an introduction to her book of essays on "film, feminism, and psychoanalysis," maintains that the term "sexual difference" is preferable. She feels that "gender" can be "put on a level with other differences" – that is, with *social* differences – and the advantage to the category "sexual difference" is that it cannot.[3] As much as we acknowledge our debt (and that of many essays in these two volumes) to the psychoanalytical school of feminist film criticism to which Penley belongs, the idea that the psychic construction of sexual difference can be so neatly separated from the social strikes us as somewhat at odds with the feminist dictum that "the personal is the political." Any strict dichotomy between the psychic and the social, the "subjective" and the political, is contrary to that proposition. Teresa de Lauretis has called this the "fundamental proposition of feminism," and she asserts that it "urges the displacement of all such oppositional terms, the crossing and re-charting of the space between them. No other course seems open if we are to reconceptualize the relations that bind the social to the subjective." [4]

Judith Butler finds that "gender" cannot be "conceived merely as the cultural inscription of meaning on a pregiven sex (a juridical conception); gender must also designate the very apparatus of production whereby the sexes themselves are established."[5] Thus "gender" cannot be placed on either side of a "social/psychic" dichotomy, but rather is part of the process that produces that very dichotomy, as well as a whole system of dichotomies, including "male/female." Butler's radical questioning of gender and "sex" represents an important theoretical project: the deconstruction of any "prediscursive" essence attached to these terms. Her antiessentialist project also includes questioning the idea that "women" are the "subject of feminism."[6] Our focus, however, remains on "women" and "feminism," not out of any sympathy with essentialism, but rather on pragmatic – and political – grounds. We are concerned with the *social* reality (realities) of women (and not any monolithic female identity or prediscursive essence).

3. Constance Penley, *The Future of an Illusion: Film, Feminism, and Psychoanalysis* (Minneapolis: Univ. of Minnesota Press, 1989), xix.

4. Teresa de Lauretis, *Alice Doesn't: Feminism, Semiotics, Cinema* (Bloomington: Indiana Univ. Press, 1984), 56.

5. Butler, *Gender Trouble*, 7.

6. Butler, *Gender Trouble*, 1–7.

It was out of concern with the social experience(s) of women that feminism began – specifically, out of a concern with the oppression of women. This is by no means the only form of oppression, but nonetheless it is a real one, and one that still persists, in spite of any gains that have been made. Feminism's theoretical investigation of the cultural parameters and ideological foundations of women's experience(s) should never lose sight of real political struggles and real suffering. By "real" we do not mean anything "prediscursive" (although it may well include the "extra-discursive"). Systems of discourse require analysis (especially in terms of their relation to power), and the psychoanalytical insight into the split subject has been invaluable theoretically. Nonetheless there is a reality to social oppression that should not be effaced. Only a Faurisson could be interested in denying the reality of the crimes committed against the Jews, gypsies, and homosexuals in Nazi concentration camps. Similarly, we would assert that the suffering of Central Americans at the hands of death squads armed by the U.S. (especially during the 1980s) was real. The suffering of women is real – the suffering, for example, caused by pervasive sexual violence against women in many cultures (including the so-called "developed" countries) over many centuries. Our point is not that these examples of social oppression are the "same," but rather that, in spite of our skepticism about "positivism," there is a "positivity" to certain social and political realities, certain material conditions, that we feel it is irresponsible to discount. A connection to the political struggle of women has always characterized feminism. De Lauretis sees the productive tension between the "critical negativity" of feminist theory and the "affirmative positivity" of feminist politics as fundamental to the feminist project.[7] We agree: *both* are necessary.

History and the German Context

Our emphasis here on the political, the social, and the material is indicative of our training in certain German intellectual traditions that have influenced both German filmmaking and German feminism. Above all we are referring to the Marxist tradition and its "historical materialism." As in the United States, the

7. Teresa de Lauretis, *Technologies of Gender: Essays on Theory, Film, and Fiction* (Bloomington: Indiana Univ. Press, 1987), 26.

"second wave" of feminism began in the Federal Republic of Germany (West Germany) when women activists in the late 1960s distanced themselves from the male-dominated New Left. They rejected the rigid Marxism characteristic of many male activists in the student movement, for whom the "woman's question" was only a "secondary contradiction."[8] Nonetheless, a strong concern with historical analysis and material conditions remained important for many West German feminists – and feminist filmmakers – in a way less evident in the U.S., for instance, which has an intellectual tradition in which Marxism has been much more marginal.

Historical materialism has influenced our thinking about these two volumes to some degree, but we would not assert that it is equally relevant to all of the articles we have collected here. In any event, beyond the influence of the Marxist tradition in Germany, there are other, more obvious reasons why a concern with history would be so important for German intellectuals and filmmakers, female and male: above all, it has to do with the German experience under National Socialism. Intellectuals, writers, and filmmakers old enough to remember those years, or the immediate postwar chaos and instability left in the wake of fascism and the war, have often felt it their duty to come to terms with that historical legacy. The fascist impact on filmmaking specifically cannot compare to its larger crimes – above all genocide – but it was a negative one nonetheless. Many of the best directors fled Germany in the 1930s (Lang, Sirk, Wilder, Siodmak, etc.), and they left behind a mostly mediocre and politically compromised group of film directors who would dominate the film industry in West Germany into the 1960s. There are thus a number of reasons why any study of German cinema must emphasize history. It is our hope that this emphasis is obvious in both of our volumes – not just in Volume II, which deals specifically with the relation between German social history, German film history, and the depiction of German history on film, but in Volume I as well, which is concerned with a broad range of films made in the era of the "New German Cinema," that is, from the 1960s into the 1980s. Just as gender dynamics are a major focus of our "history" volume, so the vol-

8. See for example Renny Harrigan, "The German Women's Movement and Ours," *Jump Cut* 27 (1982): 42–43; and Edith Hoshino Altbach, Jeanette Clausen, Dagmar Schultz, and Naomi Stephan, eds., *German Feminism: Readings in Politics and Literature* (Albany, N.Y.: SUNY Press, 1984).

ume on gender and representation in the New German Cinema cannot ignore history.

Nonetheless, our stress here on history is not intended to imply support for the monolithic, totalizing model of history proclaimed by nineteenth-century positivism. That model claims "scientific objectivity" for its assertion of a single "History" – thus relegating so many other histories to silence. Following Walter Benjamin, we see this type of traditional historicism as being concerned with the history told of, by, and for the "victors," the conquerors: history from the perspective of the colonizers, not the colonized, of the owners, not the workers – and of patriarchal authority, not those who are most typically silenced by that type of authority: women. The historical approaches we favor are informed by a concern with those who have been the "losers" for most of Western history; they also openly acknowledge their own political agendas in the present. Habermas called this Benjaminian attitude to history "posthistoricism."[9] Today it might be more fashionably labeled a "new historicism," but perhaps a better label would be "feminist" historicism, for, as Judith Newton argues, much of what is "new" about new historicism was already pioneered by feminists in the 1970s trying to unmask the "objectivity" of traditional historicism.[10]

Because of the number of essays we want to publish, we have divided them into two volumes. The first volume is titled "Gender and Representation in New German Cinema," and by "New German Cinema" we mean the period from the 1960s into the 1980s. This era of German filmmaking is the one for which we provide by far the most thorough coverage, in large part because of our interest in the extraordinary number of women filmmakers who were able to start making films in the Federal Republic of Germany (West Germany) and West Berlin during those years; many of these directors made films that are informed by feminist perspectives. We also include in Volume I some coverage of films and filmmaking during the same era in the former German Democratic Republic (East Germany) and

9. Jürgen Habermas, "Modernity: An Incomplete Project," in *The Anti-Aesthetic: Essays on Postmodern Culture,* ed. Hal Foster (Port Townsend, WA: Bay, 1983), 5–6.

10. Judith Newton, "History as Usual? Feminism and the 'New Historicism,'" in *The New Historicism,* ed. H. Aram Veeser (New York: Routledge, 1989), 152–54.

Austria. Volume II is titled "German Film History/German History on Film," and it deals both with important films from earlier periods of German film history – the Weimar Republic, the "Third Reich," the Federal Republic in the 1950s – and with representations of German history in films of the New German Cinema. During the late 1970s and the early 1980s such films – made by both women and men – were produced in great number; they were primarily marked by a concern with confronting the direct and indirect legacies of the Third Reich, the most significant historical experience in twentieth-century German history. The centrality of that experience also bears on films made during the Third Reich (obviously), and on those made in its immediate aftermath, in the late 1940s and 1950s. It is significant for films made earlier as well, since films of the Weimar Republic obviously exist in some relation to the social and political conflicts of that era – including its gender dynamics – which led to the Nazi takeover in 1933.

What can the study of German film history from feminist perspectives bring to film studies? And the study of feminist and other forms of independent filmmaking in Germany? Among other things: an understanding of the potential (and limits) of filmmaking as an oppositional practice; the relation of specific aesthetic and commercial practices in filmmaking to the exclusion of women (on the screen, in the cinema, and/or behind the camera); the sociological, ideological, and linguistic constructions of genre and narrative, of social structures and history, of self and self-image. These are some of the issues that have been raised by women filmmakers in the German-speaking countries and addressed by feminist critics examining German film history as a whole. It is our hope that this volume can contribute to the same kind of feminist intervention in film studies and cultural studies in the United States.

Introduction

German History and GermanFilm History

The history of German filmmaking, like that of twentieth-century German art in general, cannot easily (or responsibly) be separated from Germany's political history during this century, especially from Germany's experience of National Socialism and World War II. That experience cannot be understood merely by studying the twelve years from 1933 to 1945; one must know something about earlier events that led to the success of the Nazis, especially the political and social turmoil that plagued Germany's first democratic government, the Weimar Republic, which was founded in 1918 with the defeat of the German Empire in World War I. And of course authoritarian, anti-democratic traditions in Germany have a history that begins long before 1918. After 1945, in turn, the problem of how to deal with the legacy of Nazism, its crimes, and the destruction left by the war shaped both German states. Even now that the Cold War is over – the world order that was born in the ashes of the war the Nazis began, a division of the world that ran right through the center of Germany – the fascist legacy continues to plague a reunified Germany in unexpected and disturbing ways, as outbreaks of xenophobic violence against immigrants indicate.

What does all this have to do with German film history? A great deal, as a few simple facts demonstrate: it was during the Weimar Republic when the German cinema first became important internationally, gaining a reputation that was then squandered by the influence of the Nazis on the film industry during their "Third Reich." Politically and aesthetically, some of the most interesting German films had been made by artists who fled Germany after the Nazis came to power, and it would not be until the 1960s and 1970s that German cinema would again attract international acclaim with a "New German Cinema." In turn, the group of West German filmmakers responsible for this renaissance were characterized especially by their rejection of the films made by the generation that collaborated with the Nazis, and some of their best films are the ones that attempt to confront the Nazi legacy in postwar Germany most directly.

A more detailed (but still of necessity brief) overview of German film history not only illustrates the above connections, but also contextualizes the essays in this volume. By the 1910s, an "art" cinema had developed in Germany, obsessed from the beginning with using cinematic illusion to problematize the boundaries between nightmare and reality – although at the same time it was ambivalent about that very fusion of art and technology on which the cinematic medium depends. This ambivalence, as well as economic pressure to compete with much more powerful foreign cinemas after World War I, led to experimentation with new techniques and attempts to borrow elements pioneered by modern artistic movements in other media. It was for these practices that German cinema became famous. Experimentation, however, did not mean freedom from the control of studios, producers, and political interests that looked askance at any clear attempts to undermine the status quo.

The legacy of this period of German cinema was great. Its attempt to bring Expressionism to the screen, at first a successful way to create an "art cinema," ultimately led to the development of the horror genre in international filmmaking. By the mid-1920s, the "expressionist" or "fantastic" phase in German cinema ended, and more "realistic" films were made. These films were influenced by American melodramas, but they often manifested a brutal social realism unparalleled in Hollywood cinema. Certain more politicized trends of this phase of late Weimar cinema influenced the style of social realism that would later characterize much of the cinema of the German Democratic Republic (East Germany). A combination of stylistic elements developed in the "fantastic" phase (e.g., chiaroscuro lighting and subjective camera) with certain favorite themes of the "realist" phase (especially crime) – and the immigration of German directors to America as the Nazis gained power – was to have a profound influence on the development of film noir in Hollywood.[1]

As Patrice Petro has so persuasively demonstrated, however, German cinema during the Weimar Republic (1918–1933) was not merely "art cinema"; furthermore, in both "art" films and more popular films of the era, gender dynamics are especially significant. This is true not only because of the phenomenon Petro calls "male subjectivity in crisis." The mobilization of male anxieties – and misogyny – was pervasive in Weimar cinema, but, as Petro stresses, its films addressed female spectators as well. Women made up the "major audience" of that cinema, and they must have responded to films depicting destabilized gender roles (and weakened male authority) somewhat differently.[2]

The essays in our volume dealing with this period of German film history focus on these and related issues: female spectatorship, the crisis of male subjectivity, and the sociohistorical context of the destabilization of traditional gender roles. Analyzing Ernst Lubitsch's 1919 comedies, *The Oyster Princess* and *The Doll*, with the idea of determining a "woman's position" in the two texts, Sabine Hake finds much that is subversive both of bourgeois "high culture" and patriarchy. Bruce Murray interprets Karl Grune's *The Street* (1923) as a "male fantasy" that manifests attitudes toward women typical of the proto-fascist right in Germany; and Tracy Myers compares the depiction of women in G.W. Pabst's *Joyless Street* (1925), traditionally lauded for its "social realism," to the actual social and economic situation of women in Austria and Germany during the early 1920s. B. Ruby Rich recreates the historical context for Leontine Sagan's *Girls in Uniform* (1931): the flourishing gay and lesbian subculture of

1. Besides Patrice Petro, *Joyless Streets* (Princeton: Princeton Univ. Press, 1989), other important sources on Weimar cinema include: the classics Siegfried Kracauer, *From Caligari to Hitler* (Princeton: Princeton Univ. Press, 1947) and Lotte H. Eisner, *The Haunted Screen* (Berkeley: Univ. California Press, 1969); John D. Barlow, *Expressionist Film* (Boston: Twayne, 1982); Thomas G. Plummer, ed., *Film and Politics in the Weimar Republic*, (Minneapolis: Univ. of Minnesota Press, 1982); Thomas Elsaesser's two articles, "Film History and Visual Pleasure: Weimar Cinema," in *Cinema Histories, Cinema Practices*, ed. Patricia Mellencamp and Philip Rosen (Frederick, MD: University Publications of America, 1984), and "Social Mobility and the Fantastic in Weimar Films" in *Wide Angle*, 5, no. 2 (1982), 14-25; the special issue on Weimar film theory, *New German Critique* 40 (1987); and the special issue on Weimar mass culture, *New German Critique* 51 (1990).

2. Petro, *Joyless Streets*, 13-17.

Weimar Germany, soon to be destroyed by the Nazis. Rich's positive reading of the film as an important historical achievement in affirming lesbianism is questioned by Lisa Ohm, who finds that the film reproduces anti-lesbian discourses. Whether or not the film is pro- or anti-lesbian, the fact remains that, once the Nazis came to power, Leontine Sagan and many of the people involved in making *Girls in Uniform* soon left Germany.

The mobilization of cinematic production and distribution by the Nazis after 1933 remains a discouraging example of how cinema can be used successfully for ideological manipulation of the public. Just as Goebbels desired, it was not the outright political propaganda film, but Nazi "entertainment cinema" that demonstrated a more subtle – and insidious – model for cinematic propaganda.[3] In the so-called "entertainment" films of the Third Reich, the determining influence of fascist ideology is usually clear, and fundamental to that ideology is the misogyny already evident in the gender dynamics of Weimar cinema. But at least in Weimar cinema, women are seen as important, if only in terms of the threat they present to male subjectivity; in Nazi cinema, they are not even allowed to be threatening. Women are reduced to trivial roles, as Anke Gleber demonstrates in her discussion of three "entertainment films," *The Old and the New King* (Hans Steinhoff, 1935), *The Broken Jug* (Gustav Ucicky, 1937), and *Fräulein von Barnhelm* (Hans Schweikart, 1940). Misogyny is not unrelated to modern anti-Semitism, which often views the Jew as a feminized and/or lascivious "Other." But the mobilization of misogyny in combination with crude anti-Semitism, as one finds in Veit Harlan's notorious anti-Semitic film *Jew Süss* (1940), leads to some especially interesting contradictions in a cinematic text, which Régine Mihal Friedman demonstrates in her analysis of Harlan's film from the perspective of feminist psychoanalytical theory.

Government involvement in filmmaking in Germany predated Nazi cinema, but under the Nazis, who had nationalized "Ufa" and the other major film companies in 1937 and then

3. See David Welch, *Propaganda and the German Cinema, 1933–1945* (Oxford: Clarendon, 1983); Marc Silberman, "The Ideology of Re-Presenting the Classics: Filming *Der Zerbrochene Krug* in the Third Reich," *German Quarterly* 57 (1984); Karsten Witte, "How Nazi Cinema Mobilizes the Classics: Schweikart's *Das Fräulein von Barnhelm* (1940)," in *German Film and Literature: Adaptations and Transformations*, ed. Eric Rentschler (New York: Methuen, 1986), 103–16; and Linda Schulte-Sasse, "The Never Was as History" (Ph.D. diss., Univ. of. Minnesota, 1985).

turned them into a single state monopoly by 1942, government control was much more complete.[4] After the war, the state film monopoly was broken up in the zones controlled by the Western Allies, and the resulting weakened film industry had a hard time competing with foreign films, especially American ones. Therefore, in the state that was created from the three Western zones of occupation, the Federal Republic of Germany (West Germany), the film industry became to some degree dependent on state subsidy. West German films in the 1950s were also made for the most part by directors whose careers had begun during the Third Reich. Their films became known for provincial mediocrity, best typified by the popular genre of *Heimat* films, which glorified a quaint and idyllic version of life in rural villages (thus offering an escape from the chaos of reconstruction in bomb-damaged German cities – and escape from the legacy of the Third Reich as well). As Heide Fehrenbach argues in her essay on the "scandalous" melodrama *The Sinful Woman* (1951) by Willi Forst, the provincialism of West German cinema in the 1950s had as much to do with the pressure brought to bear on the film industry by the Churches as with its inability to compete with foreign films (especially from the U.S.). The Churches intervened in turn out of a concern that male authority and the traditional family needed to be reestablished in postwar Germany.

Government subsidy of the commercial film industry in West Germany did not save it from near collapse by the early 1960s, as competition from television became serious. In the mid-1960s, a new model of state support for filmmaking was tried, an attempt to subsidize more independent film production. This attempt led to what we now call the "New German Cinema," although it was not until the 1970s that its funding became relatively secure, owing to an agreement with the state television networks and the relatively supportive attitude of the governing Social Democrats in Bonn. From the beginning the New German Cinema defined itself in opposition to the aesthetics and politics of the generation that had dominated filmmaking from the 1930s through the 1950s. At its best it confronted twentieth-

4. "Ufa" is an acronym for "Universum Film Aktiengesellschaft," meaning "Universal Film, Inc." The company was founded originally toward the end of World War I, funded in part by the German Empire in order to counter Western film propaganda. During the 1920s it became the most powerful of the German film production companies, and it came under the control of the ultraright wing Hugenberg media empire in 1927.

century German history, especially the fascist legacy, with a new urgency and honesty; it produced a number of "New German" cinematic riddles directed at a culture that in many ways never came to terms with its embrace of Hitler and of fascism.

German History in New German Cinema

The films that most directly confronted the troubled German past were made in the late 1970s and early 1980s. In the generally escapist 1950s, there had been few filmmakers willing to deal with the past in any but the most harmless and superficial ways (Wolfgang Staudte would be the most obvious exception). In 1965 and 1966, three of the films we associate with the first critical successes of the New German Cinema took a more serious look, but in two of them, ambitious and challenging formal strategies resulted in films that were not exactly accessible to the broader public: Kluge's *Yesterday Girl* and Jean-Marie Straub and Danielle Huillet's *Not Reconciled.* Meanwhile Volker Schlöndorff's *Young Törless* was much more accessible, but the historical point was still somewhat disguised in an adaptation of a turn-of-the-century novel (albeit a very prophetic one by Robert Musil).

It was only in the late 1970s that the New German Cinema produced a wave of historical films that obviously thematized the Third Reich. Most of these films reflected the personal concerns of a generation of Germans born in the 1930s and 1940s who felt a need to come to terms with the legacy of their parents, and a number of these films were openly biographical and/or autobiographical. This phenomenon can be explained in a number of ways: a West German literary trend of the 1970s called "New Subjectivity" validated the personal and the outright autobiographical in writing; even more obvious was the influence of feminism with its dictum that "the personal is political." A good deal of the literature inspired by the women's movement in Germany was autobiographical, and this trend extended to feminist filmmaking as well. One very specific set of events that triggered a great deal of historical introspection on the part of filmmakers like Rainer Werner Fassbinder, Margarethe von Trotta, and Kluge occurred in the fall of 1977, when the spiral of terrorist violence by the Red Army Faction (the "Baader-Meinhoff gang") and overreaction by the West German state came to a climax in such a way that civil liberties seemed in danger as they had not since 1933.[5] Directly resulting from this concern with 1977 and its relation to earlier periods of German history was the film *Germany in Autumn*, released in 1978 and the product of a collective which included Kluge, Fassbinder, Schlöndorff, Edgar Reitz, and others. Although von Trotta did not participate in the making of *Germany in Autumn*, while accompanying her husband Schlöndorff during the shooting of his segments, she met the sister of the Red Army's Gudrun Ensslin, Christiane Ensslin, whose story would form the basis of her 1981 film *Marianne and Juliane*. Fassbinder's work on *Germany in Autumn* influenced his own trilogy on West German history, which began with *The Marriage of Maria Braun* in 1979 (*Lola* and *Veronika Voss* were the other two parts, both released in 1981). Kluge's *The Patriot* , also released in 1979, is clearly a continuation of what he began in *Germany in Autumn*.

We have organized the second section of this volume, which deals with the representation of German history in New German Cinema, chronologically, but not in terms of the year of each film's production – all seven of the films discussed here were made within a period of six years, and five of them were made between 1979 and 1981. Instead we have organized them in terms of the chronology of the historical subject matter they attempt to depict; therefore we begin with the latest of the films, von Trotta's *Rosa Luxemburg*, made in 1985, which represents a number of episodes in the life of that famous woman, a Polish Jew who became one of the most important – and independent – socialists in Germany from the turn of the century until her murder in 1919. Anna K. Kuhn's article asserts that von Trotta's film reclaims Luxemburg, a socialist thinker and activist who expressed little interest in women's issues, for feminism.

Von Trotta has said that Luxemburg's murder by right-wing troops in 1919 was the first murder committed on the road to Nazism in Germany.[6] In Helma Sanders-Brahms's film *Germany,*

5. For more discussion of the events of 1977, see for example Anton Kaes, *From Hitler to Heimat: The Return of History as Film* (Cambridge: Harvard Univ. Press, 1989), 23–28, and Richard W. McCormick, *Politics of the Self: Feminism and the Postmodern in West German Literature and Film* (Princeton: Princeton Univ. Press, 1991), 177–80. For extended analysis of the "history films" of the late 1970s and early 1980s, see Thomas Elsaesser, *The New German Cinema: A History* (New Brunswick: Rutgers Univ. Press, 1989), 239–78, and especially Kaes, *From Hitler to Heimat*, the whole of which is devoted to the phenomenon.

6. Cited in Daniel Egger, "Reinventing Rosa," review of *Rosa Luxemburg, The Nation*, 25 April 1987, 546–49; see 548.

Pale Mother (1979), we find ourselves no longer on the road to Nazism, but rather right in the middle of the Third Reich, and we experience that era from the very personal perspective of a woman – a character who quite clearly is based on the filmmaker's mother. Richard W. McCormick argues that Sanders-Brahms's juxtaposition of a fictionalized reconstruction of her mother's biography with the larger historical discourse of German fascism and the war (including actual documentary footage) represents the very feminist project of fusing the personal with the political. Similarly, Joyce Rheuban asserts that Fassbinder's *The Marriage of Maria Braun* (1979) uses melodrama subversively to enable political critique – both of the conventional narrative of postwar German history and of patriarchal ideology as well. Gabriele Weinberger discusses Marianne Rosenbaum's autobiographical film *Peppermint Peace* (1983), which covers nearly the same period as does the Fassbinder film, but does so much more subjectively, and from the perspective of a small girl. Weinberger demonstrates how the film's feminist and pacifist critique of sexual and political repression in the Cold War era manifests itself in the often humorous confusion of a baffled child trying to make sense of the adult world around her. Jutta Brückner's film *Years of Hunger* (1979) is also autobiographical, and it makes a similar point about the mid-1950s, but from the troubled perspective of a teenager who undergoes an identity crisis as she enters puberty in an era especially repressive of female sexuality. Barbara Kosta focuses on Brückner's attempt to expose the forces that damage women's relationships to their bodies, noting that the filmmaker draws parallels between that repression and the repressive politics of West Germany during the 1950s. We also reprint an interview with Brückner by Marc Silberman in which she discusses *Years of Hunger* and her earlier films.

Von Trotta's *Marianne and Juliane* (1981) moves from the 1950s to the 1960s and 1970s. The main focus is on the 1970s and on conflicts around political violence – committed both by leftist terrorists and by the state. Barton Byg finds von Trotta's response to the "German Autumn" of 1977 too conventional in its aesthetics and ultimately cooptive of the oppositional history it cites: feminism and the student protest movement. Helke Sander's *The Subjective Factor* (1981) also examines that oppositional history, focusing mainly on a slightly earlier period: the genesis of the women's movement within the student movement, as well as the decline of the latter into dogmatic sects and terrorist cells. But in looking at the late 1960s, Sander always foregrounds the position of the early 1980s in the film, the perspective from which the history of the 1960s is being reconstructed, her own historical position as she makes the film. Richard W. McCormick argues that this foregrounding is crucial to understanding Sander's complex and formally ambitious film.

History and Feminist Film Criticism in Germany

Our appendix focuses on the history of a very significant type of feminist intervention in Germany, one that does not involve filmmaking, but rather film criticism. Published since 1974, *Frauen und Film* is the oldest feminist journal on film – not only in Europe, but anywhere in the world; we include two essays that focus on the history of its evolution from the 1970s through the 1980s. Miriam Hansen's article is reprinted here because of its coverage of the first decade of *Frauen und Film*; she locates the journal's origins within the feminist film culture that developed in the 1970s. Hansen's piece first appeared in 1984, just as *Frauen und Film* had completed some major changes, including a move from West Berlin to Frankfurt. Ramona Curry's article contrasts the Frankfurt-based journal with the older Berlin version, finding in the former a much more theoretical approach to feminist film criticism. The journal had begun in Berlin as an organ much closer to the practical and political concerns of women actually making films; in Frankfurt it has become a journal of feminist film criticism that rivals in its theoretical sophistication Anglo-American and French feminist film theory, with which it carries on a dialogue. Indeed, at the moment, it is the most serious journal of theoretical film criticism in Germany, feminist or otherwise.

There are a number of reasons for the path the journal has taken, and there are a number of advantages and disadvantages associated with both its earlier form and its current one. What is clear is that the interventions of feminist film critics associated with this journal have been ongoing and significant, and that no history of the development of German film culture over the last twenty years can ignore *Frauen und Film* or the feminist film culture from which it originated. By the same token, the role played by feminist critics and feminist filmmakers in the debates over German history and its representation (debates that *Frauen und Film* has helped to shape, by the way) also represents an intervention that must be taken into account, just as gender itself is a category that must be considered in any discussion of history and representation. It is our hope that this volume demonstrates these assertions.

Part I

Film History Before New German Cinema

1

The Oyster Princess and *The Doll*: Wayward Women of the Early Silent Cinema

sabine hake

Much has been written about how the cinema provides pleasure in terms of the needs of the male psyche. Sabine Hake is more interested in exploring female pleasure in the cinema in this analysis of two early silent comedies made in Germany by Ernst Lubitsch, The Oyster Princess *and* The Doll *(both in 1919). Her project is to analyze "the relations between narrative, visual pleasure, and woman's position" in the cinematic text. She asserts that comedy (rather underrepresented in critical work on German film) can be subversive – especially early silent comedies, produced before the formal and economic consolidation of what we now call the Hollywood model, which would become dominant internationally. While not ignoring aspects within the two Lubitsch comedies that are affirmative of the status quo, Hake concentrates on those elements that – in their uninhibited celebration of orality and consumption, and in their polymorphous playfulness with gender roles – are subversive of bourgeois "high culture" and patriarchy (as well as narrative realism). Such elements must also be seen in relation to that new audience of working women so important to the early silent cinema.*
—The Editors

With the growing interest in the early silent cinema, a number of "small" films of the 1910s have been rediscovered both by audiences and critics that repeatedly cause astonishment at their subversive cinematic qualities. As a result, film scholars have felt compelled to rethink certain assumptions about the conventions of cinematic representation and, with new theoretical concepts adopted from semiotics and psychoanalysis, to question the primacy of the dominant realist text.[1] It has become obvious that insistence on the universal validity of an historically developed form of cinematic representation, brought to perfection by the classic Hollywood film, proves particularly limiting in the assessment of early silent cinema and the different spectatorial relations addressed by it. Here feminist film theory's growing influence has been crucial in analyzing the relations between narrative, visual pleasure, and woman's position in the text. Through an explicitly gendered perspective on issues of production and reception, the respect for the technical mastery displayed in the more prestigious silent film productions (*Intolerance, Passion*) need no longer dominate the notions of "spectacle"; instead, critical attention can now focus on the persistent appeal of genres of "spectacle" outside of historicism and masculinity. The interest in film history as a history of pleasure rather than of great works, however, also requires the rejection of normative categories of taste and quality.

For the German silent cinema, this problem can be approached most productively through the films of Ernst Lubitsch. Already during his early years, Lubitsch was considered one of the masters of the costume drama and its appealing mixture of history, colportage, and spectacle. His most famous films from that period include the period films *Passion* (*Madame Dubarry*, 1919) and *Deception* (*Anna Boleyn*, 1921), and furthermore the oriental tales *The Wife of Pharaoh* (*Das Weib des Pharao*, 1921) and *One Arabian Night* (*Sumurun*, 1920). Slogans such as "the German Griffith" or "the great humanizer of history" accurately refer to the director's mastery of blending superb mass direction, tender human touches, and an explicit eroticism into an extremely successful product. In this essay, I will discuss two lesser known Lubitsch films from that period, films that seem like crossbreeds between his monumental dramas and sophisticated comedies. I am referring to *The Oyster Princess* (*Die Austernprinzessin*, 1919) and *The Doll* (*Die Puppe*, 1919), two films that deserve further attention for their surprising subversive qualities. Produced in 1919, the founding year of the Weimar Republic, both films are the result of Lubitsch's continuous work with a group of collaborators, including scriptwriter Hanns Kräly,

1. I am referring here to the work of Thomas Elsaesser, Miriam Hansen, Judith Mayne, and others.

cameraman Theodor Sparkuhl, set designer Kurt Richter, and his favorite comic actors, Ossi Oswalda as the title figure and female lead and Victor Janson as the quintessential father figure. Ignored by contemporary as well as more recent film criticism, *The Oyster Princess* and *The Doll,* as "small" films produced for women audiences, neither display the vast expenditures of personnel and materials necessary for international success nor feed a fascination with the diabolical considered typical of the silent German cinema. Yet precisely because they also relinquish a concomitant economy of visual and narrative structures aimed at the streamlined production of pleasure, they represent points of resistance in the process of cinema's integration in middle class culture. In this context, *The Oyster Princess* and *The Doll* deserve special attention because of their rejection of realism, narrative linearity, and character development.

With their wayward female protagonists, these films – and Lubitsch's expressionist fantasy *The Mountain Cat* (*Die Bergkatze,* 1921) should be added here – clearly comment on modern women and thus already anticipate the rise of "girl culture"[2] in the 1920s. The emancipated consciousness of the films' heroines would then serve as a model that modern women, primarily the new social group of female employees, tried to emulate in fashion and behavior. Playing with other designs of femininity, *The Oyster Princess, The Doll,* and *The Mountain Cat* therefore call into question a number of preconceptions about Weimar cinema, particularly in relation to images of women and female spectatorship.

I.

Approaching the specific qualities of *The Oyster Princess,* the term "spectacle" seems most appropriate to describe its particular appeal. I will be using this term as a starting point for some associative comments rather than as a fixed theoretical concept. Obviously, the term "spectacle" invokes both the notion of the carnivalesque introduced by Bakhtin and the specter of univer-

2. The term *Girlkultur* was a term frequently used in Germany during the 1920s. It referred both critically and enthusiastically to the interrelations between women's emancipation, Americanism, the new body consciousness, and consumer society. See for instance Fritz Giese, *Girlkultur. Vergleiche zwischen amerikanischem und europäischem Lebensgefühl* (Munich: Delphin-Verlag, 1920).

sal commodification described by Guy Debord in *Society of the Spectacle*.[3] Between those two poles of interpretation, the cinematic spectacle suggests a rejection of the anthropocentric view of the world. Usually organized around the film's main protagonist and only in place to highlight his or her uniqueness and grandiosity, the cinematic spectacle, however, ultimately serves affirmative functions as regards the cult of the individual. Only the silent cinema is, at times, able to integrate this tension satisfactorily between the human and the mechanical by subjecting everything to the hegemony of the eye. In all genuine cinematic spectacles, the most secret desires and the most public social relations are mediated through images; everything becomes visual representation. The distinction between the representation of human beings and material objects is surrendered in favor of an unrestricted assemblage of visual stimuli. Consequently, vision becomes the privileged human sense. In that context, the cinematic spectacle defies narration. Designed to support a story (the biography of Henry VIII in *Deception*, of Madame Du Barry in *Passion*), it tends to interrupt the flow of the narrative. This is primarily achieved through a visual iconography that glorifies quantity as quality and that plunders the archives of artistic forms, historical motifs, and sociocultural stereotypes for the most stunning combinations and effects. Exactly through its extreme commodity fetishism, then, is the cinematic spectacle able to escape the requirements of probability, verisimilitude, and psychology. In doing so, it succeeds in representing and thus satisfying desires, both repressed and produced by modern society, that have been denied by the requirements of bourgeois realism.

The Oyster Princess, Lubitsch's second feature-length comedy, allows for such a foregrounding of spectacle and its implications

3. See Guy Debord, *Society of the Spectacle,* trans. Black and Red (Detroit: Black and Red, 1970; co-published by *Radical America,* Vol. 4, No. 5 (1970), in an issue entirely devoted to this translation) and Mikhail Bakhtin, *Rabelais and His World,* trans. Helene Iswolsky (Cambridge: M.I.T. Press, 1968), 6. The notion of the carnivalesque and the subversive potential of laughter has been the source of much nostalgic appropriation. Note, in this context, Umberto Eco's highly critical comments on the transgressional theory of carnival and its reversals. Referring to what he calls the *trompe- l'oeil* effect of the comic, Eco cautions that the comic text only presupposes liberation but never actually intends to attain it: "The hyper Bachtinian ideology of carnival as actual liberation may, however, be wrong." In "The Frames of Comic 'Freedom'," in *Carnival!,* ed. Thomas A. Sebeok (Berlin, New York, and Amsterdam: Mouton, 1984), 3.

for narrative and visual pleasure.[4] Through its emphasis on bodies and objects, omnipresent in an overwhelming multitude, and their constant motion, spectacle here almost seems to take revenge against traditional notions of morality, propriety, and humanism. Full of conflicting elements of old slapstick crudeness and the new trends towards sophistication, Lubitsch filmed *The Oyster Princess* at a point of transition in the economic and social status of the cinema.[5] This fact also explains the complexity of the film and its crucial position at the threshold between his earlier slapstick films and his future drawing-room comedies. Paradigmatic for all of Lubitsch's German films, *The Oyster Princess* invokes an almost pre-Oedipal eroticism around images of oral, bodily, and visual sensations.[6] Held together by the threefold celebration of consuming, dancing, and looking, the film maps out a concept of the erotic that is not repressed by questions of legitimacy but partakes shamelessly in a permanent flow of desires and gratifications: sex, money, and power.

Turning, consequently, first to the representation of consumption in *The Oyster Princess,* the function of the display and destruction of commodities becomes evident. The film begins with a close-up of the Father, Mr. Quaker, the Oyster King. The camera moves back, positioning him at the center of activity. He is surrounded by groups of servants who comb, wash, feed, and pamper him like a baby. The next shot shows a group of secretaries, all taking the same notes. The figure of repetition, therefore, serves here both as ironic comment on capitalist surplus and the reminder of paradisiacal abundance. Lines, circles, triangles, clusters, and spirals, the whole repertoire of geometrical configurations is employed to control the tension between

4. *Die Austernprinzessin* (Projections-AG Union Berlin, 70 min.). Release: 25 June 1919. Director: Ernst Lubitsch. Scenario: Hanns Kräly. Camera: Theodor Sparkuhl. Sets: Kurt Richter. With Ossi Oswalda (Ossi, Mr. Quaker's daughter), Victor Jansson (Mr. Quaker), Harry Liedtke (Prince Nucki), Julius Falkenstein (his valet), Curt Bois (conductor). Distributed in the United States through West Glen Films.

5. Major contributing factors to the growing respectability and profitability of cinema were the founding of the powerful Ufa film studio in 1917, the rise of a motion-picture architecture modeled on the theater, the popularity of spectacular historical films or intimate bourgeois dramas, and the increase of various forms of writing on film (fan magazines, newspaper reviews, sophisticated film criticism).

6. This even continues in his American films, for instance in the pivotal dinner scenes of *Trouble in Paradise* (1932), *Angel* (1937), *Ninotchka* (1939), even *That Uncertain Feeling* (1941).

repression and eruption, between ceremony and chaos, thus constantly making visible the fulfillment of desire and the aestheticizing of its denial. Through images of immediacy, unity, and non-differentiation, the evocation of pleasures which exist prior to the Oedipal mold becomes irreversibly linked to consumer goods. Here the stereotype of the American millionaire provides the almost mythological backdrop for the feast of pure quantity, as Lubitsch excessively picks its formal elements (the black servants, oysters as the peculiar source of Mr. Quaker's wealth) from the public image of American imperialism. Such scenes, in wavering between envy and disgust, contain special significance in relation to the dire economic situation in 1918/19: shot in the middle of financially chaotic times, *The Oyster Princess* was regarded at its premiere as an extremely lavish production. Due to the high unemployment rate, it was possible to work with more cheap extras than would ever be possible again in German film.

The film's central figure is the American girl, characterized as the embodiment of shameless consumption. Her motto "instant and permanent gratification" and her frontier-style manners of achieving it refer to those aspects of Americanism that address the myths of quick wealth, social climbing, and aggressive individualism. The film's central problem is introduced when Mr. Quaker tries to calm his daughter, who is having one of her violent fits. Furious about the marriage of a millionaire's daughter to a count, she demands a prince. Emphasizing her determination, she systematically destroys all objects within reach. Such proof of her vitality and potency (much in the style of robber-baron entrepreneurship!) meets with her father's approval. Facing the camera, he politely hands her one last vase and comments: "Take it! Please!" Already in the following scene, the consulted marriage broker presents a file card: "Prince Nucki, looks: first class; assets: none." The man, thus, enters the narrative in the way traditionally reserved for women: as an object of desire. The equation between the loss of social and economic power and emasculation is expressed in another, complementary social stereotype in the European-American confrontation, the impoverished European aristocrat whose only remaining assets are his refined manners and a sensual eroticism.[7] Since

7. It would be interesting to compare Lubitsch's mild irony with the more caustic representation of European aristocrats in Stroheim's films.

Prince Nucki is still too class-conscious to break a date with his bohemian friends, he sends his valet to investigate the actual wealth of the Oyster Princess by proxy. Having arrived at her vast estate, the false prince nervously begins to trace the star-shaped floor ornaments while waiting in her drawing room. His turning and spinning accelerates, until nausea clouds his senses. Lubitsch cuts this sequence with the dressing room sequence, where the Oyster Princess is surrounded, as her father before, by innumerable maids scrubbing, combing, creaming, perfuming and, finally, dressing her. Especially in this sequence the reference to the new developments in industrial production are more than obvious. The woman's body is the product, while different groups of workers (maids), distinguished by different uniforms (aprons, frocks) referring to their functions, enter the process of production (woman's beautification) at different stages of production (cleaning, massaging, dressing) to perform those functions, which are emphasized by close-ups of hands at work. The dressing room sequence clearly is an ironic comment on early models of the conveyer belt, where the workers still carry the product through the steps of a production assembly (at one point, the Oyster Princess is, for instance, carried from the cleaning section to the massage section).

Eventually, product and consumer are united; ironically, it is the woman/product who does the buying. After skeptically inspecting the supposed prospective groom with a monocle (surveying his bald head!), the determined girl nevertheless follows through with her plan. The marriage takes place with businesslike efficiency; the wedding party begins with the choreography of a spectacular dinner. The bride whispers saucily: "Say something!" and the false groom replies with a full mouth: "I haven't had such good food in ages!" Consumption becomes the dominant relation towards the world. Its operating principle is transformation. In the end, there are only empty plates and full stomachs. Grafe/Patalas write: "For the wedding party, Lubitsch hired 300 real waiters. Behind each guest another waiter stands for each course. After each course the dish vanishes and so does the waiter. The next row steps up. The notion of consumption as real, devouring consumption is thus made obvious. Consumption has something literary in Lubitsch films, something exhilarating."[8]

8. Frieda Grafe and Enno Patalas, *Im Off. Filmartikel* (Munich: Hanser, 1977), 267.

The vertigo caused by consumption and the ornamental display of objects eventually both explode in the central dance sequence at the wedding party. What begins as a chorus line of waiters winding up and down the stairs with plates of food, of cooks preparing meals and guests chewing relentlessly, develops more and more into an abstract ritual. Through rapid editing, mise-en-scène, odd camera angles, lighting, and special effects, movement becomes dance and dance the celebration of life. While the false groom literally digests his rags-to-riches fate through gluttony (here Lubitsch cuts to Prince Nucki chewing on a tiny mackerel), a foxtrot epidemic breaks loose. In a split-screen shot, Lubitsch combines three elements of the narrative in a tableau of dancing legs in close-up: in the lower part of the frame the kitchen personnel (an indicator also of their social station), in the middle the frustrated bride with a waiter, and in the upper part the ecstatic guests. Each Lubitsch film leads up to such a dance, a party, or a costume ball. It is the culminating point of the narrative and, at the same time, the moment of its suspension. These waltzes, polkas, charlestons, and foxtrots speak of an explosive vitality, an intoxication through movement and rhythm. Yet through their controlled steps and turns they also secure the continuing existence of that thin line between celebration and chaos that is under attack even through the conductor's violently swinging hips and yet is defended by the mechanical regime of baton, drums, and dancing steps. With Lubitsch one is only alive when dancing. And through dancing the transgression of limitations of class, gender, and race becomes possible.

As a continuation of the mistaken-identity plot, the next morning sees Ossi attend a club meeting of "Millionaire Daughters Against Alcoholism." There she meets an intoxicated Prince Nucki and, after a wild boxing match with the other women, secures him as her private patient. It is love at first sight. Both recognize each other first as lovers and then as husband and wife in the following romantic bedroom scene that should rightfully have occurred the night before. For the finale, Lubitsch quickly passes over a very private dinner with Mr. Quaker and lets the young lovers retire to the sleeping quarters. *The Oyster Princess* closes with a repetition of its opening shot, that is, with the father's look aimed directly at the spectator. He addresses the camera candidly to share his voyeurism; peeking through a keyhole to supervise his daughter's erotic performance, he comments: "That's impressive!"

The gaze is the beginning of seduction. It marks the direction of desire, fixes its aim. The gaze – and this narrative is almost entirely constructed through looking – does not necessarily have to fall upon a man or woman. Culinary pleasures prove just as tempting. And even more, looking itself becomes a pleasurable act. Socially sanctioned or not, paintings, photographs, reflections in mirrors, etc. exist to arouse, maintain, or deflect desire. Yet in most Lubitsch films, they not only stand in for the desired object but threaten to replace it. In *The Oyster Princess* the lure of the images suggests – rather immorally – that it is perhaps only the promise that we desire, not its fulfillment. What is doomed to fail in the melodrama, namely imagination, becomes the great victor in all German Lubitsch comedies. What appear to be mocking comments on sublimation (the false groom's overeating, his glance at the dissatisfied bride through the keyhole) may well be a questioning of that order of primary and secondary pleasures. In the end, it is the same: looking, consuming, and dancing are all expressions of desire, almost interchangeable. With its anarchic equivalence of all pleasures, *The Oyster Princess* advocates a concept of imagination that values appearances higher than the truth and, furthermore, seems to regard substitutes as equally tempting, perhaps even more satisfying. Significantly, this anarchy can also be understood as a comment on the secret of the cinema's attraction. Thus, the longing glances on the screen are also the ones of the spectators; Mr. Quaker's look into the camera only confirms this secret bond of visual pleasure.

These spectacular elements in *The Oyster Princess* are not infused into the narrative through dramatic characters, but the specific characteristics of visual representation. Aside from the central function of props, decor, and extras, one crucial aspect of this is the specific function of screen acting. While it differs from stage acting as regards the performance and representation of the human body, comic film acting stands even more in opposition to the stage through its references to the mechanical and, moreover, tends to disrupt the sexual order when the comic hero is a woman. In that sense, *The Oyster Princess* is clearly dominated by the frantic and narcissistic activities of the female protagonist, played by comedienne Ossi Oswalda. One of the most popular film comediennes, she was neither the sexless creature of the American slapstick comedy nor the civilized, fun-loving flapper of the 1920s sophisticated comedies. Always looking slightly dishevelled, her fun could be devastating and, as such, was closer to the anarchy of her male American counterparts. Miriam Hansen in her essay "Silent Cinema: Whose Public Sphere?"[9] has commented on the popularity of such androgynous film stars and roles and links their significance to the early cinema's function as a place for women. Ossi Oswalda, but also Asta Nielsen, Pola Negri, and Lya de Putti were among the most popular German film stars who acted out a fashionable ambiguous eroticism often emphasized by cross-dressing plots. They offered an imaginary screen to stage women's ambivalent position between the private and the new public spheres, between emancipation and traditional femininity. Recent studies on the classical German cinema, however, have tended to neglect film comedies as an important outlet for these conflicts while, at the same time, focusing on the more somber aspects of a liberated male sensuality.[10]

In *The Oyster Princess,* Oswalda's performance is characterized by a physical presence and sexual aggression that, as structuring impulses, hold together the fragmented and often marginal narrative. Employing elements of slapstick acting but exclusively in the service of desire (not, as is generally the case, as a response to adversities), her performance in itself functions as a place of signification, as a site of conflicting inscriptions. The bathing scene is a good example for that ambivalence. Decor, lighting, and Oswalda's semi-nudity, hidden by steam and precious robes, visually allude to an oriental bathhouse sensuality. Yet through the rapid editing and Oswalda's own efficient movements, Lubitsch, at the same time, mocks what he pretends to represent. Oswalda's body at rest is woman as spectacle; but her body in action is efficiency gone crazy. As witness to the body consciousness of the New Woman, her performance thus is informed both by images of sexual libertinage and the

9. Miriam Hansen, "Silent Cinema: Whose Public Sphere?" *New German Critique* 29 (Spring/Summer 1983): 147–73.

10. I am referring here to films like *The Student of Prague* (1913), *Der Andere* (1913) or *The Cabinet of Dr Caligari* (1919), films that are dominated by narratives of male loss of identity. Cf. Thomas Elsaesser's description of the hysterical male in Weimar cinema in "Film History and Visual Pleasure: Weimar History," in *Cinema Histories, Cinema Practices,* ed. Patricia Mellencamp and Philip Rosen (Frederick, MD: University Publishers of America, 1984), 47–84.

notions of a streamlined functionality required in the new industrial professions for women (again: mechanization, the assembly line). The conflict becomes evident in the excesses staged around images of sexuality and consumerism. The exaggerated set designs, hundreds of extras, mise-en-scène, and montage, in short, the film's sheer volume works as an expression and, at the same time through its formal rigidity, as repression of the female body.

On the level of narrative, however, the admission of woman's desire is partly taken back through her relation to the father. The total absence and, in fact, spiteful rejection of mother-images implies paternal dominance. The father-daughter relationship, central to Lubitsch's German comedies, plays with oppositional figures of passivity and hyperactivity, voyeurism and exhibitionism, status quo and anarchy. The father is the one to construct meaning, while the daughter is the one to deconstruct it through excess. In that regard, the film can be interpreted as the return of the repressed feminine in a patriarchal setting gone hysterical. The narrative employs devices, or rather, disguises, from taming-of-the-shrew plots but only to subvert them through new readings relevant to the 1910s and 1920s. Thus, through mise-en-scène, that is, through spectacle and new paradigms of performance, the human and the material worlds in this film are reunited to provide a projection screen for the invocation of woman's desire. The film mocks traditional notions of romance and eroticism through its mad conspicuous consumption. In doing so, it points toward pleasures outside of the identification with characters or objects. Purely visual pleasures are addressed that were described time and again by contemporary 1910s authors as the infamous visual lust of the Roman arenas and medieval public executions. This gaze or stare was attributed to women and the lower classes alike, thus describing their shared exclusion from dominant bourgeois culture and modes of art appreciation. The image of an Otherness ruled by desire – the film's subversive force – and the images of commodity society and automated production become inextricably intertwined and constitute the film's multiple readings.

In concluding this part of the discussion, I would like now to take the insights gained in this analysis of *The Oyster Princess* and use them to speculate on the film's attraction to its contemporary and, in particular, female audience. Reading this film as a "spectacular" narrative raises issues of visual pleasure and gender, and perhaps with the implication that textual analysis and problems of reception need no longer be mutually exclusive. For that reason, I would like to imagine *The Oyster Princess* as one of the films that inspired critic Franz Reichwaldau's ironic comments on the progressive function of the motion picture theater. He writes: "The movies have unjustly been called the theater of the little man; they are, in fact, the theater of the little woman and the big woman. . . . Fighting for emancipation, women, too, slowly reach the acknowledgment of their desires. The cinema satisfies them in the most tender ways."[11] Reichwaldau was referring to the explicitly erotic pleasures addressed and satisfied by the films of his time through their play with visual pleasure. Yet the underlying derision of his descriptions also tells of the more disquieting aspects linked to the emergence of new women audiences. The equation of film's qualitative downfall and women's petty longing for fun and diversion, frequently made during the 1910s and 1920s and phrased with irony or moralistic contempt, was a typical result of the ambivalences the new medium and its uncontrollable pleasures produced. They point perhaps toward film's actual qualities as a new forum for representing previously silenced groups of society. Obstinate women were taking their place on the screen and in front of it, always transgressing the traditional relationship of representation and identification through the subversive powers of sheer visual pleasure. The early cinema – a "brothel for the ladies?" And for feminists – a glimpse of the female gaze, of a woman's cinema at last?

One answer can been found in the films' specific relations to childhood. They define, across genres, but admitted openly only in silent film comedy, an understanding of desires that is distinctively fed by an anarchic notion of excess, a reminder of the body's resistance to total control. This other realm is, at worst, childish but, at best, polymorphously perverse. Gertrud Koch has argued in "Exchanging the Gaze: Re-Visioning Feminist Film Theory" that we need to redefine our concept of identification, given the evidence of spectatorial identification with objects as well. She claims: "If film attaches itself to such early layers of experience, then questions of identifying with charac-

11. Franz Reichwaldau, "Das ideale Kino," *Die Weltbühne* 16, no. 19 (1920): 84.

ters in fixed sexual roles have to be reconsidered. . . . We may, in fact, owe the invention of the camera not to the keyhole but the baby carriage."[12] Consequently, a reexamination of the parameters of spectacle and performance in silent film might reveal a subversive potential operating against the Oedipal claim. It may also help understand why the cinema can be a woman's place.

II.

Released in the same year as *The Cabinet of Dr. Caligari* (*Das Kabinett des Dr. Caligari*), *The Doll* could very well be called a forgotten masterpiece.[13] In sharp opposition to the critics' glorification of *Caligari*'s seductive male gloom, *The Doll* has been dismissed as primitive, superficial, amusing at best; yet, in light of rather striking similarities to *Caligari, The Doll,* in fact, represents the other, the feminine side of a similar project. Set in imaginary worlds, both films employ extreme stylization and fantastic plots to achieve their peculiar dream-like effects. They play with the theme of mastery and the revolt of its creations (Caligari and the somnambulist Caesare, Hilarius and his mechanical dolls); at the same time, they are told by the master narrators themselves (the surprising denouement of *Caligari* as a madman's story controlled by a clinical authority, Lubitsch's appearance as the storyteller in *The Doll*). Working in the tradition of Hoffmann's uncanny tales, Meliès' cinematic trickeries and the attractions of vaudeville and the fairground, *Caligari* and *The Doll* function within the genre of the fantastic but, as finished products, conjure up very different worlds and almost diametrically opposed pleasures. Against *The Cabinet of Dr. Caligari*'s male universe of horror and madness, *The Doll,* oscillating between comedy and fantasy, represents a polymorphously perverse paradise: indeed *Caligari*'s alter ego.

The above interpretation notwithstanding, a typical assessment of *The Doll,* to be found in a similarly typical film history, would criticize its heaviness, its mixture of styles and levels of representation, and take these as proof of a faulty verisimili-

12. Gertrud Koch, "Exchanging the Gaze: Revisioning Feminist Film Theory," *New German Critique* 34 (Winter 1985): 149.

13. Ernst Lubitsch, *Die Puppe* (Union-AG, 80 min.). Release: 4 Dec. 1919. Script: Hanns Kräly. Camera: Theodor Sparkuhl. Sets: Kurt Richter. With Ossi Oswalda (Ossi, the dollmaker's daughter), Herman Thimig (Lanzelot), Victor Janson (Hilarius, the dollmaker). Distributed in the United States through West Glen Films.

tude. The illusion fails, as Kirk Bond has maintained: "It [*The Doll*] is heavy and labored and while it, too, had a parade of fantastic bits, the fantasy does not come off."[14] One purpose of this paper is to question such a verdict against the film's level of "refinement" and, in doing so, to point toward other forms of the production of meaning – in particular those that admit pleasures outside of the tyranny of narrative and the fetishization of woman. Dismissed as unrefined, childish, and thus marginal to serious scholarship, *The Doll* poses a productive challenge for new approaches, particularly in its relation to pleasures that exist outside of the Oedipal mold.

In life and in the realm of metaphors, children and dreamers often serve as representatives of a consciousness closer to the primeval flow of desires. Similarly, certain films can be interpreted as clandestine attempts to salvage traces of that lost childhood happiness. They do so by foregounding the spectatorial relationships exclusively based on male voyeurism and by introducing other perspectives and other possible readings. The fairy tale atmosphere, the naiveté, and the irreverent playfulness of *The Doll* indeed transform its audience into children and dreamers, since its parameters are founded upon belief and the deliberate erosion of common logic. With consequences reaching beyond the blatancy of the film's disrupted narrative, grotesque acting, and visual design, these remembrances of a world based on wish fulfillment establish an even more fundamental opposition to the adult order. In contrast to traditional judgments of taste, Uta Berg-Ganschow's reading of *The Doll*, for instance, represents a more contemporary tendency to highlight the film's "folk tale humor" ("Komik wie auf dem Bauerntheater") or "Christmas tale-sets" ("Dekoration wie aus dem Weihnachtsmärchen"),[15] perceiving them as attributes of a subversive potential rather than a lack. Reduced to its plot, *The Doll* could be interpreted as an ironic comment on gender relations from a chauvinistic point of view. The problem is fear of women, or, as the film's hero programmatically proclaims: "I will not marry a woman!" The rich Baron of Chanterelle demands the marriage of his juvenile nephew Lanzelot (Hermann Thimig). Pursued by forty virgins, the "mama's boy" seeks

14. Kirk Bond, "Ernst Lubitsch," *Film Culture* 63/64 (1976): 144.

15. Uta Berg-Ganschow, "Die Puppe," in *Lubitsch*, ed. Hans Helmut Prinzler and Enno Patalas (Munich and Luzern: Stiftung Deutsche Kinemathek, 1984),187–88.

refuge in a cloister where greedy monks ("We give freely but little!") persuade him to marry a doll instead, so that they can spend his dowry on food and drink. Lanzelot agrees and visits the dollmaker Hilarius (Victor Janson), who has just finished a beautiful, life-sized mechanical doll modeled after his daughter Ossi (Ossi Oswalda). Critically inspecting the dollmaker's collection, Lanzelot puts down the conditions of sale ("I want a doll with a respectable character!"). At the same time, the pert apprentice, after a wild pas-de-deux, accidentally breaks the arm of the Ossi-doll. Out of compassion for the desperate boy, the real Ossi agrees to take the doll's place. Lanzelot immediately falls in love with her and transports his new toy to the cloister where the girl delights the monks with her mechanical dances. In the meantime, the old Baron of Chanterelle is dying from grief over his nephew's disappearance. The sight of his irreverent relatives who are fighting over the furniture and china, however, revitalizes the ailing man, as does Lanzelot's return with a bride. A splendid wedding is prepared. The bridegroom successfully manages to conceal the bride's mechanical nature while Ossi enjoys unobserved outbursts of human vitality by dancing, eating, and flirting. The wedding night finally brings the delicate complications to a climax when Lanzelot longingly lies down to dream of the kisses of a real woman. A mouse in the bedroom, finally, brings about the happy ending: Ossi jumps up, a "proof" that she is, after all, a real woman. In the next scene, Hilarius, with a severe case of somnambulism since his daughter's disappearance, similarly loses control: from the madness of his nightly balloon rides he falls to earth, only to be miraculously reunited with the happy couple. The film closes with the father's remarks toward the camera: "Now I'm rid of all problems."

The narrative and visual organization of *The Doll* is dominated by the image of the mechanical doll. Developed within a tradition of slapstick that thrives on the equation of the human and the mechanical, much of the film's humor plays with the choreographic potential of mechanical movement (repetition, stalling, malfunction) and the conflicts arising from the difference between woman and her double. The film's other source of humor is based on a play with gender roles that oscillates between a fatalistic perpetuation of clichés about sexual difference and their critical exposure through parody. Departing from the exaggerated stereotypes of the "devouring mother" ("What do you want from my baby?") and the "emasculated son," the film's contribution to sexual politics seems to result in the realization that the best wife is a doll. Yet the final victory of the real woman also suggests the superiority of physical desires, both for eroticism and for consumption. In this context, the image of the doll may initially be introduced into the plot as an expression of sexism but is utilized for a complex play of suspension, reversal, imitation, and travesty.

Already in the cinema of the 1910s, woman had been firmly established as the signifier of the erotic in the genres of the melodrama, the period film, and the chamber-play film (*Kammerspielfilm*). Only film comedies, and in particular those with no references to reality, allowed for narratives in which issues of sexuality and female emancipation could be momentarily resolved. They were able to define a field of fictitious transgressions of sexual identities that is characteristic of the silent film in Germany of the the 1910s and 1920s. The recurrent motif of masquerade is most evident in the so-called *Hosenrolle* (women playing men) but also can take on less obvious forms. The aesthetic and erotic ideal of androgyny or the popularity of the tomboy character are only two avenues through which film responded to the demand for new role models and changed sexual attitudes that came together in the myth of the New Woman.[16] The doll is, in this context, only the most extreme form of a female masquerade that bears subversive potential. By pretending to be somebody else, the heroine is equipped with a framework that allows her to take the liberties traditionally denied to her by society. As her self-chosen mirror image, Ossi is even more alive, expressing her joy through a physicality that almost serves as a reminder of another repressed identity.

However, while the image of the doll succeeds in satisfying the desire for transgression, it is also held in place by two important formal devices. The first rests on the fact that the doll is the master's creation to a degree unparalleled by biological paterni-

16. A frequent motif in Lubitsch films, female strategies of masquerade usually contain negative connotations in that their liberating effects are only achieved through pretense (*The Merry Jail,* 1917), scheme (*Deception,* 1919), or ugliness (*Kohlhiesel's Daughters,* 1920) and are sacrificed at the first sight of love. For a discussion of masquerade, see also Mary Ann Doane, "Film and the Masquerade: Theorizing the Female Spectator," *Screen* 23–24 (Sept./Oct. 1982): 74–87.

ty. Here Lubitsch continues the strong tradition of exclusive father-daughter relationships begun with *The Pride of the Company* (*Der Stolz der Firma,* 1914). Whereas all his films are built on the denial of motherhood and traditional femininity, only *The Doll* ironically comments on these absences by actually representing the daughter/doll as one of her father's commodities.[17] The position of Hilarius as the ultimate creator becomes most obvious in his sales presentation for Lanzelot. By the turn of a large wheel, a group of dolls is set into motion. This cranking movement, of course, is a reference to the cinematic apparatus itself, with Lubitsch in the position of Hilarius. At the same time, this image of giving life also points to the film's central signifier – woman – when the animated corps de ballet aggressively approaches and encircles Lanzelot with daring Cancan steps. The second formal device is the film's generic reference to the motif of the double (*Doppelgänger*). In the context of its unique position in Expressionist cinema, the double represents the dark and repressed side of the male psyche, an unconscious that is characterized by greed, lust for destruction, and a fatalistic drivenness. While the typical conflict of the male double was, for the most part, elaborated in melodramatic and fantastic modes of representation, comedy became the domain of the female double.[18] Whereas the female double (within the framework of comedy) tends to signify liberation and the invocation of the pleasure principle, the narrative of the male double (the prime example being *The Student of Prague*) is inseparably linked to death as its only chance of denouement. Yet the disclosure of female masquerade, the end of her double existence, is pacified in the gesture of the heterosexual kiss and the promise of marriage.

Two modes of intervention into the narrative are responsible for the film's subversive quality, the first already taking place in the opening shot. *The Doll* begins with an exemplary token

17. Examples for a tradition of dominant father-daughter relationships are numerous throughout Lubitsch's career: *The Eyes of the Mummy* (*Die Augen der Mumie Ma,* 1918), *The Oyster Princess* (*Die Austernprinzessin,* 1919), *The Smiling Lieutenant* (1931), *Design for Living* (1933), *Bluebeard's Eighth Wife* (1938).

18. Its rules were exemplarily tested by Lubitsch in his film version of the popular play *Kohlhiesel's Daughters,* with actress Henny Porten in the double role of the pretty and ugly sister. For a discussion of the male double, see Thomas Elsaesser, "Social Mobility and the Fantastic: German Silent Cinema," *Wide Angle* 5, no. 2 (1982): 14–25. For a distinction between the fantastic and the marvelous, with the latter obviously closer to the female narratives of the fantastic, see Tzvetan Todorov, *The Fantastic. A Structural Approach to a Literary Genre* (Cleveland and London: Press of Case Western Reserve University, 1973).

appearance of its director. Lubitsch is shown as he opens a magic box and begins setting up a miniature model with trees, a house, a bench, and two costume dolls. Through a close-up of the entrance door and an invisible superimposition, the film makes the transgression from model to reality; at the end, identically dressed actors leave the house. The fact that Lubitsch presents himself as the great magician and film as the art of sorcery is underscored by the prologue's ending. The actor falls into the studio pond and his shivering plea toward an overcast sky ("Dear sun, please shine, so that I won't catch a cold!") is fulfilled by the parting clouds and a smiling sun. A world of immediate gratification is thus presented, one of basic desires and a phantasmagoric unity of imagination and reality. Its precondition is belief, a belief that is aware of the modes of its own production, but nevertheless is not invalidated by the supremacy of reason. To what degree the forces of imagination succeed can be measured by the intensity of the sun rays that make the man's clothes steam.

The disruptive function of a commentator – reminiscent of the live narrator known from the early nickelodeons (*Kientopp*) – is maintained throughout the film in the figure of the dollmaker's apprentice. He serves as the filmmakers's representative, commenting upon the development of the plot and the characterization of the protagonists. At the same time, this figure can be interpreted as an ironic self-reference to Lubitsch's own background as a comedian.[19] There is no gesture that is not ridiculed by the boy's exaggerated imitations, which almost drive the plot into a playful nihilism. In his performance, one finds the self-indulgent moves of the grand charmer (kissing first the daughter, then the mother, and commenting: "Nobody should feel left out") and the sovereignty of the experienced businessman (when receiving customers). As a comment on slapstick acting, he involves Hilarius in a frantic chase through the kitchen which ends with many broken dishes. And as a reference to the melodrama, he first commits suicide by drinking paint (Hilarius: "Are you crazy to drink these expensive paints?"), then by jumping out of the window of a ground-level room. But his desperate question "What is a bad life worth?"

19. After all, Lubitsch began his career with playing comical stock characters. As Meyer, Moritz or Sally Pinkus, he usually worked in a shoe-salon or clothing-store winning, in the end, the daughter and the business.

finds its quintessential Lubitsch answer in an attractively displayed apple that catches his attention. He grabs it and begins to chew, now smiling.

The second mode of narrative disruption can be located in the film's shifting levels of representation. The film, instead of striving toward naturalism, moves clearly in the direction of abstraction and caricature. Lubitsch himself commented upon this realm of fantasy: "It was pure fantasy, most of its sets were made of cardboard, even some out of paper. Even to this day I still consider it one of the most imaginative films I ever made."[20] Trees are suggested by round and triangular shapes, surfaces are painted, a horse is obviously played by two persons in a horse costume, and the sky is occupied by naively drawn clouds and a sun and moon that smile over the activities of the human beings. Particularly the night- and dream-sequences are dominated by animation; examples are the balloon flight of Hilarius and the graphic night silhouette of the small town. The actors are fully integrated into this fantastic scenery through their imaginative costumes and grotesque acting style. The denial of all conventions of realism is even taken a step further in the film's literary representation of popular sayings. When Lanzelot anxiously knocks at the door of the dollmaker's shop, something falls out of his trousers leg: a gingerbread heart, which he then quickly returns to his chest.[21] Upon exclaiming "This is indeed hair-raising!" the hair of Hilarius literally rises and turns grey. And later, with Ossi's happy return, his hair (in a reversed trick sequence) falls and returns to its natural color. Sometimes however, Lubitsch's humor proves less harmless. More than playing on the comical transformation of verbal expressions into images, his visual tricks serve as sharp criticisms, for instance when he exposes the greed of the barons' relatives by devising a tableau of twelve nagging mouths in close-up.

With its multiple levels of representation and playful appropriation of literary tropes, a film like *The Doll* represents a challenge to film theory and the historiographical work on the German silent cinema. Its uniqueness must be seen within a gridwork of diverse genre references and as an experimental exploration of film's material possibilities. The film's simultaneous

20. Herman G. Weinberg, *The Lubitsch Touch* (New York: Dover, 1977), 285.

21. Cf. the saying "Ihm fällt das Herz in die Hose," translated as: "The heart falls into his boots."

satisfaction and repression of revolt are proof of a complexity that defies its innocent surface. In this sense, the formal framework of the fairy tale is far from primitive, but extremely well balanced between rationality and imagination. And within those enclosures, masquerade for women can be appropriated as precisely that chance for self-distantiation that it theoretically holds. *The Doll*, then, tells the refreshing story of how the transformation of women into objects of male desire can turn against that same order. First, the female protagonist finds a realm of liberty and creativity by playfully mirroring the male projections that constitute her new identity. Then, this mirror effect is ironically taken to its limits in the ways the heroine, as doll and human being, performs and thereby undermines this notion of the ideal woman. Finally, the happy ending of *The Doll* suggests that real women are preferable to dolls, an insight, however, that is only possible after women have disputed the male order.

Searching for traces of femininity and the female gaze, then, represents a complex undertaking: the search for the female spectator, a social and historical category, and for the feminine as metaphor for the cinema and visual pleasure, hence a literary category. As part of two distinct discourses, women as historical subjects and the feminine as a narrative device are, and this I want to emphasize, not identical. In what ways they entertain a relationship to each other is a different issue altogether, yet their unreflected conflation has produced more confusion for feminist scholarship than clarity. Furthermore, to recuperate a liberated female spectator for the project of a feminist film theory (or feminism, for that matter), indeed falls prey to the same gender essentialism that, in the first place, made possible the metaphorical representation of the cinema as the feminine. Writing about silent film, visual pleasure and the feminine then means no less than an archeological adventure, a constant reading through the displacements and condensations performed within and by the texts, a thinking through of projections and superimpositions, and a willing acknowledgment of disparities and ambiguities. Films like *The Oyster Princess* and *The Doll* are crucial to that project.

2

The Role of the Vamp in Weimar Cinema: An Analysis of Karl Grune's *The Street (Die Straße)*

bruce murray

In his essay on Karl Grune's The Street *(1923), Bruce Murray draws on Klaus Theweleit's* Male Fantasies *in his effort to expose the psychoanalytical as well as sociohistorical determinants of the function of the "vamp" in Weimar cinema – and what that implies about misogyny in Weimar society. The psycho-social dynamics of the Weimar Republic are especially interesting because they undoubtedly played a role in the rise of the political order that followed: Hitler's "Third Reich." Murray, like Theweleit, sees misogyny in the Weimar Republic as one of the patriarchal attitudes integral to National Socialist ideology – and the personality type that enabled it to become dominant.*
—THE EDITORS

Since the 1970s the interest in the portrayal of women in German literature has increased. In addition to focusing attention narrowly on female authors and their portrayal of gender roles, Germanists continue to investigate the quality of female figures in the works of male authors from Bertolt Brecht to Peter Handke.[1] Among many others, Klaus Theweleit's study of *Freikorps* literature has stimulated a lively discussion by investigating the

1. See, for example, Sara Lennox, "Women in Brecht's Works," *New German Critique* 14 (1978): 83–96; Sabine Schröder-Krassnow, "The Changing View of Abortion: A Study of Friedrich Wolf's *Cyankali* and Arnold Zweig's *Junge Frau von 1914*," *Studies in Twentieth Century Literature* 1 (1981): 33–47; A.J.K. Moeller, "The Woman as Survivor: The Development of the Female Figure in Heinrich Böll's Fiction," *DAI* (1979): 1492A–93A; and Michael Klein, "Peter Handke: *Die linkshändige Frau*: Fiktion eines Märchens," in *Studien zur Literatur des 19. und 20. Jahrhunderts in Österreich,* Johann Holzner et al., eds. (Innsbruck: Kowatsch, 1981), 235–52.

influence of psychological constraints on the way male authors write about women and everything that is foreign to the male perspective.[2]

Theweleit suggests that the process of identity formation in industrialized, patriarchal societies fosters a system for perceiving and evaluating women that finds frequent expression in literature written by males. In a revision of Freudian positions, he claims that the male child's exit from the symbiotic phase of development is extremely significant for male concepts of woman.[3] Borrowing heavily from the work of Gilles Deleuze and Felix Guattari, Theweleit asserts that even before the male child can discern human subjects, distinguish between mother and father, and develop the Freudian oedipal complex, he begins to perceive parts of the mother's body as other. As the symbiosis between mother and male child continues to dissolve, the mother's body remains a center of attention for the infant. According to Theweleit, at this stage the infant male is little more than a "wish-producing machine" who identifies the mother's body both as the source of pleasure, when the mother responds promptly to his wishes, and as the source of displeasure when the mother hesitates or neglects to satisfy his wishes.

Theweleit discusses the quality and function of this process in great detail, considering its further progress in the patriarchal family and in the other institutions of modern Western societies. It is sufficient here to note that, according to his perspective, the male child in such societies often exits the symbiotic phase either too slowly or too quickly and, as a result, develops only a fragmentary identity. The partially formed male identity never transcends its focus on diametrically opposed images of woman either as nurturing or threatening and projects similar images in the act of perceiving and evaluating everything that is familiar and foreign to him. According to Theweleit, these are precisely the images that dominate the literature of the *Freikorps* males.

2. Klaus Theweleit, *Männerphantasien,* 2 vols. (Frankfurt/M: Roter Stern, 1977 and 1978). An English translation of both volumes is now available. See *Male Fantasies.* Stephen Conway in collaboration with Erica Carter and Chris Turner, Theory of History and Literature, vols. 22 and 23 (Minneapolis: Univ. of Minnesota Press, 1987 and 1989). The focal point of Theweleit's study is the analysis of novels, poems, diaries, etc., that were written by the mercenaries (*Freikorps*) of reactionary aristocrats and military leaders during the early years of crisis in the Weimar Republic.

3. Theweleit outlines his revision of Freudian positions most succinctly in the *Zwischenergebnisse* of *Männerphantasien,* 1: 253–88.

Theweleit's insights about the connection between sexuality and literary production have influenced film studies as well.[4] The most detailed application of Theweleit's approach for film analysis is that of Andreas Huyssen in his essay, "Technology and Sexuality in Fritz Lang's *Metropolis*."[5] Huyssen discusses, among other things, the significance of personified technology in the robot-vamp Maria. He suggests that the film associates the Expressionist fear of technology with the fear of a female sexuality threatening to male domination through what was perceived as its role in initiating chaos. In *Metropolis*, upper-class men lust after the machine-woman when she performs a belly dance, and later they follow her through the city's streets, shouting, "Let's watch the world go to the devil!" The robot-vamp also turns the workers in the catacombs beneath Metropolis into a raging, machine-destroying mob.

Huyssen concludes that it is no accident when, near the end of the film, the robot-vamp burns as the citizens of Metropolis watch. Threatening female sexuality must be destroyed so that the male leaders of the city can regain control: "After the dangers of a mystified technology have been translated into the dangers an equally mystified female sexuality poses to man, the witch could be burnt at the stake and, by implication, technology could be purged of its threatening aspects. What remains is a serene view of technology as a harbinger of social progress."[6] The promise of social progress is symbolized by the union of Freder, son of the city's leader, and the "real," asexual Maria in the film's final scene.

Commercial Weimar filmmakers recognized the potential of mystified female sexuality years before *Metropolis* was made in 1925/1926. Immediately following World War I, when censorship laws were abolished, many film companies began producing *Aufklärungsfilme* ("educational" films about sexuality that producers marketed as personal hygiene films, i.e., to combat venereal disease, etc.). The majority of such films focused on female prostitution and reproduced male images of woman as

4. Of course, the discussions about the relationship between semiotics and psychoanalysis in recent studies, too, have contributed significantly to investigations of gender roles and their influence on the production and reception of film. For a good introduction to work on semiotics and psychoanalysis, see Kaja Silverman, *The Subject of Semiotics* (New York: Oxford Univ. Press, 1983).

5. Andreas Huyssen, "Technology and Sexuality in Fritz Lang's *Metropolis*," *New German Critique* 24–25 (Fall/Winter 1981–82): 221–37.

6. Ibid., 236.

either absolutely good or evil. With titles such as *The White Slave Woman* (*Die Weiße Sklavin*) and *The Parisian Toy* (*Das Spielzeug von Paris*) filmmakers attracted men whose repressed libidinal drives manifested themselves in the desire to enslave women or make toys of them. With titles like *Passion and Love* (*Leidenschaft und Liebe*) and *Sensuality and Lust* (*Sinnlichkeit und Sinnengier*) they aimed at men and women who yearned for the passion and sensuality that was absent from the relationships of many in modern German society.[7] The recipe for "enlightenment" employed by these filmmakers was to present fictional heroes and heroines with whom spectators could identify. The protagonists fell prey to evil female sexuality in the world of prostitutes, pimps, and other criminals. There they were threatened, abused, and exploited. In the end fathers rescued their victimized daughters, and young men narrowly escaped, returning to the security of the patriarchal family.

Although the *Aufklärungsfilme* affirmed traditional values, conservative religious and political organizations argued that they tempted more than they deterred. Protest from such groups led to the reintroduction of censorship and to increased attempts to control attitudes about sexuality.[8] However, the commercial success of *Aufklärungsfilme* influenced production more than censorship. Producers continued to make films about socially unacceptable forms of sexuality, but they devised less provocative titles and emphasized more the alleged dangers of sexual deviance. The result was the emergence of a new type of *Aufklärungsfilm* that Siegfried Kracauer referred to as the "street" film.[9] Kracauer derived the name from Karl Grune's *The Street* (1923).

Between 1919 and 1924 German cinema began to assert its independence from relatively close relationships to the institutions of literature and theater.[10] At the same time, the decreasing value of German currency lowered the cost of domestic pro-

7. For a discussion of these and similar films, see Curt Moreck, *Sittengeschichte des Kinos* (Dresden: Paul Aretz, 1926), 130 ff. There is no production information available for many of the films cited by Moreck, including the films that I have mentioned. As a result, I have omitted them from the list of works cited.

8. Siegfried Kracauer, *From Caligari to Hitler: A Psychological History of the German Film* (Princeton, N. J.: Princeton Univ. Press, 1947), pp. 43–47.

9. Ibid., 157–160.

10. For a good introduction to the development of the cinematic institution in Germany between 1919 and 1924, see Peter Bächlin, *Der Film als Ware* (Frankfurt/M.: Fischer, 1975), 34–53.

duction, enabling German producers to undercut competitors in foreign markets and profit measurably. Competition stimulated the gradual process of standardization. The star system blossomed, commercially successful films set standards for genres, and the guidelines for efficient production grew increasingly rigid. But, at least until the middle of the Weimar era, moderately liberal conditions for artistic experimentation prevailed.

During the second half of the Weimar era the conditions for experimentation slowly disappeared. Hollywood producers competed intensely for control of the German film market once the value of the German currency stabilized after 1924, and the process of standardization accelerated. German producers strove increasingly to maximize their chances for commercial success by innovatively recasting popular narratives, marketing stars, universalizing the appeal of their products, and offering commercial entertainment instead of edification. Within this context the "street" film genre flourished. It appealed to the petit-bourgeois desire for release from the constraints of everyday life by featuring petit-bourgeois protagonists who fled the "monotony and drabness" of their homes for the "glamor and excitement" of the street. It also addressed the petit-bourgeois fear of proletarianization by portraying the threat of social disenfranchisement for those protagonists who left the security of their homes.[11]

The "street" films avoided the overt portrayal of politically-motivated distinctions between characters and their environments – distinctions that might correspond to the perceptions of a specific interest group while contradicting the views of others. However, the apparently depoliticized "street" film narrative promoted a specific ideological orientation. Despite the film's innocuous title, an analysis of *The Street* reveals that, in its role as a paradigm for a new genre, it promoted the maintenance of patriarchy and associated the threat to patriarchal authority with the mysterious and dangerous woman of the street.

Karl Grune worked diligently to develop a pictorial language in cinema that could communicate with the complexity of spoken language. He avoided titles and filled his films with imagery. Nevertheless, *The Street* begins with a short exposition-

11. For an excellent series of essays on the petite bourgeoisie in the Weimar Republic, see Siegfried Kracauer, *Die Angestellten*, in *Schriften*, ed. Karsten Witte (Frankfurt/M.: Suhrkamp, 1971), 1: 205–81.

al text, characterizing its male protagonist as typical and introducing spectators to its binary system: "There comes a moment in the life of nearly every man, be he good or bad, when, appalled by the monotony and drabness of his daily life, his soul yearns for something different – he longs for the unknown, for the glamor and excitement of the other man, the man in the street." When the text disappears, the image of a man lying on a sofa in a dark room replaces it. The size of the room, its furnishings, and the man's appearance identify him as a middle-aged member of the petty bourgeoisie. Kracauer calls him a philistine.[12] The man is listless, and his face is expressionless. Everything about him communicates boredom. As the narrative unfolds, the man's monotonous daily life becomes associated with his wife. The unknown world of the street is linked with the mystified, dangerous aura of a prostitute.

The next sequence begins with a shot centering on a simply dressed woman who is framed in a heart. In contrast to the motionless man in the dark room, the woman energetically prepares dinner in a well-lit kitchen. The woman opens the kitchen door, a stream of light covers the man on the sofa, and the woman, who is now recognizable as the man's wife, enters. She covers the table with a bright tablecloth and presents a large tureen of steaming soup. The framing heart, the animated gestures in the kitchen, and the association with light and warmth all characterize the wife as a virtuous, hard-working, and nurturing woman. She embodies the patriarchal female ideal.

During the next sequence, the narrative perspective changes from that of a bystander to that of the man. Shadows of figures on the street begin to appear on the ceiling and attract the man's attention. Spectators first discern the shadow of a woman. A second shadow, that of a man, appears. The man tips his hat, the woman departs, and the man skips away after her. The encounter between a prostitute and her customer stimulates the listless husband's first motion. He reaches up to touch the male shadow and, when the shadow skips away, his arm drops again suddenly. He seems to identify with the male shadow and to long for the excitement of the street where male customers dominate female prostitutes. The perception is reinforced by what follows.

The man rises from the sofa and moves to the window. He

12. Ibid., 120.

looks out the window at the traffic on the street. The filmic gaze once again identifies with his perspective. A montage of images replaces the view of the traffic, portraying the man's perception of the glamor and excitement that he associates with the street. Among the images are roller-coaster cars splashing into water. As the montage continues, the face of an attractive woman appears. The roller-coaster cars splash into the water, and a spray covers the woman's face, creating an image of the sexual desires connected with his longing for glamor and excitement.

At this point the husband faces a choice. Should he eat the meal that his wife has prepared for him or flee into the street where mystified female sexuality awaits him? The narrative by no means remains impartial in its portrayal. The expositional connection between the street and the unknown, the contrast between the warmth and light of the wife on the one hand and the dark shadow of the prostitute on the other, and the suggestion that the husband's perception of the street is only an image created by his distorted sexual desires all imply that his decision to flee is a mistake. As the narrative develops, plot structure, editing, imagery, and lighting reinforce the evaluation.

In the street the petit-bourgeois adventurer encounters a prostitute. She lures him into a nightclub where he loses his money in a card game. She then invites him and a wealthy provincial man to her apartment. There the prostitute's pimp/husband and his partner attempt to rob the wealthy man. They accidentally kill him and frame the naive protagonist for their crime. The protagonist's next stop is the police station. In his jail cell the totally dejected man prepares to take his life. However, a policeman interrupts his attempted suicide with the news that the real murderers have confessed. He is released and returns to the security of his petit-bourgeois home and wife. The episode cures the adventurer of his fantasies about the street. His perception of that world as a glamorous and exciting place where he could satisfy his sexual desires was imaginary. The street, according to the narrative, is a dangerous place, inhabited by evil women who control petit-bourgeois men more than such men can control women.

The editing techniques employed in *The Street* encourage spectators to agree with the male victim's final evaluation of the dangerous street and its threatening women. The organization of sequences gives the spectator information about the people in the street that is withheld from the unsuspecting adventurer. Before the protagonist encounters the prostitute, for example, the narrative reveals that she is looking for a man whom she can lure into a card game with her gambling pimp/husband. When she confronts the wandering man and claims that she has been robbed, we know that she is lying. Juxtapositions of shots depicting the prostitute's child, who crosses intersections alone and must be rescued by the police, with shots of the prostitute and her admirer reinforce the spectator's condemnation of her. As the naive, petit-bourgeois man gradually falls into her trap, the spectator's desire to warn him grows. The inability to intervene creates a tension that strengthens the perception of the prostitute as a dangerous threat and of her admirer as an unwitting victim.

Imagery and lighting also signal to the spectator that the street and its women are dangerous. Throughout the film, light and darkness distinguish the wife from the prostitute. When the fleeing husband reaches the street, night is falling. Darkness intensifies the atmosphere of insecurity, mystery, and danger that persists until he leaves the jail the next morning. As the prostitute leads her admirer through the darkness, various images warn him of danger. When he makes advances toward the prostitute in a poorly lit park, the headlights of a police car shine on them. The eyes of an optician's sign glare at the man as he follows the prostitute to the nightclub. The headlights and the glaring eyes appear as symbols of an ever-present authority that condemns the man's behavior. In the nightclub the man pauses to observe his new environment. The room begins to spin. When he removes his wedding ring to conceal his identity, he sees an image of himself and his wife in the center of the ring. Everything he experiences suggests that he should abandon his pursuit of the prostitute. The threatening world of the street with its dangerous female sexuality will destroy him. He belongs in the world depicted in the ring: next to his wife at home.

For male spectators who rejected the rationalization and fragmentation of life in Weimar society and felt especially threatened by its frequent economic and political crises, the message was clear. To abandon the existing social order and contemplate change meant potential chaos and destruction. Support for the social status quo was the lesser of two evils.

Between 1924 and the end of the Weimar era, a wide variety of "street" films, including *The Tragedy of a Prostitute* (*Dirnentragödie,* 1927), *Asphalt* (1928), and *The Blue Angel* (*Der blaue Engel,* 1930) encouraged petit-bourgeois male spectators to content themselves with unsatisfactory working and living conditions. In each case, the association between threatening environments and threatening females on the one hand, secure environments and nurturing females on the other, underscores the dominance of relatively undifferentiated perceptions of reality. But how did such perceptions achieve a dominant position in Weimar culture?

During the final years of the Weimar Republic, the economy deteriorated, the republican government dissolved, and everyday reality became increasingly confusing. In the process, the number of simplistic evaluations that portrayed crisis in terms of binary oppositions and posited radical solutions increased dramatically in all forms of modern mass media. So, too, did the number of people who accepted such evaluations and supported alternatives that were based on a strong desire for the security of a nurturing nation and a deathly fear of "foreign elements."

If one accepts the Theweleitian perspective, explanations for the popularity of such ideological perspectives (usually associated with National Socialism) that focus narrowly either on the charismatic power of a few individuals, the deterministic force of economic factors, or Freudian psychological models seem insufficient. The analysis of Weimar culture, including *Freikorps* literature, monumental films such as *Metropolis,* and the "street" film genre suggests just how significant even pre-oedipal psychological processes may be in the development of fascistic behavior. It is possible, if not likely, that disturbances (albeit socially influenced disturbances) in the earliest stages of male identity formation contributed to a male system for interacting with reality that helped to shape the petit-bourgeois perception of the Weimar Republic as it appeared in films such as *The Street.* It is equally plausible that such a system contributed to the National Socialist perception of reality and continues to affect the way we perceive reality in the industrialized, patriarchal societies of the present.

3

History and Realism: Representations of Women in G. W. Pabst's *The Joyless Street*

tracy myers

Tracy Myers's essay on G.W. Pabst's Joyless Street (Die freudlose Gasse, *1925) places this film, traditionally lauded for its "social realism," against the actual social and economic context that it purports to depict: the Austrian inflation of the early 1920s. She compares the Austrian situation to the German one, since Germany was the country in which the film was made (by Pabst, an Austrian) and marketed, just a few years after the chaotic inflation in both countries had ended. Her primary emphasis, however, is a comparison of the social and political situation of women in Austria and Germany with the roles women characters play in Pabst's film.*
—The Editors

When G. W. Pabst's *The Joyless Street* (*Die freudlose Gasse*) was released in 1925, it stunned audiences[1] and was variously subjected to censorial deletion of large portions of its text or complete banning throughout Europe and in the Soviet Union and America.[2] *Vorwärts*, the Social Democrats' official newspaper in Berlin, described the film as presenting

> a breathtaking portrait of the inflationary period sweeping through Vienna like a devastating torrid wind. We still stand too close to

1. Eileen Bowser, Program notes for The Museum of Modern Art's 7 Jan. and 12 Jan. 1980 screenings of the film, 1.

2. See for instance Siegfried Kracauer, *From Caligari to Hitler: A Psychological History of the German Film*, (Princeton: Princeton University Press, 1947), 167; Paul Rotha, *The Film Till Now*, 2d ed. (New York: Funk and Wagnalls, 1951), 86–87; and Arthur Sus, Program notes for Roosevelt University Film Society's 6 Oct. 1965 screening of the film, 2.

> these events, and have experienced them too much in our own bodies, to be able to face them yet with appropriate distance; we are still whipped into fury by the contents of the film, still roused to deep compassion for the countless victims of this pestilence that gnawed at humanity's physical and moral health, still shake our fists at the shameless exploiters of this crisis and the impudent lechers who everywhere captured their prey.[3]

The implication of this assessment, and the assumption from which most subsequent commentary has proceeded, is that it was the film's unusually realistic depiction of the social and economic conditions of the period portrayed that caused it to elicit negative popular and official response.[4] Yet, while a reading of *The Joyless Street* as exemplary of "the new realism" in German cinema during the second half of the 1920s recognizes the film's historical accuracy, the realism alleged is of a circumscribed nature. That is, although the film addresses issues of obvious and general social interest, it also subtly raises questions of gender construction and sexual politics that are subordinated to the manifest concerns of its text. The purposes of this article are first, to investigate the way in which such questions are highlighted by the film's characterizations, and second, to explore the connotations of those characterizations as reflections of the social and economic experience of women in Germany's Weimar Republic. The intent of this twofold analysis is to redefine *The Joyless Street*'s realism to account for a broader understanding of the history which underlies it.

Set in Vienna in the hyperinflationary year of 1923, *The Joyless Street* was adapted by Pabst from a novel written by Hugo Bettauer and serialized in that city's most influential newspaper, *Neue Freie Presse* (*New Free Press*).[5] The film portrays the econom-

3. *Vorwärts* (3d supplement, unpaginated): "ein packendes Gemälde der Inflationszeit, wie sie durch Wien wie ein verwustender Glutwind gegangen ist. Wir stehen diesen Ereignissen noch zu nahe und haben sie am eigenen Leibe zu sehr erfahren, um ihnen schon mit erforderlicher Distanz gegenüberstehen zu können, noch werden wir von dem Inhalt des Films aufgepeitscht, noch zum tiefsten Mitleid fortgerissen mit den zahlosen Opfern dieser Pest, die die physische und moralische Gesundheit der Menschen angefressen hat, noch ballt sich uns die Faust gegen die schamlosen Ausbeuter dieser Notlage und die frechen Lustlinge, die sich überall ihre Beute holten."

4. See Bowser, Program notes, 1; and Kracauer, *Caligari to Hitler*, 167. An important exception to this generalization is Patrice Petro's disclosure of the gender–related Foundation of the censorship of the film, published after this article was written. See Petro, *Joyless Streets*, 199–219, exp. 213–16.

5. Lee Atwell, *G. W. Pabst* (Boston: Twayne, 1977), 25 and 29–30; and Kracauer, *Caligari to Hitler*, 167.

ic and moral decline of Vienna's middle and working classes that resulted from the financial destabilization of Germany and Austria after World War I. Framed within and intercut by a contrast between life in the street and that of the privileged nightclub atmosphere of conspicuous consumption, the experiences of Greta Rumfort and Marie Lechner (Greta Garbo and Asta Nielsen, respectively) are chronicled through a complex series of textual and pictorial oppositions and the presentation of parallel narratives.[6]

Greta is the daughter of a retired, widowed civil servant (Jaro Furth); Marie's parents are a washerwoman and an apparently unemployed, crippled father (Sylvia Torf and Max Kohlkase). The contrast between Greta's and Marie's stations in life – and the conditions that can be argued to propel them to their very different ends – are highlighted from the beginning of the film: having unsuccessfully waited all night outside the local butcher shop to purchase meat, Greta is greeted by her father with resignation and a plea for patience, whereas Marie meets with an angry outburst by her father and plaintive glances from her mother. Proceeding from this initial opposition, the film becomes, on its surface, an investigation of the lengths to which Greta and Marie will go to remedy their respective economic situations.

Greta's story is that of the pure and selfless servant to familial obligation. On the same day that her father's investment of his entire pension has been lost in what proves to be a stock market swindle, Greta quits her office job after her boss repeatedly attempts to exploit her sexually. Upon learning of the loss of the family's money, Greta undertakes in a variety of most resourceful ways to secure an income for the family. She first attempts to borrow money from Frau Greifer (Valeska Gert), a procuress and couturière, who openly flirts with the stunning and seemingly sexually vulnerable Greta. Frau Greifer arranges for Greta to meet with "a very influential visitor" (the lascivious

6. This structure makes very difficult the establishment of a temporal sequence, particularly with respect to the narrative concerning Marie. I believe that structural incongruities and instances of seemingly obscure character motivation are due in large part to the fact that the print on which this study is based was reconstructed (with English intertitles) from the original shooting script by Papst's assistant director, Marc Sorkin, from copies preserved by the Cinematheque Français and the Cineteca Italiana. Even after restoration, the equivalent of two of the original ten reels is missing from this print (Atwell, *Pabst,* 36). It should be noted that the version on which my study is based differs significantly from the German version of the film. The different versions available here and in Germany affect interpretation; see Petro, *Joyless Streets,* 216, no. 55.

butcher, portrayed by Werner Krauß) to her establishment – the implication being, of course, that Greta will prostitute herself in order to feed her family. Although the attempted transaction is ultimately aborted through Greta's reticence, Frau Greifer nonetheless loans Greta money in return for her promise to join Frau Greifer at her next soiree.

In the interim, the Rumforts rent the family's spare room to an American soldier, Lt. Davy (Einar Hansen), who is immediately attracted to Greta. The apparent resolution of the family's financial difficulties is thwarted, however, when Councillor Rumfort's stockbroker calls, requesting settlement of the former's account. Indeed, each occasion on which the family has hope for financial stability is frustrated by calamity: the rent received from Lt. Davy is consumed in payment of the broker's bill; the money "loaned" to Greta by Frau Greifer is used to replace a window accidentally broken by Greta and Lt. Davy's friend in a playful moment; upon hearing Lt. Davy (rightfully) accuse Greta's younger sister of pilfering some of his provisions, Councillor Rumfort evicts him in angry disbelief at his attempt to blight the Rumfort name, thus eliminating rent as a source of income. When Councillor Rumfort collapses from nervous exhaustion, the family's limited funds are further depleted by payment of the doctor's bill.

Greta, now at a complete loss for alternatives, returns to Frau Greifer and succumbs, albeit most unwillingly, to the only apparent option left to her. While trying to evade a man who is a client hotly pursuing her, Greta stumbles onto the stage of the club, where she is seen by Lt. Davy. Angered by what he now believes to have been a pretense of virtue, he chastises Greta for her immorality, to which she responds, "Yes – like so many other Viennese girls, to save our parents from starving." As Lt. Davy starts to leave Frau Greifer's in disgust, Councillor Rumfort arrives there, seeking his daughter. Embracing Greta in warm acknowledgement of her devotion and sacrifice, he both apologizes to Lt. Davy for unfairly evicting him and explains the reason for Greta's seeming deception. Lt. Davy and Greta are reconciled, and the last shot of the film shows them in an embrace before a lighted window.

In opposition to this story line is the complicated narrative concerning Marie, whose motives and actions are ultimately depicted to be as self-serving as Greta's are self-denying. After being reprimanded by her father, Marie writes to her boyfriend Egon Stirner (Henry Stuart), an office clerk, telling him that she can no longer bear her miserable situation at home and will visit him the next day. While Marie returns to the butcher shop, Egon dines at a local restaurant with his boss, Viennese financier Herr Rosenow. Among Rosenow's guests are South American speculator Don Alfonso Canez, with whom Rosenow engineers the stock swindle that victimizes Councillor Rumfort; Regina Rosenow, Rosenow's daughter and another of Egon's lovers; Herr Leid, Rosenow's attorney; and Leid's wife, Lia.

Egon stands to benefit from his associations with these people in a number of ways. His "inside knowledge" of Rosenow and Canez's stock market deal will bring him financial gain, which will in turn make him a more acceptable match for Regina, who has implored him to prove his love for her by becoming rich. The adulterous and seductive Lia, with whom Egon plans a rendezvous – in full view, and with the approval, of Regina – likewise offers the prospect of profitable financial connections, as well as sexual satisfaction.

This set of relations simultaneously excludes and ensnares Marie. She visits Egon as he prepares for his meeting with Lia, and promises to be Egon's servant and dedicate herself to his happiness if he will let her stay with him. Egon claims that only money can make him happy, explaining that a mere $100 investment could make him rich. Marie resolves to obtain for him the money he needs to invest in the stock market.

Just as Greta's determination to prevent her family's starvation had led her to Frau Greifer's to sell herself, Marie's desire for Egon's affection and her resolution to help him achieve his financial goal also impel her to the procuress, from whom she intends to borrow the $100 Egon needs. While at Frau Greifer's, she is discovered and propositioned by Canez (who is there "sampling the famous Viennese nightlife"), whom she hesitantly accommodated at the Hotel Merkl – the site also of Egon and Lia's rendezvous. Later, Egon, Regina, Rosenow, and Leid are informed at the restaurant that Lia has been robbed and murdered at the Hotel. Regina's shocked look at Egon suggests she thinks he is the murderer.

A second transaction between Marie and Canez is interrupted by a police investigator, Frau Greifer, and the proprietress of the Hotel Merkl, who has identified Lia's murderer as someone fitting Canez's description. After deflecting suspicion from himself, Canez departs Frau Greifer's with Marie, who is clearly distraught by the investigator's intrusion. He purchases flamboyant gowns for Marie and offers her fabulous jewelry, but she is unresponsive to these material offerings and tells Canez, who is angered by her indifference, that she wishes only to return to the Hotel Merkl that evening. Canez takes her there, and Marie hysterically claims to have "witnessed" the murder of "that society lady," asserting that Egon is the murderer. After nearly strangling Canez in a trancelike frenzy, Marie leaves the hotel in an almost somnambulistic stupor.

Regina, in the meantime, has become convinced that Egon is Lia's murderer. When she encounters him in the street, she suggests they leave town together so as to avoid Egon's arrest and prosecution. Alleging his innocence, Egon rejects that suggestion and is eventually arrested. While in jail awaiting trial, he is visited by Regina, who now claims to believe Egon is innocent, declares her love for him, and tells him that she has left her family in order to be with him.

Marie, still haunted by Lia's murder, stands vigil outside the Hotel Merkl for several nights. She collapses on the street and is taken to her parents' home by a friend. Upon reading in the newspaper of the likelihood of Egon's conviction because of the strength of the evidence against him, she writes her parents a note apologizing for "the evil" she has done them and goes to the police to confess her murder of Lia. Egon, who is present during the confession, thanks Marie and kisses her hand, to which she responds, "I have always loved you – even when I lied." Having confessed her crime, Marie in essence delivers Egon to Regina.

Intercut throughout both these personal narratives are scenes of the lines outside the butcher shop and of the interior of Frau Greifer's club. At various points throughout the film, shots of these locations are juxtaposed in an almost documentary fashion that highlights their contradictions: as working people wait in line for meat, Frau Greifer steps down from her automobile and is led to the head of the line; as Canez departs his expensive restaurant to take in Vienna's nightlife, the camera pans the pitiful line outside the butcher shop; as the crowd at Frau Greifer's toasts "the beautiful women of Vienna," the camera picks Greta – a beautiful woman – from the food line as she is about to faint.

The seemingly secondary text constructed by these oppositions is in fact the foundation of the film's denouement, and gives broader scope to Greta's and Marie's individual stories. The film's final, cataclysmic scene begins in the street outside the butcher shop, where a desperate woman begs for meat for her starving child, to the nodded agreement of the crowd (which includes Marie's parents). Her plea rejected by the butcher, the woman becomes crazed, enters his shop, and murders him. This cathartic act unleashes the crowd's accumulated rage and propels it through the streets to the club of Frau Greifer, where she is at the same moment introducing a chorus of angel-winged female performers to her audience. The crowd storms the club and hurls rocks at its windows, generating hysteria within the club equal to that outside it. As Frau Greifer's patrons flee the club under the mob's assault, the camera offers scenes of the hastily deserted club, cutting finally to Greta and Lt. Davy in each other's arms. Greta's and Marie's personal difficulties are thus universalized in the conflict between the privileged and the impoverished.

Analysis of *The Joyless Street* has typically focused on its classification as a "street film" and/or, as mentioned above, on the verity of its portrayal of social conditions in Vienna in 1923. Commentators on the street film genre are themselves divided on the meaning of the street. Siegfried Kracauer, for example, sees it as "a region harboring virtues that had deserted bourgeois society."[7] Barthelemy Amengual, by contrast, writes that "the street is woman, the street is prostitution, the street is destiny. It promises the better and almost always brings the worst."[8]

Diversity of opinion on the street's significance is mirrored in assessments of *The Joyless Street*'s realism. Kracauer views the film from a socioeconomic perspective, as a contrast between the privileged and the destitute. He writes that "[s]urrounded by sadness, the elderly Councilor Rumfort . . . would be lost if it were not for his daughter,"[9] thus positing Greta as the family's savior. Like Kracauer, Herbert G. Luft interprets the film as a depiction of Vienna's situation in 1923.[10] Unlike Kracauer, however, he emphasizes the sexual dimensions of the film's charac-

7. Kracauer, *Caligari to Hitler*, 157.
8. Quoted in Atwell, *Pabst*, 35.
9. Kracauer, *Caligari to Hitler*, 167.
10. Herbert G. Luft, "G. W. Pabst: His Films and His Life Mirror the Tumult of 20th Century Europe," *Films in Review* 15, no. 2 (February 1964): 94–5.

terizations. He describes the butcher as a consumer of "human flesh" whose currency is "his own merchandise," Frau Greifer as "the slimy procuress," and Marie as "the prostitute who commits murder." His view of Councillor Rumfort as the "refined public servant of the old regime who, although he has lost everything, manages to save his daughter from dishonor and corruption" casts Greta as the object of salvation rather than its instrument, as in Kracauer.[11]

The validity of interpretations of *The Joyless Street* that focus on its realism cannot be denied, for as a document of Vienna's economic conditions in 1923, the film is substantiated by historical fact. The crisis of 1923 was the consequence of a conflation of the domestic and international political and economic circumstances surrounding the Austro-Hungarian Empire's involvement in World War I and the establishment in its place of the Austrian Republic (among others) in 1918.[12] Large government deficits resulting from wartime expenditures; the economically depressing effects of the Treaty of St.-Germain, signed by Austria and the Allies in 1919; inflation caused by the increased printing of money in 1920, which was required to compensate for reduction of foreign assistance to the Republic and cessation of the extremely lucrative war-profits tax; and further growth in deficits in 1921-1922 resulting from depletion of revenues from that tax produced a series of currency depreciations from 1918 to 1922. Although these conditions were not unrelenting and were temporarily alleviated by a large British credit to Austria early in 1922, their net effect was a 2,400 percent increase in prices from July 1921 to July 1922.

Finally turning for assistance to the Allied Powers in 1922, the Austrian government entered an agreement with them which

11. See Rotha, *Film Till Now,* 264–65; and Roger Manvell and Heinrich Fraenkel, *The German Cinema* (New York: Praeger, 1971), 41–42 for further comments on *The Joyless Street*'s realism. In contrast to such critics, Harry Alan Potamkin feels that ultimately, the "petty-bourgeois class [as portrayed in the film] was contemplating itself pathetically, hardly with stern realism." Harry Alan Potamkin, "Pabst and the Social Film." *Hound and Horn* 6, no. 2 (Jan.-Mar. 1933): 294. He attributes the film's decline into melodrama to what he considers Pabst's unwillingness to transcend the conventions of structure and characterization in such a way as to enable him "to extract and reorganize . . . the probable data that might have continued the social drama" (294; see also 296–97).

12. See Otto Bauer, *The Austrian Revolution.* 1925, trans. H. J. Stenning (New York: Burt Franklin, 1970), 253–74 for a thorough discussion of these events. Because Bauer was a leader of the Social Democrats at the time these events took place, his account is expecially compelling.

itself had mixed economic consequences. While the loan for which it provided helped to stabilize Austria's currency, the agreement's prohibition of the further issuance of currency suppressed industry by reducing purchasing power. As a result, unemployment in Vienna increased by 400 percent from August 1922 to February 1923. By December 1923, only 44 percent of unionized workers were fully employed, while 33 percent were employed part-time and 22 percent were unemployed. Between the end of 1922 and mid-1924, 100,000 civil service employees were dismissed from their jobs.[13]

Clearly, then, the conditions portrayed in *The Joyless Street* justify its designation as a realist film as perceived by Kracauer, Luft, and other critics. However, Amengual's equation of the street with woman, prostitution, and destiny, and Luft's emphasis on the sexual nature of human relations in *The Joyless Street* direct the viewer's attention to another level of realism – one which focuses on the film's characters, through whose actions the "realist" fabric of the film is woven. Amengual's observation specifically invites reconsideration of the status of women in the film, both as individuals within the fiction it creates and as what seem to be presented as types within society. Analysis of *The Joyless Street*'s characters and the relations between them suggests the film's position on women to be that generally, they are the instigators of dubious moral pursuits and the vehicles of moral, emotional, psychological, and physical distress, whether permanent or temporary. Indeed, the characterizations in *The Joyless Street* can be viewed as falling along a spectrum whose endpoints are vice and virtue. With the sole exception of Greta, the female figures in the film are concentrated on the morally suspect end of that spectrum.

Marie is motivated solely by her desire to gain Egon's love: she thoroughly ingratiates herself to his financial objectives and fawns over him physically, while he brushes her off. In pursuit of her goal, she first prostitutes herself, then murders one of her

13. In addition to Bauer, see also Gordon Craig, *Germany 1866–1945* (New York: Oxford Univ. Press, 1978), 434–68 for an in-depth discussion of "The Crisis of 1923" in Germany. The situation in Germany at this time was even worse than that in Austria, probably due to the heavier burden that war reparations placed on Germany's financial and natural resources. For example, in November 1923, 29.3 percent of all unionized laborers were employed full-time, 47.3 percent were employed part-time, and 23.4 percent were unemployed. At the same time, a head of cabbage cost 50 million marks.

competitors for Egon's attention. Hers is not a selfless love, but a self-centered passion whose means know no bounds. Although she is somewhat redeemed by apologizing to her parents for the sorrow she has caused them and by confessing to the murder of Lia, the viewer's lasting impression of Marie is of a pathetic young woman desperately seeking love at any cost to herself and others.

Regina Rosenow is, like Marie, greedy; unlike Marie's greed, however, Regina's is primarily material. Her measure of Egon's love for her is the extent of his efforts to become rich, and she goes so far as to, in effect, offer him sexually to Lia in order to enable him to do so. She is willing to sacrifice both her moral integrity and her family's love in order to protect Egon from arrest, despite her initial conviction that he is guilty of murdering Lia. Even her change of heart concerning Egon's guilt is, in view of her obvious self-interest, dubious.

Lia Leid is the amoral, adulterous temptress. Although it is she who initially solicits Egon, the implicit prostitute/"John" relation is ultimately transformed in their tryst: she allows Egon to pawn her jewels to raise cash for his stock market venture, thus in essence paying him for sleeping with her.

Frau Greifer is the exploitative procuress and lusting homo- or bisexual. Luring young women into her "business" with the enticement of financial and material favors, she enacts vicariously her own sexual desire through the transactions she arranges. In the scene in which she tries to effect such an exchange between Greta and the butcher, the camera dissolves from Greta to the butcher to Frau Greifer, who has fallen into a trance that intimates her fantasizing of the sexual act – whether between Greta and the butcher, Greta and herself, or the butcher and herself is not completely clear. But the shot strongly suggests in light of Frau Greifer's earlier flirtation with Greta and subsequent offer of herself to the butcher that the scene marks the fusion of her sexual desires.

In contrast to these characters is Greta, whose virtue is enunciated not only textually but also technically, in the lingering, caressing shots of her anguished face. Unlike Marie, whose sexual and moral prostitution is selfishly motivated, Greta offers her virtue in order to rescue her family from complete financial ruin. The redemptive goodness of her actions is inferred by the facts that she ingeniously rebounds from each financial setback and that Lt. Davy's questioning of her scruples is eventually resolved in the understanding of her motives. In contrast to the wages of Marie's sins and fall, Greta's narrative argues clearly the belief that virtue, although challenged, ultimately triumphs.

It must in fairness be noted that representations of men in *The Joyless Street* are not particularly complimentary. To the contrary, each of those characterizations can be argued to fit into a negative stereotypical cast of its own. In almost every instance, however, the more undesirable qualities of a given male character are largely overshadowed, and the consequences of the manifestation of those qualities mitigated, by the traits of his female foil. The negative aspects of Egon's financial aspirations, for example, and the lengths to which he goes to attain them, pale in comparison to Marie's murder of Lia as a means toward her own goal. Canez's deviousness is similarly diluted by Marie's willingness to service him as another means to her objective. Egon's wide-eyed sexual interest in a variety of women and his seemingly universal appeal to them are rendered almost glamorously, while the measures those women take to possess him border on the absurd.

While this contrast between the implied excusability of male idiosyncrasy and the seeming inescapability of female disingenuousness is not uniformly applicable to the film's characterizations – the butcher, for example, simply has no redeeming qualities – it is sufficiently recurrent to suggest a generalized belief within the film in womankind's threat to the mutable but inviolable prerogatives of her opposite gender. I believe that the further contrast between Greta's ultimate goodness and the perniciousness of Marie, Regina, Lia, and Frau Greifer, and the depiction of tragedy and conflict as resulting from the pursuit by each of the latter of their personal objectives, constitute the articulation of a historically pervasive and paradoxically dualistic perception of woman: on the one hand she is exulted as the giver of life, protector of morality, and source of physical nurturance; on the other hand, this idealized vision of woman is countered by the perception of her sexuality and sexual difference as potentially dangerous to the physical, moral, material vigor of humanity. The consequence of this paradox in the social sphere is that, rather than being viewed as capable of participating in social institutions in ways that empower them or contribute significantly to change, women are relegated to the performance of functions to which their presumed biological and psychological constitution is believed to dispose them.[14]

The Joyless Street is not unique as an artistic vehicle for presentation of the variety of possible embodiments of woman inferred by the paradox discerned here. Precedents abound throughout the history of literature and the visual arts, from Homer's Odyssey and Leo Tolstoy's Anna Karenina in the former case, to seventeenth-century Dutch paintings of taverns and domestic interiors and Edvard Munch's menacing depictions of women in the latter. The insistence with which *The Joyless Street* exposes the dimensions of that paradox, however, is particularly striking when it is considered in the context of the experience of women in Germany's Weimar Republic. Such an investigation highlights points of contact between the film and historical fact that shed new light on the notion of the film's realism.

A word is in order here on the grounds for analyzing a film set in Vienna in terms of German history. The similarity of conditions in the Austrian and German Republics in 1923 might logically be viewed as an inevitable by-product of a centuries-long history of (sometimes uneasy) propinquity between the Habsburg and Hohenzollern empires that preceded them. This relation, which took final form in the Austro-German Alliance during World War I, did not perish with the empires in the wake of the revolutions which created those Republics in late 1918. To the contrary, a prominent and ongoing political objective of the socialist faction in the Austrian revolution was unification with the "German Motherland."[15] Insofar as the identity of heritage and tradition that informed the new Republics' political

14. Renate Bridenthal and Claudia Koonz, "Beyond Kinder Küche Kirche: Weimar Women in Politics and Work," in *When Biology Became Destiny: Women in Weimar and Nazi Germany,* eds. Renate Bridenthal, Atina Grossmann, and Marion Kaplan (New York: Monthly Review, 1984), pp. 33–65; Karin Hausen, "Mother's Day in the Weimar Republic," trans. Miriam Frank with Erika Busse Grossmann, ed. Marion Kaplan with Ellen Weinstock, in *When Biology Became Destiny*; and Renate Pore, *A Conflict of Interest: Women in German Social Democracy, 1919–1933* (Westport, CT: Greenwood, 1981), 73–78.

15. Bauer, *Austrian Revolution,* 61–65; see also 269–271.

16. On the relationship between the German and Austro-Hungarian empires, see Robert A. Kann, *A History of the Habsburg Empire 1526–1918* (Los Angeles: Univ. of California Press, 1974). For discussions of Austro-German contributions to Habsburg cultural developments from the mid-eighteenth century to 1918 see especially pages 370–79 and 544–61.

aspirations likewise inspired and mediated their social and cultural perceptions, beliefs, and expectations,[16] the proposition on which the present analysis is based is that questions of gender construction and sexual politics elicited by *The Joyless Street* are equally relevant to German and Austrian experience. However, because the Weimar Republic was the film's primary market in the German-speaking world (as well as Pabst's home from 1920 to 1933), it is on circumstances in that country that the remainder of this study focuses.

The Weimar Constitution was, at the time it was ratified (1919), widely remarked for "the consistency and thoroughness of its embodiment of the idea of popular sovereignty."[17] Particularly revolutionary in its extension of civil liberties for women, it prescribed equal and direct suffrage for all German citizens (Articles 17 and 22), and declared the equality of men's and women's civic rights and responsibilities (Article 128). In addition to the guarantee of these individual rights, the Constitution addressed certain communal rights: Article 119 gave constitutional protection to the institution of marriage, which it claimed is based on the equal rights of both sexes, and charged the State with maintenance of the family and the protection and care of motherhood.[18]

Simultaneous with, and in direct contradiction of, the liberalization of women's rights and protections, however, was the retention of certain Imperial statutes which effectively limited those rights: abortion continued to be illegal, access to contraceptives remained limited, and the rights of women in marital and divorce matters continued to be circumscribed.[19] Restriction of women's control over their bodies was complemented by their enforced economic dependence on men: Paragraph 1358 of the civil code allowed men to prohibit their wives from working, and Paragraph 1363 gave them control over their wives' wealth or earnings.[20]

In retrospect, these contradictions were prophetic of the ambiguous economic position that Weimar women would come

17. Craig, *Germany 1866–1945*, 415.

18. See Rene Brunet, Appendix, *The New German Constitution*, trans. Joseph Gollomb (New York: Knopf, 1922); and Otis H. Fisk, *Germany's Constitutions of 1871 and 1919* (Cincinnati: Court Index Press, 1924).

19. Bridenthal, Grossmann, and Kaplan, eds., Introduction, *When Biology Became Destiny*.

20. Pore, *Conflict of Interest*, 82.

to occupy. On the one hand, women were theoretically entitled to the same employment opportunities as men; on the other demobilization orders issued by the Ministry of War in 1919 specified that female industrial workers (who had entered the work force to meet the wartime shortage of men) with other means of support – i.e., husbands – now had to yield their positions to unemployed veterans.[21] While mechanization and standardization of industry promoted general economic recovery after 1924, it effectively restratified labor along sexual lines by forcing great numbers of women into lower-paying assembly-line jobs.[22] Indeed, working women were often condemned as "double earners" denying men employment.[23]

The essential conservatism reflected in ambivalence toward women in the economic sphere did not respect political parties' boundaries. Leftist dogma subordinated the issue of women's rights to the greater class struggle. Attributing women's inferior socioeconomic status to the effects of capitalism rather than to oppression of women by individuals, it pressed not for legislation which would equalize men's and women's rights, but for measures that would reinvigorate familial traditions undermined by capitalism.[24] Even such attempts as were made by the Social Democrats to involve women in the battle for a socialist state served in the final analysis to maintain the sexual status quo. For example, the working-class welfare organization (*Arbeiterwohlfahrt*) was founded in 1919 to provide both social services for those in need and a point of entry for working-class women into the field of social work. While on its surface the *Arbeiterwohlfahrt* facilitated meaningful participation by women in the party's work, its focus on social work amounted to the continued constraint of women's energies and initiative by the limitations of their traditional domestic role.[25]

The various parties of the right and center were more blatant in their loyalty to traditional perceptions of women's roles. These parties' first objective was to put down the socialist revolution and achieve in its place a spiritual revolution, and both centrist and rightist factions considered women crucial to the achievement of this objective. Women's participation, however,

21. Ibid., 91–92.
22. Bridenthal, Grossmann, and Kaplan, Introduction, 9–10.
23. Pore, *Conflict of Interest*, 97–98.
24. Bridenthal and Koonz, "Beyond Kinder Küche Kirche," 38–39.
25. Pore, *Conflict of Interest*, 71–73.

did not require that they be granted equal rights; rather, it entailed the assertion of their "femininity" and fulfillment of their "feminine" duties.[26] These factions thus "sought to make motherhood more attractive," and the obligation of women to return to "children, kitchen, and church" (*Kinder, Küche, Kirche*) "was upgraded from a responsibility to a calling."[27]

Finally, as modernity came to intrude on conventional notions of propriety in the realms of culture and sexual behavior, women, the primary consumers of culture, became "the nexus of the 'morality question.' They were simultaneously seen as guardians of morality and as the chief agents of a 'culture of decadence'."[28]

It is on this last point that *The Joyless Street* and the history of Weimar women converge most distinctly in addressing the paradox, and its consequence, identified above. The explicit message of the policies of Weimar's right and center was that women's proper place is in the home, where their skills could be utilized toward the maintenance and strengthening of the familial values that it was believed would make possible Germany's spiritual survival. No less illusory was the left's program with respect to women: women's value to the socialist cause was considered to lie principally in the utility of their "feminine" talents for the betterment of society. In both cases, conventional uses of women's skills functioned to defuse the threat to sexual distinctions that might be posed by a grant to women of true social and political equality.[29] The "good" woman recognized her position in the broad scheme of things and, in meeting the requirements of that position, did her part for family and society.

Representations of women in *The Joyless Street* speak clearly to the ambiguous and contradictory status of Weimar women, and suggest the proportions of the paradox underlying perceptions

26. Bridenthal and Koonz, "Beyond Kinder Küche Kirche," 41.

27. Ibid., 43. It must be noted that women of these political parties took part fully and willingly in the program which this policy advocated. As Bridenthal and Koonz observe, statistics show that "German women did not merely lose the fight for equality; they joined the opposition" (34). The premise of their study, in fact, is that "the conservatism of Weimar women must be seen in the context of the fraudulence of their supposed emancipation. Despite the rhetoric about women's emancipation, patriarchal ideology continued to dominate all institutions of German economic and political life" (34–35).

28. Bridenthal, Grossmann, and Kaplan, Introduction, 13.

29. Bridenthal and Koonz, "Beyond Kinder Küche Kirche," 44; and Pore, *Conflict of Interest*, 74.

of their proper role in the Republic. Greta, the nurturing, self-sacrificing, "good" daughter, becomes a heroine without seeking gain for herself. She "knows (and keeps) her place," focusing her efforts on the well-being of her family, and is rewarded by reconciliation with Lt. Davy, with whom the film's closing shot implies she will pursue a traditional family life. In contrast, Marie, the self-interested, suspiciously motivated, "bad" daughter, brings ruin on herself and nearly on Egon; she almost causes Egon to lose his battle for Regina's approval by allowing criminal suspicion to fall on him. At film's end, Marie is alone with her guilt, while Egon and Regina, like Greta and Lt. Davy, enjoy the prospect of a life together. Lia and Regina function in similarly contrasting (although subordinate) ways: whereas Lia is victimized, in part, by her own sexual desire, Regina is, notwithstanding her questionable motives, rewarded by reunion with Egon for her loyalty to him in the face of rather dire prospects.

Viewed in terms of the paradigm created by the positions on women held by Weimar's various political parties, characterizations of women in *The Joyless Street* transcend the simple issue of the "good" versus the "bad" woman to suggest a prognosis for Germany's physical and spiritual survival. In this reading, Greta becomes a symbol for the promotion of moral recovery and sustenance of gender-based tradition that it is implied will ensure the Republic's success, whereas Marie signifies the threat posed to that recovery and tradition by the thoughtless pursuit of selfish will. The material viability of the Republic and the likelihood of its spiritual and moral resurgence are thus contingent on the extent to which the symbolic "Greta" prevails over the symbolic "Marie."

In his critique of *The Joyless Street*'s "realism," Ed Lowry argues that its depiction of the plight of the middle and working classes in truth simply masks the implied merit of complacency:

> The inevitably unhappy end of characters who invariably try to escape their social roles suggest[s] the workings, not of a social order created by men, but of an overpowering Fate. Thus social realism becomes metaphysical tragedy, and what seems to be a materialist analysis becomes, in fact, a warning against all those who would strive for change.[30]

The charge of conservatism is especially relevant to the film's representations of women. Those women – Greta and Regina –

30. Ed Lowry, Cinema Texas Program Notes 2.2 (28 Sept. 1976), 4.

who are faithful to their men are rewarded with approval, love, and security. Those who recklessly pursue their desires without apparent consideration of the consequences of doing so – Marie, Lia, and to a lesser extent, Frau Greifer – meet with uncomfortable, if not tragic, ends. As has been shown, conservatism was likewise the primary conditioning fact in the lives of Weimar women. Regardless of their political affiliations, the reality of their existence was not liberation, but merely a different application of the attributes which prescribed their traditional role.

The Joyless Street's "realism" is thus appropriately viewed as two-dimensional. On its surface, the film presents a historically accurate picture of conditions in Vienna and Germany in 1923. Delving beyond such superficial analysis to the interpersonal dynamics of the circumstances depicted, however, the viewer discovers a covert comment on the proper position of women in society. The distinction between these levels of interpretation issues from the difference between "realism" and history, for *The Joyless Street*'s true realism lies not in its factual precision, but in that its representations of women reflect with great fidelity the assumptions and ambiguous expectations that dictated to Weimar women the role they would play in the new Republic.[31]

31. This paper is dedicated to my father, whose integrity, perseverance, and love never cease to inspire me. Special thanks also to Jane Roos for her encouragement and thoughtful comments.

4

From Repressive Tolerance to Erotic Liberation: *Girls in Uniform (Mädchen in Uniform)*

b. ruby rich

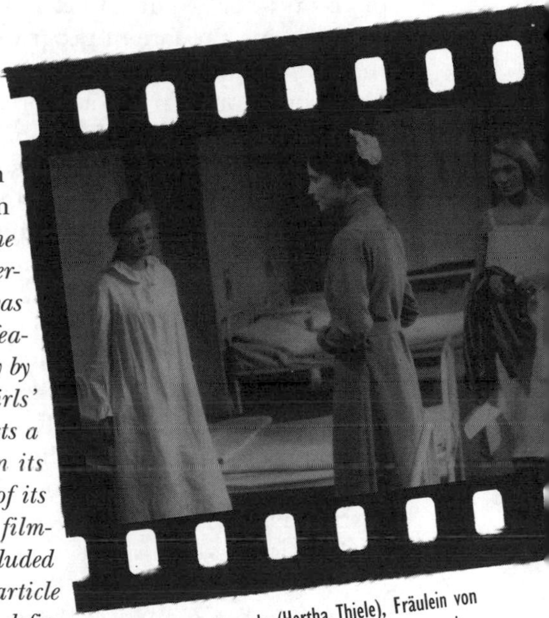

In the dormitory: Manuela (Hertha Thiele), Fräulein von Bernburg (Dorothea Wieck), and Edelgard (Annemarie Rochhausen). Leontine Sagan's *Girls in Uniform* (1931). (Photo courtesy of Museum of Modern Art/Film Stills Archive)

Leontine Sagan's Girls in Uniform (Mädchen in Uniform, *1931) was one of the very few films made during Germany's Weimar Republic that was directed by a woman; it also featured a cast made up exclusively by women. Set in a Prussian girls' school, the film definitely suggests a homoerotic attachment between its two main characters. Because of its significance in the history of filmmaking by women, we have included two essays on the film. In her article on the film (reprinted here in its definitive 1984 version), B. Ruby Rich attempts to "re-claim" the film from traditional film criticism. Not only does she provide an openly lesbian reading of the film, but she grounds this reading with an impressive discussion of the film's historical context, including discussion of a historical legacy too long ignored: the legacy of the long struggle for homosexual rights in Germany. She also describes the flourishing homosexual subculture in Berlin during Germany's Weimar Republic, its subsequent suppression under the Nazis, and the relevance of that experience for political struggles being waged over sexuality and sexual identity today.*
—The Editors

> What in God's name does one call this sensibility if it be not love? This extraordinary heightening of all one's impressions; this intensification of sensitiveness; this complete identification of feeling? . . . *I* was Manuela, as she is Manuela, and everything that has happened to her has in essence, and other circumstances, happened to me. This incredible feeling of sisterhood.[1]
>
> —Dorothy Thompson, upon meeting Christa Winsloe

There are moments when one historical period seems to beckon to another, offering the semblance of lessons to be learned or errors to be avoided. Certainly, that is true today for those of us reviewing the fate of progressive political organizations in the Weimar period preceding Adolph Hitler's coming to power in the inflation-torn and authority-hungry Germany of 1933. In particular, the history of women's-rights groups and homosexual-emancipation organizations is one that needs to be better known and analyzed. It is a testimony to our ignorance of the period that Leontine Sagan's film, *Mädchen in Uniform* (1931), is generally assumed to be an anomaly, a film without a context, or else a metaphor, a coded tale about something *else*, something other than what appears on screen. If we are to understand *Mädchen in Uniform* fully, then it is important to keep in view the society within which it was made: the celebrated milieu of Berlin *avant-la-guerre*, Berlin with dozens of gay and lesbian bars and journals, the Berlin of a social tolerance so widespread that it nearly camouflaged the underlying legal restraints (which were to grow, rapidly, into massive repression). I would stop short of claiming an outlandish Rosetta

1. Jonathan Katz, *Gay American History* (New York: Avon, 1976), 843. Acknowledgement is due here to two people who contributed the very heart of this article: Karola Gramann, who has written me extensively from Frankfurt and shared her own knowledge and research on *Mädchen in Uniform*; and Bill Horrigan, who brought numerous sources to my attention and even located copies of rare materials like the original playbill and published play script – his materials improved my work immeasurably. In addition, I owe thanks to Ramona Curry, who provided encouragement and translations, and to Rennie Harrigan, who offered background information and suggested avenues of research. The section of this article which deals with specific textual analysis of the film was originally presented as a paper at the 4th Annual Purdue Film Conference, March 1979, on a panel devoted to early German cinema. Thanks to Jim Franklin for his encouragement at that time. This article was first published in *Jump Cut,* no. 24/25 (March 1981), 44–45, as part of a special section on Lesbians & Film; without the context and spirit of that special section and my coeditors on it, this article could not have been written. A shorter version was published in *Radical America,* vol. 15, no. 6 (1982), 17–36.

Stone status for the film, no matter how tempting, lest the reader lose faith. Yet it might be emphasized, *Mädchen in Uniform* is an exemplary work, not only for what it presents to us on the screen but also for the timely issues that its analysis must confront. It is the film revival most central to establishing a history of lesbian cinema.

Mädchen in Uniform was filmed by Leontine Sagan in Germany in 1931, based upon the play, *Yesterday and Today,* by Christa Winsloe (alias the Baroness von Hatvany) and republished as a novel, *The Child Manuela,* also by Winsloe. The film, like the play, enjoyed a tremendous initial popularity, both within Germany and internationally; yet it has been nearly invisible in the past few decades within the academic study of German cinema. The film has frequently fallen into a seeming limbo between the silent German Expressionist cinema and the notorious products of the Third Reich studios. Despite its remarkable sound quality (praised by Lotte Eisner as the work in which "the prewar German sound film reached its highest level")[2] and in spite of its evocative cinematography (which Kracauer cited as transmitting "the symbolic power of light"),[3] *Mädchen in Uniform* faded from the text books, the revival houses, and even eventually from distribution entirely. During the early 1970s, however, Sagan's classic was resoundingly redeemed by the cycle of women's film festivals, gathering a solid following and the critical attention it had long lacked. The result, today, is that the film is back in distribution in a beautifully reconstructed print (in contrast to the butchered, mistitled print that made the rounds of the early festivals) and is accorded a secure spot in the history of pre-Reich cinema.

In part, the film's reputation rests upon unusual stylistic components. Sagan's montage-inflected structure manages to break away from the usually stagey and claustrophobic *mise-en-scène* of early sound films. Her montages, no doubt Soviet-influenced, establish a persuasive counterpoint to the more theatrical scenes and mold them into a cinematic rhythm. Dramatically, her use of a large cast of nonprofessional actresses lends the film a fresh and documentary-like tone, while the performances of the lead actresses won widespread praise.

2. Lotte H. Eisner, *The Haunted Screen* (Berkeley: Univ. of California Press, 1969), 326.

3. Siegfried Kracauer, *From Caligari to Hitler* (Princeton: Princeton Univ. Press, 1947), 227.

Sagan was a pioneer in her use of sound, not only as a functional synchronous accompaniment, but also as a thematic element in its own right. However, most important to the film's reputation through the years has been its significance as an antiauthoritarian and prophetically antifascist film. And, to be sure, the film has suitable credentials for such a claim. Any film so opposed to militarism, so anti-Prussian, so much in support of the emotional freedom of women, must be an antifascist film. Furthermore, it was made through the Deutsche Film Gemeinschaft, a cooperative production company specifically organized for this project – and was the first German commercial film to be made collectively. Add to such factors the fact that the film was made on the very eve of Hitler's rise to power, just prior to the annexation of the film industry into Goebbel's cultural program, and the legend of Sagan's proto-subversive movie is secure. In emphasizing the film's progressive stance in relation to the Nazi assumption of power, however, film historians have tended to overlook, minimize, or trivialize the film's central concern with love between women.

Today, we must take issue with the largely unexamined critical assumption that the relations between women in the film are essentially a metaphor for the real power relations of which it treats, i.e., the struggle against fascism. I would suggest that *Mädchen in Uniform* is not only antifascist, but also antipatriarchal in its politics. Such a reading need not depend upon metaphor, but can be more forcefully demonstrated by a close attention to the film text. As I propose to read it, *Mädchen in Uniform* is a film about sexual repression in the name of social harmony; absent patriarchy and its forms of presence; bonds between women which represent attraction instead of repulsion; and the release of powers that can accompany the identification of a lesbian sexuality. The film is a dual coming-out story: that of Manuela, the adolescent who voices "the love that dares not speak its name" and who, in distinguishing between fantasy and desire, dares to act upon the latter; and that of Fräulein von Bernburg, the teacher who repudiates her own role as an agent of suppression and wins her own freedom by accepting her attraction to another woman. In this reading, the film remains a profoundly antifascist drama, but now its political significance becomes a direct consequence of the film's properly central subject, lesbianism, rather than a covert message wrapped in an attractive but irrelevant metaphor. If *Mädchen in Uniform* is the first truly radical lesbian film, it is also a fairly typical product of late Weimar society, a society in which "homosexuality . . . became a form of fashionable behavior" linked to "the Weimar idea of making a complete break with the staid and bankrupt past of one's parents' generation."[4] As such, it offers a particularly clear example of the interplay between personal and collective politics – and the revolutionary potential inherent in the conjunction of the two.

The film centers upon the relationship between two women. Manuela (Hertha Thiele) is a young student newly arrived at a Potsdam boarding school that caters to the daughters of German officers who, in the mid-1920s, are largely impoverished, as is the school itself. With her mother dead, her father unable to look after her, and her aunt/guardian icily uncaring, Manuela is left craving affection. Fräulein von Bernburg (Dorothea Wieck) is the school's most adored teacher, champion of a maternalistic humanitarianism opposed to the school's Prussian codes. Harsh, ascetic, militaristic, the boarding-school environment is enforced by a totalitarian principal (Emilie Unda) dedicated to toughening up her charges.

Manuela quickly develops a passionate attachment to Fräulein von Bernburg, who simultaneously nourishes and discourages her admirer. Manuela's infatuation is even more intense than the crushes that her fellow students have upon the esteemed Bernburg. Furthermore, she carries matters to an unprecedented level by announcing her passion publicly, to all the school. The declaration occurs when Manuela, drunk and in male attire, celebrates her thespian success in the school play by offering the news of her affections as a convivial toast. For such a transgression, Manuela is confined to solitary in the infirmary by the school principal, who forbids students and faculty alike from so much as speaking to her.

The mounting crisis impels Fräulein von Bernburg to confront the principal and challenge her authority, a climax which coincides with the desperate Manuela's own decision to solve the problem by committing suicide. Distraught at having to give up her beloved teacher, Manuela climbs the school's forbidding staircase (a central leitmotif in the film) and is about to throw

4. Alex de Jonge, *The Weimar Chronicle: Prelude to Hitler* (London: Paddington, 1978), 138.

herself from its uppermost railing when her schoolgirl companions, disobeying the injunction, come to her rescue. Their arrival is paralleled by the rush of Fräulein von Bernburg to the scene, confirming her affection for Manuela and her identification with the students' action. The aversion of imminent tragedy is a triumph for the forces of love and community, signalling the coming of a new order. The event seals the fate of the evil principal, who retreats down the hall into the shadows even as Fräulein von Bernburg remains in the light, united through crosscutting with Manuela and the students grouped above her on the staircase.

As should be clear from the summary, the action of *Mädchen in Uniform* transpires entirely within an all-woman environment and, indeed, a thoroughly "feminine" atmosphere. However, the very first establishing shots of the film serve to inform us of the real power of absent patriarchy and remind us that an all-woman school in no way represents a woman-defined space. The montage of visual icons in the first few frames establishes an exterior world of military preparedness, steeples and archways, bugle calls and the marching rhythm of soldiery. And this world of regimentation extends to the neat rows of students who, two by two, file past the gateway into the domain of the school. The link between the exterior authority and the interior order is explicitly visualized only once, but it informs our reading of the entire film (particularly as represented by the emblematic use of off-screen sounds and on-screen symbols, like the staircase).

On her first day of school, Manuela listens to the principal's speech outlining her required duty and identity: "You are all soldiers' daughters and, God willing, you will all be soldiers' mothers." The girls are there to be taught the Prussian values in order that they might transmit the "correct line" to their future progeny. They are destined to be the transmitters of a culture, not its inheritors. The learning is not for them as women in their own right, but for their function as reproducers of bodies and ideologies. The extent to which the absent patriarchy (which at no point in the film takes the shape of actual men on screen) dominates the women's world is a theme constantly reiterated by Sagan in her many visualizations of classically Romantic leitmotifs. Barred shadows cross the women's paths, a sternly overbearing staircase encloses their every movement, a frantic montage marshals their steps into a militaristic gait, and even the school songs reinforce the authority of a demanding fatherland with a handful of schoolgirls in its grasp. The film's very title underlines this theme, with its play of meanings on the word "uniform" meaning (as a noun) the clothing of a regimented educational/military/professional institution, or (as an adjective) the regulated, all-alike behavior of uniformity dictated by the rules of the patriarchal order.

The ultimate incarnation of the absent but controlling patriarchy is the school principal. Her identity as the "phallic woman" is suggested by her reliance on an everpresent cane with which she measures her steps and signals her authority, and by the phallocentric codes of *Kinder, Kirche, Küche* ("children, church, kitchen") which she is dedicated to instilling. Her mandates and bearing call to mind a vision of Frederick the Great, to whom she has been compared. Perhaps coincidentally, her jowly face and disassociated affect are equally reminiscent of that other prophetic cinematic persona of demented authority, Doctor Caligari. Like the mad Doctor, this principal is accompanied by an obedient assistant, a dark hunchbacked figure who carries out her orders. Unlike Caligari's missions of murder, the principal's agenda is more properly "feminine" in its details of manipulation and reconnaissance. The henchwoman is a warped figure; like the principal shuffling with her cane, the assistant presents an image of womanhood carrying out patriarchal dirty work and physically warped by her complicity. Her hands huddled close to her chest, her eyes pinched and shoulders stooped, the assistant becomes a physical marker of emotional damage. In *The Cabinet of Dr. Caligari* madness and hypnotism were held responsible for complicity in murder; Sagan is willing to pinpoint a more precise cause in the dogma of an authoritarian ideology. Just as nuns have long provided an easy example of a woman's order subject to entirely male authority (in the form of priest, Pope, or God the Father, Son, the heavenly bridegroom), so, too, the institution of the woman's boarding school is shaped to the mold of the militaristic patriarchal society, poured like molten liquid into its empty spaces to keep it whole.

How, then does the power structure within the school itself function? Specifically, what are the roles assumed by the beloved Fräulein von Bernburg, champion of the emotions, and the hated Principal, enforcer of discipline? Traditionally, critical readings of the film have identified Fräulein von Bernburg as a sort of freedom fighter, a humanitarian standing up to the forces of repression, and have targeted the Principal much as I have described her, a tyrant ruling over a regime of denial. I would take issue with this romanticized view and trade its simplistic hero/villain dichotomy for a different model, i.e., a system of repression based instead on the "good cop, bad cop" pattern, with the Principal as the "bad cop" and Fräulein von Bernburg as the "good cop."

To comprehend the logic of such a system in the case of the boarding school, it is necessary to return to the point made earlier in the Principal's opening speech. As she made clear, the young women are being bred ("educated") as transmitters of the patriarchal German culture everpresent in encoded form within the world of the school. In order to ensure this training, preserve the young women's "honor," and most effectively carry out their special socialization, it is necessary for society to shape women within an all-female setting; in fact, prior to feminist movements, this was no doubt the primary reason for "separatist" institutions. What, however, is the danger to the patriarchal society presented by such an institution? It is a sexual danger: the threat that the heterosexuality required of these women may, in the cloistered pressure-cooker atmosphere of the boarding school, become derailed into a focus upon their own sex. The possibility that heterosexuality on the part of women may become transferred ("warped" as the father might say) into homosexuality presents a powerful threat to a system geared for procreation and the rearing of male offspring: "Gender is not only an identification with one sex; it also entails that sexual desire be directed toward the other sex."[5] The danger of the boarding school is that a concentration on the former entails a corresponding relaxation of the latter. Perhaps it is because the women's boarding school is the Achilles' heel of patriarchy that it figures in so much lesbian literature and cinema.

In *Mädchen in Uniform*, the code name for this sexual threat is "emotionalism." When Fräulein von Bernburg early in the film

5. Gayle Rubin, "The Traffic in Women: Notes On the 'Political Economy' of Sex," in *Toward an Anthropology of Women*, ed. Rayna R. Reiter (New York: Monthly Review, 1975), 180.

catches two schoolgirls exchanging a love letter, she confiscates the paper and, to their relief and delight, rips it up without reading a word; smiling but strict, she warns them to desist in the exchange of such letters because they can lead to "emotionalism." Again, later in the film, the student ringleader, Ilse, uses the same expression with the same negative message. She is engaged in declaiming a series of mock toasts during the post-play banquet, all phrased in the language of the school's official ideology, and thus she reprimands Manuela for the acting style of her male impersonation: "Remember, next time, less emotionalism."

In line with the model of repression that I suggest, Fräulein von Bernburg's task as the "good cop" seems to be to keep "emotionalism" in check and to make her charges more comfortable in their oppression. She acts as a pressure valve and as the focus of dissident energies in order that the overall system will not be endangered. Fräulein von Bernburg has two guises, then, for coping with the social and sexual schism. Socially, she polices the heart, i.e., the emotional life of her students. As she puts it at one point to Manuela, "You mustn't persuade yourself it isn't nice here." It is her presence in the school's cabinet of power that keeps the girls from rebelling against an order that would otherwise be totally abhorrent. Likewise, it is her presence as a confidante that permits her to discern and block any tentative moves in the direction of revolt, as, for example, when she persuades the headstrong Ilse not to run away from the school. Thus she functions as mediator between the top and bottom of the school hierarchy.

It is made clear, however, that the methods by which Fräulein von Bernburg exercises her functions are sexual. For instance, she succeeds in persuading Ilse to stay by slapping her on the ass and speaking to her seductively. This is her second guise: she capitalizes upon the standard form of transference that leads adolescent girls to develop crushes on their teachers. Her positioning of herself as the exclusive object of schoolgirl affection may be seen as a tactic of repressive tolerance carried out in the arena of sexuality. Under the camouflage of her tolerance is the reality of repression. If the girls focus their sexual desires upon her – where they can never be realized – then the danger of such desires being refocused upon each other (where they *could* be realized) is averted. The figure of the teacher remains ever more powerful, more attractive, more worthy of adoration, than any mere fellow student. It is, in fact, very nearly a relationship of adoration in the religious sense, with forms of expression that are thoroughly ritualized and contained, as, for example, the evening bedtime scene makes clear.

The scene is set in the dormitory on Manuela's first night in the school. It is filmed with the soft focus and radiant light of a Romantic painting, for example a Friedrich. The lights are dimmed by Fräulein von Bernburg to make the scene more seductive. All the girls are poised on the edge of their beds, kneeling in identical white gowns, heads upraised to receive the communion of her lips touching their foreheads, which she holds firmly as she administers each ritualistic kiss. This extreme fetishizing of the kiss by the nature of the teacher's gestures and the film's style is emblematic of the unspoken codes of repressive tolerance. The kiss is permitted, to each alike, but it is at once the given and the boundary. Nothing more may be allowed or even suggested, although the tension of that which is withheld suffuses the scene with eroticism and grants the teacher her very power. The kiss is both minimum and maximum, a state of grace and a state of stasis. The entire equilibrium is founded upon this extreme tension, which is snapped when Manuela, overwhelmed by the atmosphere and her feelings, breaks the rules. She throws her arms around Fräulein von Bernburg's body in a tight embrace and receives not a punishment but a kiss – a kiss, not merely on the forehead, but full on the lips.

Of course the school's system of sexual repression does not crumble from this one transgression; it is much too securely established. Less so is Fräulein von Bernburg, whose situation is a difficult one. It is apparent that the sexual repression she forces upon the students she also forces upon herself. Yet Manuela causes a surplus of feeling which she cannot control. Sagan carefully presents Fräulein von Bernburg almost entirely in terms of Manuela. The first time she appears in the film, she is looking at the newly arrived Manuela on the stairway. The extent to which she begins to identify her own desires and sensitivities with Manuela's takes the shape of a literal superimposition. When Sagan presents a scene of Manuela as student in Fräulein von Bernburg's classroom, it is the anguish of the conflicted pair that she portrays through an extraordinary dissolve that predates the more widespread (and more pernicious) use of the motif by Ingmar Bergman in *Persona*.[6] In the scene while struggling vainly to retrieve a memorized passage from a mind gone blank in the beloved teacher's presence, Manuela's vision begins to blur. Fräulein von Bernburg's sight, subjectively rendered, blurs as well, as her face becomes superimposed and fused with Manuela's staring back at her. It is she, as teacher, who breaks the locked gaze, averts her eyes, and reprimands Manuela with a "not prepared again," thus reasserting her authority and utilizing her rank to shield her emotions.

The next meeting of the two takes place in Fräulein von Bernburg's office soon after, where she has called Manuela in order to give her one of her chemises (in response to an attendant's expressed pity for the young girl's lack of undergarments, due to her lack of a caring mother). By giving Manuela one of her own chemises, she attempts to channel her concern and affection into the quasi-permissible form of a maternal gift which, however, is clearly an erotic token. The conversation that transpires between the two provides further evidence of the code of repressive tolerance exercised toward the students' incipient homosexuality. From the start, it is clear that "emotionalism" rules the encounter, as Fräulein von Bernburg begins by reprimanding Manuela, who has burst into tears at the gift of the chemise: "What an excitable child you are." Manuela confesses she is not crying out of unhappiness, and finally is coaxed to explain by the teacher's concern: "Is there a reason you can't confide to me?" It is the loneliness of the nights that plagues her, the moments after the goodnight kiss: "I stare at your door and would like to get up and go to you, but I'm not allowed . . . I like you so awfully much." She is tortured by the passage of time: "I think of when I get older, and have to leave the school, and you'll kiss other children." Her expression of love, desire, and jealousy is quite explicitly phrased (although, in the older prints of the film, it was largely unsubtitled). Unprepared for such a declaration and unwilling to face the consequences of receiving such information, Fräulein von Bernburg lays down the law of the land: "I think of you, too, Manuela. . . . But you know I can't make exceptions. The others would be jealous."

6. The comparison with *Persona* is pointed out by Nancy Scholar as well, in an article which marks the 1970s revival of the film. See her "*Mädchen in Uniform*," in *Sexual Stratagems: The World of Women in Film*, ed. Patricia Erens (New York: Horizon, 1979), 219–23.

Her response is telling. She doesn't say that she does not share the girl's feelings of attraction; if anything, she implies that she does. She does not invent a boyfriend to assert a defensive heterosexual identity. She asserts only that she is under obligation to love all the girls equally in order to maintain her position as object of their affection; therefore, she cannot break that egalitarianism in order to reciprocate Manuela's passion. The system that she must serve – as its token humanitarian – represses her own sexuality as well as that of the students. She is as much the victim as the promulgator of its repression, unlike the Principal, whose phallic identity cancels out any homoeroticism. However, despite her struggle to repress her own emotions, Fräulein von Bernburg does act. The gift of the chemise is a turning point: it leads to the crisis of the school play, which is the central moment of the film, the moment which changes its direction from repressive tolerance to one of erotic liberation, the choice taken by Manuela throughout and by Fräulein von Bernburg, more complexly, at the film's end.

The school play, a favorite device of the boarding school genre, necessitates the pleasurable moment of cross-dressing in male attire. Manuela plays the lead role of Don Carlos in the 1787 play of the same name by Friedrich Schiller, scion of the *Sturm und Drang* school and leader with Goethe of Weimar classicism.

The choice of this play by Sagan and Winsloe to be the play-within-the-film is particularly significant.[7] *Don Carlos* is identified with the youthful Schiller, in that it represents the peak of his early idealistic period (indeed, after it, Schiller went into a period of doubt and reevaluation that kept him from writing plays again for a full decade). *Sturm und Drang* was a literary

7. It should be noted that *Don Carlos* appears to be yet another innovation of the film, as opposed to a borrowing from the play. In the published play script of *Girls in Uniform*, the production (which takes place entirely off-stage) is described as a light French drama of courtly love with Manuela featured as a knight in armor. Apart from the clearly delineated statements on forbidden love that I outline in the text, the choice of *Don Carlos* also serves to throw into relief the differing consequences for the outlaw lover of both periods. In the Schiller drama, death by *auto-da-fé* awaited heretics of the reigning order. By the time of *Mädchen*, however, the lover marked by the heresy of lesbianism already faced a modern narrative expectation: in the absence of a functioning Inquisition, she is expected to perform her own execution via suicide. The quotation recited by Manuela about death as the payment for Paradise thus accrues additional meaning.

movement that presaged German Romanticism in its emphasis upon the individual in conflict with a rationalist, unjust order. Both Schiller and Goethe stressed emotional harmony and a community of sympathy as the basic social values to put forward in opposition to the oppressive rationalism of the Enlightenment; *Don Carlos* is considered the very embodiment of that theme. Based upon the life of Don Carlos, son of the Spanish King Philip II, the play counterposes the son's liberal idealism with the brutal tyranny of his father's reign. In the play, Don Carlos forms an alliance with the older and wiser Marquis Posa, who conspires with him to advance a humane order and overthrow the ruler. In Schiller's play, the Marquis – learning that their plans are suspected – saves the prince by drawing all guilt upon himself, consequently suffering execution by the king's decree in order to save the prince. The play ends tragically, with Don Carlos refusing to relish his fatally bought freedom, showing his true face to the king, and thus suffering a similar death at the hands of the bloodthirsty Inquisition.

Thus far, then, *Don Carlos* would seem the perfect corollary to the film's much advanced theme of humanitarian idealism counterposed against a fascist reign. In such an interpretation, Manuela would essentially play herself, while the Marquis Posa would represent the Fräulein von Bernburg role and the King would represent the Principal. Schiller, like Winsloe/Sagan, thus assumes the mantle of proto-antifascist for his eloquent, romantic opposition to the maddened illogic of absolute order. The Principal's invited guests seem prone to this same interpretation, for they cluck disapprovingly over their tea that "Schiller sometimes writes very freely."

However, the subsequent scenes following this admonition, as well as the choice of the scene from *Don Carlos,* suggest the same sort of alternate reading that I have been suggesting for *Mädchen in Uniform* as a whole. The scene immediately following the tea-talk is one of the schoolgirls, giddy from a dose of spiked punch, dancing in each other's arms, disobeying the rules, and generally enacting their guardians' worst fears. The scene chosen from *Don Carlos* is not one dealing in political matters, but rather, the rarified scene in which Don Carlos at last wins an audience with the Queen and declares his forbidden love to her. Reprimanded for his rashness in compromising them both by coming to see her, Don Carlos tells the Queen that "Even if it means death, I shall not go from here: One moment lived in Paradise is not to dearly bought with death." These are the lines spoken by Manuela (as Don Carlos) in the scene we see of the school play. A significant key to the narrative of *Don Carlos* is the fact that the Prince's beloved is his father's newly acquired wife: she is, literally, his mother, which makes their love forbidden as, in the words of Schiller's play, "the world and nature and the laws of Rome condemn such passions." Sagan clearly annexes this sentiment by choosing the scene in which Don Carlos proclaims his love for Elizabeth, the name both of the Queen Mother and of Fräulein von Bernburg. With Manuela cross-dressed as the passionate suitor (in a performance heralded by all for its remarkable sincerity!), the sequence represents the central theme of forbidden love encoded within the sanctity of German high culture.

Drunk with punch and the euphoria of her success, Manuela decides to extend her role into real life: she rises to deliver an impassioned toast in which she declares her love for Fräulein von Bernburg and announces the gift of her chemise as proof of its reciprocation. She abandons caution to proclaim, "I know she likes me." She echoes and surpasses Don Carlos in her insistence on sharing the news: "Nothing else matters . . . I'm not afraid of anything. . . . Yes, everyone should know." In a coming out that is the opposite of Don Carlos's vow of silence, she concludes with a celebratory generosity: "Long live Fräulein von Bernburg, beloved by all."

Despite the school's aura of eroticism, it is this act of pronouncement which constitutes the unpardonable transgression. It is the *naming* of that which may well be known, this claiming of what is felt by the public speaking of its name, that is expressly forbidden.[8] For her speech, which is witnessed by the dread Principal, Manuela is immediately imprisoned, significantly enough within the confines of the infirmary – in a reference to the pseudo-scientific view of homosexuality as a species of mental imbalance, a disease, but one that nevertheless can be punished as a crime. Indeed, the first view of Manuela in the hospital traces her position in bed below heavy bars of light emblazoned on the shadowed wall above her head. The immediate

8. For a fuller discussion of this issue, see my article on "The Crisis Of Naming in Feminist Film Criticism," *Jump Cut* 19 (December 1978), 9–12, and a considerably revised version, "In the Name of Feminist Film Criticism," *Heresies* 9 (Spring 1980), 74–81.

wish of the Principal is to blot out history, to expunge the traces of the "scandal" and pretend that nothing ever happened. It is a wish that is initially reflected in Manuela's own coming to consciousness, as she emerges from her hangover with the complaint that she cannot remember what has happened or what she has done. So powerful is the taboo that amnesia is the consequence of its transgression.

The public speech, in fact, can be seen as an extremely powerful transgression, one which, unlike the private actions between Manuela and Fräulein von Bernburg, publicly disrupts and subverts the prevailing order of the school. The Principal's regime could tolerate the widely acknowledged schoolgirl crushes and libidinous undercurrents as long as they remained marginalized and subservient to the dominant ideology. The homoeroticism had been portrayed graphically ever since the time of Manuela's arrival: Ilse told her how envious other girls were, asking if it were true that "the Golden One" really "kisses you good night, oh god, oh god . . ."; the laundrywoman explained the heart and initials on her school uniform, "E.V.G.", by laughing that "the girl who wore this dress must have been infatuated with Fräulein Elizabeth von Bernburg, thus the initials"; and pairs of girls were repeatedly shown holding hands, embracing by windows, or passing love notes. An unendorsed *de facto* eroticism could be contained within the reigning patriarchal order, but a double challenge could not be abided: the challenge of Manuela's public naming of that eroticism and the challenge of Fräulein von Bernburg's material action in presenting the chemise over and above the limits of egalitarianism. For this reason, amnesia was a possibility only for Manuela. Everyone else remembered quite well what had occurred.

Unable to turn back the clock, the Principal opts for quarantine: Manuela is sentenced to solitary confinement, as though homosexuality were a communicable disease spread by social contact. As Manuela becomes distraught in the final phase of the film, Fräulein von Bernburg struggles, more consciously than her young student, to come to terms with her sexuality and acknowledge her feelings for her own sex. In their final meeting with Manuela, held clandestinely in defiance of the Principal's prohibition, she tries to tell the girl the exact nature of a "crime" she seems unable to understand: "you must be cured . . .

of liking me so much." At the same time, she makes a telling complaint about Manuela's speech. She does not reproach Manuela for what she has brought upon herself, as we might expect, but instead says: "What you have done to me, you know." There is more meaning to the statement than the fact of Manuela's speech, which to be sure has damaged her standing at the school but yet is not wholly different from countless other private declarations she no doubt has withstood. Rather, Fräulein von Bernburg may well be referring to the terrible inner conflict into which Manuela's speech has thrown her. It is a conflict not unlike that felt by so many in-the-closet homosexuals of both sexes in this country following the opening up of sexual boundaries during the Stonewall eruption and the succeeding gay liberation movement of the late 1960s and early 1970s. This period carried for many an undesired pressure to identify a previously privatized sexuality (in Fräulein von Bernburg's case, to make that identification not only to others, but to herself as well). From the moment of this reproach, the teacher's struggle to "come out" and emerge from the raging conflict within her becomes the central theme of the film. It is a theme concerned with finding the courage to oppose an unjust authority, a courage shared, finally, with the other students of the school.

Fräulein von Bernburg's inner struggle reaches its peak immediately after this meeting with Manuela, which has concluded badly, with the girl rushing out of the room in desperation and the teacher's race to call her back blocked by the arrival of the Principal. In fact, her confrontations with the Principal have been escalating ever since the "theatrical" incident. She has begun assuming more radical stances in opposition to the Principal's edict. Earlier, arguing over her permissiveness toward Manuela, she had declared: "What you call sin, I call love, which has a thousand forms." She was speaking in general terms of her philosophy of maternal nurturance versus the Principal's punitive discipline, but the more explicit meaning of the statement also holds true. Intent on subjugating the teacher to her authority, the Principal now threatens her: "I will not permit revolutionary ideas." Fräulein von Bernburg then breaks rank in the only truly decisive way possible, responding: "I resign." Herewith, she makes her choice to reject her role as the "good cop" and seek a genuine humanitarianism *outside* the corrupt system of the school, which in turn means seeking also her genuine sexuality as she has come to recognize it.

As the teacher and the Principal enact their battle of will and authority, Manuela prepares to throw herself over the stairwell. It is this point that the film's second superimposition of the faces of Manuela and Fräulein von Bernburg takes place. Again, it is Fräulein von Bernburg who "experiences" the blurred vision and "sees" Manuela's face projected through her own image. This time, however, having made her choice to break with the patriarchal order, she does not avert her gaze or try to separate herself from the vision. Instead, she recognizes this "vision" as a psychic signal of her bond with Manuela.

What does the superimposition mean in this context? The Principal had earlier warned the teacher to "dissolve" her contact with Manuela, suggesting the nature of this shot. The blurring of definition and melding of identities has usually had a negative impact when applied to women in cinema. In Ingmar Bergman's *Persona*, for example, the loss of individual identity is the threat that haunts women's intimacy like a destructive specter: getting too close to another woman means losing oneself. In addition, there is always the companion myth of narcissism. The superimposition shots here may also be a tacit recognition by Sagan of the myth of homosexuality as a narcissistic doubling, an attempt to solidify one's identity by the addition of its likeness in another. Rather than balking at the vision, however, Fräulein von Bernburg recognizes the merged faces as a signal of power by combination. She does not read the superimposition as erasure (the patriarchal warning) or negative bonding (the mirror phase prolonged), but rather as positive depiction of the strength exercised by such a *redoubling* of energy and identity. She trusts the sign and acts on it. Shouting Manuela's name, she rushes from her office (and the startled Principal) to the stairwell, intent on rescuing Manuela, where of course she discovers that the schoolgirls have arrived ahead of her and saved the day.

There are only these two superimpositions in the entire film, and significantly they are both assigned to Fräulein von Bernburg at times in which Manuela is in distress. It is Fräulein von Bernburg, and the force she has come to represent, who prevails in the film's final scene: the rescued Manuela is cradled by the schoolgirls as the defeated Principal, bereft of her authority, slowly retreats down the long, gloomy hall. The darkness of the hall deepens in her wake, her cane taps faintly on the floor, the sound of bells and finally bugles can be heard in the distance. As the bugle calls signify, it is a provisional victory, and yet the patriarchal order *has* been ruptured within the school by the liberation of eros among the women.

In terms of the interpretation that I have been suggesting, as well as the more traditional interpretation of antifascism, the ending of the film is extremely important. Yet the nature of the ending has been frequently obscured in cinema histories. Many reports of the film have cited a supposed "other" ending in which Manuela successfully commits suicide, and some critics have even cited the existence of a "Nazi" suicide ending and and "export" version like this one. Yet as several German sources testify, such was not the case.[9] However, the original play *did* have Manuela kill herself and ended with the Principal setting a cover-up in motion at the play's end; but this is one of many differences between the play and the film that I will discuss later. In point of fact, the film *Mädchen in Uniform* concludes with an ending of rescue. What does this ending signify? Such an ending confers a unity upon the film's two themes – the widely acknowledged one of anti-authoritarianism as well as the previously ignored one of erotic liberation – and shapes them into a consistent and harmonious whole.

It has frequently been argued that the preferred ending for a proto-Nazi film was suicide, i.e., the ultimate abandonment of hope that leads the individual to throw herself/himself into the depth of oblivion or, conversely, into the hands of a superhu-

9. Variations on the theme of a double ending have been repeated by a number of critics, including Nancy Scholar and Sharon Smith, *Women Who Make Movies* (New York: Hopkinson and Blake, 1975); Caroline Seldon,"Lesbians and Film: Some Thoughts," in *Gays and Film*, ed. Richard Dyer (London: British Film Institute, 1977), pp. 5–26; and Parker Tyler, *Screening the Sexes* (New York: Holt, 1972). While American and English critics display a striking unanimity on this point, the German critics of the period of the film's release make no such acknowledgement. Both Eisner and Kracauer specify the averted suicide at the end of the film they are discussing, while neither makes reference to any such "home market" alternate ending. In private correspondence, Karola Gramann wrote me that she was unable to find anyone in Germany who had seen the alleged suicide ending. However, in a 1980 interview with the still lively Hertha Thiele (living in East Berlin and still active in theater), Gramann discovered that a suicide ending was indeed filmed – but never included in the final film, for the reason that the scene was too pathetic-looking to the filmmakers. As best as can be determined, no one in Germany ever saw the film with such an end-

man savior. That was the scenario against which a film like *Kuhle Wampe* (by Slatan Dudow with script by Bertolt Brecht) rebelled, by refusing to end on a note of despair and insisting instead on the persistence of faith in the future. So, too, Sagan. Her anti-Naziism is nowhere more apparent than in the ending, which posits not only the maintenance of hope but also the vindication of resistance as a very different "triumph of the will" from Leni Riefenstahl's brand. In Riefenstahl's film of the same period, *The Blue Light* (1932), the heroine (played by Riefenstahl) finally throws herself from a cliff, despairing, isolated from others of her kind, done in by an unsympathetic society. Not so Manuela: the schoolgirls of the boarding school integrate her sensibility into their own consciousness; instead of closing ranks against her, they come to her (and, by extension, their own) rescue. The cliffhanger ending is at once a powerful statement of political resistance, both individual and collective, and a validation of lesbianism as a personal and public right.

The Principal earlier had condemned Fräulein von Bernburg's feelings and actions as "revolutionary," and so they may indeed be. In a patriarchal society which depends upon women for the reward and procreation of its (his) own kind, a break in the link is disastrous: "What would happen if our hypothetical woman not only refused the man to whom she was promised, but asked for a woman instead? If a single refusal were disruptive, a double refusal would be insurrectionary."[10] The ending of the film serves to validate Fräulein von Bernburg's difficult development from humanitarian disciplinarian to a free, stronger, and woman-identified woman. The progression of the scenario depends upon her inner struggle and final evolution in response to the catalyst of Manuela's passion. At the film's end, Fräulein von Bernburg stands triumphant with the schoolgirls witnessing the Principal's melancholy retreat. She wins this position *not* by maintaining her power in the hierarchy but by rejecting it, *not* by tightening the reins of her repression but by casting them down, *not* by cooption but by refusal. Her place on the staircase at the end may be seen, then, as a reward for her "coming out" and acknowledging her sexuality, just as Manuela's rescue at the end represents a social legitimation of her passion. *Mädchen in Uniform* presents a positive vision of lesbianism that has been largely disregarded for years, a film victim

10. Rubin, "The Traffic in Women" 183.

of a subtle critical homophobia that has insisted upon perceiving the literal as the merely metaphoric.

An analysis of the film today clarifies the meaning and can easily annex Sagan's work to our contemporary tradition of lesbian culture. But historical differences nevertheless persist between the perspectives of Sagan making a film cooperatively in Berlin on the eve of the Third Reich and most of us today. Differences are apparent even in the shifts of meaning between Christa Winsloe's original play and its metamorphosis into *Mädchen in Uniform.* Yet most surprising, perhaps, are the similarities that slowly become recognizable upon reexamining both film and its period – similarities which in some cases are crucial for us to recognize as we proceed into the 1980s.

Sagan's movie is in many respects a more radical work of lesbian celebration than Winsloe's play, while at the same time it focuses far more on the codes of patriarchal power than the stage production. The stage play (both the original, *Yesterday and Today,* and the international version, *Girls in Uniform,* which was widely performed after the film's release)[11] actually fits quite tidily into the model of the "lesbian fairy tale" that Elaine Marks traces to its Sapphic origins in her important essay on lesbian literature:

> Although there is no evidence in Sappho's poems to corroborate the notion that she did indeed have a school, religious or secular, for young women, the gynaeceum, ruled by the seductive or seducing teacher has become, since the eighteenth century, the preferred locus for most fictions about women loving women. . . . The younger woman, whose point of view usually dominates, is always passionate and innocent. If, as is usually the case when the author of the text is a woman, it is the younger woman who falls in love, the narrative is structured so as to insist on this love as an awakening. The older woman as object of the younger woman's desire is restrained and admirable, beautiful and cultivated . . . the exchanges between the older and the younger woman are reminiscent of a mother-daughter relationship. The mother of the younger woman is either dead or in some explicit way inadequate. Her absence is implied in the young woman's insistent need for a goodnight kiss. The gynaeceum, particularly when it is represented by a school, also controls time. Time

11. Quotations and data are derived from personal copies of the original playbill. Blackstone Theatre, Chicago, "beginning Sunday Night, March 11, 1933," and the published play: Christa Winsloe, *Girl in Uniform: A Play in Three Acts* (Boston: Little, Brown, 1933).

> limits are set by the school calendar whose inexorable end announces the fatal separation, which may involve a death. Temporal structures reiterate the almost universally accepted notion that a schoolgirl crush is but a phase in the emotional development of the young woman, something that will pass. The dénouement in these lesbian fairy tales is often brought about by a public event during which private passions explode.[12]

If the contours of Marks's paradigm bear a striking resemblance to the film (which in fact was viewed as an adolescent tale far more than a lesbian one), its elements fit the play even more so. For example, in the play a subplot involves Manuela's pursuit by a diligent, if unwanted, male suitor: her equestrian instructor, no less. In the play, Fräulein von Bernburg is not unmotivated in her feelings for the girls: she secretly wants to be the head of the school herself. She does not resign in the final confrontation with the Principal, but merely tries to increase her power base through the face-off; and Manuela throws herself out a window before anyone has had the chance to rescue her. Since the play can end with only Manuela having stepped out of line and dead for her actions, it is far more easily recuperable into the tradition of lesbianism as tragic, powerless, passive, and in particular, fatal to its adherent. As Marks emphasizes, the "constraints" of the genre signify the "marginal status of lesbians and lesbianism."[13]

While incorporating the classic elements of the "fairy tale" in *Mädchen in Uniform,* Sagan goes further. She changes a few areas of the story line and utilizes the visual and editing codes particular to cinema in order to extend the meaning of the original text.[14] One of the film's strongest features is its success in making palpable the functioning of patriarchal codes despite the

12. Elaine Marks, "Lesbian Intertextuality," in *Homosexualities and French Literature,* ed. George Stambolian and Elaine Marks (Ithaca, NY: Cornell Univ. Press, 1979), 357–58.

13. Ibid., 357.

14. I refer here to Leontine Sagan alone, but that is inaccurate. Carl Froelich is listed as "supervisor," but other sources of the period make claims for codirector or even director status for Froelich, although there is no firm evidence to support such a claim. It should be noted that Froelich stayed in Germany after Hitler's ascendancy and directed films that met the standards of the Third Reich. In addition, there is a fascinating detail for speculation. According to Erwin Leiser's *Nazi Cinema* (New York: Macmillan Co., 1974), Carl Froelich directed a film about Frederick the Great, *The Hymn of Leuthen,* which showed for the first time on 3 February 1933, four days after Hitler became Chancellor of the Reich – suggesting that the intelligence that created *Mädchen* must have

absence of any male or militaristic figures. The use of the central staircase is one such case, with a symbolism both visual (its barred railings and threatening abyss) and philosophical (its use by the girls prohibited from using the formal front staircase). The stairwell suggests a confining enclosure, carceral in its grates of iron and shadow, as well as the functional confinement of virtually all the girls' activities. At one point, the schoolgirls drop an object from the top in order to test a formula for calculating the time a falling body takes to reach bottom. The staircase is thus both a representation of the prevailing order and its power of organization and also a portent of tragedy in its depth and shadows. The camera frequently views the marching of the girls through the iron forms, further emphasizing their molding into Prussian "women of iron." And, of course, the very first meeting between Manuela and Fräulein von Bernburg occurs on the staircase, their bodies positioned midway between forbidding shadows at screen left and a bright window screen right.

In addition to such visual compositions, Sagan inserts a series of montages that provide a bridge between the fairly theatrical scenes involving the central characters and the documentary-style observations of schoolgirl behavior. The large cast of schoolgirls – all nonprofessional actresses – functions as an alternate discourse to set against the patriarchal regimentation. The students horse around, express homesickness, carry on multiple intrigues with each other, play jokes, dress and undress, and relate to each other in a tone that shifts between childishness and eroticism.[15] At one point, a locker room scene of bedtime activities is imme-

---

belonged to Sagan and not to Froelich. Given the analogy of the Principal to the Frederick stereotype, however, the progression is fascinating. It has been said (by none other than the Reich actor Emil Jannings) that an historical line may be drawn "from Frederick the Great to Bismarck to Hitler." Given that, here is the fascinating detail: a 1942 film on Frederick (Veit Harlan's *The Great King*) detailed the episode of the Prussian king's defeat at Kunersdorf in 1759 and in particular shows the disdain that Frederick manifested for one regiment which "preferred life to victory" and had not thrown itself into suicidal combat. Stripped of stripes and insignia for this action, the regiment's colonel commits suicide. The name of the colonel and his regiment? Bernburg. Such a detail makes one wonder what Froelich's contribution could have been, as Sagan seems so clearly to have had her way thematically.

15. At one point, in the first locker room scene, the model of heterosexuality comes under discussion and, obliquely, attack. There is a photo of a male actor in Ilse's locker, a male pinup some girls are giggling over, and finally, highlighted, an illustration in Manuela's book that depicts a woman being rapaciously carried of by a swashbuckling man on horseback – a rather dark statement on the power principles of heterosexual fantasy and reality.

diately followed by a montage that marshals the disorganized activities into a marching order of mouths in extreme close-up barking orders, feet hurrying to obey, identical lines of students filing past, and so on. The montage ends with a shift to the famous dormitory scene of Fräulein von Bernburg's goodnight kisses, a scene which is itself ambiguous in its resolution of eroticism with regimentation.

Most significant are the montage sequences which frame the encounters between Manuela and Fräulein von Bernburg, and indeed, frame our entire encounter with the film. The montage which opens the film communicates a view of the exterior towers of Potsdam; the old stone putti and statue which resembles a tiny soldier and the sounds of church bells and bugles portray an atmosphere of patriarchal readiness within which the school building itself is located. Traces of the same montage appear as narrative interruptions at key moments in the evolution of Manuela and Fräulein von Bernburg's relationship. For example, just after Manuela has thrown her arms around the teacher in the goodnight scene, Sagan inserts a rapid cut to the towers and statues. Later, when Fräulein von Bernburg gives the student her chemise, Sagan similarly terminates the scene with a cut to the stone towers and the sound of bells tolling. The montages appear to be cautionary, clues to the audience that emotions between women are never free of the shadow of patriarchal aggression. Their intrusion into the film is an antidote to viewing this all-female space as a "free zone" within a patriarchal society, which can be seen to dominate not only in the concrete form of the staircase or Principal, but in the equally threatening form of external authority that waits just outside the school gates.

Even at the film's end, when the two women and their student supporter seem most victorious, the ominous sound of the bugles reappears to accompany the Principal's retreat. While Siegfried Kracauer contends that the prominence of the motif at the end of the film proves that "the principle of authority has not been shaken" within the school,[16] I would suggest otherwise: the motif reminds the audience just how provisional the victory is, and just how powerful are the patriarchal forces with which any new order within the school must contend. It is a warning that separation from the dominant order does not automatically grant freedom from its dominance. It should have

16. Kracauer, *From Caligari to Hitler*, 229.

been a warning to lesbians then living in Germany that the time for strong collective action was upon them, as the forces of fascism gathered outside the windows. Instead, the Third Reich indeed came to power, and most of those responsible for *Mädchen in Uniform* left the country.

Who were they? Little has been written and little is known about the women behind this work. Their sexuality has been as thoroughly veiled as the lesbian theme of the film itself. Rumors, anecdotes, and bits of stories form the customary trail of unofficial history. Blanche Wiesen Cook is instructive regarding what *not* to look for. Commenting upon *Mädchen in Uniform*, Ann Elisabet Weirach's *The Scorpion*, and other works of this period and genre, Cook warns against accepting the tragic tales of unrequited love and tragic abandonment as autobiographical fictions: "The truth is that these passionate little girls were not always abused and abandoned. They did not commit suicide. They wrote books about passionate little girls, death, and abandonment."[17] Not infrequently the lives of the authors and their models display a depth and breadth of options not readily visible in their constructed tales – when, that is, their lives are recoverable at all.

Leontine Sagan was born in Austria in 1889 and was married at some point to a doctor from Vienna. She trained as a stage director and actress and worked with such directors as Bernofskey and Max Reinhardt, teaching for a time at Reinhardt's drama school. As an actress, she appeared alongside Salka Viertel in an early production of the Ibsen play *John Gabriel Borkman* and also in a rare production of Franz Blei's *The Wave.* The circumstances of her taking on the direction of *Mädchen in Uniform* are not now available, although she was certainly a popular figure in the Berlin theater scene. She left Germany soon after and went to England, where Alexander Korda sought to capitalize on her success by engaging her to direct *Men of Tomorrow,* a sort of "boys in uniform" film about Oxford; not surprisingly, the success was not repeated. Judging by the published script and cast list for a production of *Mädchen in Uniform,* Sagan also worked in theater in London. The play, retitled *Children in Uniform,* listed as being "produced by Leontine Sagan" at

17. Blanche Wiesen Cook, "'Women Alone Stir My Imagination': Lesbianism and the Cultural Tradition," *Signs* 4, no. 4 (1979), 722.

18. Information on *Anna and Elizabeth* is taken from David Stewart Hull, *Film in the Third Reich* (Berkeley: Univ. of California Press, 1969), 37–38, and also from private correspondence with Karola Gramann.

The Duchess Theatre, London, opening 7 October 1932. Soon after, Sagan left England. She moved to the United States for several years and thence to South Africa, where she cofounded the National Theater. She died in 1974 in Johannesburg. As far as is known, she never made another film.

The two leading actresses of *Mädchen in Uniform*, Hertha Thiele and Dorothea Wieck, starred together in another film shortly afterward. Directed by Frank Wysbar in 1933, *Anna and Elisabeth* returned to the traditional view of intimate attachments between women as debilitating and demonic: Hertha Thiele played a young girl with miraculous powers who drove Dorothea Wieck to attempt suicide because Thiele failed to resurrect her husband! The women are portrayed as having an unnaturally close, almost supernatural, relationship; lesbianism is explicit only as the power of darkness. Both actresses were still alive in the early 1980s, and much additional material has been made available by Karol Gramann, the *Frauen und Film* editor who interviewed Thiele.[18]

Christa Winsloe is the best remembered of the *Mädchen in Uniform* women, perhaps simply because her intimates wrote memoirs. Erika Mann, who herself played one of the teachers in the film, remembered Winsloe (the Baroness von Hatvany) in her memoirs of 1939 in a fashion that would please Blanche Cook. Smiling and confident, dressed in white shirt and tie, Christa Winsloe looks out at us from a photograph captioned "once a Mädchen in uniform." Erika Mann recalls Christa's life as a "beautiful and amusing society woman" who ran an expensive household in Munich and hosted salons in Budapest and Vienna as the wife of Baron Ludwig Hatvany, a Hungarian writer and "grand seigneur." She made animal sculptures and held exquisite dinner parties, at one of which Mann remembers her announcing her plan to write a play about her own childhood boarding-school experiences. Trying to explain the play's phenomenal success, Mann suggests:

> How was it? . . . Because Christa Hatvany had guarded in her heart, and now rediscovered, a simple, strong and genuine feeling, and because she could so express it that hundreds of thousands of peo-

18. Information on *Anna and Elizabeth* is taken from David Stewart Hull, *Film in the Third Reich* (Berkeley: Univ. of California Press, 1969), 37–38, and also from private correspondence with Karola Gramann. [The 1980 interview with Thiele appears in *Frauen und Film* 28 (1981): 32–41. – Eds.]

> ple [sic] recognized the pain and ecstasy of their own childhood, their own first love, which had, in their own hearts, been overlaid, but never stifled. The poignant feeling of recognition. . . .[19]

If Mann holds to the favorite view of lesbian as a phase through which "hundreds of thousands" of women pass during adolescence, she at least manages to hold out a phrase of reservation regarding the impulse which is yet "never stifled."

Certainly it was never stifled in Christa. Nor in Dorothy Thompson, the U. S. journalist who was married to Sinclair Lewis when, in 1932, at her own ten-day Christmas party, she fell in love with Christa, who was then on the verge of getting a divorce from the Baron. Dorothy Thompson's diaries of the time reveal her struggle to name her experience, to try to understand how she can be "happily married, and yet wanting that curious tenderness. That pervading warm tenderness – there are no words for it."[20] When the party guests had left, Dorothy followed Christa to Budapest. In March, the two met in Italy, where they shared a villa at Portofino for several months. Upon leaving the villa, Dorothy brought Christa back to the U. S. with her. In August, the two women traveled back to Austria together. When apart, they wrote constantly. In early 1934, Sinclair Lewis had to be out of town for several months and Dorothy stayed in New York with Christa. "They were a couple," said their friend John Farrar. "If you asked Dorothy for dinner, you asked Christa too."[21]

After two years, however, relations between the two began to break down, with Dorothy answering one of Christa's letters: "I feel that something between us has broken. . . . . I had a strange dream last night. I dreamed I was putting out into a very rough sea in a frail ship, and the crew were all women. I was afraid, and woke up, sweating."[22] By this time, Thompson was persona non grata in Germany, having been expelled on her last trip by Adolph Hitler himself because of an uncomplimentary interview (and, no doubt, her habit of laughing at Bund rallies). Christa couldn't return to her home, so went instead in 1935 to live in southern France. Their continued intimacy was so strong

19. Erika and Klaus Mann, *Escape to Life* (Boston: Houghton Mifflin, 1939), 50–51.

20. Katz, *Gay American History*, 841.

21. Marion K. Sanders, *Dorothy Thompson: A Legend in Her Time* (Boston: Houghton Mifflin, 1973), 190.

22. Ibid.,193.

that, in 1940, when the Nazi occupation of France made it impossible for Christa to withdraw money from her Munich bank, Dorothy began sending her money every month to live on.

Christa Winsloe's life had a sad end, but nothing at all like a Marks fairy tale formula: she was murdered on 10 June 1944 by a common criminal named Lambert, who pretended to be operating as a member of the French resistance. His claim led to ugly speculation that Winsloe had been a Nazi spy and to an old friend's writing Dorothy Thompson at the end of the war (1946) to inform her of the death and beg help in clearing Christa Winsloe's name. The friend explained the rumors by Christa's liaison at the time with a French-Swiss girlfriend, Simone Gentet, who was alleged to be a spy:

> Christa once described her as a hysterical, dissolute morphine addict and alcoholic, but she certainly knew nothing of Simone's other activities, should the rumor be true . . . we know with such absolute certainty that Christa was the most violent enemy of National-Socialism and that she would never have made the slightest compromise. On the contrary, we were always worried that the Gestapo would grab her and we still believed this is what happened to her because she had helped many Jewish friends get out of the country.[23]

Thus, the author of *Mädchen in Uniform* was killed by a man claiming to be a resistance fighter but whom her friends believed to be a Gestapo agent, an ambiguity that lends to her death the same confusion that continues to surround the relationship between homosexuality and the Nazi era.

As an example of their conflation, Rossellini's *Rome, Open City* established an early tradition of identifying homosexuality with fascism through his narrative of hearty male resistance fighters betrayed by a lesbian morphine addict and her Gestapo lover. Bertolucci continued the tradition by consistently portraying fascists as suffering from sexual repressions of "perversions" in his films (with time out in *The Conformist* for a lesbian resistance fighter in the person of Dominique Sanda, although he did equip her with a male mentor and suggest that her attraction to women was her weakness). The connections have not depended upon cinema, either Italian or German, for promulgation. The stereotype of Nazi campiness, of SS regalia as s-&-m toys, of the Gestapo as a leather-boy thrill, of the big bull dyke as concentration camp boss,

23. Ibid.

etc., all seem to have a firm hold in our culture's fantasy life and historical mythology – this despite the facts of the third Reich's large-scale massacre of homosexuals as pollutants of Aryan blood and a stain on the future master race. Hitler apparently agreed with Manuela's boarding-school Principal in seeing homosexuality and lesbianism as "revolutionary." He did not hesitate to purge his own ranks, as on the infamous "night of the long knives" of June, 1934, when Ernst Röhm (the SA chief of staff and a well-known homosexual) and his followers were murdered to make the SA, as Hitler put it, "a pure and cleanly institution."

Why the Nazis wanted to eliminate homosexuals along with Jews, communists, and various national minorities is a question that seems fairly well answered and understood now in the light of Nazi ideology and the "final solutions" it proposed for the united, fascistic, patriarchal Aryan race. Why gay men or any women should have joined the Nazi party at all is quite another question. What circumstances led to the existence of a Röhm? What sort of outlook could have lent credence to Christa Winsloe's murder as an act of Resistance, or alternately, as an act of Nazi vengeance? What sort of lesbian community inhabited Berlin during the Weimar Republic and the rise of the Third Reich? What sort of women's movement was there too combat the Nazi ideology of woman's place? What were social and legal attitudes toward homosexuality? Who liked *Mädchen in Uniform,* and why? To answer these questions fully lies outside the possibilities of this article, but to address them at least in part is crucial to our understanding of the film and to our recognizing just how exemplary was Leontine Sagan's combination of personal liberation and collective action.[24]

Germany had a radical women's movement in the early years of the century, beginning with the country's first large rally for women's suffrage in 1894. The movement for women's rights was part of a larger movement for overall reform known as the *Lebens-*

24. The three basic texts to consult on issues of feminism and homosexuality in Weimar Germany are: Richard Evans, *The Feminist Movement in Germany 1894–1933* (Beverly Hills, CA: Sage, 1976); Lillian Faderman and Brigitte Eriksson, *Lesbian Feminism in Turn-of-the-Century Germany* (Tallahassee, FL: Naiad, 1979); and James D. Steakley, *The Homosexual Emancipation Movement in Germany* (New York: Arno, 1975). Relevant information in this article is culled almost entirely from these sources. For a superior review and perspective piece, see Carol Anne Douglas, "German Feminists and the Right: Can It Happen Here?" *off our backs* 10, no. 11 (December 1980), 18–20. She discusses at length the political crosscurrents I have barely managed to summarize here.

reformbewegung (the Life Reform Movement), which encompassed groups working on behalf of women and homosexuals as well as youth, natural health, clothing reform, and nudity. There do not seem to have been lesbian political organizations as such, but many lesbians were active in women's suffrage and feminist groups (notably Anita Augspurg and Lida Gustava Heymann, who fought for suffrage and opposed World War I as "a men's war fought between men's states"), and many others worked with the Scientific-Humanitarian Committee founded by Magnus Hirschfeld (the key figure in homosexual rights struggles). As early as 1904, Anna Ruling had addressed the Committee at a meeting on the common struggles of women's and homosexuals' rights groups, complaining that women's organizations were "not lifting a finger . . . doing nothing, absolutely nothing" in support of homosexual emancipation.

In 1909, however, a bill was proposed to criminalize lesbianism, which up until then had not been subject to the Paragraph 175 laws against male homosexuality. Seeing the bill as a clear retaliation against the gains of the women's movement, Dr. Helene Stöcker (who in 1905 had founded the league for the Protection of Maternity and Sexual Reform) spoke at a meeting held jointly with the Committee to support its petition drive against the proposed bill and to denounce the criminalization of lesbianism as "a grave error." The arguments on behalf of both women and homosexuality were diverse and at times contradictory, with variations in ideology so wide that some elements could be supportive of the new Russian Revolution as a model while other elements drifted into support of National Socialism. Stöcker's argument for keeping lesbianism legal rested on the defense of "individual freedom in the most private part of private life – love life"; Hirschfeld rested his arguments on scientific theories of human sexuality/psychology and upon a human-rights-type plea for tolerance; certain other groups based their homosexuality upon theories of male supremacy and past models of soldiery and lovers-in-arms leading to an early Nazi identification; while other groups initially supportive of sexual freedoms for women, like those in the "sexual hygiene" movement, turned antiabortionist for racial reasons and ended up merging with the proto-Nazi "racial hygiene" groups.

Varying definitions of private and public life – and private versus public rights – are key to the differences. Hirschfeld, unlike many others, threw all his energies into effecting social education and legal changes (although with a tone of apology and tolerance-begging foreign to our styles today). The years of the Weimar Republic witnessed a flowering of women's rights and of struggles for homosexual emancipation, as well as a bursting forth of a large lesbian and gay subculture quartered largely in Berlin. And the sexual theories of the time are fascinating. In 1919, Hirschfeld opened the doors of his institute of Sexual Science and won substantial support for the theory of "a third sex" that was neither male nor female: he called homosexuals "Uranians" and based much of his strategy upon this notion of a literally alien species.

The move to criminalize lesbianism had been dropped with the advent of the Republic and the end of World War I, which had seen women move so totally out of the former spheres as to make such a bill ineffective as a stay-at-home device. Therefore, much of Hirschfeld's Committee's efforts went toward the repeal of Paragraph 175 (prohibiting male homosexual practice). The Coalition for Reform of the Sexual Crimes Code (founded in 1925) worked to legalize acts between "consenting adults." The German Communist Party, following the lead established by revolutionary Soviet laws in support of homosexual rights, had a strong presence on the Reichstag committee for penal code reform – which succeeded in recommending for approval the repeal of Paragraph 175 (but unfortunately, its approval came on 16 October 1929, when the crash of the U. S. stock market changed the whole nature of the political scene in Germany, leading to the tabling of the resolution and the quick rise of the Nazi forces). As anti-Semitism, misogyny, and homophobia grew alongside the move to the right in Germany, Hirschfeld became an ever more popular target. Attacked in 1920, his skull fractured in 1921, fired upon in 1923, attacked verbally by a Nazi delegate to the Reichstag in 1927, he had the dubious honor of seeing the library of his Institute become one of the first victims of book-burning on 10 May 1933, just four months after Hitler became chancellor.[25]

The cycle of free expression followed by total persecution experienced by Magnus Hirschfeld was symptomatic of the treat-

25. Interestingly enough, Hirschfeld appeared in a film he must have taken a part in producing. *Different From the Others* (directed by Richard Oswald in 1919) starred Conrad Veidt as a homosexual blackmail victim who is "saved" by the intervention of a philanthropic doctor played by Hirschfeld himself. It was wide-

ment of the larger gay population and culture he had come to symbolize. Jim Steakley provides a partial answer to the obvious reaction (how could such a thing happen?), pinpointing the Weimar contradiction "between personal and collective liberation" – a contradiction manifested in the simultaneous existence of a widespread social tolerance of homosexuality (including the flourishing of gay culture, the growth of bars, and de facto police acquiescence, at least in Berlin) alongside repressive laws and the frequent failure of most legal actions on behalf of lesbians or gay men.[26] The history of Berlin's gay male subculture is fairly well known today; according to Steakley, there were some forty gay bars and between one and two thousand prostitutes in the city by 1914, as well as perhaps thirty homosexual journals published during the course of the Weimar years. However, the same "invisibility" that granted lesbians immunity from the criminal laws has also granted the Weimar lesbians a less welcome immunity from the history books.

Recent research has begun to yield materials that can outline for us the contours of the lesbian community that was so lively during the same period, especially in the larger cities of Berlin and Munich. Louise Brooks (who starred as Lulu in G. W. Pabst's *Pandora's Box*, which offered a glimpse of Berlin's decadent ways) has reminisced about the mood of Berlin, recalling for example a lesbian bar, the Maly, where "there was a choice of feminine or collar-and-tie lesbians."[27] Alex de Jonge provides a more embroidered account in a male visitor's account of the Silhouette, which was "one of Berlin's most fashionable night spots." He, too, describes the scene of role-dressed couples on a night out, but makes an important point: "You could see women well known in German literature, society, the theater and politics. . . . There was no suggestion of vice about the place. It was a usual phenomenon in German life."[28] While the Silhouette admitted men if accompanied by a lesbian regular, other women's bars did not; de Jonge mentions Die Grotte and Entre

ly banned, but evidently more for reasons of anti-Semitism (directed against Hirschfeld) than homophobia, if such a distinction can indeed be made. The film was remade in 1927 as *Laws of Love,* again starring Veidt, but minus Hirschfeld, whose absence in this version led to Veidt's character's suicide.

26. Steakley, *Homosexual Emancipation Movement,* 78–79.

27. Louise Brooks, "On Making Pabst's *Lulu,*" in *Women and the Cinema,* ed. Karyn Kay and Gerald Peary (New York: Dutton, 1977), 81.

28. de Jonge, *Prelude to Hitler,* 140.

Nous as two of the "more exclusive" places, about which he therefore can provide no information.

Ilse Kokula has provided one of the most complete accounts of the period in her brief but tantalizing summary, "The Uranian Ladies Often Meet in Patisseries."[29] She expands upon the meaning of "uranian" by tracing its root as an epithet of Aphrodite taken to mean "celestial" or spiritual, and she reiterates Hirschfeld's popular theory of "a third sex." The estimate of homosexuality in Weimar Berlin is placed at fifty thousand out of a population of two and a half million (although the methodology behind the statistics is not specified). While bars, hotels, and saunas serviced gay men, there were also, more surprisingly, various services for lesbian seeking to meet each other. For example, there were *Vermittlungsbüros,* or agencies that fixed up single lesbians. There were personals columns in which lesbians advertised for partners. One such ad from the period listing the following: "Fräulein, decent, 24 years old, looking for pretty Fräulein as girlfriend." There were also a number of social clubs for lesbians that met in cafes and *Konditoreien* (patisseries), such as one group of "Israelite" (Jewish) lesbians who met from 4:00 to 6:00 in the afternoon to talk and play chess. Balls were held regularly, run by and for lesbian women. There was a general attitude of self-recognition, with many lesbian couples eager to convince the world how well-adjusted they were and to combat the stereotypes of depravity and tragedy.

From 1918 on, lesbian journals were part of the culture, usually presenting a perspective that was part political and part educational; they had such titles as *Frauenliebe* (womenlove), *Ledige Frauen* (unmarried women), and *Die Freundin: Weekly Journal for Ideal Friendship Between Women. Die Freundin* was published continuously during 1923–32 by the *Damenklub* (women's club, or bar) "Violette" – itself a coded name, as violets were considered a sign of lesbianism at that time. Some of Ilse Kokula's information is evidently derived from first-hand sources, as she is able to comment that many older lesbians still remember the cafes "with great pleasure," and that one such woman, Kati R., remembers that the secret lesbian balls continued into the 1950s and 1960s, with as many as two hundred women attending. What emerges, then, is a picture of lesbian life as a wide-

29. Ilse Kokula, "Die urnischen Damen treffen sich vielfach in Konditoreien," *Courage* 7 (Berlin: July 1980); copy courtesy of Karola Gramann.

spread phenomenon, surprisingly aboveground and organized around its own publications, clubs, and rituals. This is reflected in virtually none of the films or official histories of the time.

Despite such a spirit of freedom and such an ambience of lesbian permissiveness, at no point, either in its own time or in ours, has *Mädchen in Uniform* been critically (i.e., publicly) discussed as a lesbian text. And yet the histories specify its initial *succès de scandale*, implying an at least unofficial recognition of the film's true meaning. Why has this meaning been so hidden, so difficult to retrieve? The extent of the obstacles in the path of the gay historian seeking to reinterpret film texts has been emphasized recently by Vito Russo's uncovering of the original New York State censor's notes on the American release of *Mädchen in Uniform*.[30] Almost line for line, scene for scene, the shots and subtitles that I have specified as revolutionary and most fundamentally lesbian were the sections of the film that the censors wanted to cut. Initially condemned, the film was approved by the censors for release in August 1932 only after all evidence of lesbianism had been cut. Their notes were specific; for example, "Reel Four: Eliminate all views of Manuela's face as she looks at Miss Von Bernburg in the classroom." The censors at least understood the power of the superimpositions! But, in a cruel irony of manipulation, the contemporary critics reviewed the butchered film positively, using its now antiseptic contents to ridicule all who had been holding the film up as an example of "neuroticism . . . a celluloid *Well of Loneliness*."

Ever since, most critics have been eager to harness its tale of schoolgirl struggle to an assumed "universal" of humankind's fight against fascism, rather than some perverse championing of inverted emotions. With hindsight, however, we can equally read the film as a celebration of and warning for its most sympathetic audience: the lesbian population in Germany in 1931. Like Manuela and Fräulein von Bernburg, the lesbian community was proud and outspoken, romantic and idealistic, equally opposed to a bourgeois morality as well as to outdated models of woman's proper place. The schoolgirls may have been stand-

30. Vito Russo, *The Celluloid Closet: Homosexuality in the Movies* (New York: Harper and Row/Colophon, 1981), 56–59. Russo's book came out after this article's initial publishing. It is an important work, beautifully researched and filled with primary data, but unfortunately marred by a bitchy misogyny. Nevertheless, the photograph of a very butch Dorothy Arzner arm-in-arm with Joan Crawford on the 1937 set of *The Bride Wore Red* is itself worth the price of the book.

ins for the lesbian women they could grow up to become (if they passed through Erika Mann's famous "phase" intact). If the boarding school was chosen as a literary and cinematic motif because it was more socially acceptable than the grown-up reality, then how ironic that it is all that remains for us. We need more research into our history. We need more information on films of the period that have been almost entirely forgotten, like *Anna and Elizabeth* or *Different from the Others*.[31] We need to heed carefully Blanch Cook's warning not to judge the authors entirely by their texts, lest literary conventions of the time blind us to the unexpected. We need to recognize *Mädchen in Uniform* not only as a beloved fairy tale but also as a powerful expression of its own time – an individual record of a collective aspiration.

Mädchen in Uniform has been extremely influential for other writers and films as well as for lesbian viewers down to the present day. Colette herself wrote the text for the subtitles of the French release print.[32] None other than Hollywood mogul Irving Thalberg was a fan of the film. He quizzed Salka Viertel, as she worked on the screenplay of *Queen Christina,* as to whether she had seen Sagan's film. "Does not Christina's affection for her lady-in-waiting indicate something like that?" he asked, and urged her to keep it in mind" because, "if handled with taste it would give us very interesting scenes."[33]

Stephen Spender came to New York in February of 1982 to speak about "Experiencing the Cinema In Berlin."[34] The film he most vividly remembered was *Mädchen in Uniform,* which he and Christopher Isherwood had gone to see during their 1931–32

31. See note 25. A print of *Different From the Others* survives in an East German archive. A print of *Anna and Elizabeth* survives in an archive at Koblenz. A special form of *Different From the Others* was made for screenings in Montreal and New York City in 1982; *Anna and Elizabeth* has yet to be seen here.

32. The French subtitles and a preface explaining Colette's role in writing them can be found in *Colette au cinéma,* ed. Alain and Odette Virmaux (Paris: Librairie Ernest Flammarion, 1975). Unfortunately, the entire *Mädchen in Uniform* section has been omitted from the English-language edition, trans. Sarah W. R. Smith (New York: Frederic Ungar, 1980).

33. Salka Viertel, *The Kindness of Strangers* (New York: Holt, 1969), 175. Viertel's memoirs are discreetly restrained on virtually all topics of sexuality and therefore shed no light on the nature of her relationship with Greta Garbo. Viertel wrote the screen treatments for Garbo's films and was her frequent companion. In his dirt-digging *Hollywood Babylon* (New York: Dell, 1975), Kenneth Anger wrote that "Garbo's genuine reserve held the gossips at bay for the most part. There was however, occasional speculation about how close her friendship really was with writer Salka Viertel"(246).

34. The event was the International Center of Photography's symposium, "Avant-Garde German Photography: 1919–1939," held at the Guggenheim Museum. Quotations are based on notes.

residence in Berlin. Spender recalled that they had slipped away from some other event to see what he described as "the most remarkable film we'd ever seen," due in large measure to the "extraordinary impression" made upon them by Hertha Thiele; indeed, he went so far as to describe the film as "full of extraordinary images based on this girl's face." Of special relevance to us is Spender's description of a Berlin caught up in a cinematic fever inspired by the Soviet films that showed two or three times a week. "Unlike futurist art," said Spender, the Soviet and progressive Weimar films "really did make you think they would change your life." With a certain nostalgia for a time *before* everyone became "suspicious about photography," Spender pinpointed the importance for him of *Mädchen in Uniform* and the progressive films with which he identifies it: "The great thing about photography in this period was that it seemed an expression of freedom." It is only in today's historical considerations that this film and others like it have come to be graded on formal qualities disassociated from any political meaning. Spender's remarks are useful in reminding today's viewers (and scholars) that Sagan was working at a time when "the camera was linked to the idea of a revolution that was still possible."

Like Spender, we can acknowledge what Colette, Thalberg, Viertel, and Garbo all seem to have known: that *Mädchen in Uniform* was a film about women's love for each other. And what Louise Brooks knew: that such love was no rarity in Weimar Berlin. And what Alex de Jonge knew: that it was no vice. And today we can also begin to consider what Jim Steakley knew: that there was a disturbing gap at the time between "personal" and "collective" liberation.

Mädchen in Uniform emerges from such a review of Weimar's lesbian subculture not any longer as an anomaly, but as a survivor. The film assumes a new importance when seen not as a curiosity but rather as a clue, an archeological relic pointing back to an obliterated people and pointing ahead, for us, to a much-needed perspective on our current situation.

The first lesson of *Mädchen in Uniform* is that lesbianism has a much larger and finer history than we often suspect, that the film indicates as much, and that we need to do more work on reconstructing the image of lesbian culture that has been so painfully erased. The second lesson is that in looking backward and inward we cannot afford to stop looking forward and outward. The bells and bugles that sound periodically throughout the film, casting a prophetic pall upon the love of Manuela and Fräulein von Bernburg, are waiting just outside the gates for us as well. As I have suggested, the ending of the film can be interpreted as a warning to heed the forces mounting outside our narrow zones of victory and liberation. Such an interpretation, if it was perceived at the time, went unheeded by the film's lesbian audience in 1931. Today, the work in building a lesbian culture cannot afford to ignore the context of such labor in a society veering so strongly in the opposite direction.

Today, we must begin to consider the contemporary gap between "personal" (or lifestyle) freedoms and "collective" (or legal political) rights. We must begin to examine what the links and coalitions are, in our own time, between lesbian, gay male, and feminist organizations. We must learn strategy and remember that when the pre-Weimar misogynist, F. Eberhard, wanted to attack the women's movement, he accused the emancipated women of being lesbians and, therefore, depraved. The women's groups of the late Weimar period exhibited a distressing willingness to take such attacks to heart and try to accommodate themselves accordingly. Polite cooptation sapped the strength of the groups. Too late, many lesbians must have learned that patisseries do not grant asylum.

Struggle was postponed to a fatally late date due to false perceptions of homosexuality as a "private" issue that was being adequately handled and of lesbians/gay men as somehow more protected than others because of the history of social tolerance. The celebrants of the staircase must listen hard to the rallying cries outside the school and take heed. Today, we can not afford to ignore history, nor to repeat it. While lesbianism and feminism are certainly "revolutionary" (to quote the Principal yet again), the history of Weimar politics demonstrates that they are not *inherently* so unless linked to a pragmatic political strategy and set of principles. In the 1980s our struggles for sexual freedom and gender flexibility must be integrated with the ongoing fights against economic injustices, racism, growing militarism, and all such forces that have an impact on every individual in our society. We have to do better.

This article is reprinted from the collection Re-Vision: Essays in Feminist Film Criticism, *eds. Mary Ann Doane, Patricia Mellencamp, and Linda Williams.*

5

The Filmic Adaptation of the Novel *The Child Manuela*: Christa Winsloe's Child Heroine Becomes a *Girl in Uniform*

lisa ohm

Lisa Ohm also examines Girls in Uniform, *taking issue to some extent with Rich. In analyzing both the film and the novel upon which the film was based, Ohm asserts that neither is a "coming out" text, finding in both negative attitudes toward lesbianism that derive from the medical/psychological discourse on sexuality that had become dominant by 1920. In her reading of the film, Ohm places renewed emphasis on the thematization of authoritarianism in the film; from this perspective, the film's happy ending is more problematic.*
—The Editors

The 1931 German sound film *Girls in Uniform* (*Mädchen in Uniform*)[1] is the story of a schoolgirl's crush on her female teacher in a private seminary established for the daughters of aristocratic Prussian army officers. The film's all-female cast was directed by actress and theater director Leontine Sagan[2] under the tech-

1. *Mädchen in Uniform* (*Girls in Uniform*), dir. Leontine Sagan, Deutsche Filmgemeinschaft GmbH. 1931. The cast includes Dorothea Wieck (Elizabeth von Bernburg), Hertha Thiele (Manuela von Meinhardis), Emilie Unda (Headmistress), Ellen Schwanneke (Ilse von Westhagen), Hedwig Schlichter (Fräulein von Kesten), Annemarie Rochhausen (Edelgard), and Gertrud de Lalsky (Manuela's aunt). A remake of the film under the same title directed by Geza Radvanyi and starring Romy Schneider and Lilli Palmer appeared in 1957.

2. Leontine Sagan was born Leontine Schlesinger in Austria in 1889. A student of Max Reinhardt, Sagan acted and directed in theaters in Berlin, Dresden, Vienna, and Frankfurt. After her success with *Girls in Uniform* she was invited to direct a film (*Men of Tomorrow*) based on a novel about Oxford students by Anthony Gibb (*The Young Apollo*). In 1939 she went to South Africa and founded the National Theater in Johannesburg. She died in South Africa in May, 1974.

nical supervision of the well-known director Carl Froelich. *Girls in Uniform,* Sagan's first of only two films, is based on a novel by Christa Winsloe[3] entitled *The Child Manuela* (*Das Kind Manuela.*)

Past critics were aware of the film's suggestive homoeroticism, but culled more significance from the political content, interpreting the averted suicide of the adolescent heroine at the end as a victory for humanism over the authoritarian Prussian educational system or its political extension, fascism. In his 1932 review of the film, for example, Mordaunt Hall wrote: "It is actually more of a rap on the knuckles for the militaristic notions than an exposition of unnatural affection."[4] Feminist film critic Jeanne Betancourt wrote in 1974: "The physical structure of the school, its rules and the effect of the rules on the girls are a metaphor for the strategies of Hitler throughout Germany or of any oppressive authoritarian system."[5]

Since the 1974 revival of Sagan's film, however, American feminists have given the homoerotic content priority over the political. Critic B. Ruby Rich, for example, interprets the film as a lesbian "coming out" for both the pupil, Manuela von Meinhardis, and her beloved teacher, Fräulein (Elizabeth) von Bernburg.[6] Erotic liberation is not a metaphor, says Rich, but the message of the film.

Rich, however, relies heavily on the novel for her analysis of the film. While her interpretation enriches our viewing of the film, her search for the classic elements of the lesbian fairy tale in a boarding school setting has seduced her to overlook critical revisions of the novel for filmic use. The novel concentrates on the personal tragedies in the private world of its child heroine, Manuela. The film, however, shifts interest from Manuela, whose youth and isolation in the boarding school no longer hold center stage in the visual medium, to her teacher, Fräulein

3. Christa Winsloe was born 23 December 1888 in Darmstadt, Germany, the daughter of an army officer. She attended a private girls' boarding school in Potsdam and became a sculptress in Schwabing. During World War II Winsloe lived in Southern France. On 10 June 1944 she was underway to Munich via Cluny when she and the Swiss authoress Simone Gentet were arrested and shot to death for alleged collaboration with the enemy. [cf. B. Ruby Rich's discussion above, p. 87, this volume.]

4. Mordaunt Hall, rev. of *Mädchen in Uniform,* 21 September 1932, in *The New York Times Directory of the Film* (New York: Arno, 1971).

5. Jeanne Betancourt, *Women in Focus* (Dayton: Pflaum, 1974), p. 98.

6. B. Ruby Rich, "*Mädchen in Uniform*: From Repressive Tolerance to Erotic Liberation," *Jump Cut* 24–25 (1981): 44–50. [Rich's article is reprinted in this volume in its definitive 1984 version. See above, 61–96.]

von Bernburg. Bernburg is caught in a dramatic conflict of generations, her youthful idealism colliding on the one side with the old-school harshness of her older superior, the headmistress, and on the other with her younger pupils. This shift of central interest automatically enhances Bernburg's role, necessitating the stunning, idealistic reversal at the end of the film when the suicidal Manuela is rescued by her rebellious classmates. Manuela's attempts to gain Bernburg's favor in the film (the novel stresses her need for a mother figure) reveal her precarious position as an outsider to the school's group of girls, and lead to Manuela's open confrontation with the institution of the seminary, represented by the headmistress.

This shift of interest in the more condensed and dramatic visual medium reduces the private emotionalism of the novel from central theme to a mere tactical device used to trigger dramatic action in the film. Furthermore, the homoeroticism of the novel is reduced to voyeurism by the exploitative veneer of provocative sexuality added to the film – most obvious in the famous kiss scene – to assure its commercial success. Hertha Thiele, who played the part of Manuela in the film, revealed in an interview that the film's technical supervisor, Carl Froelich, chose the title because he felt it would help assure the production financial success by invoking visions of girls's legs beneath military jackets. Thiele indicated that Sagan's lack of experience in film gave Froelich power beyond his purely technical role and that his supervisory eye was mainly on box office receipts.[7]

The recognition of these significant differences between the novel and the film does not support Rich's conclusion that *Girls in Uniform* is a "coming-out" film. Nor is Winsloe's novel a "coming-out" text. The first half of *Das Kind Manuela* hints at Manuela's boyishness. Healthy, athletic, and the tallest girl in her class, Manuela likes to wear trousers, tumble, and play Indian brave rather than tepee-tied squaw in games with her two brothers. Significantly, she is very close to her mother, who dies when Manuela is eleven years old – a critical age for the preadolescent. At age fourteen Manuela's growing independence and budding sexuality cause her governess such concern that sending her to the seminary, with its iron discipline and spartan pro-

7. Heide Schlüpmann and Karola Gramann, "Momente erotischer Utopie – ästhetisierte Verdrängung: Zu *Mädchen in Uniform* and *Anna und Elisabeth*," *Frauen und Film* 28 (1981): 30 and 40–41.

visions, seems the appropriate response. There Manuela will have little time, opportunity, or energy to indulge herself while up against the grim reality of schoolwork, discipline, hunger, cold, discomfort, and lack of privacy. She will lose her personal identity by donning an ill-fitting uniform, and her hair will be pulled back flat, plaited, and pinned up in a standard style suggesting Prussian discipline.

The second half of the novel – and the starting point of the film – relates Manuela's seminary experience. During the months following her entry as a penniless charity student, the once strong, healthy girl degenerates into a weepy, overwrought, troubled student variously described as nervous, tender, weak, sensitive, pitiable, and unable to handle the rigorous seminary system. Winsloe's novel thus follows the typical pattern for lesbian texts after about 1920, which Lillian Faderman outlines in her book, *Surpassing the Love of Men.*[8] In the end, as Faderman's paradigm foretells, Manuela commits suicide.

Winsloe's novel reflects the influences on literature that Faderman attributes to Freud and the German sexologists who published their studies on sexual inversion around the turn of the century. Manuela's love for her teacher, perfectly acceptable in a nineteenth-century novel, by 1920 had become a medical/psychological problem, and medical terminology entered literature to describe homoeroticism. Lesbianism (in the broad sense of the term, any emotionally supportive same-sex friendship, not necessarily sexual) had come to be viewed as a morbid sickness, or a congenital sexual abnormality, which, if not cured (by marriage) usually ended in isolation or death. The use of such medical terminology is bitterly ironic in the novel's seminary reception scene. The institution's royal patroness, on seeing a pale and unsteady Manuela curtsying before her, nervously asks the headmistress if Manuela is ill, and if she might not be "infectious." The headmistress hurriedly reassures her that Manuela is only temporarily indisposed, but, in fact, believes that Manuela could indeed prove to be the contagious source of a vile epidemic of emotionalism, i.e., lesbianism, and has her quarantined. In the film this particular scene loses the bitter edge since the viewer is not given the psychosocial explanatory reading of the novel. At best, the patroness's innocent question prods the viewer's recollection that Manuela is at that moment

8. Lillian Faderman, *Surpassing the Love of Men: Romantic Friendship and Love Between Women from the Renaissance to the Present* (New York: Morrow, 1981).

hung over from too much spiked punch.

There are several reasons that Manuela is unwelcome in the seminary. She is entering late; she is a charity student and thus a burden on the school's already restricted budget; and her mother is not an alumna of the seminary. Even her name is suspect since she is the first "Manuela" to enter the seminary and mix with the well-worn Prussian likes of Ilse, Helga, and Edelgard. In the crucial opening scene of the film, which takes place in a cold and bare reception room, Manuela and her aunt are subtly snubbed by the headmistress, who does not descend to greet them personally. Instead she sends her obsequious assistant, Fräulein von Kesten, with excuses that she is ill. Later in the morning the headmistress appears at prayers to sermonize and scold the girls for infractions of the rules.

Manuela has no choice at the seminary but to seek her identity and security within the group, and the group's chosen love object is Elisabeth von Bernburg. When Manuela selects the class insignia – with an "E.v.B." inked on the back – left behind by a former student and pins it on her uniform in the prescribed place (over the heart), she inherits, rather than develops, a love for her teacher. When Manuela throws her arms around Bernburg on her first night at the school (in the novel the kiss on the lips occurs several weeks later), she is accepting the group's choice of Bernburg as a love object and signaling her desire to join them in seeking Bernburg's attention.

There is good reason for Manuela to join the others in seeking Bernburg's affection and approval: her identity and security lie within the group. Moreover, liking Bernburg is certainly no chore. In contrast to the dour headmistress, whose reliance on authoritarianism is symbolized by her cane, and the meek aide, Fräulein von Kesten, whose servility is symbolized by her hunchback, Bernburg is attractive, sympathetic, and even motherly.

Bernburg, however, holds the girls in a double bind. Manuela's insistence on becoming a personal favorite collides with Bernburg's attempts to treat the girls equally and economize her own feelings. While Manuela longs for her teacher's presence, she must be satisfied with tokens that manifest her person. Thus the chemise, much like the "E.v.B." heart, becomes important more as a fetish embodying her motherlessness rather than an erotic symbol representing physical intimacy.

Bernburg's position at the seminary is indeed uncertain since her authority as a teacher is insufficient to protect her from the system's demands or the students' maniupulations. Manuela's inability in class to recite properly her memorized lines underscores the shortcomings of Bernburg's teaching philosophy and reminds her of her own alienated position on the faculty. Forced to defend her pedagogical methods in a teachers' staff meeting, Bernburg holds her own in a face-off with the headmistress and the other teachers, but she accepts their judgment that she be vindicated only if her students' performance is superior to that of the other girls.

The production of the school play, which is the high point of Manuela's seminary experience, sets into motion the chain of events that leads to her suicide attempt. In the novel Manuela projects into her role as the knight Nérestan in Voltaire's *Zaïre* her inability to comprehend Bernburg's devotion to the institution and her desire to "rescue" Bernburg from it. Bernburg and the other students marvel at Manuela's superb performance and unequivocably extend to her their full approval and acceptance. Buoyed by her success – and the added effects of the spiked celebratory punch – Manuela speaks out, determining her own fate by disclosing her love for Bernburg and her hatred of the headmistress. The horrified headmistress, suspecting a rebellion, calls Manuela's speech a scandal and declares her sexually abnormal. Manuela is to be punished/cured by isolation. Confused, overwhelmed, asking "What in the world have I done?" Manuela attempts to punish herself by self-destruction.

At the end of the novel Manuela dies alone. Her suicide is a private tragedy, and none of the others who are accused by implication – her irresponsible father, the harsh headmistress, her cowardly classmates, and even the overly cautious Bernburg, who arrives too late with too little – openly admits guilt.[9]

9. Prior to writing the film script, Winsloe had adapted her novel material for a play initially entitled *Ritter Nérestan* (*Sir Nérestan*) but first published under the title *Gestern und Heute* (Vienna, 1930). An English-language version of the play, *Yesterday and Today*, appeared in Great Britain in 1932. The film script was prepared by Winsloe in collaboration with F. D. Andam. The novel did not appear until 1933; the first English translation was published in London in 1934. In the stage version Bernburg is given a supplementary motive for her cautious behavior: she envisions herself one day as headmistress of the seminary. In the end the audience is left with the single hope for a better tomorrow when Bernburg's milder hand will rule over the seminary, and Manuela will not have died in vain. It is interesting to note here that the kiss scene was excluded from the English script of the play. The German script, on the other hand, emphasizes the kiss and Manuela's reaction more than the otherwise more introspective novel. This change makes Manuela appear as a victim of her own emotions in the play.

The film, however, finishes with a stunning reversal of the novel's tragic outcome: the last-minute rescue of the suicidal Manuela by Bernburg and her rebellious classmates, leaving the headmistress in a lonely retreat down the hallway. Critic Rich interprets this rescue as a "coming-out," yet the outcome is more persuasively the result of the adaptation of the narrative text to film. The shift of interest from Manuela to Bernburg discussed above automatically leads to an upgrading of Bernburg's heroic status and a public confrontation. In the film Bernburg attains true heroic stature when she actually resigns her teaching position, declaring that she can no longer tolerate the headmistress's intimidating methods that turn the girls into moral cowards. Her close identification with Manuela's fate, her increased character value, and particularly the emphasis on the clash of values simply demand that she anticipate – and help prevent – her pupil's death.

The more compact film creates a larger role not only for Bernburg but also for one of Manuela's classmates. The three Ilses in the novel are combined in the film into an expanded single role contrasting Manuela's characterization. Ilse von Westhagen is a mischievous little rebel, refreshing and fun. She does not confront the system, however, but tests it surreptitiously, singing her demands under the cover of other voices and whispering her barbs behind the backs of the other girls. Alert to the crossfire between institution, staff, absent parents, and students, Ilse enlists the girls to both worry about and ultimately rescue the frightened and confused Manuela. In the kiss scene, it is Ilse who baits the erotic line by cheekily pursing her lips and tipping her head back when Bernburg comes for the ritual goodnight kiss on the forehead. It is also Ilse who, with a falling firecracker, plumbs the depth of the stairwell down which Manuela will later attempt to hurtle herself. Such pranks, however, bind Ilse to her classmate's fate and ultimately lead to Manuela's rescue.

Another critical change of the novel material reveals the filmmakers' pragmatic reading of pre-Nazi politics in Germany: the substitution of Friedrich Schiller's *Don Carlos* for Voltaire's *Zaïre* as the school play. A play by Schiller would have satisfied the then active clamorings of nationalistic, anti-French groups.[10] Yet

10. Georg Ruppelt, *Schiller im nationalsozialistischen Deutschland: Der Versuch einer Gleichschaltung* (Stuttgart: Metzler, 1979), 9.

there was a risk in allowing the girls to perform Schiller, whose very name invokes images of Storm and Stress (*Sturm und Drang*) emotionalism and devoted friendship, visions of personal and political freedom and attraction to youth, and thoughts of keen social criticism and awareness of political power. That risk is hinted at by one of the straight-laced guests at the performance who remarks to the headmistress that "Schiller also writes quite freely sometimes. . . ."

The filmmakers' choice of the renunciation scene from *Don Carlos* (I, 2) reflects the basic conflict in the film. In this scene, the dutiful young queen (like Bernburg, named Elizabeth) implores her stepson, Don Carlos (played by Manuela), to renounce his love for her and turn his attentions to his princely duties. And this is precisely one way the film was explained to young girls in the 1930s: they should not allow a love for their teacher to distract them from their studies.

Schiller's political overtones are clearly evident at the end of the film when drums and bugles in the distance remind us that the power structure beyond the walls of the school remains intact despite Manuela's averted suicide and the girls' revolt. Although the rebellious students temporarily usurp authority, the headmistress is not defeated but merely beats a momentarily reflective retreat down the hallway. Her power is, in fact, increased by the new clinical interpretation of lesbianism that allows her to label others as sexually abnormal. And while Manuela's attempts to sever Bernburg's strong allegiance to the repressive institution are partially successful, Manuela herself succumbs to the seminary system. Manuela's former submission to Bernburg is now ironically replaced by her new tie to her peer group, which, in turn, is totally repressed by the dominant Prussian patriarchal system beyond the school's walls. The slide into fascism accelerates – and Manuela becomes a "girl in uniform."

This article appeared originally in Neue Germanstik, *Spring 1986.*

6

"Only Man Must Be and Remain a Judge, Soldier and Ruler of State"[1]—Female as Void in Nazi Film

anke gleber

Bruce Murray's essay investigated misogyny in films of the Weimar Republic, postulating – as many critics have done – that it played a significant role among the underlying psychosocial forces that contributed to the victory of National Socialism. Once the Nazis were in power, the official state ideology of their "Third Reich" was clearly misogynistic, and Anke Gleber's essay provides a good deal of evidence about the pervasiveness of misogyny within Nazi cinema. She examines the ideological function of women in three films of the Nazi era – three films that were supposedly "entertainment" films, not official "propaganda" films. She demonstrates that these "entertainment" films use women characters in ways fully in harmony with Nazi pronouncements on the accepted (inferior) role of women in that society.
—The Editors

I. Ideology: On Film and the Female

Striking parallels can be drawn between Rosenberg's motto and vision of an ideal society and the ostensibly apolitical Nazi entertainment film, which projects an image of the female that has thus far received scant notice even from commentators who focus on the critique of ideology.[2] It is precisely the seemingly

1. Alfred Rosenberg, "Der Mythos des 20. Jahrhunderts," quoted in George L. Mosse, *Nazi Culture* (New York: Schocken, 1981), 40.

2. For older, "non-ideological" criticism see especially David Stewart Hull, *Film in the Third Reich* (New York: Simon and Schuster, 1973). As examples of recent critical analyses without explicit emphasis, however, on the female image, see Marc Silberman, "The Ideology of Re-Presenting the Classics: Filming *Der Zerbrochene Krug* in the Third Reich," *German Quarterly* 57 (1984); 590–602, and Karsten Witte, "How Nazi Cinema Mobilizes the Classics: Schweikart's *Das*

harmless nature of these films that allows them to be read as textbook examples of a most appalling manifestation of everyday fascism. Here the myth of male supremacy that underlies both National Socialism and the Prussian tradition is given filmic expression through the inferior role played by the female, whose devaluated position in society is now cast into cinematic terms.

In Nazi cinema male dominance asserts itself through a series of stylized masculine roles. One of the first and most blatant examples of Nazi male aesthetics in film is the Rosenbergian "Ruler of State" featured in Hans Steinhoff's *The Old and the Young King* (*Der alte und der junge König*, 1935). The film celebrates the forced initiation of the future Frederick the Great into the role of a traditional political patriarch, by exorcising his male friend Katte and the influence of his artistically inclined sister. The male as omniscent and incontestable "Judge" dominates the *mise-en-scène* of Gustav Ucicky's *The Broken Jug* (*Der zerbrochene Krug*, 1937). Kleist's drama is stripped of its subtle ambivalence: the unscrupulous Adam is rehabilitated in his official function as a judicial persona, while women are cast exclusively in terms of disturbances – prosecuted plaintiffs and petty petitioners. With the same ironic distortion found in Nazi "adaptations" of the classics, Hans Schweikart recasts Lessing's Tellheim, who refuses "to serve the mighty" (*Minna von Barnhelm* V, 9), into a die-hard "Soldier," who leaves *Das Fräulein von Barnhelm* (1940) to her own ineffectual devices as an extra on the "domestic front," while he rides into yet another battle – a popular hero cheered on by the masses, in time to the music and the aims of contemporary war propaganda.

These films clearly bear out the diminished role of the female, explicitly defined in National Socialism as the absolute "other,"[3] dependent on man and acceptable only in her func-

Fräulein von Barnhelm (1940)," in *German Film and Literature: Adaptations and Transformations*, ed. Eric Rentschler (New York: Methuen, 1986), 103–116. For an attempt at an ideological critique based on the female image see Anke Gleber, "Das Fräulein von Tellheim: Die ideologische Funktion der Frau in der nationalsozialistischen Lessing-Adaption," *German Quarterly* 59 (1986), 547–568.

3. Concerning "domestic isolation," see Renate Wiggerhaus, *Frauen unterm Nationalsozialismus* (Wuppertal: Hammer, 1984), 76. With regard to the "domestic child-bearer," see Ingeborg Weber-Kellermann, *Die deutsche Familie: Versuch einer Sozialgeschichte* (Frankfurt/M.: Hanser, 1984), 73–111. National Socialist "male bonding" is examined in Rita Thalmann, *Frausein im dritten Reich* (Karlsruhe: DOKU, 1979), 76 and 103.

tions subservient to the state as homemaker in "domestic isolation" or in the so-called "cult of the mother," as a "domestic childbearer" of soldiers for the Nazi war. Ideological images of the female such as these found in writings from Rosenberg to Hitler are directly projected onto film, in keeping with its acknowledged function as a "national medium of education," even one of "guidance."[4] The key role played by the female in this ideologization of society through the filmic medium is strikingly illustrated in *Reichsfilmführer* Fritz Hippler's emphasis on this aspect to the point of assigning it normative guiding principles in his "Formative Power of Film":

> It is indisputable that women depicted in film influence the ideal of beauty for the masses. For that reason film casting should be done with the utmost consideration . . . a woman, properly chosen . . . and by continual usage [!] in films, can, by subconscious means, prove invaluable not only in respect to population politics, but also in the sense of qualitative improvement.
>
> The choice, as well as the manner of usage and its direction, should and can . . . promote the wish to have a child.[5]

Rosenberg's cynical exclusion of women from all major functions of society combined with such principles of ideological cinematography leaves little but the domestic role of mother to the women in the Nazi films analyzed.

2. Women Excluded from the Male State

The cinematic space reserved for women in *The Old and the Young King* as a paradigm of Nazi "Fridericus" films (about Frederick the Great of Prussia) is confined to scenes framed and bound by official spectacles of the male realm. Male bonding governs all levels of the film: in the center stands the patriarchal domination exerted by the old "Soldiers' King" over his son Frederick, over "his men" – soldiers – and his royal family, where he plays the role of a petit-bourgeois domestic tyrant. His temporarily lost son seeks refuge from this paternal control in a male friendship with Lieutenant von Katte, a younger version of internalized Prussian *raison d'etat*. Katte's loyalty is founded in a

4. Goebbels' speech, "On the Occasion of the War Session of the Reichfilmkammer" (State Film Organization), quoted in *Der Film im 3. Reich*, ed. Gerd Albrecht (Karlsruhe: DOKU, 1979), 76 and 103.

5. Hippler, "Reflections on Creating Films," in *Der Film im 3. Reich*, ed. Albrecht, 144–48; quote on p. 144.

Prussian sense of duty rather than a personal fancy for Frederick's sister Wilhelmine, an unobtrusive "white woman" (in Klaus Theweleit's terminology),[6] who serves as an alibi of sorts to spare the two male Prussian superegos the acknowledgement and expression of any possible latently homosexual mutual attraction.

The woman is reduced to a pale background, a mere screen onto which this male friendship is projected in dramatic and gory terms. One scene shows Wilhelmine sitting at a piano with her back to the viewer. She is positioned at the apex of a triangle between her brother and his comrade: her diminished stature directs the viewer's gaze onto the full size images of Katte and Frederick, who is standing, his body conspicuously extended by a flute in his hands. As the father enters the room, she hides behind her brother before being dragged away. The confrontation that follows is limited to male participants.

Images signifying male power and sovereignty abound in the film, starting with the opening shot: an imposing tilt up the bell tower of the Prussian garrison church in Potsdam is loaded with allusions to Prussian virtues. Accompanied by the resounding tolling of the bells, every attribute adds up to one image of phallocentric presence – Prussian law and order, drill, discipline, and punctuality coalesce into one unified expression of ultimate state control. In the next shot, the female world is presented as a negative contrast to this male order, where breakfast is announced by a military goose step and drum roll. Female incomprehension of military protocol is suggested to be a failing, a lack, through comic repetition of similar scenes. Startled ladies-in-waiting – consistent with the female cliché of women suffering from headaches – protest that they are not deaf, a reaction shared only by two frightened children.

The female role as an outsider within the Prussian order is shared by the archenemies of the state, the French and the gamblers. Both of these groups are discredited by their "luxurious" lifestyles as unproductive parasites that ruin the state's finances. In his gambling circle, surrounded by agitatedly gesticulating

6. In his examination of proto-fascistic male fantasies, Theweleit distinguishes two distinct types of women, the harmless, unthreatening "white" one, and the intellectually and sexually self-determined "red" woman. See Klaus Theweleit's *Male Fantasies*, vol. 1 (Minneapolis: Univ. of Minnesota Press, 1987), a translation of *Männerphantasien*, vol. 1 (Frankfurt/M.: Roter Stern, 1977), especially chapter 1.

players, Frederick betrays his duty as a future ruler with a round of "effeminate" males. The frills and cuffs of their costumes, their undulating wigs – a Prussian only wears his sober tresses – present a visual link to the women startled from their boudoirs, emerging with rustling crinolines (once again the circular motif) fulfilling a purely ornamental function. The women, like the gamblers, tend to be found only in groups, choreographed in loud, lavish, animated, gossipy, extravagant, cocoa-sipping circles. The *modus vivendi* personified in the frugal and thrifty Prussian statesman is completely alien to them. Even Prussian meals do not take place at a round table, but at a plain, rectangular oak one, presided over by the royal patriarch and domestic tyrant. The old King's group of male "smoking buddies" (the "Tabakskollegium") is also visually bound to a right-angled banquet table. A perfumed newcomer from Bayreuth, attired in the latest fashion with a beauty patch and a curly wig "like a female," has to be initiated into this gathering of "real men" by a few rough pranks which are played on him. "All his little ribbons and bows and pleats," comments the Soldiers' King. "I don't like that at all. Fashion is just for womenfolk."

Against such "buffooneries" stands the tough realm of male ideals. "Dying is often not all too hard," Katte explains to Wilhelmine, who continues clinging to life in a cowardly, opportunistic "female" way, while he "happily" sacrifices himself for the young king. The scene of his execution is governed by the same patterns of ideological geometry. Two grave diggers serve as macabre points of departure for a very slow and solemn tracking shot: the camera ceremoniously draws back in a very straight and Prussian orderly line from Katte's (once again, rectangularly shaped) grave, until a detachment of smartly marching Prussian guards lines the foreground. A low-angle shot gives them a towering appearance and blocks out the horizon in the background, framing the image in military terms, as if legitimizing it through its ordered structure. This military order is confronted with a memento of the trivial female world of circles: a round medallion of Wilhelmine's, which Katte chooses to close forever after a short final gaze. He returns it not to Wilhelmine, but to her male guardian, the brother. Here femininity is reduced to a contained form, a disposable item of decoration dwarfed into nonexistence by the powerful forces shaping the manifest destiny of the male state.

The complete instrumentalization of the female, her utter lack of purpose and meaning, is typified in another short sequence preceding the final apotheosis of Prussianism, in which women appear as scantily clad courtly ballet dancers or pompous ladies-in-waiting, and once again only serve as decorative background for male absolutism. The young king's wife, selected for him by the old king – "At your service, Sir" being the only response of the prospective husband – is presented as a superficial, scheming little "airhead." She enthusiastically applauds Frederick's flute performance, while being publicly decried as "completely amusical."

In the face of all the empty images of femininity offered in this film, the young king has cultivated a socially acceptable gentleman's misogyny to the extent that he "appreciates goddess Venus considerably less" than the male duties of Prussian politics. In the following scene *raison d'etat* celebrates its ultimate triumph: Frederick puts a halt to the frivolous doings on the stage and leaves the theater, physically separating himself from the female courtly circles. Upon his father's death, Frederick's ascent into the realm of male imagery is complete: a long and ceremonious tracking-shot ending in a close-up petrifies him into the well-known emblem that has been made by male historiography and cinematography to signify "Frederick the Great." Against such a statuary presence of the male "ruler of state," no single female image in this film can even attempt to hold its own.

3. Women Deprived of Male Justice

The Broken Jug also opens with a statuary image. A bell tower complete with *Glockenspiel* and mechanically revolving figures presents an image of plentitude and suggests a perfectly functioning social order. The revolving sails of a windmill, however, signal the passing into a more chaotic realm of disturbed order. This chaos takes on concrete form as the viewer is led into Adam's bedroom, which the camera scrutinizes with voyeuristic attention: untidy heaps of clothes, single shoes, household utensils, and trash are strewn across the room. The cause of this alarming disorder seems to be personified in the first human figure entering the scene, opening the door to let in light: a maid stomps across the room in heavy wooden clogs, an ungainly appearance in wide skirts. She yawns loudly, kicks the door shut behind her, carelessly drops firewood, and finally wakes

Judge Adam with a disrespectful slap on his considerable posterior, which protrudes out of the featherbed. No matter how vulgar Adam's behavior becomes later on in the film, it has already been evoked to at least an equal extent by the two maids in this opening scene. These two women, in deviation from Kleist's original, set the negative tone that permeates the rest of the drama.

With their bovine appearance and demeanor, Lise and Grete are destined to play a servant's role: to help dress their master, and to fulfill his most basic everyday needs – "Bring bread, sausage, cheese, but hurry up!" Adam punctuates his commands by slapping the first one, and then "the other one" – his way of addressing them – resoundingly across the face. They start to bawl, their dull faces remaining expressionless. For the rest of the film they tend to act as stationary props, barely human scenery, which can only be set into motion running errands and performing menial tasks by their master's voice. Their stoic and undifferentiated facial expressions seem to express the state of mind of big female domestic animals, a stereotyped figure typical of the discrimination and reduction of women in Nazi film, which renders them as mere "creatures" without individuality or a distinct personality.

The next female couple consists of young Eve, another "white woman," the submissive object of the rustic Ruprecht's matrimonial intentions, and her female counterpart, her mother, Madam Marthe. Once again and characteristically, women tend to appear only in pairs; not one seems to have enough stature to perform on her own. This Madam Marthe is a quarrelsome old woman, a midwife at that, as Adam is eager to add in a conspiratorial whisper. All in all, she is a woman of rather shady knowledge, which gives her a certain measure of self-confidence.[7] It is not surprising, then, that in the course of the film she has to be depreciated and increasingly discredited by her behavior and appearance in unfavorable situations. Marthe is introduced yelling at an intimidated Eve, who is humbly beseeching her irate fiance Ruprecht to forgive her, since she does not dare to unmask the village judge as the true culprit. The noise level is amplified as the two women argue in loud and shrill voices, contradicting each other, Martha even slapping her daughter for a presumed lie. The turmoil surrounding her entrance legit-

7. In a similar way, Auntie Brigitte, the sole witness, is dismissed as a confused, superstitious old woman, who is just seeing things and murmuring "mystical" gibberish.

imizes the chaotic condition of Judge Adam's chambers. The dissension among the female characters seems to call their credibility and thus their claim for justice into question.

The discrediting of the female protest through defamation of the plaintiff reaches its culmination in Madam Marthe's lament for the jug. It is symptomatic that not the grievance itself, but the object of her plaint becomes the focus of attention. The jug steals her show. It is fetishized into a symbolic object of an idealized and ideological *status quo ante* of yesteryear history to be regained. The present status quo, however, is not depicted as a state of injustice against (female) humans (Eve), but as a state of history which has fallen into disorder (the jug). To this end Marthe is made to recite a monotonous catalogue of damaged representations of history on the jug: provinces of the Netherlands, the Emperor Charles V, the Marketplace in Brussels. . . . This litany of historical genre scenes diverts attention from the actual cause of the grievance. Ucicky's orchestration of this scene reduces Madam Marthe's recitative to monotonous background noise: while she is speaking, *both* men – Judge Adam and Judge Walter – drum their fingers on the arm-rests of their chairs, look up to the ceiling in boredom, and impatiently run their hands over their hair. The body language here unites even these two former adversaries of Kleist's text through their complete lack of interest in the female cause. Madam Marthe's monologue remains non-diegetic throughout the scene: her lament is an off-stage sound, subservient to the male images on which the interest of the camera resides.

The solidarity of male justice against its female objects of justice is also borne out in the judges' collaborative intimidation tactics: "A judge is always, you know, a judge," Adam reminds Eve, while his colleague Walter reprimands Marthe, "How dare you, more respect for the judge," although Judge Adam's corrupt practices have not escaped his attention. This old-boy camaraderie finds its ultimate expression in the all-reconciling round of laughter with which Adam is chased through the village pond, while Walter entreats, "Bring him back, I don't want to force him to desert [!]."

Eve, on the other hand, remains dependent on male mercy; Ruprecht generously "forgives" her deeds. She is once again his "good child [!]," instead of the "whore" he called her earlier. Furthermore, Walter promises Eve that he will forestall Adam's extortionist threat to send her Ruprecht to a faraway military outpost. "Besides," he assures Eve, "the recruits being enlisted at the moment are to serve within the country." In 1937, then, this film acts as an "appeasement comedy"; the function of comedy was to be changed by 1940. The intact world of history seems to be flawlessly restored as far as the judges, the men, and the institution of rustic marriage are concerned.

The final sequence, however, glosses over the fact that the female claim, the broken jug, remains without due justice: the camera pans from the carriage, which is departing with Walter (a not too trustworthy trustee – the meaning of the name "Walter" in Kleist's German – of female interests) to the diminishing figure of Madam Marthe, clutching her broken jug, vainly trying to catch up with the judge's vehicle. All she is left with is the image of the departing judge. Court has adjourned, and her justice is postponed once again. In the final round of the *Glockenspiel*, that image of a mechanically guided "eternal order," Madam Marthe keeps circling behind her jug – unchanged and unchangeable from the beginning – while Adam forms the dominating final figure of this ensemble as the unchallengeable and ever-authoritarian judge. The restored order does not require its male "judges" to grant the restoration of female rights.

4. Women Colonized by Male War

In *Das Fräulein von Barnhelm,* Lessing's classic is recast into a "mobilization comedy."[8] The underlying theme of the film is the glorification of the man-at-arms. Images of plenitude featuring Tellheim the "soldier" predominate. Mounted on horseback, his elevated presence heightened by low-angle shots, Tellheim faces the camera – and thereby the spectator – to deliver propaganda slogans such as: "War is tough and we need to persevere," or: "If our adversaries force war upon us, we don't have a choice," and "War is not decided on the battlefield alone." Upon these declarations, there is a cut to the home front, where women are ghettoized in the coffee-klatch atmosphere of auxiliary league circles, making themselves useful by producing bandages for wounded soldiers.

Once again the role of the female in this film is a subordinate one, one which makes the role of the dominant, militaristic male possible in the first place. This is expressed in formal

8. Karsten Witte, "Die Filmkomödie im Dritten Reich," in *Die deutsche Literatur im Dritten Reich,* ed. Horst Denkler and Karl Prümm (Stuttgart: Reclam, 1976), 358.

terms by the polarity between the establishing shots of male plenitude and control, rigidly marching columns of footsoldiers and men on horseback which stretch across the landscape in seemingly endless lines, and the cheery, banal, small world of Minna and her girlfriends in their women's circles. This complementary relationship between the sexes, with its reduction of the female role, also has a functional application. This is illustrated most strikingly in a sequence where Minna's female presence at the piano frames Tellheim's battle scene, thus mellowing its impact and seemingly legitimizing war through her aesthetics. Minna is shown in a medium-long shot, sitting at a piano, which is to say, dwarfed to half of her size. Suddenly, within split seconds, her image and piano sound are dissolved into a fog that aesthetically shrouds the battle scene. Without a trace or consequence her short sequence gives way to a longer sequence of "heroic" deeds: shooting soldiers on "noble" chargers (avoiding images of falling and dying ones, as this could damage the mobilization campaign); death-defying men to whom "the flag . . . means more than death" – *kitsch* and death.[9] At the moment when Tellheim tears the flag out of his dying friend Marloff's hands, the camera returns briefly to Minna, an expression of admiration and intuitive awe of male bravery on her face. Framed by this pathos-laden female image, Tellheim's exploits on the battlefield are accentuated and given closure.

In Schweikart's film, female images have been colonized into decorations of male signification; even clichéd representations of female aesthetics exist only as packaging for male propaganda: "To the degree to which women are made to vanish, men gain in stature. This is the way that the grammar of fascism tends to proceed."[10] This principle sets the tone for the rest of the film: time after time women are relegated to the sidelines. Impassioned grannies await their soldiers at the wayside; blond girls with braids line the streets, cheering on the troops.

This film celebrates female subordination to the "higher order"[11] of men, her colonization through absolute loyalty to

9. See Saul Friedländer, *Reflections of Nazism: An Essay on Kitsch and Death* (New York: Harper and Row, 1985).

10. Theweleit, *Männerphantasien,* 1:54.

11. For the depiction of women in "Prussian films," see Gertrud Koch, "Der höhere Befehl der Frau ist ihr niederer Instinkt. Frauenhaß und Männer-Mythos in Filmen über Preußen," in *Preussen im Film,* ed. Axel Marquardt and Heinz Rathsack (Reinbek: Rowohlt, 1981), pp. 219–33.

the male war(rior). Even Lessing's self-assured heroine has to be subjugated to this propaganda program: Minna is reduced to a silly and superficial extra who uncritically adorns her "soldier" Tellheim, who had already retired from military service in Lessing's version. One particularly defamatory cross-cut associates a coffee-klatch gathering of Minna's girlfriends with a pen of gluttonous pigs. Minna and her formerly bright and irreverent maid Franziska are reduced to giggling accessories, whose images have no stature of their own and can effortlessly be appropriated by the dominating male presence.

The programmatic marginalization of women is realized in a nearly exemplary fashion throughout the film. In the closing frames, Minna is standing behind a balcony railing, waving good bye to her Tellheim. Confined to her supportive role, she is slowly pushed off to the edge of the frame, where the rest of the women stand behind a white picket fence, admiring the troops marching out of town. Here the camera displaces women into the marginal position that they have been alloted in society: in keeping with the precepts of such ideological filmmaking, the camera comes to a rest on the martial image of Tellheim on his horse, an equestrian statue, the pivotal image of the film as well as the active role in society. This heroization of the male "soldier" and his war in fascist propaganda would not be possible without the devaluation of the female and her colonization by framing and camera angles that are masculine and militaristic in both their visual and ideological perspectives.

5. Form and Propaganda

The systematic exclusion of women from active roles in public life coincides with formal characteristics shared by all three Nazi films: a central motif is the association of women with "circles" – Minna and her friends, circles of vain ladies-in-waiting – which mirror their lack of political power:

> The political life of women has been totally extinguished . . . only organizations within the National Socialist women's clubs are permitted, that is, gigantic afternoon tea parties.[12]

This tendency corresponds to the pressing of women into socially and visually marginal positions. They have to clear the

12. Ernst Bloch, "Die Frau im Dritten Reich," in *Vom Hasard zur Katastrophe: Politische Aufsätze 1934–1939* (Frankfurt/M.: Suhrkamp, 1972), 133.

stage for men to play their various political, judiciary, and military roles: Lise and Grete wait mutely in the background, and Minna waves cheerfully at her warrior's side. These scenes illustrate Hess's ideological dictum that bases a woman's right of existence entirely on her function for the man: "a woman . . . standing at her husband's side in his interests, in his struggle for existence, who makes the world more beautiful and richer in content for him."[13]

All that remains for women, then, is a retreat into their familiar circles, into domestic isolation, into a decorative function as a frame for male activity. These functions are exemplified by those images of women at the piano, Wilhelmine as an ornamental accessory for male drama and Minna as the decorative packaging of male war. Goebbels clearly assigns them this position in society: "The mission of women is to be beautiful and to bring children into the world."[14] In films which reduce women to items of decoration, to mere vegetating "creatures" – as milkmaids, as gobbling pigs – Hippler's ideological demand for a decidedly reproduction-oriented depiction of women in film seems to have been answered.

In the final analysis, even the seemingly "harmless" "apolitical" Nazi entertainment film is permeated with National Socialist ideology. It operates by denying female individuality, thus gaining more space in which the aura of the fascist male state can dominate freely. In accordance with this principle, the women in the films analyzed here have been strategically choreographed so that their filmic presence is ultimately done away with altogether: the rapid exit of the bland Wilhelmine; the dismissal of the female plaintiff; the reduction of Minna to a silly "Fräulein," so that – emptied of her original substance – she can be more effectively mobilized for male purposes. Women are denied an identity for reasons of poltical rationale: "There is no place for the political woman in the ideological world of National Socialism. . . . The German resurrection is a male event."[15] Analogous to this conclusion, the dynamics of meaning and image in Nazi cinema is the exclusive domain of male propaganda, a propaganda operating at the expense of the female image, which is defined only in terms of absence and lack.

13. NS-politician ("Reichsminister") Hess, in Mosse, *Nazi Culture,* 42.
14. Goebbels, in Mosse, *Nazi Culture,* 41.
15. Engelbert Huber, "This is National Socialism," in Mosse, *Nazi Culture,* 47.

7

Male Gaze and Female Reaction: Veit Harlan's *Jew Süss* (1940)

régine mihal friedman

Régine Mihal Friedman does a very detailed analysis of one particular "entertainment" film of the Nazi era. It is a film that had obvious propaganda value: Veit Harlan's Jew Süss *(1940). Her discussion, which includes valuable historical information on the production and reception of this film, is primarily a psychoanalytical investigation of the function of the fictional female characters within this anti-Semitic film as well as of the film's positioning of actual female spectators. In her analysis Friedman uses concepts drawn from psychoanalytical film theory (especially from Christian Metz and the feminist critic Laura Mulvey), but she does not by any means efface the politics of this fascist film. Rather she illuminates them in a very sophisticated demonstration of the feminist dictum that the personal – here psychoanalyzed – is inherently political.*

—THE EDITORS

Kristina Söderbaum as Dorothea and Ferdinand Marian as Süss in Veit Harlan's *Jew Süss* (1940). (Photo courtesy of Museum of Modern Art/Film Stills Archive)

Jew Süss: In the Wake of an Infamous Film.

Of all the German film directors who cooperated with the Nazi government Veit Harlan was the only one to stand trial at the end of World War II. He was charged with having provided the

Third Reich with one of its most effective tools for anti-Semitic propaganda.[1] After a series of trial proceedings that made newspaper headlines, future screenings of this mythic film were prohibited by the Allied courts[2] "on the grounds of crimes against humanity."[3]

Thereupon, Harlan initiated a broad campaign to justify himself. During the numerous protests that he made, he had no scruples even about opening a polemic attack against the writer Lion Feuchtwanger. It was Feuchtwanger's bestseller *Jew Süss* (1925)[4] that had triggered a reawakening of interest in this figure, his role and epoch, not only in the area of historical studies but also in literature, theater, and film.[5] When Feuchtwanger, who had emigrated to the United States, learned of Harlan's film, he published an "open letter to 7 Berlin actors." This letter first appeared in the United States in the *Atlantic Monthly* in 1941. It was eventually reprinted in September 1947, in the first issue of the journal *Weltbühne*:

> I read in the *Völkischer Beobachter* that you, my Berlin friends, played the principal roles in a film entitled Jud Süss which received a prize in Venice. This movie shows, so the paper says, the true countenance of Judaism, its sinister methods and its devastating goals. One among many of the ways it demonstrates this is by means of a scene in which the Jew, Süss, makes a young woman do his bidding by torturing her husband. In short, gentlemen, by adding a touch of *Tosca*, you have transformed my novel, Power, into a vile anti-Semitic movie a la Streicher and his *Stürmer*. . . .
>
> All of you know my novel. Five of you, possibly all seven of you, have acted in stage versions of it. In discussing specific points with me you

1. For national-socialist film propaganda cf. the important book by Dorothea Hollstein, *"Jud Süss" und die Deutschen. Antisemitisches Vorurteil im nationalsozialistischen Spielfilm. Materialien* (Frankfurt/M. and Bern: Ullstein, 1983).

2. Herbert Pardo and Siegfried Schiffner, *"Jud Süss": Historisches und juristisches Material zum Fall Veit Harlan* (Hamburg: Auerbach, 1949).

3. Court of the Federal State of Hamburg, *Sentence in the Criminal Case of Film Director Veit Harlan on the Crimes against Humanity*. 29 April 1950, 85 pages.

4. Lion Feuchtwanger, *Jud Süss* (Munich: Drei Masken Verlag, 1925); the novel is based on the play by the same author, *Jud Süss. Schauspiel in drei Akten.* Munich: Georg Müller, 1918.

5. Curt Elwenspoek, *Joseph Süss Oppenheimer, der große Finanzier und galante Abenteurer des 18. Jahrhunderts* (Stuttgart: Süddeutsches Verlagshaus, 1926). Selma Stern, *Jud Süss, ein Beitrag zur deutschen und zur jüdischen Geschichte* (Berlin: Akademie Verlag, 1929). Ashley Dukes, *Jew Süss: a tragic comedy in 5 acts* (London: Martin Secker, 1929). Arthur-Richard Rawlinson, *Scenario and Dialogues of "Jew Süss" from the Novel by L. Feuchtwanger* (London: Methuen, 1935).

proved that you understood the book, and you talked about it in high terms.[6]

Harlan's unscrupulous response mixed very specific justifications of his behavior with incontestable facts. He even went so far as to scold Feuchtwanger for passing judgment without personally having experienced the force of the Nazis:

> I think it superfluous to further describe the variations of coercion and other imaginative means that Goebbels so masterfully commanded when he wanted to execute his will. You yourself ran away from all this.
>
> . . . After nearly all of the first movie actors who had received offers – among them Werner Krauß, Emil Jannings, Willy Forst, Ferdinand Marian, Eugen Klöpfer, Heinrich George, Otto Wernicke and many more – refused with what seemed more or less to be good excuses, Goebbels staffed the film according to his own choice. He excluded the lucky ones and the others received "official orders" – which, according to my knowledge, happened for the first time in the NS film era, probably because of the significance that this decision had for Goebbels.[7]

In the end, it was Harlan's insistence that he had been "forced" to act in this way that allowed him to go free in his third trial in 1950; the film alone was banished to the iron vaults of the film archives. Although such testimony of a collaborator is of course dubious, this film can still be considered as a work commissioned by the Nazis who strictly controlled all its production stages, from painstaking examination of the screenplay and dialogues,[8] the selection and "psychological" preparation of the actors and the film director,[9] to a no less painstaking inspec-

6. "To My Friends the Actors," in *Atlantic Monthly*, Vol. 167, No. 4 (April 1941), 500–501. Subsequently in German in "Offener Brief an sieben Berliner Schauspieler," *Weltbühne* 1 (September 1947), 735–39.

7. Cited from Pardo, 63–66.

8. Veit Harlan, *Im Schatten meiner Filme. Autobiographie* (Gütersloh, 1966). The Reichs-superintendent of film at that time, Fritz Hippler, confirms the facts referred to by Veit Harlan in his book *Die Verstrickung* (Düsseldorf: Verlag Mehrwissen, 1982). Every historian of Nazi film stresses Goebbel's interventions in the screenplay, on the basis of which *Jew Süss* was reworked several times.

9. For Veit Harlan's and the actors' "research trips" to the the newly established Polish "ghettos" see Hollstein, 96, and Gerald Reitlinger, *The Final Solution* (London, 1971). As for the viewing of Yiddish film on Goebbels's command, cf. Veit Harlan and Werner Krauß, *Das Schauspiel meines Lebens, einem Freund erzählt*, ed. Hans Weigel (Stuttgart, 1958). Also in *Der Film* 41 (30 Nov. 1940).

tion of the dailies during the shooting.[10] In addition to this control, Goebbels had offered unlimited financial backing to secure the film's success, including propaganda campaigns after its completion.[11] We know the consequences of such effort: *Jew Süss* was the box office hit of Nazi cinema. From 1940 till 1944, nineteen million viewers in occupied Europe submitted, readily, to its influence. Piles of testimony attest to the film's quite direct effect: assaults on Jews immediately after the showings. Less directly, the film helped to set the mood for the extermination of the Jews.[12] The relationship between the production of the most important anti-Semitic films and the "final solution" has been underscored by Joseph Wulf, one of the main scholars who has documented Nazi culture:

> After all, it is no coincidence that all three anti-Semitic films *The Rothschildes, Jew Süss*, and *The Eternal Jew*, premiered in 1940. Obviously, Goebbels commanded that the three films be made and shown because of the planned (and later implemented) "final solution of the Jewish question" that was later also executed, even though the actual date as to when this "final solution" was decided by the officials of the Third Reich is not completely certain. . . .
>
> What is certain is the fact that the movie *Jew Süss* was shown to the "Aryan" population – especially in the east – whenever "deportations" to the extermination camps were imminent. Many witnesses – and as for Poland, the writer of these lines as well – can testify to this from their own experience. Surely this was done to instill hatred against the Jews in the "Aryan" population of the respective countries, as well as to nip in the bud any thought of assistance to the Jews.[13]

The above-mentioned letter by Harlan actually provokes – though unintentionally – yet another question that has thus far been neglected: the question of the female audience's reaction to *Jew Süss*. This is especially noteworthy, as Harlan ends his pleading on his own behalf with the remark, "Finally, let me

10. Veit Harlan particularly stresses that the scene of Süss's execution, in which he originally curses his hangmen, was changed by Goebbels's orders. Cf. *Film-Press* 27 (22 July 1950), 7.

11. Gerd Albrecht, *Nationalsozialistische Filmpolitik* (Stuttgart: Ferdinand Enke Verlag, 1969), 106 ff.; Willi A. Boelcke, *Kriegspropaganda 1939–1941* (Stuttgart: DVA, 1966).

12. For an evaluation of the varied evidence cf. my book: Régine Mihal Friedman, *L'image et son juif* (Paris: Payot, 1983), 13.

13. Joseph Wulf, *Theater und Film im Dritten Reich* (Gütersloh, 1964), 6–10.

mention that the 'hated Jew' Marian received baskets full of love letters from every city in Germany."

Jew Süss: Development and Status of the Character

As insidious as the preceding argument from Harlan's pen may be, it reveals something about the female unconscious in Germany at that time. When playing the demonic Jew, the actor Ferdinand Marian does not deny his own erotic attractiveness because his is Süss's Aryan stand-in. However, to understand this kind of attraction, let us attempt a reading of *Jew Süss* from the viewpoint of visual pleasure – a pleasure which the film does provide – seen in its contradictory and complementary aspects as elaborated by Christian Metz[14] and Laura Mulvey.[15]

On the one hand, the movie appeals to the visual desire of the male viewer, stimulating his voyeurism by giving him access to a scene whose narrative autonomy nevertheless projects a world of its own. On the other hand, such films also play with the other side of scopophilia: the identification with the protagonist that gives the viewer the experience of temporarily losing himself in order to enjoy a more satisfying, if fleeting, identity. This identity is usually constituted via a male character for whom the female "icon," adhering to the two-dimensional realm, is exhibiting herself and thereby realizing what Mulvey has called "her looked-at-ness." Hence, she satisfies both her male partner and the viewer who is identifying with him.[16] The Nazis' decision to make a movie of *Jew Süss* entailed, of course, an inevitable problem at the level of the fictional agent. Obviously, the Jew was to be the enactor of the diegesis, the semiotic tool,[17] who, by displacements and shifts of location, creates the illusion of three-dimensional space, thus permitting the play of identification. Furthermore, the experience of the movie *The Rothschildes* (July 1940) had to be kept in mind in order to avoid a similar failure. This film, as well, was based on the attempt to concentrate anti-Semitic hatred on one Jewish figure, but it

14. Christian Metz, *Le signifiant imaginaire* (Paris: 10/18 UGE, 1977) [Engl.: *Psychoanalysis and the Cinema: The Imaginary Signifier* (Bloomington: Indiana Univ. Press, 1982)].

15. Laura Mulvey, "Visual Pleasure and Narrative Cinema," *Screen* 16, no. 3 (Autumn 1975): 6–18.

16. Mulvey, "Visual Pleasure."

17. Cf. Philippe Hamon, "Pour un statut sémiotique du personnage," in *Poétique du récit* (Paris: Seuil, 1977), 115–80.

failed precisely because it systematically avoided implementing the process of visual pleasure and identification.[18]

After all, the topic of *Jew Süss* could hide under the cover of history, especially since the genre of historical film served specific ideological functions in the Third Reich.[19] And the straightforward plot – the meteor-like climb of a "court Jew," who, less than three years after he had appeared on the scene, met a brutal end through an ignominious execution in the marketplace – lent itself to any kind of interpretation and deceptive ornamentation, whereas more specific historic references would have made the representation of this figure more difficult. According to the historical documents, Joseph Süss Oppenheimer had the dubious reputation of being a heartbreaker and favorite with women. Hence, on screen he could hardly be represented as the Jewish monster prescribed for the depiction of Jews in anti-Semitic German and Nazi caricatures.

As a matter of fact, during the two centuries that lay between the execution and its filmic resurrection, a tradition of writing emerged, often para-historical and para-literary in nature, in which Süss was always portrayed as physically attractive, even when he was judged negatively in a moral sense. One of these portrayals was presented by Wilhelm Hauff, who, according to Harlan, inspired the movie. He turned Süss, in 1827, into a kind of romantic and exotic Lovelace:

> Gustav had never observed this overpowering figure so closely as now, when he became an involuntary observer held in place by the crowd who walled him in. He admitted to himself that the face of this man was naturally beautiful and of a noble shape, that even his forehead, his eyes, imperious by habit, had acquired something that commanded respect; but hostile, aversive furrows lay between the eyebrows where a free forehead should have met with the well-formed nose, the little mustache could not hide the sneer about his mouth, but the hoarse and forced laughter with which the Jewish deputy noted either gain or loss seemed truly gruesome to the young man.[20]

18. "More than in the theater the spectator in the cinema has to know whom to love and whom to hate. If, for instance, I make an anti-Semitic film I obviously cannot portray the Jews as likeable. If I portray them as unlikeable, then their opponents have to be likeable." Fritz Hippler, *Betrachtungen zum Filmschaffen* (Berlin: Max Hesse Verlag, 1942), 92.

19. Helmut Regel, "Historische Stoffe als Propagandaträger," in *Der Spielfilm im III. Reich* (Oberhausen, 1966), 117–33.

20. Wilhelm Hauff, "Jew Süss," in *Gesammelte Werke* (Leipzig: Bong Verlag, 1907), vol. 4–6: 160.

It was the Protestant theologian Zimmermann whose dissertation on Süss eventually inspired Feuchtwanger to treat the theme in depth. Zimmermann wrote in 1874:

> This is certain: on the outside, in his physique and behavior, the later Süss showed not only oriental [i.e., Middle-Eastern] features but also much of a Christian heritage, particularly of the type known as the "cavalier." The high state of mind that his vanity had cherished since childhood, and the nobility of his personality that he tried to play out in public, his courtesy, his quickness, his love of grandeur, his generosity with invitations and gifts, his disposition to extreme squandering, which never calculated and never cared about the amount of his expenditures, are not the only indications; but the deep shadows of his many-sided guilt debts are illuminated by flashes of a certain gallantry, and, though bound with chains, imprisoned, harrassed by questions, and mistreated by words and deeds, he was, in one aspect, at least, undeniably more a cavalier than all his aristocratic judges.[21]

Having to equip a Jew with an attractive exterior was a tricky matter, but the Nazi Film compensated for it by designing all the other dramatic figures according to the criteria of Nazi typology. In contrast to Süss, the assimilated and Europeanized Jew, the role of the secretary, Loew, represented the non-assimilated counterpart in his natural state. As such the pair, "caftan Jew/camouflaged Jew," visually signalling the two stages of social integration, could be recreated. Veit Harlan knew how to give this stereotypical pair, present in all anti-Semitic films, emblematic value:

> All other Jewish roles in the film are, however, played by one German character actor: Werner Krauß.
>
> Krauß will act the part of the miracle-working rabbi Loew, he will play the fraudulent little secretary Levi, and he will briefly appear as yet another figure. But it is not at all my intention to demonstrate here the brilliant accomplishment of a great actor; actually, this casting (which by the way was suggested by Krauß himself) has a deeper purpose. The intention is to show how all these various personalities and characters, the religious patriarch, the sly crook, the haggling merchant, etc., stem from the same root.
>
> In the center of the film will be a scene of the Purim celebration, a celebration of victory interpreted by the Jews as the festival of revenge on the goyim, the Christians.

21. Manfred Zimmermann, *Joseph Süss Oppenheimer: ein Finanzmann des 18. Jahrhunderts* (Stuttgart: Riegersche Verlagsbuchhandlung, 1874).

> Here I show the original Jewry as it used to be and as it is still preserved today, in its pure form, in what was Poland. [Harlan had just returned from a trip through Poland, where he examined the Jews in the ghettos of several cities.] In contrast to this primeval Jewry stands Jew Süss, the elegant finance minister of the court, the clever politician, in short: the camouflaged Jew.[22]

Jew Süss: The Corrupter

More than in any other anti-Semitic work, Süss embodies here the supposed destructive power "inherent" in the Jewish character. The anti-Semitic film *The Eternal Jew*[23] cites Richard Wagner, who asserts: "The role of the Jew in plot development is the demon incarnate of humanity's ruin." The plot in *Jew Süss* illustrates the Jew as snake and vampire who at the same time causes the moral dissolution and physical decay of those who come near him.

What is significant here is that the victims singled out by Süss, i.e., the ones whom he tempts, corrupts, or both, are predominantly women. Through the women Süss succeeds in gaining access to a city hitherto closed to Jews. Through women he will eventually make his rapid ascent at the court of Karl Alexander. In fact, this ascent is initiated by the jewelry promised by the duke to his wife, which can only be obtained on credit from the usurer of the Frankfurt ghetto. The latter makes the loan contingent on a passport to Stuttgart, a city which had been prohibited to Jews. Süss's entrance into the city is made all the easier when he unexpectedly meets Dorothea Sturm, the daughter of the city councilor.[She gives Süss a ride into the city after his carriage breaks down. – Ed.]

Subsequently, Süss advances his career by generously financing what the provincial representatives deny the duke: a body guard, an opera, and a ballet troupe meant to satisfy the sensuous appetites of the duke. However, the professional cooperation of the ballerinas is soon replaced by the libertine's conquest of Württemberg's less accessible – but for this reason all the more desirable – wives and daughters. In the end, these repeated transgressions, aimed solely at the female body, provoke a male revolt. At the court ball, protected by his mask, Faber [Dorothea's fiancé and later husband] gives vent to his

22. Wulf, 398; the interview appeared in *Der Film* of 20 Jan. 1940.
23. Fritz Hippler, *Der ewige Jude*, November 1940.

feelings: "He is gambling with Württemberg! The Jew is gambling with your daughters, and the duke is keeping the bank."[24] And in a special council session the councillors work up a rage: "They invade our country like an epidemic of locusts. . . . The Jew has his hand on the money, on the salt, on the beer, on the wine, and even on the grain. . . . And on our wives and daughters." Röder, too, delegated by the council of the estates to take their complaint to the duke, advises: "If the Jew wants to pursue his swinish nature with our wives and daughters, it is up to you to, my lord, to put an end to it."

The riot breaks out when Dorothea commits suicide by jumping into the river to drown her shame after Süss has raped her. During the filming, Veit, in an interview, made the following concluding statement:

> In the judgement against Jew Süss, the film follows historical record exactly. This sentence, it is known, had its problems, as Süss Oppenheimer was himself a lawyer, and he had arranged all his dealings leading to the financial ruin of the people so skillfully that, at first, he could not even be legally incriminated. At last he was sentenced on the basis of an ancient law that says: "When a Jew becomes involved with a Christian woman, he is guilty unto death." This illuminates an interesting parallel to the Nürnberg laws. In fact, Süss was sentenced to death over 200 years ago because of a racial crime.[25]

Jew Süss does not, however, limit itself to illustrating Hitler's ideology of the mandatory sexual segregation of the races. The film is not just an instructive example that uses the past to derive insights for the present and protective measures for the future.[26] It is also not merely that the film stages the respective passages from *Mein Kampf* about the influence of the court Jews on German aristocrats,[27] or that it projects its image of lusting young Jews who go after the Aryan virgin in order to rape and deprecate her.[28] Beyond the central power struggle in the film, which is depicted as being between two "races," what is also striking is the shockingly anti-female denunciation that this film

24. All citations are taken from the "transcript of the film *Jew Süss*" which appeared in Dorothea Hollstein's book, 270–314.

25. The remaining text of the interview on 20 Jan. 1940 was kindly passed on to me by Dorothea Hollstein.

26. Friedman, chapter 5: "De l'histoire au mythes."

27. Adolf Hitler, *Mein Kampf* (München: Zentralverlag der NSDAP, 1927), pp. 340f.

28. Hitler, *Mein Kampf*, 357.

makes. The repudiation of women, in the long run, proves to be no less than that of the Jew.

Expressing this double rejection and this double powerlessness, the following lines by Horkheimer and Adorno have become famous:

> The signs of powerlessness, sudden uncoordinated movements, animal fear, confusion, awaken the thirst for blood. The justification of hatred for women that represents her as intellectually and physically inferior, and bearing the brand of domination on her forehead, is equally that of hatred for Jews. Women and Jews can be seen not to have ruled for thousands of years.[29]

Examining the nucleus of Freud's theory of the death drive, Erich Fromm has also differentiated more carefully between the drive aimed at dominating and controlling an object and the drive that focuses on the destruction of that object.[30]

The Anti-Female Discourse: The Corruptible

From the start the film frames the extreme unreliability of woman, her corruptibility and desire for money, in several striking shots. When Süss empties his wallet onto the duke's table, offering him what the council dignitaries refused him, the gold coins are transformed via superimposition into whirling ballerinas. This impressive dissolve clearly demonstrates Süss's future intention to finance the whims of the despot. At the same time, this scene underlines the exchangeability of women and money. That woman can be bought for a trinket has of course been a motif used exhaustively in German cinema from Murnau to Dupont and Käutner.[31]

If, on the one hand, the court is a place of decadence – "This is a pigsty, not a court," the enraged Faber, screams out – in their own homes the local dignitaries, on the other hand, see traditional values subjugated to the power of the authorities and fading away. Contaminating corruption lurks everywhere. Thus,

29. Max Horkheimer and Theodor W. Adorno, "Excursus II: Juliette or Enlightenment and Morality," in *Dialectic of Enlightenment* [1944], trans. John Cumming (New York: Continuum, 1987), 112.

30. Erich Fromm, *The Anatomy of Human Destructiveness* (New York: Holt, 1973); cf. Appendix, "Freud's Theory of Aggressiveness and Destructiveness," pp. 439–78.

31. In *Faust* (1925) Mephisto puts a necklace in Gretchen's drawer. In *Varieté* Bertha-Marie is conquered with a bracelet; also keep in mind the role the pearls play in *Romanze in Moll* (1943).

the rather young daughters of Fiebelkorn, another member of the council, hasten to respond to an invitation to the court ball despite their father's admonishment: "By the duke? – Invited by the Jew! The Jew is organizing a meat market once again, this time in the castle, and our daughters are good enough to furnish the wares."

Aside from their lacking any conscience, the girls prove unable – if not unwilling – to resist the duke's talents for seduction and humiliation, when Süss abandons them to his pleasure.

As for Dorothea, she is condemned from the beginning because her heart triumphs over her "instinct," the character trait typically preferred by the Nazis.[32] At the start of the rape scene she is shown in tears, trembling and imploring Süss to free her father and her husband, who have both been imprisoned by him. The reverse shot frames Süss at a lavishly set breakfast table, while a huge, unmade bed decorated with the star of David stretches out behind him. When he then stands, tears up her letter of petition, and locks the door behind her, while telling her that the traitors shall be executed, she has finally fallen into the trap. Now at last Süss can reap the benefit of his previously arranged scenario. The circumstances of the rape are all the more ingenious as they force Dorothea "voluntarily" to submit to his power, since she entered the lion's den on her own.

Hence, *Jew Süss* shows the insidious consequences of actions that women are capable of when they are left to their own devices. Even prior to the tragedy she had expressed her astonishment at the rising cost of groceries, which elicited a reproach from her fiancé: "And whom can we thank for that? You brought him to Stuttgart!"

Numerous brief remarks and commands underscore the theme of female culpability. Leading male characters use these remarks in order to reduce each of "their" women to the level of an immature and reproached child: "Shut up," Fiebelkorn says to his daughter; and the duke tells his wife who is worried about his health: "Go away, this isn't women's business." Süss can even be more gruff: "Pull yourself together, stupid cow," he orders his blond lover, Luciana. On the occasion of a public execution of an insolvent debtor whom Süss had sentenced, it is first Luciana who is inundated with offensive remarks ("Jewish

32. "Instinct" in National Socialism serves as a positive counter-concept to "destructive, levelling intellect." Cf. Cornelia Berning, *Vokabular des Nationalsozialismus* (Berlin: Walter de Gruyter, 1964), 106.

whore!") before they are directed at Süss. Since women are irresponsible, the men have to decide for them. When Süss invites Dorothea to the court ball, Faber intervenes: "She will not go," and at the ball Sturm commands: "My child will go home."

It is probably no coincidence that in the representation of the denigrated woman, the authoritarian discourse impinges on the erotic discourse, even though the plot furnishes grounds for ascribing the entire disgrace to Jewish perversity. In tears the female character surrenders to her complete dissolution: loosened hair, clothes in disarray, half-naked, trembling breasts. Other female figures appear who are also carelessly dressed, but they stem from a world that, from the viewpoint of a virtuous Württemberg household, bears the mark of corruption, either the court or the ghetto. At one point there is a shot of a young Jewish woman in the ghetto leaning out of the window. Her old-fashioned slip exposes her breasts far less than the low décolletés of Dorothea. Yet her demeanor, her tempting pose, her dishevelled hair, the lips half-open sucking on an undefinable object, as well as the presence of the snickering old man beside her all suggest an atmosphere of unleashed promiscuity. When the duchess approaches her royal husband in order to support Süss in his schemes, she wears a loose robe and her long, black hair is freed from the constraining, powdered wig. This image implies what is in fact confirmed: a meaningful look from Süss, a sweet, conspiratorial smile from the duchess. After she has left the scene, the duke tells Süss to his face:

> *Duke*: You have even lied your way into the duchess's heart. Only the heart? *Süss*: I don't understand – *Duke* (screams): I am asking whether it was only the heart? *Süss*: How do you mean that, your highness? *Duke* (with contempt): Ah, I mean that nothing is holy to you, not even the wife of your duke, Jew. Only your own interests, your profit.

This remarkable dialogue demonstrates once more Süss's secretive and malicious art of seduction. However, beyond the evidence of Jewish treason, this interrogation demonstrates and condemns female unreliability.

Spurned by the Male Gaze

Regardless of their "innocence" on the level of the diegesis, the most important female characters are, one after the other, judged and attacked. Only the scene of the degradation changes. What is constant is the male gaze, the look of authority, which affirms the worthlessness of the women in the film and reduces them to objects. This gaze, this power, is already established during the first few minutes of the film when the president of the council reads aloud the constitution, and the council swears allegiance to it. During almost the entire film Süss is the bearer of this gaze until it is transferred to Sturm in the epilogue. It is Sturm who announces the death sentence and the edict for the expulsion of the Jews from Württemberg.

The superior position of the figure endowed with power is expressed on screen in the vertical dimension, in the commanding gaze of the privileged protagonist/viewer who occupies the highest position and thus directs his gaze downward. During the procession after the coronation ceremony, the duke notices a young woman from his carriage. Her enthusiasm so carries her away that she breaks through the security barricade. The guards violently push her back, tearing her corset and in the process exposing her breasts, a scene which provides the duke considerable merriment. In a later sequence the duke, standing on a balcony of the palace and flanked by Süss, inspects the dancers, a monocle in his eye. Later, from the same standpoint and encouraged by Süss, he ogles the roundelay of the young girls at the ball. This scene clearly portrays Süss as mediator and pimp:

> Would your highness like to observe the arrangement? In the back the old ladies, in front the appetizing youth, and on the other side your highness's bodyguards. . . . I thought, for a change, I would replace the boring thistles at the court with spring flowers from the field for your highness alone. . . .

The girl's confusion over the importunities of the duke only hastens the victory of the Jew, the damned soul:

> But Minchen, why so timid, so ashamed, when all the others are envious? Won't you show the duke your pretty little legs? (Süss signals to a coquettish female standing nearby and she hurries to lift up Minchen's skirt. The humiliated young girl breaks out in tears.)

This scenario, arranged for the protagonist's benefit, also provides the [male] spectator with his own viewing angle. From this point of view, the spectator not only satisfies his own visual pleasure, he confirms that his is the point of view of the authority figure through his mirror function as subject.[33] The dual aspect of cinematographic discourse allows the spectator to develop the unavoidable sadistic dimension – according to Metz there is no other[34] – while at the same time allowing him to deny this dimension by attributing it to Jewish vileness.

The same duality also lies behind the shot of Minchen as the young, intimidated victim who nonetheless surrenders. Between two close-ups of her face that betray her excessive embarassment a slow vertical, downward pan of the camera reveals decidedly shapely legs that show no modest signs of resistance or shame – an apparent concession to the pleasure of the spectator's gaze. The gazes from inside and outside the visual plane converge on the perfect curve of the legs extended in the stereotyped pose of a fashion magazine. The scopophilic drive is joined by another partial drive which comes from the auditory realm, the drive to "make oneself heard."[35] In the decisive rape scene there are various visual and acoustic levels that are under the control of the all-powerful gaze. Süss finally succeeds in breaking Dorothea's will by forcing her to listen to the screams of her tortured fiancé. At a pre-arranged signal (a scarf either hung up or removed from the window by Süss) heart-rending screams fill the room; and since the body is involved, the screams can even be felt from the off-screen space. In addition the spectator is rewarded with an additional feeling, since he can see what Dorothea only hears: the long shot of the tortured and screaming Faber.[36]

The Sadistic Discourse

In the preceding discussion I have established the close connection between the anti-Semitic and anti-female discourses along the lines of the (now classic) Freudian-Lacanian model as it has been appropriated for cinema by Metz and Mulvey. Therein we find an astonishingly great correspondence between the analysis of filmic texts and the constructions of a theory that "shows

33. Louis Althusser, "Idéologie et appareils idéologiques d'état," *La Pense* 151 (June 1970): 3–36.

34. Metz, *Le signifiant imaginaire*, 85.

35. Jacques Lacan, *Le séminaire*, Livre 11, "Les quatre concepts fondamentals de la psychoanalyse," (Paris: Seuil, 1973), 178.

36. This scene is taken from V. Sardou's *Tosca* from 1887, which was put to music by G. Puccini in 1900.

how the patriarchal unconscious has structured the form of film."[37]

Jew Süss brings out the close connection between voyeurism and sadism, in that the inquisitive male gaze sets up a pleasurable spectator position, and also in that the film makes a crucial distinction along the lines of the polarity of sexes, in which woman is associated with a "lack." Mulvey interprets this "lack" as fear of castration that the male unconscious wishes to escape and hence either worships woman as a protective fetish against castration or subjects her to a ceaseless investigation in order to reveal her secret. The film uses an alternative:

> Pleasure lies in ascertaining guilt (immediately associated with castration), asserting control, and subjecting the guilty person through punishment or forgiveness.[38]

This hypothesis of the sadistic dimension of film can be juxtaposed to the "suggestions" of Gilles Deleuze in his "Portrayal of Sacher-Masoch."[39] Deleuze compiled an "index of symptoms and non-referential signs"[40] to distinguish between two perversions that are nonetheless pathologically related to one another. His emphasis rests on the "institutional sense" of sadism because, in contrast to the masochistic "contract," sadism (as an "institution") expresses (and confers) a long-lasting, involuntary, and inaccessible status, like that which constitutes power and domination.[41]

In *Jew Süss* the plot actually unfolds between two legal pronouncements, which are mandatory, prescriptive, and impersonal in character. In the first one the duke swears, in front of the representatives, to uphold the constitution; the film ends with the second pronouncement after the legal transgressor has been removed and authority has been returned to the venerable, patriarchal dignitaries. Deleuze remarks elsewhere that "paternal and patriarchal themes are dominant in sadism. . . . In every respect sadism represents an active denial of the mother and elevation of the father . . . the father stands above the law."[42]

I have shown elsewhere that the hitherto unexplained

37. Mulvey, "Visual Pleasure," 6.
38. Ibid., 14.
39. Gilles Deleuze, *Présentation de Sacher-Masoch; le froid et le cruel* (Paris: UGE 10/18, 1976).
40. Ibid., 14.
41. Ibid., 77–78.
42. Ibid., 58.

absence of the mother in the center of the nuclear family recurs in a whole series of anti-Semitic films.[43] Thus in Sturm's household, the haven of family virtues, only Dorothea stands for bourgeois *Gemütlichkeit.* By comparison, Sturm embodies not only the institution but he also becomes, in the name of the patriarchal and puritanical law aimed at sexual repression, the castrating father. Even though he orders Dorothea and Faber to get married in a hurry in order to deter Süss's advances, the young couple, despite the father's absence, seems incapable of consummating their marriage. In the scene where Faber remains on the threshold of Dorothea's room, the dialogue affirms the overarching, repressive law of the father:

> Dorothea is standing in her room changing the sheets on her bed. Faber is too timid to enter the room and remains at the door. Dorothea : Why don't you come in? Are you afraid? – Tonight you will sleep in my bed and I will sleep downstairs in the living room. Faber: But Dorle, you don't even know whether your father would allow that!

At the end of his enlightening discussion, Deleuze even pushes a bit further:

> The sadist's superego is so strong that he has become identified with it; he is his own superego and can only find an ego in the external world. What normally confers a moral character on the superego is the internal and complementary ego upon which it exerts its severity, and equally the maternal element which fosters the close interaction between the ego and superego. But when the superego runs wild, expelling the ego along with the mother-image, then its fundamental immorality exhibits itself as sadism. The ultimate victims of the sadist are the mother and the ego. *His ego exists only in the external world*: this is the fundamental significance of sadistic apathy. *The sadist has no other ego than that of his victims.*[44]

In light of this, the love letters addressed to a corrupt Jew, but a Jew portrayed by an Aryan actor, can be read as an instance of rebellion against the denial and sacrifice of the female self demanded by the regime. In a system that excludes "the motherly component in constituting morality" and instead celebrates woman exclusively in her biological role of reproduction, in a system that restored the old values and at the same time invited

43. Friedman, *L'image,* 245.
44. Gilles Deleuze, *Sacher-Masoch. An Interpretation,* trans. Jean McNeil (London: Faber and Faber, 1971), 107.

young women for eugenic reasons to submit to the advances of those SS men who were considered especially pure in race, in the same system in which in the end the presence of women was not only required at home but also on the assembly lines,[45] this double bind provokes the two meanings of an ambivalent response.

During this period, female desires attached themselves precisely to fantasies of legendary debauchery and unruly sexuality, resisting, even if timidly, the Nuremberg laws invoked by Harlan. What the Jew embodied in the film and what the German women at the time saw in him was exactly the regime's denial and neutralization of the body's sexuality. Herbert Marcuse described how in a repressive society increased erotic needs and satisfactions come to be considered as perversions:

> Against a society which employs sexuality as means for a useful end, the perversions uphold sexuality as an end in itself; they thus place themselves outside the dominion of the performance principle and challenge its very foundation. . . . In a world of alienation, the liberation of Eros would necessarily operate as a destructive, fatal force – as the total negation of the principle which governs the repressive reality.[46]

It is nonetheless clear that this timid, convoluted reaction of the German women, muffled as it were in cotton, could not in any way represent even the slightest hint of an alibi for a subsequent generation of women – a generation whose films denounce their mothers and ruthlessly condemn the irresponsibility of this silent majority.

Translated from German by Angelika Rauch. This article is a translation of the German version appearing in Frauen und Film *41, (December 1986): 50–64.*

45. Renate Bridenthal, Atina Grossmann and Marion Kaplan, eds., *When Biology Became Destiny: Women in Weimar and Nazi Germany* (New York: Monthly Review, 1984), 237–69.

46. Herbert Marcuse, *Eros and Civilization* (New York: Vintage, 1962), 46 and 86.

8

Die Sünderin or Who Killed the German Male: Early Postwar Cinema and the Betrayal of Fatherland

heide fehrenbach

Heide Fehrenbach contextualizes both the film The Sinful Woman (Die Sünderin) *and the controversy it aroused in West Germany during 1951 by providing a persuasive overview of that era's film politics – and its gender politics. Under U.S. influence the new West German state (formed in 1949) allowed the film industry to censor itself; state censorship was forbidden by the West German Constitution (Grundgesetz). Willi Forst's film, as Fehrenbach's analysis of the text itself demonstrates, shared the dominant conservative ideology about gender: above all, that it was necessary to reinstitute the traditional rules that had been destabilized during the war and the immediate postwar chaos. Nonetheless the film caused a furor merely by depicting prostitution and weakened male authority, even though it "resolved" these problems in its closure. The film's "scandalous" depiction of gender roles was used by the Churches to mobilize mass public protests, enabling them to attain such influence that thereafter they were able to exert considerable authority over the film industry – and West German society in general.*
—The Editors

The big world rests upon the small world!
The big world cannot survive if the small world is not secure![1]

In January, 1951, director Willi Forst's film *The Sinful Woman (Die Sünderin)*, the story of a women's resort to prostitution,

1. From Adolf Hitler's speech to the National Socialist Women's Organization at the Nuremberg Party Rally, 8 September 1934, quoted in Tim Mason, "Women in Germany, 1925–1940: Family, Welfare and Work. Part II," in *History Workshop* 2 (1976), 24.

redemption through love, and eventual suicide, premiered at the Turmpalast in Frankfurt. Within days of its release, Pastor Werner Hess, the Protestant film commissioner, lambasted it for "call[ing] into question the last vital forces of morality during a time of distress for our Volk,"[2] and the Protestant and Catholic churches set in motion a series of public demonstrations against the film's exhibition. Clergy initiated protests in Koblenz and Bielefeld, as well as Düsseldorf and Regensburg, where street scuffles broke out and stink bombs were thrown into theaters. Screenings were interrupted by teargas in Frankfurt and Mannheim and by the release of white mice in Duisburg. Priests led schoolboys in street marches in Lüneberg, Munich, Regensburg, Ulm, and elsewhere. In Erlangen, confessional students disseminated leaflets demanding local censorship and condemning the film's "glorification of the new heathendom," while in Cologne the Archbishop issued a pastoral statement, calling on all Christians to boycott the film. By spring, the film was banned in dozens of small- and medium-sized towns across West Germany.[3]

What was it about *The Sinful Woman* that stirred such immediate and passionate response by German churchmen? The dramatic nature of the language employed against the film suggests that these clergymen were motivated by more than a predictable moral squeamishness to the depiction of prostitution on the big screen. The stakes, they argued, were much higher. They considered their mobilization an act of "self-defense" against a grave cultural threat.[4] "Cry[ing] out from a plagued heart," Protestant film commissioner Werner Hess established both the tone and the agenda for the ensuing campaign in a remarkable film review which continued with the near-hysterical plea: "who will help hinder such spiritual murder of our young people and women, tested by suffering, and our broken-bodied men?"[5]

The question was rhetorical; the churches would obviously

2. Quoted in Juliane Eisenführ, *Die Sünderin. Geschichte und Analyse eines Kinoskandals* (Magisterarbeit: Universität Osnabrück, 1982), 243.

3. "Hirtenwort des Kardinals Frings gegen den Spielfilm 'Die Sünderin', 28. Februar 1951," quoted in the source material in Klaus-Jörg Ruhl, ed., *Frauen in der Nachkriegszeit, 1945–1963. Dokumente* (Munich: Deutscher Taschenbuch Verlag, 1988), 115–16.

4. See Cardinal Frings' Palm Sunday address from the pulpit in Eisenführ, 299.

5. From a film review by Werner Hess in the *Evangelischen Filmbeobachter* 3 (1 February 1951), quoted in Eisenführ, 247.

lead the campaign. After 1945, the German churches rapidly assumed the leadership of social and ideological reconstruction, and in fact became the "great normalizers" of postwar West Germany. The Catholic Church, in particular, served both as an important signal of alarm as well as a sounding board for conservative attitudes. No other group had a comparable institutional base or exhibited such unity of action and conviction of purpose. Church influence was further strengthened by the avid support of coreligionists in state and governmental offices, who were able to translate church concerns into new legislation. By the beginning of the Bonn Republic, these well-entrenched interests dominated the process of social and cultural reconstruction.[6]

Yet Hess's images of violence and ruin, of gender and generation, are inexplicable without further scrutiny of the film and the social-sexual context in which it was produced and distributed. The anti-*Sünderin* campaign can be read as a story of the struggles involved in the postwar reconstruction of social ideology, and an analysis of the discourse surrounding the release and exhibition of *The Sinful Woman* exposes the ideological justifications for conservative social policy toward women and the family promulgated in the early 1950s.[7]

The film itself is artistically unexceptional, and its message strikes the modern viewer as hopelessly romantic and socially conservative: Marina, the female protagonist, after a short but

6. Heide Fehrenbach, *Cinema in Democratizing Germany. The Reconstruction of Mass Culture and National Identity in the West, 1945–1960* (Ph.D. diss., Rutgers University, 1990), 66–168. Also Fehrenbach, "The Fight for the Christian West: German Film Control, the Churches, and the Reconstruction of Civil Society in the Early Bonn Republic," *German Studies Review* 14, no. 1 (February 1991), 39–63.

7. For a discussion of postwar German social policy affecting women and the family, see Robert Moeller, "Reconstructing the Family in Reconstruction Germany: Women and Social Policy in the Federal Republic, 1949–1955," *Feminist Studies* 15, no.1 (Spring 1989), 137–69; Robert Moeller, "Protecting Mother's Work: From Production to Reproduction in Postwar West Germany," *Journal of Social History* 22, no. 3 (Spring 1989), 413–37. Also see Ruhl, *Frauen in der Nachkriegszeit*; Doris Schubert, *Frauen in der deutschen Nachkriegszeit. Frauenarbeit 1945–1949. Quellen und Materialien.* Vol. 1, ed. Annette Kuhn (Düsseldorf: Pädagogischer Verlag Schwann-Bagel, 1984); *Frauen in der deutschen Nachkriegszeit. Frauenpolitik 1945–1949. Quellen und Materialien.* Vol. 2, ed. Annette Kuhn (Düsseldorf: Pädagogischer Verlag Schwann-Bagel, 1986); Angela Vogel, "Familie" in *Die Bundesrepublik Deutschland. Band 2: Gesellschaft*, ed. Wolfgang Benz (Frankfurt/M.: Fischer Taschenbuch Verlag, 1985), 98–126; and Ute Frevert, *Women in German History. From Bourgeois Emancipation to Sexual Liberation* (Providence/Oxford: Berg, 1989), 255–86.

significant life of prostitution finds love and redemption with one man, and ultimately she affirms her fidelity to him by surrendering her own life in order to join him in death. The death scene frames and structures the narrative: it provides the dramatic ending of the film, but also, more significantly, the enigmatic first scene. *The Sinful Woman* opens just before Marina commits suicide in the arms of her dying lover, Alexander. Exclaiming "Oh my God, I've killed you! How did it happen?" Marina initiates a series of flashbacks which answer her own question. Her answer indicates that her actions grew out of despair over Alexander's increasing incapacitation, which their love was unable to cure.

But some influential Germans thought she answered the question badly. They did not seek an answer to the broad question of what killed "the German male." In fact, there is reason to believe that they resented and feared the question posed in that fashion. They especially did not want the particular answer offered by that film; indeed, they did not want the answer left to the movies at all.

Die Sünderin aroused extraordinarily strong passions for two reasons. First, it challenged German leaders to confront what they had preferred to suppress: the fact that traditional social ideologies and gender relations, which had been exalted and exaggerated under Hitler, had been profoundly disrupted and perhaps destroyed. Second, the film highlighted the ability of mass culture to disseminate this devastating message. For these reasons, the film provoked intense anxiety and a sharp public response from conservative elites.

The fact was that "the German male" was a real social problem in the postwar period. German women outnumbered men by 7.3 million in 1945, leading contemporaries to speak of a *Frauenüberschuß*, or surplus of women, which was particularly marked among women in their childbearing years (ages 20–40). Nearly four million German men had been killed in the war, and at the end of hostilities 11.7 million German soldiers were held in prison camps.[8] By 1950, even with the return of most of the German prisoners-of-war, almost one-third of West German households were headed by divorced women or widows. In those households in which a man was present, he was "often

8. These numbers are from Doris Schubert, *Frauen in der deutschen Nachkriegszeit*, Vol. 1, 34. See also Frevert, 257–58, 263–64.

physically or psychologically scarred, unwilling or unable to work, or disqualified from some jobs because of [his] National Socialist loyalties."[9] He could not, therefore, easily resume his traditionally defined social role as husband or father.

The crisis of the German male coincided with military defeat and occupation. Male identity was bound up with national identity. The behavior of German men in Berlin after the arrival of Russian soldiers and the beginning of widespread raping of German women testified to this. One Berlin woman recorded in her personal journal that her friend, a widow,

> agreed during this period to house a former male tenant, who from the day he returned (to Berlin) . . . put himself to bed with a "neuralgia," allowing himself to be cared for, fed, and protected. . . . Only after the Russians withdrew did he get out of bed, healthy and fully recovered.

The same diarist noted a similar change among Berlin men in public on 8 May 1945, the day the Russian troops pulled out of the city:

> For the first time in weeks . . . I've heard German men talking in loud voices, seen them move with any sign of energy. They were acting in a practically masculine way – or in a way that used to be called "masculine." Now we're going to be on the lookout for a better word, one that can still be used even in bad conditions.[10]

Male inactivity in Berlin occurred in response to enemy soldiers from a rival country and so carried with it associations of submission and national humiliation. German men, for a short time, "infantilized" themselves, and opted to behave in a passive, noncombative manner.

The infantilization of physically and emotionally disabled veterans was a common phenomenon following the German defeat in the First World War. After World War II, parallels would not have been difficult to draw. "What the war victims need . . . is not only the hand of fatherly justice, but the soft

9. Moeller, "Reconstructing the Family," 140. See also Sibylle Meyer and Eva Schulze, *Von Liebe sprach damals keiner. Familienalltag in der Nachkriegszeit* (Munich: C.H. Beck Verlag, 1985).

10. Annemarie Tröger, "Between Rape and Prostitution. Survival Strategies and Chances of Emancipation for Berlin Women after World War II," trans. Joan Reutershan, in *Women in Culture and Politics: A Century of Change*, ed. J. Friedlander, B. Wiesen Cook, et al. (Bloomington: Indiana Univ. Press, 1986), 102–104.

hand of the mother. After all, they are really sick children, not so much because of the medical problems they have, but because of the terrible shock they have endured," read one article in the German press in 1921.[11] Several years earlier, Catholic Bishop Michael von Faulhaber, who would later become Cardinal of Bavaria, complained of the "lack of emotional vigor, a frightening paralysis of will, a perverse kind of homesickness and an endless grubbing for pensions" among disabled veterans he had seen. Critical of this marked lack of volition and productivity, Faulhaber insisted that "[t]hose who have been touched by death must not be allowed to wander around with their peg-legs and music boxes as they did after previous wars. . . . Even the blind cannot be permitted to become drones. Self-pity is like being buried alive."[12]

This failure of masculine "will" was regretted as much after the Second World War as after the first. Yet in the post-1945 world, the situation was further exacerbated by the missing (or consciously withheld) "soft hand of the mother" that was necessary in earlier times to nurse the fatigued and prostrated former warrior.[13] After 1945, women were depicted as repudiating, in great numbers, their traditional roles as wife and helpmate. The war, which emasculated men, had masculinized women. In a telling article, publicist Walther von Hollander, a frequent contributor to women's magazines, blamed women for the increasing number of broken marriages in postwar Germany, noting with regret that not all women were willing to submit to their men and surrender their new-found freedom:

> Women have proven themselves during the war to be capable of enduring life-threatening situations and work normally befitting men. They have often led a sexually active life that until now – justifiably or not – was reserved only for men; only those who shut their eyes can deny it. Now there are innumerable women, perhaps they are the majority, who would be only too happy to give the burden of a masculine life back to the man; however, not all are so ready to sur-

11. Robert Weldon Whalen, *Bitter Wounds. German Victims of the Great War, 1914–1939* (Ithaca, NY: Cornell Univ. Press, 1984), 187, quoting from "Psychologische Streiflichter auf das Versorgungswesen," *Zentralblatt*, 16 August 1921.

12. Whalen, *Bitter Wounds*, 187–188, quoting from Michael von Faulhaber, *Das hohe Lied der Kriegsfürsorge* (Berlin: Kameradschaft, 1916), 19–20.

13. In August 1945, for example, Ursula von Kardorff exhorted women to "furnish the understanding, the emotional balance, the rebuilding of confidence, the encouragement needed now by so many totally beaten and desperate men." Quoted in Frevert, 262.

> render the pleasure of masculine life [and] its relative liberty. . . . Women have learned to bear responsibility. They can be relieved of this responsibility only if someone [else] actually has the strength to lead. Only then will women again happily and mildly extend their trust.[14]

In order to contribute to "normalization," women were being asked again to join the family in the roles of wife and mother and to defer to male authority.

Yet gender roles are relational; in order for women to (re)assume their traditional roles, men needed to summon the will to reassert their authority. It is not surprising, then, that when men in Berlin "crawled out of their beds and hiding places" they felt the need to reestablish their gender identities and the national identity so intimately bound up in them. They attempted to rescue their self-image and social position by reestablishing their sexual dominance. Berlin men, in the guise of a compliment that quickly gained common currency, began inquiring in public whether *they* could "offer" German women "a little abuse" shortly after the withdrawal of Soviet troops.[15]

Annemarie Tröger has observed, based upon her research in Berlin, that the war and defeat demolished the myth of German masculinity and undid "the ideological fetters of traditional femininity," allowing German women to "experience a certain sexual and social emancipation" during the first years of the military occupation.[16] Often, of course, this sexual "emancipation" was forced and brutal, with "the rights of the victor nations . . . acted out on [women's] bodies."[17] Estimates of the number of women raped after the fall of Berlin range from twenty thousand to a half million, and thousands of Berlin women resorted to prostitution in order to survive.[18]

Despite the predominantly violent and coercive quality of this "emancipation," it was not uncommon for German men to publicly vilify German women for having had sexual relations with enemy soldiers. Often these male commentators did not distinguish between rape and prostitution, nor did they, in order to

14. "Der Publizist Walther von Hollander über Ehezerrüttung, Ehetrennung, Ehescheidung, 1946," in *Frauen in der Nachkriegszeit, 1945–1963.* Dokumente, 37.

15. See Tröger, "Between Rape and Prostitution," 111–12.

16. Tröger, "Between Rape and Prostitution," 109–110.

17. Frevert, 258.

18. Tröger, "Between Rape and Prostitution," 98–99. See also Meyer/Schulze, *Wie wir das alles geschafft haben.*

carry their arguments, dwell upon the miserable material circumstances that drove women into prostitution:

> Another very bitter symptom, which is difficult to articulate, would be senseless to suppress. It is not only the case that the German man returned home defeated. The victors marched in with him, and he had to observe that a small, and not very valuable, number of women fell prey to the[se] victors. It is almost impossible to pronounce objectively on this. . . . But for the sake of the dignity of the defeated, he naturally wishes that all German women would maintain the morally necessary distance. And for those who trespass against this he feels a thoroughly understandable disdain, mixed with hate, for women who give themselves to the victors for meager material advantages.[19]

Public rhetoric such as this, which condemned women for their sexual intercourse with (and often their victimization by) victorious soldiers, was symptomatic of the drive to reestablish the "myth of masculinity" in occupied Germany. More precisely, it advocated a specific brand of "German" masculinity that linked gender roles and sexuality in a complex way to nationality and national pride. By portraying women as selling themselves for "meager material advantages," male commentators resurrected the putative connection between consumption and femininity, an assumption which would inform government policy toward women, the family, and mass culture. Moreover, they insinuated that German women were partners to a national betrayal. From here it was a short step to shifting responsibility for national humiliation onto these women.

The answer to this postwar dilemma seemed to lie in the redomestication of German women. They were to "obey their husband[s] and bear [them] children, thereby securing the existence of the *Volk*."[20] The success of German reconstruction was linked by social conservatives to the renewal of the "small world" of the normative family structure. This vision of the patriarchal family righted the skewed universe of postwar German society by reestablishing a reassuring, orderly domestic hierarchy with the father at the pinnacle.[21] The mother re-

19. "Der Publizist Walther von Hollander über Ehezerrüttung, Ehetrennung, Ehescheidung, 1946," 37.

20. Ruhl, *Frauen in der Nachkriegszeit*, 107.

21. One influential contemporary explained:

The family is an unequal community and is hierarchically organized. Unity and order of the family become ensured by means of a double hierarchy: the

tained her traditional role as socializer and nurturer of the children, but was sexually and socially redomesticated. The process was one of ideological repatriation; women could reclaim their influence as mothers of Germany's future only by submitting to patriarchal authority.

The overarching problem with this solution was that the postwar experience of many Germans contradicted the ideal. Just over half of all West Germans lived in "intact families," the divorce rate was high, and it would continue to rise for several more years.[22] Magazine articles regularly bemoaned the prevalence of "*wilden Familien*" headed by unmarried parents as well as "half families" comprised of mothers and their "illegitimate" children. This situation, which one author erroneously claimed "has never been the case up until now," was expected to have devastating results:

> One cannot remove the men from the family for ten years and think that the organization of the family (*Familiegestalt*) would remain untouched and could be easily reassembled . . . the overall shape of the family is changed, and somehow destroyed.[23]

In the midst of increasing rhetoric of family disfunction and collapse, empirical sociologist Helmut Schelsky acquired an influential voice in postwar social policy by heralding the family as "society's last bastion, the ultimate place of safety" in West Germany.[24] Schelsky's emphasis on the normative family served an important cultural function. As Robert Moeller has suggested,

> The reconstitution of a private family sphere . . . embodied a critique of the ideological alternatives presented by Germany's recent past and by a Communist East Germany in the present. In the confused categories of totalitarian theory, it was possible to reject both at the same time; the family could serve as a vehicle for anti-Nazi *and* anticommunist rhetoric.[25]

---

authority of the parents over the children and the preeminent position of the father. . . . In accordance with the intimate connection between marriage and family, this authority lies, according to Christian teachings, with the father, since he is the master of the wife.

"Klaus Mörsdorf über die hierarchische Struktur von Ehe und Familie, 1952," in *Frauen in der Nachkriegszeit 1945–1963*, 116–17.

22. Vogel, 99.

23. Erich Reisch, "Die Situation der Familie von heute," reprinted in *Frauen in der Nachkriegszeit 1945–1963*, 123–24.

24. Robert Moeller, "Reconstructing the Family," 146; and Frevert, 265.

25. Moeller, "Reconstructing the Family," 162.

West German social policy makers were indeed careful to distinguish family-oriented programs, on ideological grounds, from their Nazi precursors, as were their counterparts in the Democratic Republic.[26] Yet an examination of the discourse accompanying film matters also reveals that German social and political leaders sought to protect themselves from the cultural and moral implications of materialist and commercial culture, which they identified with democratization and Americanization. The normative family, then, was to provide a bulwark against ideologically unappealing alternatives: the Nazi, the "Commie," and the so-called "Ami (American)," an expectation that was succinctly captured in the sociological catchword "*Fluchtburg Familie.*"[27] And although, over the course of the early 1950s, Adenauer steered the Federal Republic firmly along the path of political integration with the West, church leaders displayed a pronounced ambivalence toward cultural integration. They pushed, instead, in the direction of a cultural *Sonderweg,* or special path.

The fear that godless, materialist culture would accompany democratization and spell the death of a culturally discrete, capitalist West Germany was widespread among churchmen and conservative state leaders. One Catholic bulletin praised the absence of erotic decadence in the Soviet media, commenting pointedly that one should not be surprised if those "unbroken youths someday become masters of the lustful boys" in the West.[28] This fear survived well into the 1950s. In 1956, for example, a speaker at a conference of Catholic women argued that:

> Not only is the dialectical materialism of the East a terrible danger, but so too is the materialism of the West that prepares the way for the former and that subordinates all values, even the religious, to questions of profit, and elevates the standard of living to an Idol.[29]

Church leaders were particularly active in asserting that "the time had come, after years of dissolute living and lawlessness, to once again make decency and morality felt."[30]

26. See Moeller, "Reconstructing the Family" and "Protecting Mother's Work."

27. Frevert notes that this phrase ("the regfugee-fortress: family") gained currency in the early 1950s (265).

28. Quoted in Eisenführ, 281.

29. The speech was given at the annual meeting of the Working Group of Catholic German Women (*Die Arbeitsgemeinschaft der katholischen deutschen Frauen*). See "Die Frau in der Entscheidung zwischen Zeitgeist und christlicher Wertordnung, Januar 1956," quoted in Ruhl, *Frauen in der Nachkriegszeit,* 130.

30. Quoted in "Bischöfe fordern Jugendschutz–Gesetz," *Münchner Merkur* (24

In the midst of this atmosphere of social disruption and moral crisis, activist priests led armies of schoolboys onto the streets across West Germany in protest against the film, *The Sinful Woman,* demanding a new public morality and the "protection of our women's honor."[31] In order to understand more fully why this specific film was targeted by social conservatives and identify the themes that touched an exposed nerve in the early years of the Bonn Republic, we must examine the film in some detail. We must then explore the way the film organized the sociological data and how some contemporaries interpreted this organization. *Die Sünderin* appeared at a time when German leaders pressed for postwar social normalization. By 1951, the shape this normalization would take was clear. State and religious elites had identified what was acceptable and what was abhorrent to the process of social reconstruction. Their position was neither defensive nor passive; they occupied the seats of power and knew what they wished to affirm and what to condemn.

* * *

The Sinful Woman was released to much fanfare in the popular press. It was the young German actress Hildegard Knef's first feature film since her return from the United States, to which she had emigrated with her American husband in 1948.[32] The film opens with a double death scene, in which Knef's character Marina commits suicide in the arms of her dying lover, Alexander. It then launches into a series of flashbacks, slowly building layers of meaning, which ultimately culminate in a fuller, and now comprehensible, encore of the opening scene.

The first flashback occurs in a small house on the Italian coast, where Marina and Alexander are vacationing. Alexander, an aspiring artist, suddenly rips a painting from its easel and smashes it, then clutches his head in pain. Shaken, Marina resolves to help Alexander by selling one of his paintings. After failing to interest numerous gallery owners, she finally makes the sale by bartering herself, thinking of Alexander and his pain as she agrees to submit to the proprietor's sexual advances. On reflection, she called this a "step into filth, nothing more."

Marina first encountered Alexander at a posh Munich night spot. After observing the drunken Alexander being mistreated

31. See Eisenführ, 264.
32. Eisenführ, 167–68.

and bounced from the bar, she hires a taxi and takes him to her apartment to sleep off the alcohol. The next day, when Alexander awakens, Marina realizes that although he is unkempt and unemployed, he is from a "good family," and wonders if she is really any better than him. This thought prompts another flashback, in which her earlier life is portrayed.

After her father's death and her mother's remarriage, Marina's family moves to Hamburg from Danzig. The year is 1939; Marina is a teenager. She describes how her stepfather, an anti-Nazi, lost his job as the head of a firm, forcing the family to move to a more modest house. With the onset of austerity, her mother deserts the family every evening, listening during dinner for the car horn that signals the arrival of her wealthy male friend. One evening, after the mother has left, the Gestapo come and arrest the stepfather, leaving Marina alone with her stepbrother. That night they have their first sexual encounter. She promptly learns that he is willing to offer money and jewelry for her sexual favors: her body has become a medium of exchange. Marina's family life continues to erode. The dramatic culmination occurs when her stepfather strikes his wife and storms from the house. He returns some days later to find Marina and his son in bed together. He ejects Marina from the house and beats his son, perhaps fatally.

Marina begins a profitable life of prostitution, fraternizing with Nazi, and later American, soldiers, once she moves to Munich after being bombed out in Hamburg. Marina explains that "that was the way it went until Alexander," when she realized that "love means giving . . . never taking."

The narrative returns to Marina's new life with Alexander. She learns that he was an officer in the Second World War and that his personal and professional decline began with the German defeat. This decline had grave consequences for his domestic situation: although legally married, he and his wife have separated. Marina also learns that he is terminally ill with a malignant brain tumor, which is causing a gradual loss of sight. He always carries a potent painkiller with him so he can choose the time of his death.

Marina and Alexander travel to Italy on vacation, and after several happy days, Alexander suffers the head pains that caused Marina to go off to sell his painting, the scene we saw earlier. Only now do we understand Marina's sexual surrender to the gallery owner. She needs money to pay for an operation for Alexander and is willing to sacrifice even herself: "My whole existence has only one purpose," she gushes, "to help you, to keep you alive." Yet their return trip to Munich consumes much of the profit from Marina's transaction, and she desperately tries to earn more money by resorting, once more, to her former profession. At her old hangout, she hooks up with a man who turns out to be the medical doctor who had diagnosed Alexander's condition. In the hotel room, the doctor, realizing that Marina is prostituting herself on Alexander's behalf, declines the encounter and orders the operation.

Recovered, Alexander moves with Marina to Vienna to escape the inquiries of his estranged wife, whose interest in Alexander has been rekindled due to his recovery and artistic success. The days in Vienna are happy ones. Alexander is now a prosperous artist, painting "as [if] possessed," until one day he is blinded by a sudden relapse, and convinces Marina to administer a fatal dose of pills to him. Drinking champagne before the fireplace, Alexander slowly dies, unaware that Marina has also taken the pills and is dying in his arms. She whispers: "I love you. I'm coming darling."

Although the film has since become renowned for containing the first postwar nude scene, church officials offered no objections to the exposed flesh.[33] Instead, they denounced the high degree of sexual independence exhibited by the character Marina, who engaged in conjugal relations unsanctified by marriage, including, shockingly, sexual relations with her stepbrother as well as the long term adulterous relationship with Alexander. Predictably, churchmen objected to the film's presentation of prostitution as the answer to Marina's financial worries[34] and were gravely concerned about the possible social effects of the

33. Eisenführ, 226–27.

34. In fact, the film reviewer in *Katholischer Film-Dienst* objected to the impression some young women might get from the film regarding the lucrative nature of prostitution:

"We see this danger – as in almost all prostitute films – as a positive romanticization of prostitution. . . . Who can make us believe that a prostitute can earn the 4000 DM required for an operation in the course of a few hours?"

Klaus Brüne, Review of *Die Sünderin* in the *Katholischer Film-Dienst* (2 February 1951), reprinted in Hilmar Hoffmann and Walter Schobert, eds., *Zwischen Gestern und Morgen. Westdeutscher Nachkriegsfilm 1946–1962* (Frankfurt: Deutsches Filmmuseum, 1989), 356.

film, which elevated an unrepentant prostitute to a melodramatic heroine.[35]

Marina gains economic independence, indeed wealth, by playing on the male desire. Indeed, by portraying prostitution as a matter of individual choice, the film may actually have served to allow contemporaries to draw uncomfortable – and inaccurate – parallels with the experience of German women, who bartered their bodies for food and cigarettes during the early years of the Occupation in order to support themselves and their families. Social workers in the city of Aachen reported on the "grievous confusion of notions of morality" among women who "sexually submit" themselves in order to improve their standards of living: "Mothers excuse their behavior by arguing that they must provide bread for their children." The same report bemoaned the behavior and moral judgement of young girls, stating that "it has almost become a truism, that a girl will proposition a 'foreigner' in order to secure the enjoyment of coveted food or consumer goods."[36] Such reports minimized the real conditions of want that these women faced and the overwhelming incidence of *Hungerprostitution.* Instead, they emphasized the moral degradation and implied materialism identified as the cause of prostitution.

The free use, by an independent woman, of her own sexuality was clearly a theme that caused deep disturbance among conservative political and religious leaders, and one which was not peculiar to *The Sinful Woman.* Officials at the Bavarian State Youth Office were outraged by a report they received from the Regierungspräsident of Upper Bavaria, which quoted an advertisement that had been making the rounds in local newspapers for the Italian film *Bitter Rice*:

35. The Working Committee of the film industry self-censorship body, *Die Freiwillige Selbstkontrolle der Filmwirtschaft,* which viewed the film for public release, criticized Marina's return to prostitution "for reasons of convenience . . . [as the] self-evident way out of her human and financial troubles." Specifically they criticized "the episode in Naples, in which Marina submits to the gallery owner to sell Alexander's painting . . . her walk through the Munich rubble during which she decides to earn money for Alexander's operation by means of her old bar work [prostitution] . . . the particular part of the bar scene in which Marina scolds herself . . . for being a failure . . . because she is no longer able to interest men in her [sexually] . . . and the street scene . . . with Dr. Valentin . . . and the following scene in the hotel room." Eisenführ, 226–27.

36. "Die Lage der Jugendlichen in Aachen, 1947. Sozialbericht der Stadt Aachen über die Lage der Jugendlichen 1947. HSTA/Bestand NW 43/457," which appears in Ruhl, *Frauen in der Nachkriegszeit, 1945–1963,* 31–34.

> 17 year old Silvano Mangano [sic], discovered for this film, the overnight sensation, the nubile Roman girl! A young woman, without inhibitions, totally natural, without shame! Silvano Mangano [sic], the erotic super-atomic bomb – in a stormy, passionate, tumultuous film. Everybody wants to see her – Silvano Mangano [sic]![37]

The author of the report questioned how their social programs could successfully "place a 17 year-old girl in a home or under protective supervision for moral degeneracy, while 'girls without inhibitions and . . . shame' are at the same time being publicly prized." The problem that faced the churches was how to make mothers and daughters once again out of war-shattered women, how to corral German women back into the newly reconstructed home. Films, like *Bitter Rice* and *The Sinful Woman,* which openly celebrated sexuality, were perceived as grave dangers to this effort.

Clearly any depiction of prostitution reveals a great deal about male-female relationships and the socially constructed definitions of masculinity and femininity. What was so disturbing about *The Sinful Woman* was that Marina did not fit the role of victim; Alexander, however, did. Throughout the film, the figure of Alexander emphasizes the impotence of "the German man," and his death hints at the futility or even failure of a reconstruction based on old, familiar terms.

Since definitions of masculinity and femininity are necessarily interdependent, a confident and energetic Marina, who can set a goal and achieve it through the use of her sexuality, threatens the traditional social and sexual order. One striking aspect of *The Sinful Woman* is that it inverts the traditional characterization of male as active and female as passive. In the film, Marina is the agent of change. It is she who acts – Alexander merely waits or is acted upon; he cannot help himself. Marina literally pulls him from the gutter and provides him with the means, and hence the self-respect, to resume his career as an artist. Alexander is a cinematic incarnation of Werner Hess's "broken-bodied man." And he is set off by a self-reliant woman, a contrast that serves to further infantilize Alexander, who has already been infantilized by the effects of the war. His survival and success, throughout most

37. Bayerisches Hauptstaatsarchiv (hereafter BayHStA) MK51766. Copy of Letter from Dr. Kneuer, Regierungspräsident Oberbayern to the Bayerische Landesjugendamt, dated 24 April 1951. Kneuer likely had no first hand knowledge of the film, *Bitter Rice,* nor its notorious star, Silvana Mangano, to judge from the consistency with which he misspelled her name throughout his letter.

of the film, result only from Marina's efforts and volition.

The film, then, portrayed an ideological world turned on its head, and, most frighteningly, one which had obvious parallels in recent experience. In the years following the war, at least some German women were reluctant to surrender their responsibility for their individual fates to men and reaffirm too quickly the principle of social patriarchy, especially when the projected patriarchs were not up to the challenge. One woman in Berlin told of her husband's returning from war physically and emotionally drained:

> We had absolutely nothing. It was so bad between us, especially since he didn't want to, or couldn't, do anything. . . . I went to work and did the work at home that I had to do as a housewife and a mother, but my husband didn't want to do his work – for example to find wood. . . . And so I can well observe, if I place myself back in those difficult times and attempt to make a meal out of nothing, to collect herbs just so the food has a little flavor, stand on line for hours, keep the apartment clean, keep myself clean, keep him clean, wash his filthy underwear, that I also expect him to do his men's work! And so I'd rather be alone. I got myself a divorce. . . .
>
> I was fed up with marriage . . . I am not the type of person who likes so terribly to subordinate herself to others. The men of my generation are still used to having their wives submit to them unquestioningly. I know many women of my age, whose husbands can't pour their own coffee. The men bray, "Butter me a piece of bread." Then the bread will be buttered for them. But I don't consider myself to be a *Dienstmädchen*. . . .
>
> You know, the things one used to need a man to get can be had without one, you don't need to marry.[38]

Another Berliner remembered how she felt, at the age of fourteen, when her father returned home after seven years in a prison camp. She considered his reappearance an unwelcome invasion and burden on the "women's household," comprised of herself, her mother, grandmother, aunts, and sister:

> I hardly knew him. And I was totally uninterested in him, he could have just as well stayed away. He was, at that time . . . superfluous for us; we did fine on our own. He was just one more . . . [to care for]. And the men all came back sick from being imprisoned. Most of them didn't work. My father, for example, lost an arm and had stom-

38. Meyer/Schulze, *Wie wir das alles geschafft haben*, 53.

> ach ulcers. Yes, he was ill and he couldn't work, he was absolutely incapable of it . . . it is difficult for one to say, but we were totally independent because of the war. He was an encumbrance for us, so to speak, adults. We were again subjected to patriarchal authority (*väterliche Erziehung*), which was and is totally senseless, because it is always the mother who raises the children.[39]

Physical and mental debilitation among returning German soldiers meant that the burden of providing for the family fell on women. This was no easy task in the early postwar years, when food and consumer goods were at critically low levels, and women spent long hours waiting on lines, scavaging, gardening, and bartering on the black market. Yet rather than recognize the exhausting effort needed to supply a household under these conditions, "[m]any men feared and resented their wives' self-reliance, a product of women's 'forced emancipation' during the war . . . [when they] . . . had learned to manage without fathers and husbands."[40]

While such signs of female independence were common in the immediate postwar period, other German women eagerly expressed their support and desire for marriage, especially at a time when the loss of male life in the war made this option highly improbable for many women.[41] Not all women, then, rejected the return to traditional sexual and gender relations. Many willingly surrendered the responsibilities of "women's households" for a more familiar role as wife and mother, and the hope of a more equitable distribution of productive labor.[42] Yet the eager-

39. Meyer/Schulze, *Wie wir das alles geschafft haben*, 127–28.

40. Moeller, "Protecting Mother's Work," 415. One woman described a husband who, upon returning from the war, insisted that it was solely her responsibility to manage the household and care for their children, while he sat in the corner, read the paper, and complained. Unhappy with the inequitable division of labor, the woman queried, "Haven't these men had enough of giving orders yet? He says he's entitled to a comfortable home, but to my way of thinking he's not 'entitled' to anything." Quoted in Frevert, 263.

41. Doris Schubert has suggested that women's willingness to revert to traditional roles was due, in part, to "competition" for available men. The women's press encouraged this: The popular women's magazine *Constanze* printed, in July 1949, an article entitled "A Kingdom for a Man" which referred to "panicked women" and "pasha men." See Schubert, *Frauen in der deutschen Nachkriegszeit, Bd. I*, 56.

42. After all, as Ute Frevert (258) has argued, "the end of the Third Reich heralded no new beginning, no *Stunde Null* . . . , but rather a continuation of [women's] toil under straitened circumstances." See Schubert, *Frauen in der Nachkriegszeit, Bd.I*, 48–49 and 66–67, and Tröger, "Between Rape and Prostitution . . . ," 109–110.

ness of many German women to embrace marriage and domesticity did not relieve male apprehension of permanently altered gender relations.

The historical push for redomestication of German women was echoed in the film *The Sinful Woman* and found its parallel in the parameters of Marina's powers. Marina's efforts, although considerable, are circumscribed and ultimately thwarted by Alexander's fatal physical flaw. What is striking in this connection, however, is not Alexander's loss of will to live and determination to die, but his relegation of that task to Marina, and her willingness to administer a fatal dose of pills to him. For she indicates by her action that she also recognizes the physical, psychological, and social implications of Alexander's loss of sight and accepts the necessity of his death as well as that of her own, since it was only through her devotion to him that her life has gained meaning and happiness.

Within the context of the film, then, Marina's actions may be understood as supporting "normalization," or the reversion to traditional gender and sex roles. Marina is spurred into action only in the face of dire situations, in an atmosphere of crisis or despair. During periods of time in the film depicted as "happy," Marina becomes passive and ornamental, deferring to Alexander, who, recovered and strong, takes command of both the relationship and his career. Thus the film presents such times as "normal," implying the abnormality and exceptionality of those scenes in which Marina embodies agency.

It is highly significant that Alexander resolves to die when he permanently loses his sight. Loss of sight for Alexander means not only loss of livelihood, but also loss of control and the inability to protect his property and interests – a loss, that is, of masculinity. This point is illustrated in a scene near the end of the film: Alexander and Marina have moved to Vienna, where Alexander's career has flourished. Since his successful operation, happiness and "normalcy" have been reinstated, if temporarily. Alexander has taken to painting "only Marina," thereby containing her on his canvas. He emphasizes her femininity in languorous, reclining, nude poses which highlight her passivity and ornamentality. At the same time that Marina is contained and objectified by Alexander's gaze, she is also the object of our gaze, and in one garden scene in which she poses nude for Alexander, the gaze of two male intruders who have eagerly climbed the garden wall for some visual titillation. Alexander's loss of sight means that he can no longer control and domesticate Marina, and more seriously, that he cannot protect his proprietary interest in her by aggressively chasing away other encroaching gazers, as in the garden scene. Loss of sight means loss of power, loss of control, in effect impotence and the negation of masculinity.[43]

In its treatment of masculine and feminine roles, then, *The Sinful Woman* could be read as an allegory of postwar German gender relations. The film illustrated that German masculinity had lost its potency, that "neither collective protection nor individual heroic deeds [could be] expected," as the convalescent and passive behavior of German men in the face of Russian raping raids had made painfully clear to Berlin women.[44]

Churchmen were blind, however, to the ways in which *The Sinful Woman* could be read to reinforce the conservative social ideology they advocated. The aesthetic death scene at the end serves to "right" the skewed world of male impotence and gender inversion. The healing properties of heterosexual love have transformed Marina, causing her to renounce her solitary existence and self-centered materialism to devote herself fully to her man. She sacrifices herself willingly for Alexander, and without his knowledge – a convention that was employed frequently in films of the Nazi period.[45] Thus female martyrdom brings human redemption and spiritual fulfillment.

Yet critics of the film disregarded this transformation and attacked Marina's role as prostitute and murderess. The film was read strictly in terms of how it challenged the traditional morality and normative relationships these churchmen and their political counterparts wished to reestablish. Moreover, they posited the film as a dangerous and disruptive cultural agent, accusing it of working directly on the mind of the viewer by influencing individual desire and social behavior. A state police official (*Landpolizeibeamter*) from the small Bavarian town

43. See Sigmund Freud, "The Psycho-Analytic View of Psychogenic Disturbance of Vision (1910)," in *The Standard Edition of the Complete Psychological Works of Sigmund Freud,* Vol. 11, ed. James Strachey (London: Hogarth, 1964), 211–18.

44. Tröger, "Between Rape and Prostitution," 104.

45. I am indebted to Miriam Hansen for this observation. One of the earliest feature films during the Nazi period which portrayed a surreptitious female suicide was *Hitlerjunge Quex.* While, admittedly, in this film the woman is a mother sacrificing herself for her son, the concealed and aestheticized nature of the act anticipates Marina's suicide in *The Sinful Woman.*

of Lenggries, for example, betrayed his fear of the effects of *The Sinful Woman* in a letter to the Cultural Committee of the Bavarian State Parliament:

> This film is . . . no entertainment film, and it is not a matter of whether more or less white flesh will be set before the viewer. No, *this film is an unmistakably grave assault on the foundation of our morality with regard to love* – all but the most base elements have recognized that. Because the innocent viewer, who seeks entertainment and a little excitement, sits in the theater and allows himself to be gradually lulled by the racy and dazzling poison, so that he finally accepts, without resistance, that a woman, who according to the film is supposed to truly love deeply, occasionally walks the streets in order to improve the household finances – something, however, that does no damage to her "great love." . . .
>
> The loving woman can . . . calmly walk the streets, the purity of a true love does not suffer from it – or at least that is what it's trying to say.[46]

The author of the passage blurs the distinction between the protagonist and the film, thereby feminizing the latter. The film is seductive agent, lulling the viewer into complacency so s/he cannot recognize the ideological and threat implied by the film's representation of Marina's actions and their consequences. Both the film itself and the character's behavior in the film were represented as a challenge to traditional notions of morality, of monogamy, and the socially constructed and fiercely protected ideological coupling of love and monogamous sex.

Critics were disturbed not merely by the message they read from *The Sinful Woman*, but by the effects of the film medium as well. Officials in the Bavarian town of Rosenheim objected to the film's "subtlety and cleverness." Technical sophistication was identified as an treacherous tool which could provide direct access to the viewer's psyche. And the Evangelical Men's Club in Feuchtwangen, Bavaria worried that the purportedly "realistic" style of *The Sinful Woman* would make the portrayal of the characters more convincing and encourage the audience to surrender to despair:

> We also have in our city many mothers who have mastered an extremely difficult life, similar to that which the girl Marina had to lead, [but] in a thoroughly respectable manner. We also know from

46. BayHStA MK51766. Letter from Wilhelm Kummerle, *Landpolizeibeamter*, Lenggries, to the Cultural Committee of the Bavarian State Parliament, dated 24 May 1951. Emphasis appears in the original.

first hand experience of disabled ex-servicemen, who, with quiet valor accept and bear their fate given by God.

When a film . . . portrays social misery with its muddled relationships in a totally realistic way, one would at least expect that it lead . . . to a way out and not to hopeless dead ends.[47]

The church-sponsored protests against *The Sinful Woman* only served to endorse this assessment, fostering a heightened sense of crisis. Film was not mere entertainment, but a powerful tool for inappropriate socialization.

* * *

The dreaded malady of despair and loss of will, which social conservatives feared would overtake and undermine the nation, found its victims only among the male sector of the German population, or so conservative rhetoric would have us believe. Women were thought to be susceptible to other contagions. Given the important role women were to play as mothers in the German reconstruction, any outside influence that interfered with their vocation was considered a threat to normalization. Employment outside of the home was one such threat. Mass culture was another.

An examination of the rhetoric of conservative cultural critics in both church and state strikingly reveals that they considered women and youth, and not the "broken-bodied," debilitated German men, to be most susceptible to the attractions and the "insidious" influences of film and commercial culture. This can be read from the fears, expressed in a Catholic bulletin, that "the lustful boys in the West" would fall prey to the uncorrupted, "unbroken boys in the East."[48] It appears also in the comments of some local leaders that mothers could not be trusted with the regulation of their own children's film attendance. This state of affairs was used as justification for moral intervention by an outside authority, be it church or state. A letter from the office of the President of Upper Bavaria to the Bavarian Ministry of Education and Culture maintained that

[a]s much as one, at this time, may greatly dread . . . that which

47. BayHStA MK51766. Transcript of public meeting called by the Evangelischen Männerwerk Feuchtwangen, dated 11 April 1951.

48. Quoted in Eisenführ, 281.

> smacks of censorship, a means and a way must be found to redress this deplorable state of affairs, which exposes the already greatly endangered youth to further dangers. This is not served by appealing to the reason of parents . . . [b]ecause experience shows that parents oftentimes lack the necessary understanding. . . . Otherwise it would not happen that mothers appear at film screenings with small children in their arms.[49]

How could one expect mothers to be responsible for the moral development of their charges, when they themselves were seduced by the very source of the corruption? Instead, women were urged to embrace motherhood and "serve with self-evident self-sacrifice . . . to defend the Christian world order from the *Zeitgeist* suffused with 'bolshevik collectivism in the East' and the 'Hollywood-ideal in the West.'"[50] Women who forsook their calling threatened German regeneration and were thus implicated in the postwar moral decline perceived by conservative elites.

Given male distrust in women's ability to withstand the seductive powers of the mass media and consumer culture, *The Sinful Woman* was seen as a direct threat to traditional religious and community values because it allegedly fostered a desire for consumer goods and a cosmopolitan life style.[51] It was Marina, then, as a symbol of unregulated female sexuality and rampant consumerism, who killed the German male. Conservative criticism focused almost exclusively on the representation of Marina, who moves from one urban setting to another, acquiring mater-

49. BayHStA MK 51766, letter from Regierungspräsident, Oberbayern to Bayerisches Staatsministerium für Unterricht und Kultus, dated 4 March 1947.

50. Quoted in Ruhl, *Frauen in der Nachkriegszeit, 1945–1963,* 107–108.

51. See Andreas Huyssen, "Mass Culture as Woman: Modernism's Other," in *Studies in Entertainment. Critical Approaches to Mass Culture,* ed. Tania Modleski. (Bloomington: Indiana Univ. Press, 1986), 188–207 for an analysis of discourse on "mass culture as woman" during the late nineteenth and early twentieth centuries. In West Germany, the prevailing sense that women could not adequately perform necessary tasks of social reproduction has enormous implications for the analysis of postwar policy decisions. Robert Moeller has pointed out that German sociology and family policy in the early 1950s were predicated on the assumption that women's proper place was in the home, not out in the labor force. And it was women's roles as nurturers of the family and socializers of children that were particularly stressed: "at the same time that women's reproductive work was praised as essential to the smooth functioning of the 'market economy,' it was also women's responsibility to raise children to resist the consumer temptations that the economic miracle offered . . . inculcating children with the right values was clearly among a mother's tasks." Moeller, "Reconstructing the Family," 162.

ial finery, and in effect achieving economic mobility by using her body as a medium of exchange. This at a time when the Bishop of Würzburg, fearing widespread rural depopulation, rapid urbanization, and an ensuing increase in secular behavior and belief, demanded legal means be adopted to ban films such as *The Sinful Woman*, which were "meant to enervate the body of the *Volk* and, particularly in the villages, to encourage flight from the land."[52]

Urban origin had been popularly associated, since the 1920s, with secularization, economic independence, sexual emancipation, and consumption. This polyglot of meaning continued into the postwar period. One Berlin woman, for example, transplanted to a small town in West Germany for professional reasons, noticed that

> It was not at all easy to be a single woman in a small city in West Germany. That was much more difficult than in Berlin. That was because the men above all thought that if you were a Berliner, you would also be Parisian in part. . . . And men imagine that a woman who is alone is fair game, that they can do with her what they want. But they were mistaken. . . . And it also wasn't so easy with the married women, they weren't much better. They were continually jealous, although one wanted nothing to do with their husbands, just worked with them.[53]

Bavarian Cardinal Faulhaber linked secularization and the threat to traditional morality to the pluralism of values and behavior and to the cultural changes which accompanied democratization. He maintained that in a democracy, individuals' opinions concerning immorality and obscenity were often widely divergent and that this led to an alarming situation in which "moral principles increasingly freed themselves from their roots in natural law and in Christian moral law, and thereby from God." He cautioned that this undermining of law and morality would continue and worsen, "increasingly confounding more values until it destroys the basis of our entire moral order and national community."[54] This reasoning, in conjunction with the belief that women and children were susceptible

52. BayHStA MK 51766. Copy of letter from Bischöfliches Ordinariat Würzburg to Dr. Hans Erhard, Bayerischen Ministerpräsident, dated 6 March 1951.

53. Meyer/Schulze, *Wie wir das alles geschafft haben*, 133.

54. Quoted in "Bischöfe fordern Jugendschutz-Gesetz," *Münchner Merkur* (24 March 1950).

to the pernicious influences of film and materialism, resulted in the call for state regulation of film, a kind of "discriminatory paternalism" of male supervision through state agencies.

The same year that churchmen led public protests against *The Sinful Woman*, the federal government passed a law (*Jugendschutzgesetz*) intended to protect minors from the insidious influences of the mass media. The timing was not, of course, fortuitous. The most vocal opponents of the film's exhibition comprised the most active proponents for federal regulation of the media. The Catholic hierarchy in Bavaria, for example, played a crucial role in lobbying for the legislation.[55] In an "Appeal of the Bavarian Bishops for the Protection of Youth and the Security of the People (*Volkssicherheit*)" directed to the Office of the Minister President, Cardinal Faulhaber called for the expedient enactment of a "far-reaching law for the protection of youth and public morals (*Volkssittlichkeit*) from works of trash and smut." Arguing for an empirically proven relationship between the increasing circulation of "trash and smut" and the "moral brutalization" of the young, Faulhaber warned that the somber social effects of unregulated consumption and a free market were daily becoming more "evident in the increase in youth criminality, the growing number of crimes against morality, and the climbing curve of illnesses resulting from immoral acts." While Cardinal Faulhaber's rhetoric was directly aimed at printed matter, this law was understood to apply equally to films:

> Although federal legislation for the protection of youth was enacted in 1951, the problem of film viewing by juveniles remained a hot topic for research and lobbying by state and religious youth offices. Periodic anguished cries regarding youth criminality continued throughout the 1950s. In an article at the end of the decade, the head of the Munich-based *Aktion Jugendschutz* reaffirmed the need for public commitment to the regulation of film and its increasingly popular domestic rival, television:

55. Before federal legislation was enacted, the Bavarian Ministry of Education and Culture actively pursued legal remedies for limiting film attendance by children and adolescents. Bavarian state officials, in fact, expressed their impatience regarding lack of progress by the federal government in this area during early summer, 1951. The Bavarian Ministry of the Interior had determined some months earlier, in response to *Sünderin* demonstrations, that legal means did not exist for the prevention of attendance at films unauthorized for youth. And since proposed legislation in Bonn seemed to be at standstill, the Bavarian Parliament agreed to begin drafting a Bavarian Law for the Protection of Minors. BayHStA MK51766. Memos dated 11 June 1951, 20 June 1951, and 26 July 1951.

> It concerns something fundamental: the totally elementary task of self-defense, the protection of the human against profit-hungry production and the managerial dominance of economics. . . .
>
> And now we hear, from both adults and youth, an energetic boast about their own accountability, on the one hand about the right of parents (which is occasionally adroitly exploited . . . by the film industry), and in the case of youth as aversion to any type of "tutelage."
>
> In this climate, it has completely disappeared from view that our freedom is no longer markedly threatened by restrictions and encroachments by the state, but rather by the predominance of misused freedom. We only need to think about the cunning ways that consumer coercion through sex appeal . . . is pushed by the film industry.[56]

The danger was not identified as the long arm of the state, but the cultural effects of democratization and unrestrained commercial culture. The state was appealed to as the great protector of moral order.

State paternalism extended to the social reproducers as well. In 1952, German mothers were the subject of legislation introduced in the workplace for their "protection." While the law may in fact have had a beneficial effect in preventing the firing of pregnant women, protection required women workers to bare their private lives and circumstances to the scrutiny of the Labor Ministry and factory inspectors. Moreover, its formulation rested on the conviction of social policy makers that women's primary social task was motherhood. Women's employment was viewed not as a matter of individual choice, but the result of economic hardship. Thus, women workers were treated as a "disadvantaged group, forced out to work while fulfilling their natural obligations as mothers."[57]

Furthermore, the law's enforcement was based upon a "consensus" among factory inspectors and the courts "that pregnant women needed protection *because their physical and psychological capacities were diminished.*"[58] Factory inspectors went so far as to attribute unruly behavior in the workplace – for example boisterousness or theft – to "pregnancy psychosis," and maintained that pregnant women suffered from an inability "to control

56. Paula Linhart, "Zur Praxis des Filmjugendschutzes," *Jugend-Film-Fernsehen* 3, no. 4 (1959), 19–20.

57. Moeller, "Protecting Mother's Work," 420–32.

58. Moeller, "Protecting Mother's Work," 413, 420, and 431. Emphasis added.

themselves from pursuing irrational resolutions and desires once formulated." Cleptomania was considered a particular problem, but in this case materialist pursuit was excused as emanating from the mother's "desire" to provide for her offspring.[59] The *Mutterschutzgesetz* went into effect in 1952, at the height of concern for cultural retrenchment of women's roles.

Demands for "discriminatory paternalism," buttressed by state power, were made at a time when paternal standing and authority within the family was diminished or absent. The protective legislation for youth and women was in fact an attempt to restore an impotent patriarchy with an infusion of state power.

* * *

The reconstruction process in West Germany was clearly not dominated merely by the straightforward, though arduous task of material and institutional restructuring. Reconstruction also demanded a process of redefinition. Local elites needed to address the question of national identity: what it would mean to be "German" after National Socialism. This process of national redefinition was complicated by the fact of foreign occupation, and German church and state leaders struggled to constitute a "new" Germany that would depart from the communist and capitalist ideologies of the dominant victors.

As good social conservatives, German churchmen argued that national regeneration would have its foundation in the family, and that required the resurrection of traditional gender relations. Women needed to be redomesticated after their adventures during the war. They had to be convinced that the apron was their natural uniform, that resuming their duties as wives and mothers would be a service to themselves, their families, and their country; it would ensure normalization. Cultural representations that questioned the efficacy or implications of this agenda were therefore harshly condemned by church and state leaders. Culture was feared as a corrupter of national morals at the same time that it was embraced as a means to promote a particular vision of German national and gender identity. In the postwar period, as in the Third Reich, the cinema again became a crucial focus for constructing social ideology in Germany, an ideology that would have seemed comfortably familiar to Adolf Hitler.

59. See Moeller, "Protecting Mother's Work," 413–25.

Part II

Historical Films of New German Cinema

9

A Heroine For Our Time: Margarethe von Trotta's *Rosa Luxemburg*

anna k. kuhn

Anna Kuhn defends von Trotta's Rosa Luxemburg *(1986) against criticisms that the film distorts history through its relatively conventional realism. She asserts instead that it is precisely the film's "holistic" recreation of Rosa Luxemburg that makes the film feminist – precisely the filmic creation of a multifaceted, "whole" human being with whom one can empathize. In her theoretical writings, Luxemburg, a leading activist of the German Social Democratic Party, expressed little interest in women's issues; Kuhn argues that von Trotta has nonetheless reclaimed her for feminism by depicting her as a woman, not merely a socialist icon.*
—THE EDITORS

Captured by the Freikorps: Barbara Sukowa as Rosa Luxemburg and Otto Sander as Karl Liebknecht in Margarethe von Trotta's *Rosa Luxemburg*.
(Photo courtesy of New Yorker Films)

The fierce debate surrounding Margarethe von Trotta's *Rosa Luxemburg* (1986) focused in large part on a discussion of the fidelity of the filmmaker's cinematic (re)creation to the historical figure. Did von Trotta's insistence on a holistic portrayal of Rosa Luxemburg do violence to a great socialist revolutionary by (over)emphasizing the "private" Rosa to the detriment of the public figure? Was *Rosa Luxemburg* a German *Reds*, a film that used history merely as the stage prop against which to unfold a love story? Did the filmmaker's reliance on viewer identification and conventional forms of narrative cinema undercut the film's political impact? Was *Rosa Luxemburg* melodramatic kitsch, or the successful presentation of a complex human being in her multifacetedness? These were the questions that informed the discussion.

Since the historical figure of Rosa Luxemburg features so prominently in the critical reception of the film, I will preface my discussion of von Trotta's *Rosa Luxemburg* with background information on the historical Rosa. I will assess her importance for the development of international socialism in the late 1890s and early twentieth century and address the question of her political reception before turning to an analysis of the film.

I. The Historical Rosa

Rosa Luxemburg is one of the most important figures in the history of European socialism. Born in Poland in 1871, she became active early in the Polish socialist party. Most of her adult life was spent advancing the cause of socialism in Germany, the country with the largest and best organized working class, which many, including Marx, mistakenly considered the obvious site for the proletarian revolution. An active member of the Second International, Luxemburg appeared alongside August Bebel, Karl Kautsky, Lenin, and Jean Jaurès at party congresses. She was placed in "protective custody" in February 1915 for her outspoken opposition to the First World War, and spent most of the war behind bars. While still in prison, she became cofounder of the radical leftist *Spartakus* party, precursor to the German Communist Party (KPD), which she subsequently helped found. Upon her release in November 1918, she joined Karl Liebknecht in agitating for revolution. Liebknecht urged immediate revolution; Luxemburg opposed it as untimely, but deferred to his judgment. Together they led the ill-fated January 1919 *Spartakus* uprising. After the uprising was suppressed, she and Liebknecht were brutally murdered by the *Freikorps* (Free Corps)[1] soldiers the new Social

1. The *Freikorps* was a volunteer, right-wing law-and-order group composed primarily of remnants of the old army, especially officers, many of the old Prussian caste. A counterrevolutionary force, it was one of the ultra-nationalist groups in the Weimar Republic who prepared the way for the Nazis.

Democratic government had called out to restore order. Thus Luxemburg, betrayed by her socialist comrades, became a victim of the counterrevolution.

An orthodox Marxist, Luxemburg was praised by Georg Lukács in an essay of 1921 (later recanted) as the only one of Marx's disciples effectively to continue his life's work in economic theory and economic method.[2] Combining a keen intelligence with vast knowledge, and passion of purpose with facility of expression, Luxemburg was a rigorous theoretician, a brillant orator, an effective activist, and a formidable opponent. She eventually crossed swords with the most prominent socialist thinkers of her time. In a series of articles written in 1898, and later collected as *Social Reform or Revolution*, Luxemburg delivered what was considered the definitive rebuttal to Eduard Bernstein's revisionism. Rejecting his notion of reformist socialism, the belief that the workers' cause could adequately be advanced through internal reform of the system, Luxemburg demonstrated to the satisfaction of the SPD (German Socialist Party) mainstream at the turn of the century that the collapse of capitalism called for by Marx was indeed necessary for the rise of socialism.

Her reaffirmation of orthodox Marxism, for a time at least, effectively countered the challenge from the socialist right. It earned her the gratitude of the SPD leadership and assured her place in the party. Yet ironically, many party leaders themselves secretly embraced reformism. For them Marxist revolutionary ideology was merely a convenient platform through which to win workers' votes and advance the long-term goal of amassing power within the system. Luxemburg's uncompromising belief in nonviolent, spontaneous populist revolution soon brought her into conflict with both August Bebel and Karl Kautsky. Subordinating personal friendship to political conviction, she publicly and vociferously rejected their cautious parliamentarianism and eventually broke with her former mentors and friends.

Her most famous disagreement, however, was with Lenin, whom she knew well and admired. As early as 1904, in her essay "Organizational Questions of Russian Social Democracy," she rejected his call for ultracentralism, maintaining that a political

2. Georg Lukács, "The Marxism of Rosa Luxemburg," in *History and Class Consciousness*, trans. Rodney Livingston (Cambridge: MIT Press, 1972), 27–45. Juxtaposing Luxemburg to the vulgar Marxists of her time, Lukács terms her work "a return to the pristine and unsullied traditions of Marx's own method"(33).

movement must be based on the popular will. She remained uncomfortable with Lenin's authoritarianism and reiterated her discomfort in her long draft essay "The Russian Revolution," published posthumously in 1922.[3] In 1918, one year after he had taken power, she wrote the following in her prison cell in Breslau:[4]

> [Lenin] is completely mistaken in the means he employs. Decree, dictatorial force of the factory overseer, draconic penalties, rule by terror. . . . Without general elections, without unrestricted freedom of press and assembly, without a free struggle of opinion, life dies out in every public institution. . . . Only bureaucracy remains as the active element. . . .
>
> [Lenin and his comrades] have contributed whatever could possibly be contributed under such devilishly hard conditions. The danger begins only when they make a virtue of necessity. . . .
>
> Freedom only for the supporters of the government, only for the members of one party – however numerous they may be – is no freedom at all. Freedom is always exclusively for the one who thinks differently.[5]

Luxemburg's relationship to Lenin merits close examination. Yet von Trotta omits any mention of the Russian leader in her film, an omission which I will address later in this essay.

II. Political Reception of Rosa Luxemburg

Despite her significant theoretical contributions, despite the major role she played in the Second International, despite her

3. Many of Luxemburg's comrades, especially Paul Levi, felt that it would prove harmful to the incipient Soviet state and divisive to international socialism were she to publish her views on the Russian Revolution. Against her better judgment she acquiesced to pressure they brought to bear and suppressed an essay she had written in summer 1918. Levi later had a change of heart and had the longer unfinished work Luxemburg began in September 1918 published under the title *The Russian Revolution.* See Elzbieta Ettinger, *Rosa Luxemburg: A Life* (Boston: Beacon, 1981), 222–27 for a discussion of the history of Luxemburg's essays on the Russian Revolution.

4. In all, Luxemburg spent three years and four months of the war in prison. After serving a one-year sentence for having incited public disobedience in 1914, she was detained and imprisoned without trial for the duration of the war (Ettinger, *Rosa Luxemburg,* 202). She was first detained in Wronke, where she remained until August 1917, when she was transferred to Breslau.

5. Rosa Luxemburg, "The Russian Revolution," in *The Russian Revolution; Leninism or Marxism?,* trans. Bertram D. Wolfe (Ann Arbor: Univ. of Michigan Press, 1961), 25–80; here 71; 79; 69.

unflagging activism in Wilhelmine Germany, Rosa Luxemburg has failed to receive the recognition accorded her male counterparts. In the Federal Republic (FRG) Luxemburg's unpunished murder remains a blot on the national conscience.[6] Although one of her students, Wilhelm Pieck, later became the president of the German Democratic Republic (GDR), the East was uncomfortable with her criticisms of Lenin, so there, too, she remained problematic. Officially honored, her views were misrepresented: she was celebrated as a forerunner of that country's authoritarian bureaucratic socialism.[7] Among her Polish compatriots, her staunch internationalism and rejection of nationalist politics made her unpopular, and Stalin's denunciation in 1931 made her persona non grata in the Soviet Union for many years.

Left-wing West German student radicals of the sixties constitute an important exception to this general trend of nonrecognition. For them Luxemburg became a cult figure: a symbol of the missed possibilities of the failed German revolution of 1919; the martyr of an unripe revolution; an embodiment of the unfulfilled promise of the society envisaged by Marx which they now in turn hoped to realize. Holding fast to her belief that the revolution returns again and again in dif-

6. As late as 1968 the Federal Republic sanctioned Luxemburg's murder by labeling it a "state execution." In 1974 attempts to issue a commemorative stamp of Luxemburg met with widespread resistance. Many postal carriers refused to deliver letters with this stamp, and many citizens of the FRG refused to accept letters which bore the stamp. Only very recently has Rosa Luxemburg begun to receive her due recognition: plans are currently underway to build a monument to the murdered revolutionary leader in West Berlin. Ironically, it was a Christian Democratic Senate in West Berlin that undertook what its Social Democratic predecessors for decades were reluctant to do: officially honor "Red Rosa." Margarethe von Trotta's film has unquestionably contributed to this new interest and reassessment of Luxemburg. For a discussion of von Trotta's film and its relationship to the rehabilitation of Luxemburg, see Manfred Scharrer, "Ein Denkmal für Rosa Luxemburg," *Die Tageszeitung*, 25 March 1987.

7. In the last of the former GDR, Luxemberg's role was also in flux. In the wake of the regime's reprisals against critics of the system she became an icon of resistance and the embodiment of democratic socialism. Presumably von Trotta's film, which was shown and enthusiastically received in the GDR, has contributed to this revaluation of Luxemburg in the East. The actress Barbara Sukowa, who played von Trotta's Rosa Luxemburg, was among those West German artists who sent a telegram of protest to Erich Honecker following the recent arrests of East German citizens. Those arrested had used the official 17 January commemorative celebration of the deaths of Luxemburg and Liebknecht to underscore their requests for exit visas (cf. *Frankfurter Allgemeine Zeitung*, 25 January 1988). I will address these events in the GDR later in this essay.

ferent forms,[8] they regarded themselves as Luxemburg's political heirs.

To members of the New Left, who also espoused populist democracy, Luxemburg's criticisms of the SPD must have seemed prophetic. The formation in late 1966 of the *Große Koalition* (the Great Coalition), which joined the SPD with the Christian Democrats and elected former-Nazi-turned-Christian Democrat Kurt Kiesinger Chancellor of the Federal Republic, marked an important watershed in the rise of the West German student movement. It symbolized the SPD's ultimate betrayal of its Marxist origins[9] and proclaimed the bankruptcy of the Federal Republic's only legal party of the Left.[10] This bankruptcy manifested itself most clearly in the SPD's support of the *Notstandsgesetze* (emergency laws), laws that provided for the suspension of certain civil rights in a state of emergency. Fanned by student protests in 1967 and 1968, some of which were specifically directed against the passage of the *Notstandsgesetze,* these laws were passed in 1968 with the help of the SPD. In an ironic twist of history, precisely the party outlawed by the Nazis' *Notstandsgesetze* helped implement similar laws. The history of the Left was repeating itself in West Germany: the mainstream Left was betraying its more radical contingent.

III. Von Trotta's Rosa

Margarethe von Trotta, a member of the 1960s student generation, has admitted that her perception of Luxemburg was ini-

8. In her last article "Order Reigns in Berlin," which she wrote for the Communist paper *Die Rote Fahne* (*The Red Flag*) after the brutal suppression of the Spartacist uprising in January 1919, Luxemburg took issue with the bourgeois presses' reiteration of the government's statement that order had been reestablished. The famous concluding paragraph, which von Trotta incorporated into her film, reads: "'Order reigns in Berlin!' You stupid lackeys! Your 'order' is built on sand. The revolution will 'raise itself up again clashing,' and to your horror it will proclaim to the sound of trumpets: I was, I am, I shall be. Rosa Luxemburg." *Selected Political Writings,* ed. Dick Howard (New York: Monthly Review, 1971), 415.

9. The Great Coalition was the culmination of a process that began in 1959 with the appearance of the Bad Godesberg plan in which the SPD sought to broaden its political base, proclaiming that it was no longer the party of the working class, but rather a *Volkspartei* (party of the people). See Richard W. McCormick, "The Politics of the Personal: West German Literature and Cinema in the Wake of the Student Movement" (Ph.D. diss.: Univ. of California, Berkeley, 1986), 29–64 for a concise overview of the West German student movement.

10. The Communist party was outlawed in the Federal Republic in 1956 and was not reinstated until 1968.

tially informed by the movement's perspective.[11] Yet her film biography, Rosa Luxemburg, does not simply advance the movement's perception of her; it is not merely a rehabilitation of Luxemburg as political theoretican and activist. Instead, in keeping with von Trotta's post-1960s feminist consciousness, it intertwines the personal with the political. It exposes the contradictions in Luxemburg's life by politicizing the personal and personalizing the political. Focusing on her interpersonal relationships, including her long, tormented affair with Leo Jogiches, it gives us access to the private woman behind the public figure, and thereby differs from more traditional biographies of (male) political leaders, which tend to stress the public persona, or which at any rate shy away from presenting the public man in his frailty. It does, however, overlap closely with Elzbieta Ettinger's recent literary biography of Luxemburg (1986): both rely heavily on Luxemburg's love letters to Jogiches[12] to portray the vulnerable woman behind the renowned revolutionary.

In a sense von Trotta inherited her film from Rainer Werner Fassbinder, who, at the time of his death, had been working on a film of Luxemburg's life. She must have welcomed the opportunity; she had been interested in making a film about Luxemburg since 1968.[13] Political activism was, after all, a topic she had treated both in her first independently made feature film, *Das zweite Erwachen der Christa Klages* (*The Second Awakening of Christa*

11. "Ich habe Rosa Luxemburg aus dem Landwehrkanal geholt. ("I pulled Rosa Luxemburg out of the Landwehr canal.") A Conversation between Members of the GA Newspaper and the Director Margarethe von Trotta", *General Anzeiger*, 3 April 1986.

12. Luxemburg's letters to Jogiches were unavailable to non-Polish readers until the early 1970s. They were translated into German by Mechthild Fricke Hochfield and Barbara Hoffmann and published as *Briefe an Leon Jogiches* (Frankfurt/Main: Europäische Verlagsanstalt, 1971). Elzbieta Ettinger translated the letters into English: *Comrade and Lover: Rosa Luxemburg's Letters to Leo Jogiches*, ed. and trans. Elzbieta Ettinger (Cambridge: MIT Press, 1981). These letters were therefore not available to J.P. Nettl when he wrote his two volume study, *Rosa Luxemburg* (London: Oxford Univ. Press, 1966), long considered the standard biography of Luxemburg.

13. Predictably, von Trotta's Rosa bears little resemblance to Fassbinder's. According to von Trotta Fassbinder's filmscript omitted "the dimension of her life as a woman – her desire for a complete life – wasn't there. And it used none of her writing. Everything it had to say was so simple-minded. You can't separate Rosa from her writing." See Amy Taubin, "Von Trotta, Wanting it All," *The Voice* (12 May 1987): 78.

Klages, 1978) and in her more sophisticated *Die bleierne Zeit* (*Marianne and Juliane*) of 1981.

Christa Klages, in which a mother robs a bank to prevent her daughter's day-care center from being evicted, had treated issues that formed the cornerstone of the German women's movement: the demand for decent day care; the empowering experience of female bonding; the need for solidarity with other women. While calling into question the feasibility of meaningful individual political action, it left open the possibilty of effecting social change through collective action. *Marianne and Juliane*, based on the experiences of Christiane Ensslin and her sister Gudrun, a member of the Baader-Meinhof group, had dealt with the volatile topics of German terrorism of the 1970s and state-sanctioned counterrevolutionary violence. Juxtaposing Juliane's efforts to change the system through reform with Marianne's advocacy of violence, the film questioned both legal and illegal forms of political action. Besides treating an overtly political theme, *Marianne and Juliane* illustrated the feminist dictum that "the personal is the political" by meshing politics in the public sphere with the politics of private life: the relationship of the sisters to each other and to their parents is as important a focus of study as their respective strategies for eliciting political change. Thus the prospect of portraying the charismatic and complex figure of Rosa Luxemburg, political activist *par excellence*, must have been a welcome challenge to von Trotta: it presented her with yet another vehicle for exploring these issues.

Rosa Luxemburg created a furor in the Federal Republic, where the film was criticized on political and aesthetic grounds. Von Trotta was faulted both for overemphasizing the personal to what was perceived as the detriment of the film's potential political message[14] and for failing to employ innovative cinematic techniques, i.e., for relying on a traditional Hollywood-style film narrative.[15]

These criticisms are hardly new: they have dogged von Trotta since the beginning of her film career. The tension between the

14. See for example Hellmuth Karasek's review, "In kitschigem Rosa," *Der Spiegel* 15 (1986): 255, in which he totally pans the film. In contrast, the discussions by Cora Stephan, "Der widerspenstigen Zähmung," *Der Spiegel* 15 (1986): 254–55 and Gertrud Koch, "Die Internationale tanzt," *Konkret* 1986, no. 4: 72–76 are somewhat more positive although they also take exception to the portrayal of certain historical events. Stephan criticizes the portrayal of the the November revolution and Koch faults von Trotta with a naive recounting of history.

15. See in particular Karasek.

private and the political is central to all the filmmaker's work, and the debate concerning the personal versus the political has always been a salient feature of von Trotta criticism. This debate reached a new intensity with her films *Heller Wahn* (*Sheer Madness*, 1983) and *Rosa Luxemburg*. As the only German woman of her generation making mass audience films, von Trotta employs a more traditional, naturalistic style of film narrative than her colleagues such as Ulrike Ottinger, Helke Sander, or Helma Sanders-Brahms. In part because of her reliance on familiar cinematic strategies, von Trotta has attained greater recognition abroad than her colleagues, particularly in the U.S. Since German women's cinema arose partly in reaction to Hollywood's sexist portrayal of women, formalists often castigate von Trotta for reverting to a style they consider ideologically incorrect and aesthetically anachronistic.

In the following, I will address these objections, arguing (1) that *Rosa Luxemburg* is in fact a feminist and profoundly political film; and (2) that this, her formally most conservative film, is accessible to a wide audience precisely because of its conventional form and is therefore well suited to von Trotta's purpose, to recuperate Rosa Luxemburg. Weighing the film's shortcomings against its successes, I will argue that its widespread audience success and the viewer response it elicited, invoked in the service of von Trotta's distinctly political ends, are its justification.

According to the reading of *Rosa Luxemburg* as an unpolitical film, von Trotta has distorted history, has reduced her Rosa into a sentimentalized romantic figure whose political significance is minimized if not wholly suppressed. In fact, the scrupulously researched filmscript assumes a great deal of historical knowledge. Those unfamiliar with the development of socialism in Poland, Russia, and Germany, of the bankruptcy of socialist internationalism when confronted with the nationalistic war fever that culminated in World War I, and of the shameful coalition between the Left and the Right after the war that led to the murder of Luxemburg and Karl Liebknecht at the hands of the *Freikorps* in 1919 may find it difficult to follow *Rosa Luxemburg*.

Precisely the film's historical and political framework poses problems for an American audience that is largely unaware of the European history von Trotta takes for granted. It will doubtless find the temporal shifts in the opening sequences disorienting.[16] Here von Trotta jumps from prison scenes of Rosa in

Wronke during the war to prison scenes in the notorious Czarist Citadel fortress in Poland just after the 1905 Russian revolution, in which she faces a mock execution for political agitation. This flashback is interspersed with yet another one of Rosa as a young child, and is followed by scenes in Zurich in 1899 and by the German socialist party's New Year's eve costume ball in Berlin at the turn of the century. These early scenes, with their overlay of flashbacks and their jumbled chronology, are the film's most innovative. (In contrast, the latter half of the film, which deals primarily with the years 1917–19, essentially adheres to a straightforward linear chronology.)[17] Coherence among these disparate events is vouchsafed by presenting them all through Rosa's perspective. Thus von Trotta, adopting a well-known strategy of the Hollywood melodrama, fosters the audience's identification with her protagonist by consistently using a subjective point of view to narrate her story.

To call von Trotta's *Rosa Luxemburg* "unpolitical," one must ignore a great deal. From the outset, the film emphazises the importance to its protagonist of politics in the public sphere; throughout it forcefully demonstrates the price Rosa must pay for her political convictions. Beyond that, and this is perhaps its most important function, it reveals the everyday politics of the personal sphere of her life. By documenting her constant struggle to assert herself in the male-dominated socialist party, it problematizes issues of gender, issues which Luxemburg herself chose not to address.

It is intriguing how von Trotta manages to fashion a feminist film out of a subject whose record on the so-called "Frauenfrage," or "woman's question," was, from a feminist perspective, far from exemplary. Unlike her contemporary and close friend Clara Zetkin, Rosa Luxemburg did not privilege issues of gender. In fact, as the film makes clear, she clashed with Bebel over

16. It would be helpful to provide viewers with a short chronology of Luxemburg's life and of the development of the socialist party in Germany and Poland before screening this film.

17. Despite its complicated time structure, an overriding logic to the film's chronology suggests itself. Starting in 1915, the film works backwards in time via flashbacks to 1899, and then, moving forward, it returns to 1915; the general progression is interrupted by short returns to 1915 and by short childhood flashbacks; then, having returned to the starting point, the film moves forward in a linear fashion through to the end of Luxemburg's life. It appears that von Trotta seeks to furnish viewers with necessary insights into Rosa's psychology in order to allow them properly to understand and empathize with her situation.

her refusal to address the question of women under socialism. She obviously believed women's oppression to be of a piece with the oppression of the working classes. In her view gender could not be treated as a separate issue. Both injustices would cease once capitalism had been overthrown.

The luncheon scene at the Kautskys enables von Trotta to make Rosa's position manifest while at the same time showing the limitations of that position. Against the backdrop of a lively discussion of political strategies, including the role of trade unions and mass strikes versus parliamentarianism, Clara Zetkin raises the issue of female suffrage. When she questions why the party had only formally supported the women's vote, Rosa disparagingly remarks that this topic is not relevant to the debate. Bebel's response, ostensibly in support of Clara, reveals his contempt for the "women's question" and his ambivalence toward Rosa: "Yes it is," he maintains. "I've asked you from the beginning to take a greater interest in the ladies' issues. An intelligent, argumentative female like you should admit to her sex." By having Bebel use the perjorative term "Weibersachen" ("ladies' issues") to describe women's suffrage and the epithet "streitsames Weib" ("argumentative female") to describe Rosa, the film calls into question the widespread assessment of Bebel as an advocate of women's emancipation. It makes clear that women must be liberated not only from class oppression under capitalism, but also from their social oppression under patriarchy. By pointing to the limitations of a Marxist critique, the film points dialectically to the necessity for a feminist analysis.

In addition to its feminist dialectic, the film presents von Trotta's political reception and evaluation of Luxemburg. As demonstrated by Rosa's appearance at a party rally in Frankfurt in 1913, von Trotta sees Luxemburg, along with Marx and Lasalle, as the representative of authentic socialism in Germany. Appearing center stage, she is flanked by a large picture of Lasalle on the left and Marx on the right. Von Trotta's decision to use an actual historical photograph[18] as the basis of her mise-en-scéne represents her acceptance of the 1960s reception of Luxemburg. This iconographic tribute to Rosa Luxemburg as mother of the German socialist party is underscored by the

18. See Ettinger, *Rosa Luxemburg. A Life*, unpaginated photographs between pages 160 and 161. The actual photograph depicts Luxemburg delivering a speech at the congress of the Second International in Stuttgart in 1907.

many scenes in which she is pitted against the cautious, staid, and aging representatives of the party, to emerge as the irrepressible voice of conscience and humane socialism.[19] Yet even though von Trotta's spunky Rosa invariably has the last word in her squabbles with the SPD leadership, she remains a Cassandra-like figure, whose voice, the *vox populi*, is unheeded by the party leaders. Luxemburg stands alone, a symbol of women's exclusion from real political power.

As an *auteur* filmmaker, Margarethe von Trotta imprints her oeuvre with her stamp. In *Rosa Luxemburg* she uses her historical subject matter also to address pressing issues of our time. The omissions and changes in the historical record are, I submit, intricately bound up with the filmmaker's own political agenda. Those who bring the critical norm of "objectivity" to bear, who fault the film with failing to portray adequately the "real" Rosa Luxemburg, overlook the fact that every biography is an interpretation. It is a commonplace that biography's fashioning of factual information into narrative amounts to the subjective reception of a person's life by the biographer.

In many ways von Trotta's Rosa is a woman of the 1980s.[20] According to the filmmaker, "'Rosa wanted everything – all that a woman can experience – biologically, intellectually, and emotionally. That's very modern.'"[21] She seeks (and attains) intellectual satisfaction and public recognition through work. At the same time she realizes that work is not enough, and throughout her life longs for emotional fulfillment and personal happiness. That she should seek this happiness with Leo Jogiches, a man emotionally incapable of giving her the affection she so desperately needs, constitutes the tragedy of her personal life.[22] Rosa Luxemburg very much wanted a child. In this, her thinking intersects with that of some contemporary feminists, e.g., Ger-

19. By pitting Luxemburg against the male SPD leadership, von Trotta is also giving voice to the women of the New Left who, during the student movement, were often dominated and silenced by their male colleagues before they split off to found the women's movement.

20. By "woman of the 1980s" I am of course referring to the feminist of the 1980s, not to that other "woman of the 1980s" phenomenon: the traditional woman who limits her scope to the family.

21. Taubin, "Wanting it All," 78.

22. Luxemburg's symbiotic relationship with Leo Jogiches must have fascinated von Trotta. Emotional symbiosis is a theme she has explored in depth in *Schwestern oder die Bilanz des Glücks* (*Sisters or the Balance of Happiness*, 1979) and *Heller Wahn* (*Sheer Madness*, 1983) and to a lesser degree in *Die bleierne Zeit* (*Marianne and Juliane*, 1981).

manine Greer,[23] whose assessment of the personal costs to individual women of the post-1960s women's movement, with its achievement-oriented ethos of employment parity, has led them to place a new, higher value on motherhood. In a letter of 6 March 1899 to Leo Jogiches, the historical Luxemburg articulated her dream for personal happiness:

> Our own small apartment, our own nice furniture, our own library; quiet and regular work, walks together, an opera from time to time, a small, very small circle of friends who can sometimes be invited for dinner; every year a summer vacation in the country, one month with absolutely no work! . . . And perhaps even a little, a very little baby? Will this never be allowed? Never? . . . Oh, Dyodyo, won't I ever have my own baby?[24]

Her wishes fell on deaf ears; Leo Jogiches' monomaniacal obsession with revolution did not permit personal distractions, certainly none so consuming as a child.

Von Trotta dramatizes Rosa's situation by inventing an encounter between the lovers that displays their irreconcilable differences. In a flashback to 1899, the sequence recalls Jogiches's ultimatum: "You have to decide: do you want to be a mother or a revolutionary?" For Jogiches, who thinks in terms of antinomies, motherhood and political action are mutually exclusive categories: it is, in his view, her task to "give birth to ideas, those are your children." Rosa's response is to break a mirror, into whose shattered glass she stares, an indication of how Jogiches's withholding mutilates her. Iconographically Rosa's reflection captures the history of their relationship: whereas her head remains intact, the bottom left side of her body is obliterated. The reflection in the mirror, whose jagged edges cut into Rosa's heart, can be read as follows: as her teacher and mentor, Jogiches has been instrumental in shaping her mind, but she has freed herself of his influence; she is intellectually autonomous. As her lover, he is able to deny an important part of her person by refusing to sire a child. On a more universal level the scene can be read as a condemnation of the dominant culture's binary opposition (as expressed by Jogiches) between body and mind, an opposition that is seen as

23. See for example Germaine Greer, *Sex and Destiny: The Politics of Human Fertility* (New York: Harper and Row, 1984).

24. Rosa Luxemburg, *Comrade and Lover. Rosa Luxemburg's Letters to Leo Jogiches*, 73.

destructive in contrast to Luxemburg's holistic worldview.

The historical Rosa Luxemburg was an extremely complex, contradictory, and often fiercely contentious woman. Von Trotta downplays her contentiousness, softening her often vitriolic and personal attacks on political adversaries. But the film brilliantly captures some of Luxemburg's contradictions and ambivalences. A woman who detested the bourgeoisie, she espoused many of the traditional German bourgeois family and cultural values. Quoting directly from the above cited letter, von Trotta incorporates Luxemburg's longing for this bourgeois idyll into her characterization of Rosa.

Rosa shared her desire for the comforts of a bourgeois life with the rest of her Social Democratic comrades. These champions of the working class were nothing if not bourgeois. One glance at the elegant surroundings of the Kautsky household, with its meticulously set table, or Karl's elegant library with its hardwood bookshelves and leather-bound books, or even the opulence of Rosa's small apartment with its heavy furniture and Oriental carpets, suffices to convince the viewer that these are hardly representatives of proletarian culture. On the contrary, in the true style of the *Bildungsbürgertum* (intellectual bourgeosie), they are the custodians of high culture.[25] Thus we see Rosa, listening in rapt attention as her lover Costia Zetkin recites a poem by Mörike; we hear her refer to Schiller's *Wallenstein* in one of her anti-war speeches. And on the night before their murder, in the midst of political chaos, Rosa asks Liebknecht to play something on the piano; she longs to hear the music of which she had so long been deprived in prison. Liebknecht complies with a skillful rendition of Beethoven's "Moonlight Sonata."

Von Trotta's *modus operandi* in *Rosa Luxemburg* is similiar to that

25. Von Trotta's portrayal of the socialists' bourgeois taste was entirely in keeping with the self-understanding of the Social Democrats at that time. They did not perceive any contradiction between their bourgeois aspirations and their socialist beliefs. Instead they believed that they were working for a system where all citizens would enjoy such comforts and would partake of "high" culture. Already Lasalle had called for the creation of *Arbeiterbildungszentren* (centers for the education of workers) and part of the the Social Democrats' platform was to encourage everyone to "strive for the pinnacles of culture" ("nach den Gipfeln der Kultur streben"). In a discussion following the prepublic screening of *Rosa Luxemburg* in New York on 15 January 1987, von Trotta alluded to the Social Democrats' cultural imperative and indicated that it had informed her portrayal of them.

of Christa Wolf in her "biography" of the romantic writers Heinrich von Kleist and Karoline von Günderrode, *Kein Ort Nirgends* (*No Place on Earth*, 1979) in several ways.[26] Basing her portrayal of the fictitious encounter between Kleist and Günderrode on carefully researched historical and biographical data, and drawing extensively on authentic quotations from the correspondence of both, Wolf directly incorporated these quotations into her text. Similiarly, von Trotta allows Rosa Luxemburg to speak for herself; the major part of the film's dialogue consists of verbatim quotations from Luxemburg's letters. In addition to her letters to Leo Jogiches, the filmmaker draws heavily on her prison letters to Luise Kautsky and Sonja Liebknecht.[27]

Sometimes Luxemburg's epistolary utterances are identified as such, e.g., the Wronke prison sequences showing Rosa writing to Sonja, accompanied by a voiceover of Barbara Sukowa (the actress whose brilliant performance as Rosa won her accolades from even the film's severest critics).[28] More often these utterances are dramatized: von Trotta uses a quotation from Luxemburg and interpolates the real or imagined response of her addressee,[29] duplicating Wolf's strategies in *No Place on Earth*.

Sometimes an entire scene is constructed around one of Lux-

26. Christa Wolf, *Kein Ort Nirgends* (Darmstadt/Neuwied: Luchterhand, 1979). English version, *No Place on Earth*, trans. Jan van Heurck (New York: Farrar Straus Giroux, 1982). Von Trotta is obviously familiar with Christa Wolf's work. In *Heller Wahn* she has her woman professor of German literature lecture at length on Karoline von Günderrode. She also uses a closeup of a recently reissued volume of Günderrode's works that was selected and edited by Christa Wolf, *Der Schatten eines Traumes* (Darmstadt/Neuwied, 1976). In a conversation in April 1987 with von Trotta's sister-in-law, Barbara Schlöndorff, I was told that von Trotta and Wolf are close friends. According to her, Margarethe von Trotta feels that she and Christa Wolf share similiar politics and are working to achieve common goals.

27. Although Wolf and von Trotta rely heavily on authentic quotations, their technique does not result in what is conventionally understood as "documentary" literature or film. In contrast to so-called "documentary" art forms, both women augment their accounts with fictional constructs.

28. One notable exception is Gertrud Koch, whose acrimonious assessment of Sukowa's acting talents seems gratuitously nasty. "Die Internationale tanzt," *Konkret* 1986, no. 4: 74,76.

29. Von Trotta's reliance on Luxemburg's prison letters is somewhat problematic. As Ettinger has pointed out, Luxemburg assumed many personae in her correspondence from prison. In her letters to Sonja Liebknecht she was wont to play the role of mentor and confidante. Since she considered it her function to bolster Sonja's morale during the war years, her letters may be falsely optimistic; i.e., the writer's awareness of her readers' needs may well have influenced their content (Ettinger, *Rosa Luxemburg: A Life*, 199). Von Trotta, however, uncritically takes over Luxemburg's projected self-image, because it suits her purposes to do so.

emburg's *bon mots*, e.g., the scene in which Rosa and Clara Zetkin arrive late for lunch at the Kautskys. Upon learning the reason for their delay, that they had ventured too close to military artillery practice and could have been killed, the men outdo one another in composing possible suitable eulogies, only to be upstaged by Rosa's remark: "Why not simply – here rest the last two men of the German Social Democracy." A comparison between two ensuing shots, that of the assembled women and that of the men, readily reveals that appreciation of Rosa's wit breaks down along gender lines. The women obviously derive vicarious satisfaction from Rosa's clever turn of phrase, and the men's faces uniformly register dismay at this affront to their masculinity.

In *No Place on Earth* Christa Wolf had stressed those aspects of Günderrode's life that allowed her to foreground issues of gender, refracting her figure through her twentieth-century feminist consciousness. Von Trotta's Rosa is also refracted both through the lens of the 1960s student movement and, even more strongly, through that of post-1968 feminism. The filmmaker interprets Luxemburg's life in a manner commensurate with her own political stance, specifically with a pacifist, ecofeminist perspective.

It is this perspective, I believe, that leads von Trotta to conflate the figures of Rosa's young lover, Costia Zetkin, and Hans Diefenbach, with whom the historical Luxemburg carried on a romantic correspondence from prison in 1917. The historical Costia survived the war; he died in 1980, having outlived Luxemburg by sixty-one years; Diefenbach fell in battle in October 1917. Von Trotta has Costia die in the war, using the melodramatic scene in which Rosa learns of his death as a powerful conveyor of both her own and Luxemburg's antimilitarism. The sequence shows Rosa opening a black-edged envelope that has been delivered by the prison warder along with other mail. A blurred closeup of the obituary, which makes it impossible to decipher the name of the deceased, is followed by a closeup of Costia's photograph on Rosa's desk. Thus although never explicitly stated, viewers are led, through the sequencing of images, to conclude that Costia has died at the front.[30] Precisely those strategies repudiated by formalist critics, (Hollywood-

30. By leaving it to the audience to draw the (inevitable) conclusion that it is Costia who has died, von Trotta presumably can argue that she has not misrepresented the facts.

style) realist strategies that enhance viewer identification with Rosa, make this scene effective. Having been privy to the love scenes between her and Costia, we can readily empathize with her sense of loss. Here, as in the political speech scenes, music is used to heighten the emotional effect.[31] However, the following shots of a sobbing Rosa, lying on her cot, are interspersed with documentary footage showing the carnage of the battlefield, the faces of mourning civilians, and the spectacle of widows receiving awards and condolences from military officials. Von Trotta thus breaks with straightforward illusionistic narrative strategies[32] to show that Rosa's tears are not merely for her lover, but for all the victims of the war.

Her empathy with suffering humanity is reiterated in the scene in which von Trotta, dramatizing a passage from an authentic letter to Sonja Liebknecht, has a helpless Rosa watch as two buffalo pulling a heavy burden are brutally beaten. As we are shown a closeup of Luxemburg with tears in her eyes, the voiceover (Barbara Sukowa) informs us:

> The animals stood perfectly still and the one that was bleeding stared ahead with an expression on its black face like that of a tear-stained child. I stood in front of it and the animal looked at me; tears ran down my face – they were *its* tears. One cannot tremble more painfully for one's most beloved brother than I did in my powerlessness in the face of this quiet suffering. Oh, my poor buffalo, my poor beloved brother, we are both standing here so silently and are joined only in pain, in impotence, in longing.

Here Rosa's empathy with the brutalized buffalo, a symbol of downtrodden humanity, is so complete that the two become identical (she cries its tears). Thus we can understand the psychological basis of her activism: although her situation is different from that of the masses, she totally empathizes and identifies with them and therefore seeks to ameliorate their lot. Taken together, these scenes make clear that Rosa is committed, not

31. Von Trotta's melodramatic use of music in general and in *Rosa Luxemburg* in particular has come under attack. It is true that the filmmaker employs music somewhat heavy-handedly to heighten dramatic tension in *Rosa Luxemburg*, especially in the political speech scenes.

32. The use of documentary footage is not restricted to this scene. Von Trotta later inserts newsreel footage of Berlin at the end of the war and during the *Spartakus* uprising. To what degree these historical shots serve to distance viewers and can be regarded as a break with illusionistic cinema and to what degree they can be regarded as an aestheticization of the historical, used to enhance viewer identification with von Trotta's Rosa, remains to be explored.

only intellectually but also emotionally, to socialist brotherhood.[33] In her refusal to separate the cerebral from the emotional, the heart from the mind, Rosa Luxemburg shares von Trotta's feminist holism.

One can, of course, deplore the film's historical transgressions,[34] and indeed my main caveat is its complete lack of reference to Lenin and the Russian Revolution of 1917. Yet it seems more fruitful to seek possible explanations for these changes than to find fault. The portrait of Rosa Luxemburg that von Trotta paints is that of an ardent pacifist whose commitment to peace arises from her socialism and who strives to realize Marx's vision of international brotherhood by staunchly opposing militarism and nationalism. An indomitable spirit with an unquenchable passion for life, she lives and works for freedom, seeking to help make the masses subjects, rather than objects, of history. But perhaps most significantly, in her desire to develop all aspects of her personality, she symbolizes the quest for human self-actualization of which the early Marx speaks.[35]

She is also presented (and this certainly coincides with the historical Rosa) as someone with a deep-seated, almost pantheistic, reverence for nature and all living things. Indeed, the film contrasts the peace and solace Luxemburg experiences in her communication with nature (birds, plants, her cat Mimi) with the turbulent, often unfulfilling world of politics. At first glance it might appear that in her emphasis on Luxemburg's connection to nature, von Trotta is resorting to a romantic cliché, that reductionist equation of woman with nature so prevalent in portrayals of women by men.[36] But her Rosa is hardly defined solely

33. I use the gender-biased term "brotherhood" consciously here to point to the limitations of both Luxemburg's and a Marxist socialist perspective. For a feminist critique of Marx and revaluation of Luxemburg's thought, see Chrisel Neus, *Die Kopfgeburten der Arbeiterbewegung oder Die Genossin Luxemburg bringt alles durcheinander* (*Headbirths of the Workers' Movement or Comrade Luxemburg Mixes Everything Up*) (Hamburg/Zurich: Rasch und Rühring, 1985).

34. Other noteworthy omissions from von Trotta's account of Luxemburg's life include: the suppression (apart from the brief reference in the opening shots of the film's short written biography of Luxemburg) of Rosa Luxemburg's (albeit assimilated) Jewish background; the exclusion of Luxemburg's university years, which saw the development of her political thought; despite Barbara Sukowa's consistently sustained limp, the failure to deal with Rosa's disability; the omission of the founding of the KPD (German Communist Party).

35. See for example his *Economic and Philosophic Manuscripts of 1844* and, together with Engels, his *Theses on Feuerbach* and *The German Ideology*.

in terms of her relationship to nature; this is only one aspect of her richly complex and contradictory character. In many ways Rosa's respect for nature is an extension of her politics, not the antithesis of them: it is of a piece with her pacifism, her reverence for all forms of life.

Von Trotta thus brings her Rosa into close ideological proximity to contemporary European ecological, antinuclear, and peace movements, to which she is committed. Rosa's perspective is obviously relevant to the ecological/antinuclear critique of technocracy, which argues that, for the sake of humankind's survival, we must abandon our self-destructive desire to master nature and learn to coexist with her, a critique that often meshes with a feminist analysis of patriarchal structures and male dominance. The Social Democrats' complicity in World War I and the inability of socialism to stem the tide of nationalism indicate that precisely such a critique was needed. Perhaps rather than international brotherhood, what was needed was international sisterhood.

Rosa Luxemburg's relationship to the broad-based, grassroots peace movements in both East and West is obvious. In the wake of the missile showdown between the superpowers in Central Europe in the early 1980s, peace movements gained a wide membership in the Federal Republic and the German Democratic Republic, fostering a sense of unity, of common purpose in that divided nation. In that context, a possible explanation for von Trotta's omission of Luxemburg's polemic against Lenin presents itself: she may have chosen to suppress their differences for the sake of the East-West solidarity of the peace movement.[37] In this time xenophobia and re-born nationalisms in the wake of the cold war, we cannot afford to turn a deaf ear to the voice of reason, be it that of Rosa Luxemburg or contemporary peace activists. Rosa Luxemburg's anti-nationalist, anti-war

36. See Silvia Bovenschen, *Die imaginierte Weiblichkeit. Exemplarische Untersuchungen zu kulturgeschichtlichen und literarischen Präsentationsformen des Weiblichen* (Frankfurt/Main: Suhrkamp, 1980) for a discussion of the portrayal of women in literature by men.

37. Ironically, it would ultimately have been more meaningful for East-West solidarity in the peace movement to have addressed the issue of Leninism, since independent peace groups in the East bloc tended to be critical of Soviet and Warsaw Pact behavior much the same way as Western groups were critical of the U.S. and NATO. Presumably von Trotta avoided criticizing Lenin (as Soviet icon) because she thought criticism could have been divisive to the peace move-

speeches still have a distinctly contemporary and urgent ring to them. Does political relevance compensate for a lack of historical accuracy? Perhaps. At any rate, despite certain misgivings, I must applaud von Trotta's undertaking.

Does Margarethe von Trotta see "Red Rosa" through rose-colored glasses? Clearly. *Rosa Luxemburg* is hagiographic: her Rosa is a heroine whom we are meant to admire, a woman whose many personal and political setbacks, indeed even her brutal death, in no way diminish the validity of her struggle, and whose persistence in the face of adversity is exemplary. Originally called *Die heitere Geduld der Rosa Luxemburg* (The Cheerful Patience of Rosa Luxemburg), the film celebrates Luxemburg's resilience, her idealism, and her uncompromising dedication to her beliefs. Just before she is led out of the Eden Hotel, bludgeoned with a rifle butt, shot, and dumped into the canal, Rosa responds to the commanding officer's statement that the right-wing *Freikorps* soldiers are the power in the state and not she "and her pitiful comrades." She tells Officer Papst that history will prove him wrong. It is possible to read this statement as an invocation to viewers to vindicate Rosa's murder by proving her right – after all. It would then be a mandate to us viewers to work to implement the populist democracy in which Rosa Luxemburg so fervently believed and for which she died.

IV. Concluding Remarks

When I went to see *Rosa Luxemburg* I had some sense of the historical figure. Having studied modern German history, I knew that the foundations of the doomed Weimar Republic had been laid on her and Liebknecht's corpses; I recalled the fiasco by which the Republic was called into its stillborn existence; remembered *Spartakus,* the German socialist revolution manqué, easily overcome by the more efficient forces of repression that had been operable in Prussia for so long.

I was unprepared for the strong personal effect von Trotta's Rosa would have on me. Since first seeing the film I have read several biographies of Luxemburg, as well as many of her letters and political writings. The more I read, the more I (re)viewed the film, the more intrigued I became with the ways in which the historical figure meshed with von Trotta's reading of her; even more fascinating were the ways in which she did not. Yet without von Trotta's film, my knowledge of Rosa Luxemburg would have remained schematic. It left enough questions unanswered to impel me to learn more about her. My experience was not unusual: *Rosa Luxemburg* rapidly became von Trotta's most popular film in the United States. It had unusually long runs in New York and San Francisco, and bookstores in both cities had a run on books by and about her.[38] In this country at any rate, people attempted to inform themselves about this important historical figure. By serving as a catalyst for this information gathering, von Trotta's film fulfills the definition of cinema as mass media and is in harmony with Rosa Luxemburg's populist leanings. Perhaps it will also serve as a catalyst for a critical reassessment of the prevalent monolithic and generally perjorative notion of "narrative cinema" and a theoretical rethinking of the value of (at least some types of) identification in cinema.

V. Epilogue

As events during the last few years of the late German Democratic Republic demonstrated, Rosa Luxemburg's legacy is very much alive today. In the context of that government's reprisals against critics of the regime (directed primarily against members of autonomous peace groups), the figure of Rosa Luxemburg came to symbolize resistance to the forces of oppression. On 17 January 1987, the anniversary of Luxemburg's and Liebknecht's deaths, East Berlin police arrested some one hundred demonstrators who had taken part in official commemoration ceremonies. The demonstrators, many of whom wanted to emigrate to the West, used the ceremony to draw attention to their situation and to voice their dissatisfaction with conditions in the GDR. They challenged officials by carrying placards with pictures of Luxemburg and Liebknecht and brandishing banners inscribed with such well-known Luxemburg quotations as "freedom is always exclusively for the one who thinks differently.'" Most of those arrested belonged to the "group for citizens' rights in the GDR," a civil libertarian group dedicated to the dismantling of repressive state controls. While many of those try-

38. Admittedly, my information concerning the demand for books on and by Rosa Luxemburg following screenings of von Trotta's film in New York and San Franciso is anecdotal. In the case of New York, it is based on a conversation with a manager of Barnes and Noble bookstores, who stated that an unprecedented number of these books had been sold. In San Francisco, it is based on my unsuccessful attempts to locate these regularly stocked books in local bookstores.

ing to emigrate were granted visas in the wake of this widely publicized incident, others, like the songwriter Stephan Krawczyl and his wife Freya Klier, wanted to stay in the GDR and work to democratize their country.[39] Unfortunately, Krawczyl and Klier could not stay: faced with the choice of prison or expatriation, they emigrated to West Germany. Doubtless others who share their sentiments remained behind. For these dissident socialists, Rosa Luxemburg became what she once was for the New Left in the West. As the symbol of the road not taken, she has a utopian function: she keeps alive the memory of a more humane future. As the spiritual heirs of Rosa Luxemburg, these citizens of the GDR were living testimony to the truth of her prophecy that the revolution returns again and again in different forms.

39. For a discussion of these events in the former GDR, see "'Laß ihre Politik scheitern'" (Let Their Politics Fail), *Der Spiegel* 5 (1 February 1988): 18–27.

10

Confronting German History: Melodrama, Distantiation, and Women's Discourse in *Germany, Pale Mother*

richard w. mc cormick

The film Germany, Pale Mother *by Helma Sanders-Brahms (1979) has been praised as a feminist confrontation with the most awful period of twentieth-century German history – fascism, World War II, and the war's aftermath – a depiction of that era from a woman's point of view. It has also been attacked as a melodramatic trivialization of that most crucial history. In his discussion of the film, Richard McCormick argues that Sanders-Brahms interrupts the fictional reconstruction of her mother's experience of fascism and the war with various distantiation techniques that relativize the story's melodrama. The film is melodramatic, but Sanders-Brahms has structured her film so that it foregrounds – rather than effaces – both its discursivity and the filmmaker's position of authority in its construction.*

—The Editors

Eva Mattes as Lene and Anna Sanders-Brahms as Anna in Helma Sanders-Brahms's *Germany, Pale Mother*.
(Photo courtesy of New Yorker Films)

I. "Public" and "Private"

"*Germany, Pale Mother* – the title is significant for that whole generation of those who are between thirty and forty, in whose childhood the 'fatherland' was a land of mothers."[1] In his 1981 review, Christian Bauer touched on the relationship between Helma Sanders-Brahms's film and the historical position it articulates: the search for personal identity by members of her generation – a search that eventually involved the need for a dialogue with their parents, most specifically with regard to those questions so long unspoken pertaining to the years of fascism and the war.

The role that fathers played had been at issue in much West German literature in the latter half of the 1970s.[2] As that decade ended and the 1980s began, certain women filmmakers attempted to make films about their mothers and their relationship to their mothers, most notably in films such as *Germany, Pale Mother* (*Deutschland, bleiche Mutter*, 1979) by Helma Sanders-Brahms, Jutta Brückner's *Years of Hunger* (*Hungerjahre*, 1979), Recha Jungmann's *Something Hurts* (*Etwas tut weh* – 1980), and Jeanine Meerapfel's *Malou* (1981).[3]

1. "*Deutschland, bleiche Mutter* – dieser Titel hat Bedeutung für die Generation der heute Dreißig- bis Vierzigjährigen, in deren Kindheit das Vaterland ein Land der Mütter war." Christian Bauer, "Auf der Suche nach verlorenen Müttern," rev. of *Deutschland, bleiche Mutter*, directed by Helma Sanders-Brahms, *Süddeutsche Zeitung*, 3 Jan. 1981.

2. For example: Elisabeth Plessen's *Mitteilungen an den Adel* (1976), Heinrich Wiesner's *Der Riese am Tisch* (1979), Ruth Rehmann's *Der Mann auf der Kanzel* (1979), Siegfried Gauch's *Vaterspuren* (1979), Paul Kersten's *Der alltägliche Tod meines Vaters* (1980), Peter Henisch's *Die kleine Figur meines Vaters* (1980), Brigitte Schwaiger's *Lange Abwesenheit* (1980), Peter Härtling's *Nachgetragene Liebe* (1980), Christoph Meckel's *Suchbild. Über meinen Vater* (1980). For a detailed discussion of this "genre," see Michael Schneider, "Fathers and Sons Retrospectively: The Damaged Relationship between Two Generations," *New German Critique* 31 (1984): 3–51, a translation by Jamie Owen Daniel of "Väter und Söhne, posthum. Das beschädigte Verhältnis zweier Generationen," in his book *Den Kopf verkehrt aufgesetzt* (Darmstadt: Luchterhand, 1981), 8–64; and also Sandra Frieden, *Autobiography: Self Into Form. German Language Autobiographical Writings of the 1970s* (Frankfurt/M.: Lang, 1983).

3. Wolfram Schütte reviews Jungmann's film, Brückner's film, and Sanders-Brahms's film in "Mütter, Töchter, Krieg und Terror," *Frankfurter Rundschau*, 25 Feb. 1980. For other discussions of the topic of daughters vs. mothers in film, see Jan Mouton, "The Absent Mother Makes an Appearance in the Films of West German Women Directors," *Women in German Yearbook* 4 (1988): 69–81; and Eva Hiller, "mütter und töchter: zu 'deutschland, bleiche mutter,' (helma sanders-brahms), 'hungerjahre' (jutta brückner), 'daughter rite' (michelle citron)," *Frauen und Film* 24 (1980): 29–33.

It should also be noted that Peter Handke had dealt with the story of his

Sanders-Brahms's film, in recounting the story of her mother, confronts the issue of fascism and the war in the most direct manner, for the filmmaker chooses to depict her mother's experience of precisely those years. Her mother's attitude toward the National Socialists was hardly supportive, but nonetheless problematic in its "apolitical" indifference to most of what they initiated. The relevance of Sanders-Brahms's project to feminism is evident in its presentation of an aspect of the history of the Second World War so often neglected: a woman's experience.

She does not, however, recount this history by effacing her own interest and place in it for the sake of creating the illusion of "objective" history; she uses her mother's life as the focus of the narrative and foregrounds her own position of authority in reconstructing her mother's story. Sanders-Brahms's investigation of her relationship to her mother – the "dialogue" her narrative voice carries on with her mother's life – openly controls the trajectory of the film. This fusion of a historical and political investigation with an intensely "subjective" exploration of the mother-daughter relationship is exemplary of the feminist attempt to combine the personal and the political, to analyze the political nature of women's experience in the "private" or domestic sphere, and to bring women into "history," the "public" realm traditionally defined by male experience.

Sanders-Brahms explores her mother's "private" experience at its intersection with fascism and the war, and at the same time she edits her film so that the fictional reconstruction of her mother's story confronts the documentary record of the war. She provides documentary evidence of the horrors of the war that the National Socialists had been so eager to start; the impossibility of escaping the havoc they wreaked by withdrawing into a private realm of happiness (the dream of Sanders-Brahms's "apolitical" parents) is also amply demonstrated. Her film thus deals with the intersection of the personal and the political on many levels, reflecting the interests of feminism as well as the program announced by both male and female activists of her generation since the 1960s. It also alludes to the

mother's experiences, including those in the Third Reich, in his book *A Sorrow Beyond Dreams* (*Wunschloses Unglück*) in 1972, considerably before the wave of German books and films about mothers and fathers in the late 1970s and early 1980s.

alliance of feminism and the peace movement that had developed by the beginning of the 1980s, in that it demonstrates the impossibility of trying to separate "women's issues" from other historical and political concerns – above all fascism and militarism. Those phenomena in turn cannot be discussed apart from questions of gendered socialization, as Klaus Theweleit's *Male Fantasies* so ably demonstrates.[4]

As Judith Mayne has written, "Feminist theorists have always stressed that the division of life between the realms of private and public is a false dichotomy."[5] The place of women, according to this dichotomy, is of course the "private," domestic realm, a realm of blissful warmth, free from the evils of politics, which are associated with "public" life. Women are "privileged" by this association with the warmth and intimacy of the home and its attendant "freedom" from politics, and they are indeed responsible for its maintenance, although *authority* for the home does not reside with them. This "privilege" furthermore masks their exclusion from the realm of power, bathing it in a positive light. Fully supportive of such an ideology, the Nationalist Socialists enshrined the place of women in the home. Hitler awarded women on the homefront with medals (the "Mutterkreuz") for having babies just as he rewarded men for their valor on the battlefields; the dichotomy between women's domestic role and men's activity on the fields of history was thus sanctified by the highest authority.[6]

Sanders-Brahms's film does not depict Hans and Lene, the characters representing her parents, as Nazis; the question of

4. Theweleit, *Male Fantasies* (Minneapolis: Univ. of Minnesota Press, 1987), translation by Stephan Conway, et al., of *Männerphantasien* (Frankfurt: Roter Stern, 1977). This two-volume study examines letters by and biographies about German soldiers and members of fascist paramilitary groups. The documents are analyzed in order to determine what images of women are contained therein, and to speculate about the roles these images play in the men's psychological make-up.

5. Judith Mayne, "Female Narration, Women's Cinema: Helke Sander's *The All-Round Reduced Personality – REDUPERS*," *New German Critique* 24–25 (Fall/Winter 1981–82): 160.

6. There is of course a contradiction here: Hitler/Public Power intrudes into the private realm to reward women for "public service," thus in itself undermining and exposing the dichotomy. There are scenes in the film that could be interpreted as alluding to/exposing this contradiction: the montage of the birth with the bombing; the "Silent Night" broadcast "uniting" Hans and Lene. (*Radio* is of course one of the new means by which public power intruded into the private sphere – before the war, anyway – and not just in Germany: Roosevelt's "fireside chats" would be another example.)

their complicity with the regime has rather to do with their acceptance of the public/private dichotomy in its traditional form. Sanders-Brahms writes in her "Exposé with Foreword" that her intention is to address the situation of those oft-neglected people in the Third Reich whose goals had little to do with politics, who wanted "the simple life . . . love, marriage, a child."[7] In other words, people who wanted little to do with the party, people who simply wanted private happiness. In the second sequence of the film, after a political argument between his friend Ulrich, a Nazi, and his socialist supervisor, Hans states that politics do not interest him: "I just want my peace and quiet – and the brunette. . . . The Führer can't have anything against that."[8] Lene, for her part, does not want a man in the party, as she tells her sister Hanne, but not out of any interest in resisting it, as becomes clear soon thereafter. Lene and Hanne hear glass breaking, in what seems to be a reference to *Kristallnacht* (9 November 1938), when Jewish businesses, homes, and synagogues in Germany were attacked by organized mobs. The two young women look out the window and see Rahel Bernstein, a Jewish classmate of theirs, being carried away by men on the street; it is Lene who closes the shutters to the disturbances outside, suggesting to Hanne that they continue their talk about suitable mates.

The illusion that politics and the turbulence of historical forces can simply be shut out, and that Hans will be able to live in peace with his dark-haired sweetheart, is one that is soon shattered in the film. Hans and Lene's domestic bliss is ultimately in the way of the plans of the "Führer"; Hans is drafted and sent to the front. Lene now finds herself alone in the domestic sphere, a poor refuge from the world, since the forces of history continue to intrude into it (she gives birth during an air raid, for instance). Soon her home is literally destroyed, and Lene finds herself in front of a pile of rubble. When, after the war, the traditional domestic sphere is reestablished, there is still no "peace"; Hans's and Lene's experiences have been too diverse, and the order restored in the new society after the war

7. "das einfache Leben . . . Liebe, Ehe, ein Kind." Helma Sanders-Brahms, *Deutschland, bleiche Mutter. Film-Erzählung* (Reinbek bei Hamburg: Rowohlt, 1980), 9.

8. "Mir ist das eigentlich egal. Ich möchte meine Ruhe haben. Und die Schwarze. –Nur leben, verstehst du? Da kann der Führer doch nichts dagegen haben." Sanders-Brahms, *Film-Erzählung*, 30.

makes the home not a refuge but a site of strife.[9] For Lene, at least, it will be as confining as a prison.

The film's narrative can be divided into three parts: Lene's entry into the domestic sphere – her courtship, marriage, and the birth of her daughter; her wanderings with her child in search of food and shelter after her home has been destroyed; and her life after the return of Hans, when the domestic sphere is restored.[10] Once the war has ended, Lene is still active in the world outside the home, negotiating in the black market, helping with other women to rebuild Germany out of the rubble; but when Hans returns from captivity this phase of her life ends. He gets a job, and soon there is a new house for the family, a house where Lene serves him coffee, where his authority over Anna is established, as demonstrated by his insistence that the child write neatly. The strength and the skills Lene had developed outside the domestic sphere while caring for herself and her child now are irrelevant.

It is the image of her face, deformed on one side by paralysis, that she confronts in the mirror in her new home after the war, and this mirror image is the emblem of the last part of the film.[11] In her face is reflected the crippling effects the restoration of the old private sphere has brought with it, in a conservative West German state where experiences of the war and the immediate postwar era are repressed – lessons like the bankruptcy of militarism and the value of women's contribution to survival and reconstruction. Authority is restored within the home as Germany is once again militarized.[12]

9. Sanders-Brahms's voice, in the role of the narrator, states: "That was the return of Biedermeier domesticity. The war began to rage indoors, just when there was peace on the outside." ("Das war die Wiederkehr der Wohnstuben. Da ging der Krieg innen los, als draußen Frieden war.") Sanders-Brahms, *Film-Erzählung*, 113.

10. For this analysis I am indebted to Barbara Kosta's unpublished essay, "*Deutschland, bleiche Mutter*: An addendum to history," Berkeley, Univ. of California, 1983.

11. "She had learned how far her strength could carry her and that she needed nothing but herself and her hope, this child or this man; and now, as this hope became fulfilled, but her strength was no longer needed, she lost her face." ("Sie hatte erfahren, wie weit ihre Kraft reichte, daß sie nichts brauchte als sich selbst und eine Hoffnung, dieses Kind oder dieser Mann, und nun, wo diese Hoffnung sich erfüllte, aber ihre Kraft nicht mehr gebraucht wurde, verlor sie ihr Gesicht.") Sanders-Brahms, *Film-Erzählung*, 10.

12. Cf. Rainer Werner Fassbinder's *Marriage of Maria Braun* (*Die Ehe der Maria Braun*, 1979): Just after the death of her lover, and just before the return of her husband, when Maria will learn that she has been betrayed by the men in her

The division of the narrative into three parts centering on Lene's place inside and outside of the domestic sphere corresponds more or less to the formal composition of the film as well: the beginning and end of the film consist entirely of fictional reenactments of scenes from the life of Sanders-Brahms's mother, but in the middle section of the film, documentary footage of the war and its immediate aftermath intrude into the fiction. It is the war that destroys the illusion of private happiness insulated from politics and history; it is the war that interrupts the private melodrama of Lene and Hans and forces Lene out into the public realm on her own. In that Sanders-Brahms's fiction reenacts her mother's personal experience in the war years, her juxtaposition of that personal story with the "public," documentary record of those years reflects both the intrusion of the historical reality into her mother's life and her entrance into the "public realm" of history.

One of the first sequences in the film where documentary and fictional footage are intercut is the birth sequence. Shots of Lene in labor, Lene in her most "private," most personal pain, are juxtaposed with documentary footage of Allied planes bombing Germany. Not only does the documentary footage of the bombers put Anna's birth into historical context, that birth contextualizes the bombing as well: the experience of women and children was not "separate" from the history of the war. Indeed, in the Second World War, when bombing of civilian populations occurred on a scale unimaginable in previous wars, women and children were in effect conscious targets of military strategy. Sanders-Brahms's fictional sequences of the birth thus give us a mostly unrecorded side of the historical reality of the war, without which, however, much of what is recorded does not make sense: why would non-military targets be bombed if there were no civilian population to terrorize in the midst of its daily life – working, eating, cooking, making love, sleeping, giving birth?

It would seem, in fact, that one of the most important points made by Sanders-Brahms's film is that the "public," historical record must be confronted by the experience of women, which

life – and that the power she thought she had was illusory – the spectator hears on the soundtrack a historical radio broadcast by West Germany's first chancellor, Adenauer. In it he declared that no one could stop West Germany from rearming whenever it liked; earlier in the film one had heard Adenauer in another broadcast made a few years before in which he had promised that West Germany would never rearm.

it has tended to neglect, in order to make sense of both. The most striking of such "confrontations" in the film occurs when the fictional Lene addresses the documentary image of a small boy interviewed in Berlin at the end of the war; the intercutting of fictional and documentary footage is such that the two characters seem to be in dialogue. Beyond the parallels at the level of the narrative between two homeless characters no longer "sheltered" within the domestic sphere, this "dialogue" between the boy and Lene represents as well the project of Sanders-Brahms's film: just as her fictional character, Lene, asks questions of the documentary record of the past, she too is holding a "dialogue" with her mother's past. In the role of the narrator, the filmmaker's voice-over addresses her mother from the beginning of the film: "From you I learned to speak"; "But this is your love story, mother."[13]

She is addressing not merely her mother's experience, but that of many women as well, as her description of the film in her Foreword indicates: "A story, constructed from personal experiences and experiences of many women with whom I have spoken, from whom I have tape-recorded and written testimony."[14] And of course she is not only addressing the past shared by German women, she is holding a dialogue with the collective German past as a whole, as is obvious in her use of Brecht's poem "Germany, Pale Mother" for the title and for the opening sequence of her film. This dialogue with the past is in turn reflected in her aesthetic intervention in history, in her intercutting of the fictional with the documentary. This formal technique achieves a subversion of the dichotomy between personal memory and public record that is similar not only to the project of other filmmakers,[15] but also to one of feminism's main objectives: the undermining of ideological dichotomies.[16]

13. "Von dir habe ich sprechen gelernt"; "Aber dies ist deine Liebesgeschichte, meine Mutter." Sanders-Brahms, *Film-Erzählung,* 112.

14. "Eine Geschichte, konstruiert aus persönlichen Erfahrungen und aus den Erfahrungen vieler Frauen, mit denen ich gesprochen habe, von denen ich Tonbandprotokolle, Aufzeichnungen usw. besitze." Sanders-Brahms, *Film-Erzählung,* 25.

15. To name a few: Alexander Kluge's *The Patriot* (*Die Patriotin,* 1979), Jutta Brückner's *Years of Hunger* (*Hungerjahre,* 1980), Helke Sander's *REDUPERS* (1977), and *The Subjective Factor* (*Der subjektive Faktor,* 1981).

16. Liz Mittman, discussing French feminist theoretician Hélène Cixous, describes the latter's project as a radical undermining of dichotomous thinking: "In her examination of the mythical structures which have supported Western society, she focusses not simply on that which is positioned as Other in the Self-

II. Melodrama and Distantiation

Sanders-Brahms's film has had a controversial reception; many critics – including feminist ones – have attacked it. In a long essay that is exemplary for the concerns it raises, Ellen Seiter criticizes the film for its use of "realist and melodramatic codes." This use, she argues, has the tendency to depoliticize the film: "My concern . . . is with the way that the filmmaker's use of melodramatic codes obscures the ability to read the family narrative in political, rather than pathetic terms."[17] Seiter is certainly right that the film makes use of melodramatic codes; Lene's story is primarily one of suffering, indeed, one of excessive suffering. The question is: is this melodrama the only content of the film? How is the melodrama used, and does its presence "obscure" a political reading of the film?

The problem of melodrama is a thorny one. Seiter's position is an antirealist one, and as such is similar to a left-wing modernism that sees melodrama and realism only as elements of a depoliticized mass culture. The emotionalism of mass culture is opposed to the rationalism of modernist distantiation techniques; a very "modern" dichotomy is at work here. One consequence of this either/or logic is the conflation of melodrama with realism, achieved as the result of the necessity of placing them both on the "mass culture" side of the dichotomy. This is problematic; after all, for many advocates of a politically committed realism, nothing could be less "realistic" (and apolitical) than melodrama. "Antirealists," meanwhile, considering realism inherently bourgeois and depoliticized, have often champi-

---

Other scheme of things, but on the cracks which that split is attempting to hide, on that which threatens stability." Mittman, "History and Subjectivity: Differences in German and French Feminisms" (unpublished essay, Univ. of Minnesota, 1986), 6. This essay was presented at the 1986 conference of Women in Germany, in Portland, Oregon.

17. Ellen Seiter, "Women's History, Women's Melodrama: *Deutschland, bleiche Mutter*," *German Quarterly* 59 (1986): 573. A somwhat similar position is taken by E. Ann Kaplan in her essay, "The Search for the Mother/Land in Sanders-Brahms's Germany, Pale Mother (1980)," in *German Film and Literature: Adaptations and Transformations*, ed. Eric Rentschler (New York: Methuen, 1986), 289–304. Kaplan finds the film insufficiently "non-realist" and essentialist, yet comes to quite different conclusions than Seiter, finding that the "historical address" conducted by the film gets in the way of the exploration of the mother-daughter relationship; Seiter, on the other hand, feels that the latter makes the film problematic precisely because its mystifying and melodramatic qualities obscure the troubling German past in which the film is set.

oned melodrama as politically subversive precisely because its stylization and excess are not "realistic."[18]

The same dichotomy is evident in Christian Metz's short but influential essay "Story/Discourse," which combines a psychoanalytical approach with a valorization of the distantiation techniques Brecht championed in his aesthetic theories. Discussing the traditional "Hollywood film," Metz makes use of the distinction between story (*histoire*) and discourse (*discours*):

> In Emil Benveniste's terms, the traditional film is presented as a story, and not as discourse. And yet it is discourse, if we refer it back to the filmmaker's intentions, the influence he wields over the general public, etc.; but the basic characteristic of this kind of discourse, and the very principle of its effectiveness as discourse, is precisely that it obliterates all traces of the enunciation, and masquerades as story.[19]

The Hollywood film *is* a discourse, designed for a desired reception by a mass audience by various "enunciators" who collaborate in its production, and distributed by a vast and complicated institutional network; but it is a discourse that pretends not to be one, masquerading instead as a "story" as completed – and as invulnerable to intervention or mediation by contemporary human subjects – as "history." As much as possible, evidence of its designed construction is hidden; it must appear to "happen" as though it had no human author, drawing its authority instead from "history," "fate," or "reality." At the same time, it appears to happen *now*, in the present, before the eyes of the spectators, having an aura of immediacy; as Metz writes, this type of fiction presents "the narrated without the narrator, rather like in dreams or phantasy."[20]

The value of the distinction between "story" and "discourse,"

18. See Christine Gledhill, "The Melodramatic Field: An Investigation," in *Home is Where the Heart is: Studies in Melodrama and the Women's Film*, ed. Christine Gledhill (London: BFI, 1987), 5–39, especially 5–13, 28–38. See also Thomas Elsaesser's famous 1972 essay, "Tales of Sound and Fury: Observations on the Family Melodrama," in (e.g.) Gledhill, 43–69.

19. Christian Metz, "Story/Discourse: Notes on Two Kinds of Voyeurisms," in *Movies and Methods, Vol. II: An Anthology*, ed. Bill Nichols (Berkeley: Univ. of California Press, 1985), 544; originally published as "Histoire/Discours," in *Langue, Discours, Société*, ed. Julia Kristeva et al. (Editions du Seuil, 1975). Metz sees the roots of the "Hollywood film," the "traditional film," in the realistic novel of the nineteenth century, which indeed Hollywood's products have replaced (546–47).

20. Metz, "Story/Discourse," 544–45.

as well as its relevance to art in this century, is obvious (as is its proximity to the modernism/mass culture dichotomy, which blurs distinctions between various cinematic forms in its postulation of a monolithic "classical realism"). The "New German Cinema" is often seen as opposing the "classical" (Hollywood) tradition; many of its filmmakers drew on Brecht's concept of distantiation in their resistance to its formal conventions. Women filmmakers often felt an additional antipathy to the conventions of Hollywood filmmaking, seeing its representation of woman as fundamentally patriarchal.[21] Helma Sanders-Brahms, by opening her film with a Brecht poem (read by his daughter, Hanna Hiob), would seem to be aligning her film with the Brechtian tradition, in which through the use of distantiation techniques the audience's attention is drawn to the discursive nature of what it is watching – e.g., that a play or a film is being narrated, and has been constructed by an author within the institutional apparatus of the theater or the cinema.

But the New German Cinema ought not to be confused with the avant-garde: it was for the most part an attempt to create something that would not fit at either pole of the rigid dichotomy between the avant garde and the commercial, something that would, in Fassbinder's words, let the audience "feel and think."[22] Fassbinder's specific contribution to the New German Cinema was the attempt to fuse melodrama with Brechtian distantiation. Nor indeed was Brecht himself totally opposed to narrative realism; his goal was to interrupt, not eliminate all illusion.[23]

21. One need only cite filmmaker/theoretician Laura Mulvey's classic essay, "Visual Pleasure and Narrative Cinema" (1975), in *Film Theory and Criticism*, ed. Gerald Mast and Marshall Cohen, 3rd. ed. (New York: Oxford Univ. Press, 1985), 803–16.

22. See Norbert Sparrow, interviewer. "'*I let the Audience Feel and Think'* – An Interview with Rainer Werner Fassbinder," *Cineaste* 8 (1977): 20–21. See also Thomas Elsaesser, "American Grafitti und Neuer Deutscher Film: Filmemacher zwischen Avantgarde und Postmoderne," in *Postmoderne. Zeichen eines kulturellen Wandels*, ed. Andreas Huyssen and Klaus R. Scherpe (Reinbek: Rowohlt, 1986), 310–12, 315–16.

23. Linda Hutcheon considers this intention of Brecht an anticipation of a "postmodern" strategy, that is, to work "*within* conventions in order to subvert them." *A Poetics of Postmodernism: History, Theory, Fiction* (London: Routledge, 1988), 5, 7. Furthermore, even "undiluted" melodrama has been considered a form that can distance an audience – precisely through its antirealistic excess, which implies the inadequacy of realist representation, as Petro stresses. Patrice Petro, *Joyless Streets: Women and Melodramatic Representation in Weimar Germany* (Princeton: Princeton Univ. Press, 1989), 30; see also the discussion of melodrama, 25–36.

In any case, the melodrama in Sanders-Brahms's film is hardly uninterrupted. There are many elements that distance the audience from unhindered identification with either its melodrama or its creation of an "illusion of the real." An examination of the film's formal structure makes clear how close the film's project is to that of Fassbinder and Brecht, how often the discursive nature of its "story" is foregrounded. It is a politicized melodrama with a feminist agenda. The subjective realm of feelings and relationship is presented, but not in a romanticized way: while the spectator can easily identify with certain characters, s/he is also clearly shown the limits of each character's point of view. Such limitations are foregrounded, as is the constructed nature of the fictional illusion.

The most obvious device for distantiation used by Sanders-Brahms is voice-over narration, a technique that one often finds in the films of Jean-Luc Godard, known since the 1960s for his adaptation of Brecht's theories for the screen. Sanders-Brahms, like Godard, does the voice-over herself, but in a manner drawing much more attention to herself personally; it is no secret that the narrator addresses her parents, nor that Anna represents the filmmaker as a child. Indeed, if one pays attention to the credits at the end of the film, one learns that Anna is played at one point in the film by Anna Sanders-Brahms, Helma's daughter. The autobiographical nature of the film is thus doubly underscored, as Sanders-Brahms tells her mother's story while using her own daughter to represent her part in that story.

Sanders-Brahms's role as the "enunciator" of the film, as the one who constructs it, is therefore foregrounded in a way not evident in other films; consistent with what B. Ruby Rich calls "feminist modernism," the narration is connected to the perspective of a specific human subject rather than a more abstract, depersonalized instance of authority.[24] Beyond the autobiographical aspect of the film, however, Sanders-Brahms's voice-over also foregrounds its role in constructing the discourse, and by this I mean that it literally reveals choices made as to what is shown and what is not shown by the fiction. One of the best examples of this occurs after the newly married Hans and Lene have arrived in their new home. Their tender scene of lovemak-

24. B. Ruby Rich, "She Says, He Says: The Power of the Narrator in Modernist Film Politics," *Discourse* 6 (1983): 44; reprinted in Volume 1 of this collection.

ing, which begins with their gentle attempts to undress each other, is interrupted by the narrator:

> I can't imagine your embrace. I can't imagine how your skin and yours touched. You are my parents. I am between you. I haven't gotten married. That I learned from your example.[25]

Learning that the narrator decided not to marry because of her parents' marriage, the spectator is hindered in the enjoyment of, and identification with, the romance on the screen; this happy couple will obviously not remain so. But not only does the voice-over undercut the mood of the scene, it tells the audience explicitly why only the beginning of the lovemaking is shown, why the filmmaker chooses to direct the scene as she does and cut it when she does.

Another example of distantiation involves the choice of Ernst Jacobi for the role of Hans, who represents the filmmaker's father. Jacobi appears much older than Eve Mattes, and this mismatch in age may distance the spectator further from the romance between Hans and Lene. More significantly, Sanders-Brahms's voice-over alludes to this directly: "You were as young as she, father. But in my memory your face is always as old as it was when you came back from the war."[26] In this instance Sanders-Brahms exposes the rationale for her casting. The fiction is unmistakenly her construct, not a story presenting itself as unmediated reality. It is, as Seiter writes, the "daughter's version of the mother's story," but that fact is never disguised.[27]

The film's use of voice-over thus draws attention to its own existence as a fictive discourse. At the same time, it distances the audience by providing a perspective on the events being narrated separate from that of the main characters. The other major element in the film with a similar function is the documentary footage, which, as discussed above, breaks up the fiction at the same time it contextualizes and is contextualized by it. The illusion of reality in the Hollywood film (a "beautifully closed

25. "Eure Umarmung kann ich mir nicht denken. Wie deine und deine Haut sich berührt, kann ich nicht denken. Ihr seid meine Eltern. Zwischen euch bin ich. Ich habe nicht geheiratet. Das habe ich an euch verlernt." Sanders-Brahms, *Film-Erzählung*, 112.

26. "Du warst so jung wie sie, mein Vater. Aber in meiner Erinnerung ist dein Gesicht immer so alt, wie es war, als du aus dem Krieg kamst, in den sie dich dann schickten." Sanders-Brahms, *Film-Erzählung*, 112.

27. Seiter, "Women's History, Women's Melodrama," 571.

object," as Metz writes)[28] depends in part on its apparent self-sufficiency; in Sanders-Brahms's film the fiction is called into question by the documentary footage that intrudes upon it. Both perspectives, the fictional and the documentary, relativize each other; the voice-over has a similar relationship to both of these visual components of the film.

At some points the voice-over seems to conspire with the fictional narrative, as for example during the period when Lene and Anna are homeless. It seems problematic that this period is presented as being so idyllic, but here it is the documentary footage which provides the corrective: "And so Lene and I loved each other in the bathtub and flew like witches over the roofs."[29] The voice-over here intensifies rather than undercuts the mood created by the shot of Lene and Anna happily playing together in the bathtub (at the apartment of Lene's rich relatives); the objections of some critics that the reality of the war is effaced by a mythologized mother-daughter symbiosis seem warranted.[30] The voice-over here is providing the perspective of the daughter, the way she remembers those times. This perspective is nonetheless immediately undercut by the sequence of documentary footage which follows the voice-over: an aerial shot, taken from a plane flying over Berlin in about 1945, displays for the spectator a historical reality that contradicts the child's idealized memories. "Flying over the roofs," as the child asserts she had done, would have meant flying over miles of bombed buildings, many of which had no roofs, as the spectator can readily ascertain during this silent sequence of eerie footage showing Berlin in ruins (similar to a later sequence of greater length). The spectator is not allowed to participate in the joy shared by the mother and daughter – which is idyllic only in the memory of the child, in any case – without being confronted with visual

28. Metz, "Story/Discourse," 546.

29. "So liebten Lene und ich uns in der Badewanne und flogen wie die Hexen über die Dächer." "Der Text, den ich im Film spreche," Sanders-Brahms, *Film-Erzählung*, 113.

30. This is Seiter's opinion, 570–72; Eva Hiller expresses the same opinion in her article "Mütter und Töchter," *Frauen und Film*, 24 (1980): 30–31. For a similar reading, see also Angelika Bammer, "Through a Daughter's Eyes: Helma Sanders-Brahms' *Germany, Pale Mother*," *New German Critique* 36 (1985): 103–106. Claudia Lenssen alludes to a similar interpretation in her conversation with Helen Fehervary and Judith Mayne, "From Hitler to Hepburn: A Discussion of Women's Film Production and Reception," *New German Critique* 24–25 (Fall/Winter 1981–82): 176.

evidence of how ghastly a world it was that she remembers so selectively.

Besides the use of voice-over and documentary footage, there are many other ways in which Sanders-Brahms attempts to distance the audience from too uncritical an immersion in the melodrama of the narrative. Choice of actors has already been mentioned with regard to Ernst Jacobi; more disorienting for the audience is the use of Eva Mattes in the roles of a Polish peasant and a French partisan whom Hans and his fellow German soldiers execute. The first time Mattes appears playing someone other than Lene, it is especially confusing, since up to this point in the film her identification with the role of Lene has appeared complete, in accordance with the naturalistic acting one expects in conventional films. Precisely because of this, the audience is unsettled. Hans, breaking down and crying over his role in the shooting of the peasants, then explains to his comrades that one of the women looked just like his wife; this explanation only reinforces the rupture of naturalistic codes, for the audience is positive that it is *precisely* the same woman it knows as Lene.

Sanders-Brahms thus makes a statement about war: Hans's role as a soldier includes invading the "domestic sphere" of the enemy, driving out women and children – as his wife and child will be driven from their home – and killing them. Women "just like" his wife are the enemy; women are somehow on "the other side," opposing that for which he must fight. In the case of the French partisan woman, this is even clearer, for she is *actively* opposing his side. The harsh socialization he undergoes as a soldier (he soon looses the sensitivity he displays at his first murder of civilians) plays no small part in the growing distrust he feels for his wife, and later for both wife and child.

Another distantiation technique in the film involves the use of Jürgen Knieper's music on the soundtrack, which often adds a somber, at times dissonant perspective to the narrative. One of the most striking uses of the soundtrack comes very early in the film, when, during the dance at the rowing club where Hans first speaks with Lene, there is no dance music at all; all one can hear are some ominous chords that are obviously non-diegetic. The eeriness of this sequence, in which happy couples dance to music that the spectator cannot hear, as black-uniformed Nazis stroll amidst them, signifies the threat political forces pose for all these normal, private romances.[31]

In addition, there are two major sequences of the film that have distancing functions: the opening poem and the fairy tale, which is narrated in its entirety to Anna by Lene in the middle of the film. The Brecht poem functions appropriately enough like the titles that precede the scenes in almost all of Brecht's plays: the historical and political context of the story about to begin is emphasized. It is not only the story of Lene and Hans; it is the story of Germany. Furthermore, the poem suggests through its use of gender the complex interrelationship between fascism, militarism, and gendered socialization that the film explores: Germany is a mother, despoiled by her sons. The use of the poem does not, however, set up any simplistic allegory in which Lene is to be read simply as Germany; Lene is for one thing portrayed too much like a real human being, and any attempt to interpret the story neatly as an allegory breaks down rather quickly, as Angelika Bammer has noted.[32] Such use of a poem at the beginning of a narrative adds another perspective through which to view the fiction; it is meant to add complexity precisely through the impossibility of any seamless relation to the narrative, precisely because there is a "gap" (*Leerstelle*), in that relation.[33]

31. This is made more explicit through mise-en-scène and editing. The scene opens with an extremely close shot of a huge swastika flag (such that the gnats of the summer night are very evident as they crawl all over it); through editing, shots of the two Nazis in black are alternated with shots of the couples dancing, until finally the two are shown striding through the couples. Sinister political forces penetrate even the locus of romance, where indeed Hans has been asking Lene if joining or remaining outside of the Party will help his chances with her.

32. Bammer, "Through a Daughter's Eyes," 96. Cf. Fassbinder's *Maria Braun* – which Bammer also cites – a more convincing example of the allegorization of a woman character. Kaplan, arguing similarly to Seiter, asserts that the unproblematized use of the allegorical trope (Mother: Germany) used in Brecht's poem is adopted by Sanders-Brahms and not undermined (291). I would argue that the depiction of both Lene's complicity (passive – not helping Rahel – and active – looting Duckstein's) in National Socialist policies (persecution and expropriation of the Jews), and her own victimization by Nazi policies and by the results of those policies (war, bombardment, invasion) places her in *both* roles in Brecht's poem: that of the shamed, victimized mother, and that of the sons who do the victimizing. (See below, note 43, for a more thorough discussion of Lene's complicity.)

33. Cf. Wolfgang Iser's famous essay, "Die Apellstruktur des Textes" (1970), in which he develops his concept of the "Leerstelle," acknowledging the influence of Roman Ingarden. See Iser, "Appellstruktur," in *Rezeptionsästhetik*, ed. Rainer Warning (Munich: Wilhelm Fink, 1975), 235ff. This essay appears in English translation as "Indeterminacy and the Reader's Response in Prose Fiction," in J. Hillis Miller, ed., *Aspects of Narrative* (New York: Columbia Univ. Press, 1971), 1–45.

The fairy tale, "The Robber Bridegroom" ("*Das Räuberbräutigam*"), is described by Sanders-Brahms herself as a deliberate distantiation technique.[34] It interrupts the fiction as would any story-within-a-story, but the interruption is more noticeable because of the way it is narrated. For one thing, it *is* narrated, not enacted; furthermore the text of the tale (as recorded by the Brothers Grimm) is narrated in its entirety by Lene to Anna;[35] the audience may not know this specifically, but it certainly knows that Lene is not speaking her own words. While the audience hears Lene telling the story, it sees the visual settings of her wanderings with Anna – visually, in other words, the main fiction continues, while a different story is heard. This other story, the fairy tale, provides obvious commentary on the visual events, and thus on the main narrative of the film as well.

In the tale, a father unwittingly "gives the hand" of his daughter in marriage to a man who lives in the forest with a band of robbers who capture, hack apart, and eat young, virgin girls. While Lene narrates the tale, what is seen by the spectator? The corpse of a soldier, a smokestack, an oven, documentary footage of a bombed city (Berlin), the rape of Lene by drunken American soldiers: certainly not an inappropriate visual accompaniment to this particular fairy tale, and one that makes clear connections between the tale and the historical situation of the main narrative of the film.

Certain of these connections are quite explicit: for example, when Lene recounts how the robber tells the girl to find his house in the woods – "And so that you shall find the way, I will spread ashes for you"[36] – she and Anna come upon a factory, and the camera pans slowly, ominously up the length of a very tall smokestack; the mention of ashes and the obviously emphasized shot of a smokestack clearly allude to concentration camps, allusions reinforced by the prominent oven door at the base of the furnace once the two enter the factory, combined with Lene's first recitation of the tale's refrain: "Turn back, turn back, young bride, you are in the house of murderers!"[37]

34. Sanders-Brahms, interview in Renate Möhrmann, *Die Frau mit der Kamera* (Munich: Hanser, 1980), 156.

35. See "Das Märchen," in Sanders-Brahms, *Film-Erzählung*, 92–96; see also Sanders-Brahms's remarks on Eva Mattes learning the fairy tale, "Eva und Ursula," in ibid. 124.

36. "Und damit du auch den Weg findest, will ich dir Asche streuen." Sanders-Brahms, *Film-Erzählung*, 93.

37. "Kehr um, kehr um, du junge Braut, du bist in einem Mörderhaus." Sanders-Brahms, *Film-Erzählung*, 93.

This refrain, repeated throughout the tale, stands not only as a warning for the girl in the tale, but also as a warning – admittedly one which comes too late – for Lene, whose story is quite similar, as a woman whom the audience first encounters as a "young bride," a woman who also finds herself in "the house of murderers": Nazi Germany, symbolized visually in the fairy tale sequence by a smokestack and an oven. While the man who marries Lene is not like the men who eat the flesh of young girls in the fairy tale, and is in fact portrayed sympathetically for most of the film, he nonetheless becomes a part of a war machine (against his will, but without his resistance) that does consume people, and indeed spews him out a very different person from the sensitive young man he had been.

The question of gender is obviously one that lurks not far beneath the surface of the fairy tale, which speaks to ancient fears of women in societies where decisions about their bodies and lives are made in dealings between men, dealings in which they have no part. In Lene's experience, the historical forces that determine her life make a soldier of her husband, involving him in a war where he becomes the enemy of women and children; the war creates a situation in which women and children are at the whim of competing armies. Even in the armies who fight to defeat fascism, there are men who act like soldiers in any conquering army – as Lene explains her rape to Anna, "It's the right of the victor, little girl. They take possessions and women."[38] In the fairy-tale sequence, Sanders-Brahms indicts war and the patriarchal types of male socialization upon which it depends, and she demonstrates its consequences for women.

She also suggests a strategy of resistance. The girl in the tale is saved with the help of the old woman, who is apparently a servant of the robbers, but who takes pity on her and reveals to her the true story of the robbers' reign of terror, as it were; then she hides her, and the girl herself sees that the old woman is not lying. Later, the girl is able to see justice done for the crimes against women by telling the story again, cleverly disguising it as a dream until the last moment, when she produces tangible proof – the severed finger of the woman whose murder she witnessed. The girl is saved by the old woman's taking pity on her, but the girl herself exercises a more effective solidarity. She

38. "Das ist das Recht des Siegers, kleines Mädchen. Man nimmt die Sachen und die Frauen." Sanders-Brahms, *Film-Erzählung*, 96.

manages to see that the robbers are stopped from further acts of violence against women, and she does so by telling *publicly* what she has seen.

The emphasis in the tale is on sharing knowledge, on voicing a warning, on telling one's story, and on providing proof: the tale can be read as an appeal to women to share knowledge of their history by recording it and gathering evidence. To take control of one's story, one must put it into words, one must tell it. The young girl in the tale takes control of the horror she has witnessed by telling it again, and through her clever control of the telling of the story, she traps the perpetrator of the horror. Helma Sanders-Brahms cannot claim to have achieved such utopian results by telling the story of her mother's life, but the self-reflexive parallel between the fairy tale and the project of her film is clear.[39]

"My mother. I learned to be silent, you said. From you, I learned to speak."[40] Thus does Sanders-Brahms's voice-over address the first close-up of the character representing her mother. Beyond the obvious meaning of the statement, it can also be read as self-reflexive with regard to the making of the film: the forces of history, operating on many levels (some more, some less "private") have affected Lene's life in such a way that she, like so many women before her, has become silent. But her story is not lost, because her daughter has chosen to articulate it; indeed, Sanders-Brahms "comes to speech" herself in trying to understand her mother's story. Through the telling of the disappointments and horrors that silenced her mother, she gains some control of that part of women's history, and takes a step to insure that its lessons (by no means only for women) are not lost. The story – and the history – she tells represent an active intervention in history, one that has an unhidden agenda for the present: a feminist and a pacifist one.

39. It is for this reason that I disagree with Angelika Bammer's interpretation of the fairy tale sequence as depicting women outside of history and powerless to intervene against the historical evils that affect and victimize them (Bammer, "Through a Daughter's Eyes," 106–108). The young woman in the story intervenes – and has an effect – by telling the story; this must also relate to the film director's telling of the story she chooses. For another interpretation of the fairy-tale sequence, see Barbara Hyams' sensitive, close reading, "Is the Apolitical Woman at Peace?: A Reading of the Fairy Tale in *Germany, Pale Mother, Wide Angle* 10, no. 3 (1988): 41–51.

40. "Meine Mutter. Ich habe schweigen gelernt, sagtest du. Von dir habe ich sprechen gelernt. Muttersprache." Sanders-Brahms, *Film-Erzählung*, 112.

III. Mystification or Trauerarbeit?

The special significance of the discussion of distantiation and melodrama for this film revolves around the following question: does the film's melodrama efface the historical reality of German fascism, anti-semitism, and the war in its idealization of mother-child bonding, as critics like Ellen Seiter have written?[41] Or can it be classified as a *Trauerarbeit,* a "work of mourning" that attempts to come to terms both with Sanders-Brahms's relationship to her mother and with a very dark period of German history as well?[42] In my opinion, the film is a *Trauerarbeit.*

In spite of its focus on the gentile Lene, the film is not silent about the plight of the Jews, and indeed depicts Lene in a decid-

41. "The daughter's version of the mother's story, with its emphasis on the psychological experience of merging and of irrevocable loss, is nowhere more problematic than in this film, where the relationship in its idyllic phase is played out against the background of wartime Germany. The film confines the mother to the realm of the emotional and psychological; her liberation from the domestic sphere only enables her to become a heroic, full time nurturer. . . . This vision of women in war is most troublesome in a film which fails to enact . . . the impact of World War II on women who were *not* middle class, German, unengaged in political resistance, or, I need hardly add, gentile." This is Seiter's formulation of the problems she sees in Sanders-Brahms's film, which in her opinion illustrates "the problem with all forms of feminism which mythologize the mother." Seiter, "Women's History, Women's Melodrama," 571–72. Angelika Bammer comes to similar conclusions, although her evaluation of the film as a whole is less negative than Seiter's. See Bammer, "Through a Daughter's Eyes," 106–109. E. Ann Kaplan, interestingly enough, comes to a somewhat contrary position *vis à vis* the placing of the mother-daughter relationship within the historical context, writing: "What the film needed to foreground . . . is the mechanism whereby patriarchy represses woman's desire for the mother's body" (Kaplan, "Search for the Mother/Land," 302). This argument is based on her assertion that the historical is carried by the unproblematized allegorical dimension throughout the film.

42. Christian Bauer asks: "May this luxurious attempt to come to terms with a childhood be considered also a process of working through collective experience?" ("Darf man diesen luxuriösen Versuch von Kindheitsbewältigung als Aufarbeitung kollektiver Erfahrung ausgeben?") He phrases the question in light of many of the negative reactions the film received in West Germany, but in his article, he concludes that the two projects, the personal and the collective, can coincide. Indeed, he appreciates Sanders-Brahms's openly admitted subjectivity ("eingestandene Subjektivität") (Bauer, rev. of *Deutschland, bleiche Mutter*). In general, however, the reaction to the film was negative, as Seiter reports (Note 9, p. 581), citing Janet Maslin's review, "'Germany, Pale Mother' set in the Nazi era," *New York Times,* 18 March 1984, and *Variety,* 21 March 1984, as examples of the American reception. Olav Münzberg (one of the film's defenders) summarized the reception in West Germany, analyzing it in terms of "defensive reactions" ("Abwehrreaktionen"). See Münzberg, "Schaudern vor der 'bleichen Mutter,'" *Medium* 10 (1980): 34–57. The French reception was much more favorable: the film won first prize at the 1980 Women's Film Festival in Sceaux.

edly unfavorable light in this regard.[43] As I have argued, the complicity of her parents in the crimes of fascism is thematized in the film, as is the fact that they were not engaged in political resistance. Does the film uncritically idealize the mother-child relationship? The time spent together by mother and daughter during the war appears glorified from only two perspectives: that of the child, which is understandable, and that of the grown-up daughter who remembers how active her mother was during the war and how paralyzed she became afterwards.[44] There is no escaping this latter perspective, however; it is a historical reality that, though life was certainly hard toward the end of the war for German women, they played a greater role outside the home than they were to play a few years after the

43. This occurs first when she closes the shutters on what is most likely the rape of Rahel Bernstein. A second instance where the plight of the Jews is thematized is when Lene is embroidering her new blouse to wear for Hans's return on leave. So intent is she on finishing this project with the red thread she had bought at Duckstein's that she listens without comprehending when her sister tells her that the Ducksteins, being Jews, are gone. She goes to their store and finds it boarded up, but an old woman in the building lets her in to rummage through what is left in the store; the red she seeks is not there, but the old woman convinces her to make do with blue, bidding her farewell with a "Heil Hitler!" Lene's exclusive interest in a "private" dream – pleasing Hans – causes her implication in the Nazi expropriation of the Jews. It is on a very small scale perhaps, but her attitude toward their plight has changed from one of unwillingness to help, or even to look, to one of willing readiness to profit actively from it. And here, too, the violence of the society around her is revisited upon her in a small way when the fruit of her plunder, the emboidered blouse, is ripped off of her by her husband, whose attitude toward women and sex is changing even as he tries to resist the socialization toward them typical of the soldier.

44. And these are not the only perspectives that structure the story, for Lene's ambivalence toward her role as mother is certainly depicted. Her difficulty carrying her child and possessions on the bridge into Berlin is clear, as is her exasperation with the child. She agrees with Hans when he tells her that breastfeeding the child is draining her strength; she explains her dancing with the child not as an expression of idyllic happiness, but as a survival mechanism as things get ever worse: "I'm telling you, the worse it gets, the more I sing. And not just for the child. For myself." ("Ich sag dir, je dicker es kommt, um so mehr sing ich mit dem Kind. Nicht mal bloß wegen dem Kind. Für mich selber" – Sanders-Brahms, *Film-Erzählung*, 67.) Her clinging to the child is not merely selfless. Nor is her caring for the child merely shown as emotional, psychological nurturing, with no indication of any other activity. The skills she develops during their wandering have to do with concrete, economic survival: she is willing to take clothing from corpses, she finds shelter for her child, she deals on the black market; she is also seen helping to rebuild the ruined city, in a montage where she and her sister and daughter appear to be helping a large group of *Trümmerfrauen* ("rubble women") passing bricks, a moment captured on some very famous documentary footage.

war. This is a moment in history that Sanders-Brahms's film attempts to explore, and rightly so.

In depicting the "house of murderers," the film suggests that German fascism and the war were related to broader phenomena like militarism and patriarchy. A forgotten part of women's history is depicted, but in so doing, the film does not gloss over the horror of war, nor is it shown as "separate" from the experience of women. On the contrary, it is precisely in the middle of the film, when Lene is surviving outside of the home and traveling with her daughter, that the documentary record confronts the fiction with footage of the results of the fascists' war. This is the proof, as it were, that the horrors of war that shaped her mother's story were real, not a dream. Just as the girl in the fairy tale can disprove her disclaimer – "it was only a dream"[45] – by producing the severed finger of the murdered woman, so Sanders-Brahms produces archival footage that provides "physical proof" of the destruction fascism can cause.[46]

This article is an abridged version of a section in Richard W. McCormick, Politics of the Self: Feminism and the Postmodern in West German Literature and Film. *Copyright © 1991 by Princeton University Press.*

45. "Das träumte mir nur." Sanders-Brahms, *Film-Erzählung*, 96.

46. This interpretation of the severed finger as "physical proof" was first suggested to me in a lecture given by Anton Kaes in his course on New German Cinema at the Univ. of California, Berkeley, in the spring of 1983.

11

The Marriage of Maria Braun: History, Melodrama, Ideology

joyce rheuban

Kathe Geist finds Wenders's women characters to be artificial constructs (see her article in Volume I of Gender and German Cinema*). Similarly, Joyce Rheuban finds the character Maria Braun in Fassbinder's 1979 film to be more a construct than a representation of a "real woman." Rheuban, however, evaluates this positively, interpreting this construct as Fassbinder's critique of traditional gender roles. She analyzes how his film uses melodrama self-consciously, mobilizing and subverting it at the same time with excess, opening space for the political dimension of the film: Fassbinder's revisionist history of the Federal Republic and his attack on patriarchal ideology. Thus we have in* The Marriage of Maria Braun *an ideological depiction of woman that attacks the cinematic and ideological traditions it cites.*
—The Editors

On the train: Volker Spengler as the conductor and Hanna Schygulla as Maria in Rainer Werner Fassbinder's *The Marriage of Maria Braun* (1979).
(Photo Courtesy of New Yorker Films)

I.

With *The Marriage of Maria Braun,* Rainer Werner Fassbinder achieved something he had not accomplished with any previous film – a great success with critics and public, at home as well as abroad. The film opened the 1979 Berlin Film Festival and later that year won the prestigious Federal Film Prize. Within one month of its release, *Maria Braun* had been seen by a half million viewers and had grossed three million marks (over a million dollars). A syndicated article in the *Westfälisches Volksblatt* bore the headline "People Are Coming Back to the Movies for Maria Braun,"[1] and credited Fassbinder's film, along with Volker Schlöndorff's *The Tin Drum,* also released that year, as the first postwar German films to enjoy wide popular success in Germany. With this triumph, Fassbinder for the first time gained full credibility as a commercial force in the German film industry.

In the United States, *Maria Braun* had a similarly enthusiastic reception, both critical and commercial. It was the closing night attraction at the 1979 New York Film Festival and on commercial release played for more than a year at its first-run house. It became the first postwar German film to surpass the one-million dollar mark in U.S. rentals. A full-page ad in *Variety* declared: "Fassbinder has made a lot of movies – now he makes a lot of money."[2] The consequence of this success was that *Maria Braun* (again, together with *The Tin Drum*) opened the American film market to other German films, and introduced *Das Neue Kino* (New German Cinema), heretofore known to a limited number of American *cinéphiles,* to vastly larger numbers of American viewers.

While Fassbinder's success abroad led to some involvement in international productions (*Despair,* for instance, in 1977, and his last film *Querelle,* 1982), his subsequent work remained intensely German – in subject, in script, in locations, and he continued to work with German technical crews and casts. This is not surprising when one considers that from the very beginning, his focus was largely confined to the individual, domestic, and social ills of West German society of his time. If anything, his ambitions and larger budgets with and after *Maria Braun* served to expand his compass with reference to those concerns. Thus, in 1981, he conceived a historical project whose object was to present German history of the last century and to delineate the social and cultural continuities that he believed connected his society with the German past.[3]

1. "Man strömt wieder ins Kino: In die 'Ehe der Maria Braun,'" *Westfälisches Volksblatt* (Paderborn), 10 October 1979.

2. *Variety,* 2 May 1979, 43.

3. *Variety,* 2 September 1981, 32.

For this project, *The Marriage of Maria Braun*, subtitled *BRD* [Bundesrepublik Deutschland (Federal Republic of Germany)] *1*, was a crucial step. Fassbinder would directly link two other films about postwar Germany to *Maria Braun* through their subtitles: *The Longing of Veronika Voss: BRD 2* (1981) and *Lola: BRD 3* (1981). All three films dramatize the conditions of life within the prosperous bourgeois world of postwar Germany and are further linked through their use of the experiences of individual women as the measure of the state of society. In addition, Fassbinder often repeats a motif or an historical reference to reinforce the milieu common to different parts of his trilogy. For example, the same soccer game that we hear over the radio in the last scene of *Maria Braun* is also heard in *Lola*, signifying both the chronological overlapping of the films and the sociohistorical continuity which links their narratives. A fourth film, *Lili Marleen* (1980), though not officially a part of this grouping, nevertheless seems an appropriate "prelude" to the postwar trilogy. It is set during World War II and ends when the war does, thus overlapping with the beginning of *Maria Braun*.

Nor are these Fassbinder's only historical films. Before *Maria Braun*, he made *Bolwieser* (1977) and *Despair*, both set during the Weimar Republic of the 1920s, a period he was to return to for his fourteen-part television adaptation of Alfred Döblin's important novel, *Berlin Alexanderplatz* (1980).[4] A most ambitious historical project was an aborted television series, undertaken in 1976 and based on the Gustav Freytag novel *Debit and Credit (Soll und Haben)*. The series was to trace the history of a family and their business firm from the mid-nineteenth century until the 1930s in order, according to Fassbinder, to "show that National Socialism wasn't an accident but a logical extension of the German bourgeoisie's attitudes, which haven't altered to this day."[5]

Fassbinder's remark indicates the significant links among all these historical films: whatever their period, they dramatize the circumstances and concerns of middle-class life and stress the integral relationship between that life and the course of Ger-

4. Two more films were left uncompleted when Fassbinder died: "Rosa L.," whose subject was Rosa Luxemburg and the German revolution of 1918, and "Hurrah, We're Still Alive," a project based on a best-seller about the German "economic miracle" (the *Wirtschaftswunder* of the 1950s and 1960s).

5. Christian Braad Thomsen, "Five Interviews with Fassbinder," in *Fassbinder*, ed. Tony Rayns (London: British Film Institute, 1980), 95.

man history over the last one hundred years. While Fassbinder was generally regarded by the press and by his fellow Germans as anything but an average middle-class citizen, it was nevertheless as a member of the middle class that he perceived its problems and criticized its values. Like many others of similar disposition, he was convinced that middle-class existence was based on an exploitative capitalist economic structure and an equally exploitative patriarchal social structure. Though such convictions accord, in a general manner, with Marxist social theory, Fassbinder is hardly a simple expounder of political or ideological doctrine. This was true even in his early ventures. He first gained public recognition as an avant-garde artist in the German counterculture of the late 1960s, and his theater work reflected a radical sensibility. His Action Theater troupe was even threatened with the suspension of its license because of the subversive thrust of its productions.

Yet it became clearer and clearer that Fassbinder's importance lay in his paradoxical position vis-à-vis middle-class society. "I'm a German making films for German audiences," he once declared, asserting the persistent aim that drove him to become the most active and prolific filmmaker of his time. His unflagging energy thus pursued a double-edged purpose: to consistently criticize the assumptions and values of the middle class while continually seeking the means to affect and win over that very audience of "average" Germans who were the object of his critisism. A naive aspiration, perhaps, but not a disingenuous one.

We can find the basis of this urgent project in Fassbinder's personal history. Born at the end of World War II, his cultural education reflected a typical bourgeois upbringing. He found the imprint of this upbringing, however vehemently he later repudiated it, to be indelible: "Bourgeois life is what one deals with in one's films . . . you can't crawl out of your own skin."[6] Yet, if Fassbinder could not completely separate himself from his own past, he was able not only to feel the potency of bourgeois values but to sense those values as delusive and ultimately destructive. As a filmmaker, he saw his task to be the awakening of his middle-class audience to the destructive implications of their own unexamined values. By the time he made *Maria*

6. Craig Whitney, "Fassbinder: A New Director Movie Buffs Dote On," *New York Times,* 16 February 1977, sec. C, 17.

Braun, Fassbinder had found the means to engage his audience with such material without openly attacking their values. This development helps to explain the popular success the film enjoyed.

In his exploration of middle-class society, Fassbinder, while never hesitating to denounce patent evils like fascism and racism, concentrated primarily on the underlying "sentimental idealism" that he believed helped to foster such evils. Sentimental idealism can be thought of as a debased version of values associated with nineteenth-century German Romanticism. It includes such vague and unquestioned notions as "the virtue of personal sacrifice," "the ennobling power of love," "freedom of the individual will," along with indulgence in sentiment for its own sake and a belief in the ostensible moral simplicity and heroic glories of a mythicized past. Because these values so pervade German society – and, indeed, middle-class society in general – Fassbinder maintained that in the collective mind of the public they are equated not with a particular ideology, but with universal truth. For him, this assumption is reinforced by the artistic productions of bourgeois culture that continually manifest these values and thus support the foundations of the bourgeois world – capitalism, patriarchy, and economic individualism. Fassbinder sought to encourage audiences conditioned by this culture to recognize that their attitudes, their assumptions, and their aspirations grew directly from this reinforced socialization process, not from any "inherent nature." As he said: "I try to illustrate . . . that we have been led astray by our upbringing and by the society we live in. . . . When I show people, on the screen, the ways that things can go wrong, my aim is to warn them that that's the way things *will* go if they don't change their lives."[7]

Fassbinder wanted his audience to see their own predicament in the dilemma of characters who are misled by sentimental illusions. In his films, characters frequently waste their lives for the sake of a great love (*Maria Braun, The Merchant of Four Seasons, In a Year of Thirteen Moons*), or come to a tragic end when the illusions that nurtured them conflict with their own instincts and the material realities of life in middle-class society (*Effi Briest*). The costs of false idealism emerge again in Fassbinder's last films, those he identifies as part of his historical project. Willie,

7. Thomsen, "Five Interviews with Fassbinder," 93.

the heroine of *Lili Marleen,* and Von Bohm, the naive building commissioner in *Lola,* are, like Maria Braun, victims of their own dreams of romantic fulfillment. Willie's devotion, like Maria's, is betrayed by a conspiracy of men while her other sentimental illusion, that of a glorious show business career in Nazi Germany, goes down with Hitler and the Fatherland. Von Bohm's great love for Lola is betrayed by Lola herself and a cabal of small-town opportunists who symbolize *Wirtschaftswunder* capitalism and culture. The predicament of the characters in *Lola* – the moral confusion, the feeling of a loss of stability and direction, and the search for something to substitute for a discredited idealism – is, in fact, the same predicament experienced by the characters in Fassbinder's contemporary melodramas filmed somewhat earlier in his career (*Why Does Herr R Run Amok?, The Merchant of Four Seasons, Fox and His Friends, Fear of Fear, I Only Want You to Love Me,* among others).

These similarities suggest that Fassbinder's interest in historical context lies less in exploring the distinctive qualities of a particular period than in stressing the continuity between past and present. In this enterprise, Fassbinder was contradicting the commonly accepted view of twentieth-century German history, which defined German life as being marked by a series of significant ruptures, most notably that which occurred in 1945. That year, which saw the nearly total destruction of Germany at the end of World War II, is known as Germany's "*Stunde null*" or "zero hour" – a moment to mark a void or a new beginning. The customary assessment of postwar German history found its "economic miracle" to be a testament to the country's democratic transformation and saw a different society from the one that marched under the banner of Nazism. But Fassbinder transforms the meaning of 1945 by linking it to another date significant for the development of his historical films – 1977, the year that marked the height of the German government's anti-terrorist campaign. The political events of 1977 (the Mogadishu hijacking, the Schleyer kidnapping, the supposed suicide of three imprisoned Baader-Meinhof terrorists) demonstrated for Fassbinder how quickly and with how little resistance what he regarded as fascist oppression could again emerge in Germany. To Fassbinder, "Year Zero" was not the beginning of a new German society, but merely a temporary setback, during which time the old order renewed itself with financial aid and military support from its new American partners before continuing on in the old familiar way.[8]

Thus, Fassbinder sees 1945 as crucial for understanding the 1970s, but also sees the 1970s as crucial to an understanding of 1945. That year can be taken to represent the end of a romantic tradition that had been drained of meaning, partly through cultural exhaustion, and partly through the open acknowledgement of the perversions of the Nazis, who had exploited the vague hallmarks of sentimental idealism for their own ideological purposes. But in Fassbinder's view, it was not until the 1970s that the significance of 1945, the end of such idealism as a viable ideology, could finally be understood. The parents of Fassbinder's generation had been too busy with the war, reconstruction, and the economic miracle to reexamine their beliefs; as a result, the burden of this confrontation with a bankrupt idealism fell on their children. Fassbinder turns to history because the unresolved problems of older generations are still unresolved; through history, he can show his audience how the present status quo came to be.

Since Fassbinder was obviously not primarily interested in recreating earlier decades for their nostalgic appeal, his method of making a "period film" is not the conventional one of invoking historical events (battle scenes, vignettes of important historical figures making momentous decisions, public acts of bravery or treason) to lend credibility to the narrative. In fact, such momentous events are never depicted in a Fassbinder film and are rarely even referred to in a direct way. The most important "historical" event featured in *Maria Braun* (and then only through a radio broadcast) is a soccer game; in *Lili Marleen*, it is Willie's command performance for the Führer.

The catastrophic or triumphant occurrences emphasized in Fassbinder's films are private experiences. (And even these are often presented in terms of a character's reaction to news of an event – Maria is *told* of the pact between Oswald and Hermann – rather than depicting the event itself.) The significant moments

8. Fassbinder observed: "Germany in particular finds itself in a situation in which there is very much that is very reactionary. In other words, I would say that the opportunities that Germany had in 1945, when the war and the Third Reich came to an end, were not taken advantage of. Instead . . . the structures and the values on which this country, now as a democracy, ultimately rests have remained essentially the same." Peter W. Jansen, "Exil würde ich noch nicht sagen," *Cinema* (Zurich) 2 (1978): 12.

for Maria Braun occur in her personal life: the report of Hermann's death, Bill's actual death, the meeting with Oswald, her husband's return. These private events are played out against the background of the war, reconstruction, and growing prosperity. Germany's astonishing economic recovery is evoked through the persistent background sound of a pneumatic drill and through the signs of the Braun family's gradually improving lifestyle – the changes in their clothing and their physical surroundings.

Fassbinder's disregard for the direct representation of public events does not mean that he disregards history; instead he creates a different kind of historical reconstruction, composed as a mosaic of iconic details. In one long tracking shot, Maria and her friend Betti walk through the city streets, talking of their personal lives. But the streets are devastated and the two women are wearing their "Suchschilder" – cardboard signs with a missing husband's or sweetheart's photograph and bold lettering asking for his last known whereabouts. As they walk and talk, a U.S. Army truck rumbles by, and they pass a group of women picking through the rubble – the "women of the ruins" (*Trümmerfrauen*) who, in the absence of men, began the reconstruction of Germany. This densely packed image forcefully provides the historical context, even though it is neither observed nor commented on by the two characters.

Immediately before this shot of Maria and Betti, there is a brief sequence in which two young boys playing in a bomb crater set off firecrackers when a man stops his truck to strip a fence for firewood. The driver ducks, as in a reflex action, then shouts at the boys and drives away. During this entire seemingly inconsequential sequence, the truck radio is heard on the soundtrack: a voice in English from American Armed Forces Radio describes a U.S. proposal to turn Germany into an agrarian breadbasket for Europe. Throughout the film, as here, the ambient sounds from Fassbinder's sound track are as significant as the details of his images in evoking particular moments in German history. In the Braun apartment immediately after the war, the radio is constantly playing in the background, providing the latest pop songs intermingled with the roll call of the names of missing servicemen. In later and more prosperous times, radio broadcasts carry quotations from Chancellor Adenauer's speeches to the Bundestag, the new German parliament, during debates on rearmament. The characters once again do not attend to these voices, not even to register the way Adenauer reverses his position in the course of time. Often in Fassbinder's films, the sights and the sounds that constitute the most recognizable signatures of a period are so familiar to the characters themselves that they go unheeded. In *Maria Braun*, the cumulative force of these details of image and sound give a powerful impression of its being immersed in history. In fact, the film was praised in Germany for its historical accuracy.

Nevertheless, the macrocosmic events of official history – the benchmarks of the transformation of postwar Germany – take place off-screen and have no immediately perceptible impact on the daily lives of Fassbinder's characters. Consider Maria Braun's marriage: she and Hermann continue to live apart under three different political regimes: Nazism, the American occupation, and the Bundesrepublik. Through and despite all this, Maria herself remains faithful to her ideal of one true love. Historical change only serves to heighten our awareness of how things remain the same, both in Maria's own life and, by extension, between the old and the new Germany.

Fassbinder's most emphatic assertion of this continuity is expressed in the final sequence of *Maria Braun*, once again through a radio broadcast that the characters ignore. The voice of sportscaster Herbert Zimmermann is heard counting down the remaining minutes of the 1954 world championship soccer match between West Germany and Hungary. His voice continues throughout the reading of Oswald's will and finally counts down the seconds to the end of the game, an end that coincides with the gas explosion at the end of the film. Even as the explosion blows Maria's house to bits, Zimmermann's voice hysterically proclaims victorious Germany as *Weltmeister*, literally "Master of the World."

II.

Beginning with *The Merchant of Four Seasons* in 1971, Fassbinder learned to control the erratic and eclectic tendencies that basically were the driving forces behind his first eleven films. These works, all made in a period of two years (1969-1970), gave ample expression to his many interests: they reveled in experimental uses of lighting, editing, camerawork, and mise-en-scene, much of it in loving imitation of his favorite Hollywood directors; but at the same time, the very anarchic quality of these films expressed a radical departure from the aims and conventions of Hollywood narrative cinema. However much they satisfied his immediate needs to explore cinema as an alternative form to the theater, the films themselves failed to engage social issues in a manner that could reach beyond the limited audience interested in their idiosyncratic style. As Tony Pipolo has observed, "Clearly, Fassbinder's subsequent desire to reach a large audience necessitated relinquishing such a ['reflexive' avant-garde] posture and the adoption of a mimetic style consistent with the priorities of narrative cinema."[9]

Among the newfound approaches to which Fassbinder adapted his social and historical concerns was the Hollywood "family" or "domestic" melodrama. Through the appeal of this traditionally popular genre, he proposed to place before a much wider audience the analysis of contemporary German society that his earlier films had carried to the restricted public of the art houses. Fassbinder's exploitation of the conventions of melodrama was to serve the ends of his "good myth," a salutary myth which, unlike the others that had molded the national consciousness, would effect a cure rather than spread a disease.[10]

In using the melodrama in this way, he was not breaking entirely new ground. He had already perceived in the melodramas and "women's films" made by Douglas Sirk in Hollywood the possibilities for criticizing the unquestioned values of a middle-class culture within the framework of a popular genre with admitted entertainment aims. In an essay on Sirk's films written in 1971,[11] Fassbinder praised their cinematic qualities and Sirk's uncanny ability to sympathize with his characters while turning the mise-en-scene into social commentary. It was this quality that made him realize the subversive potential in the genre and that it was by no means a capitulation to bourgeois values if one could question and contradict the system on which those values depend.

But since Fassbinder, unlike Sirk (and other American direc-

9. Tony Pipolo, "Bewitched by the Holy Whore," *October* 21 (Summer 1982): 95.

10. Wilfried Wiegand, "Interview with Rainer Werner Fassbinder," in *Fassbinder*, Peter Iden et al., trans. Ruth McCormick (New York: Tanam, 1981), 77.

11. Rainer Werner Fassbinder, "Six Films by Douglas Sirk," trans. Thomas Elsaesser, in *Douglas Sirk*, ed. Laura Mulvey and John Halliday (Edinburgh: Edinburgh Film Festival, 1972).

tors of domestic melodrama like John Stahl and Vincente Minnelli), was not working within the Hollywood studio system and therefore not subject to industry strictures, he was not obliged to resort to the subterfuges made necessary by official and unofficial censorship. And because he was responsible for his own scripts, he was also not bound to "tack on" a superficial happy ending or falsely reassuring resolution to the problems raised in the film. Even Sirk's films often have some version of these conventions in which the death or self-sacrifice of one of the characters leads to a highly emotional cathartic ending that often overwhelms the viewer and displaces his or her attention from the original focus on to an oceanic feeling of redemption (recall, for example, the denouements of *Written on the Wind, The Tarnished Angels, All I Desire, All That Heaven Allows,* and *Imitation of Life*). Fassbinder therefore took some of melodrama's cherished conventions – the predominance of a female protagonist, the obligatory happy ending, the profusion of coincidence – but employed them in his own unique way, opting more for irony and detachment over immersion and catharsis. In accentuating these conventions, his films reveal the potentially subversive dimension of the genre, even in the more pedestrian examples of it that proliferated in Hollywood.

An examination of how these conventions often unwittingly exposed the rifts in social and domestic structures is useful here. For example, the female protagonist of many Hollywood melodramas manages to dominate the narrative by competing successfully, for a time at least, in a male world. Sexual roles are reversed and thereby put into question. Michael Curtiz's *Mildred Pierce* (1945), a film that American critics have compared with *Maria Braun,* serves as an example. When the men in her life prove weak or irresponsible, Mildred is forced to assume the duties of the breadwinner, raises her child alone, and finally becomes a successful businesswoman. (Though in the end, typically, she is punished for her ambitions.) In such family melodramas, the problems and contradictions of middle-class life are central to the plot. The family, most sacred of middle-class institutions, is the locus of the dramatic conflict; the home is not an idealized haven but rather the scene of disharmony. Family members fall victims to emotional isolation, exploitation at each other's hands, and sexual frustration. Their suffering is sublimated into silent despair or violent outburst. And the spectators are encouraged to recognize that the contradictions and defeated aspirations displayed on the screen are in fact their own.

The second of the conventions – the happy ending – offers a resolution that proves far more complex than is immediately apparent and is often disturbingly ambiguous, sometimes even overtly ironic. In the Hollywood domestic melodrama, the happy ending returns the woman to a place, *her* place, from which she can no longer threaten society's sexual equilibrium. But whether the central conflict is truly resolved is open to doubt. The closure – the neat tying of all narrative threads, the explaining away of all aberrations from the "natural" order – leaves unattended those desires that once expressed cannot be unsaid. The effect of an ostensible happy ending that through ambiguity or irony denies satisfactory closure is to leave the spectator with a sense of incompleteness. This dissatisfaction leads the audience to question an ideology that proposes the home as the peaceful retreat of the male worker and the sole workplace appropriate to the ambition of a woman; it also suggests that sexual roles are a product of ideology, not an immutable function of human nature. In Fassbinder's more blatant version of the ambiguous Hollywood ending, the conflict between the individual and bourgeois society often ends with the death of the protagonist. Even where the character survives and becomes reconciled to his or her milieu, the conflict takes its toll in the form of psychosomatic illness, depression, nervous breakdown, or violence against the self and others. However, in Fassbinder, such dire conclusions are not excuses for a sudden upsurge of pathos, or for cathartic resolution, but remain distanced from the viewer in the Brechtian tradition.

A third convention of melodrama – the reliance on coincidence as the basis of plot development – tends to undermine one generally recognized objective of fiction: the suspension of disbelief. The accumulation of coincidence, its outrageous nature, its implausible regularity, has the effect of arousing doubt in the most receptive spectator, thus undermining the simple identification of viewer and protagonist. What the character regards as chance, the viewer may indeed come to regard as the fulfillment of the character's desires. And these desires, however unconscious, are shaped by social reality – a social reality grounded in bourgeois culture. Fassbinder will use the melodramatic devices of coincidence and an ending that denies satisfactory closure to heighten his audience's consciousness of the unseen psychological and ideological forces at work in the story, and, through the story, in their own lives.

III.

The special kind of causality at work in *Maria Braun* can easily be seen even in a skeletal outline of the film's narrative, in which, if we take it at face value, Maria's spectacular rise and fall are brought about by a series of lucky and unlucky coincidences. From the opening sequence depicting Maria's and Hermann's wedding amidst an aerial bombardment, itself an example of melodramatic hyperbole, to their "reunion" in the final sequence, the narrative is dependent at every turn on the fortuitous and the coincidental. At one point, believing Hermann to be dead, Maria has an affair with Bill, a black American soldier, and in the midst of an intimate love-making scene, Hermann suddenly appears. In the confusion, Maria accidentally kills Bill, but Hermann insists on taking the blame and is sent to prison, thereby separating the married couple for the second time. This particular plot contrivance precipitates Maria's subsequent involvement with Oswald and her concomitant rise to prosperity and success. The last scene provides the final twist. After a ten-year absence, Hermann appears unexpectedly at the door of her villa and announces that he has made his fortune in Canada and has returned since now he is a proper husband for her. Coincidentally, on the same day, Maria also receives the executors who have come to read the will of the recently deceased Oswald. The reading reveals that Hermann had agreed to go away and make a new start in life, financed by his rival, so that the ailing Oswald could continue as Maria's sponsor and lover for the remaining years of his life. Shortly after the will is read, Maria lights a match at the gas stove, which she had not completely switched off after lighting a cigarette there some time earlier. In the ensuing explosion both she and Hermann are killed.

This ending seems at first to conform to the familiar modes of melodrama. For example, the reading of a will is a conventional prelude to closure, a way of distributing rewards and of solving economic problems, thereby legitimizing emotional bonds. Oswald's will serves this conventional function, bestowing wealth on the people he values and seemingly guaranteeing their future happiness and security. However, this traditional function of the will is quickly discounted. Hermann and Maria do not react to the disclosure of the will with surprise and elation: he is stolid, since he already knows its contents – it confirms his agreement with Oswald; she is distracted at first and obviously bothered, for through the will she discovers that she has been deluded about the degree of control she assumed she had always had over her own life. Both Maria and Hermann offer to renounce their share of the legacy, a characteristic gesture of sentimental self-sacrifice, yet at the same time, an ironic reminder that they both are now so prosperous that they do not need the money.

This final convergence of events triggers the unexpected and ambiguous conclusion and ultimately inverts the axioms of melodrama on which the film has relied. The "reunion" of the "lovers" does not resolve the various lines of tension as in a conventional melodrama. And the disaster that follows does not merely close the narrative. On the contrary, it reopens the narrative and places under suspicion the mechanics of illusion and sentimental idealism that have motivated the characters' actions and led them to this moment – the very mechanisms, in fact, that traditionally support the established conventions of melodrama itself.

In this crucial final sequence, the revelation of the pact is less important than the revelation that the characters' actions and the final outcome have been brought about not by coincidence but by the psychological forces and ideological factors at work, and often in conflict, throughout the course of the film. It is not by coincidence that Hermann appears at Maria's door immediately after Oswald's death or that the executors of Oswald's estate follow right after him. From this perspective, the characters' conscious and unconscious desires are seen as the causal connections between the day's events. It is also apparent that the behavior of the men has been influenced by the same sentimental idealism that dominated Maria's thoughts and actions. The cruel "twist of fate" that sends Hermann away from Maria again after Bill's death is therefore explained by the fact that Hermann's image of himself as women's protector requires him to take the blame and punishment for his wife's deed. Similarly, his long separation from Maria after prison is a consequence of his belief in an ideal of male self-sufficiency. Hermann can accept money from Oswald, but not from Maria. He accepts Oswald's offer and goes away because he cannot allow himself to be dependent on a woman. The inflated language of Oswald's will in which he justifies buying off Hermann by praising his humility and noble self-sacrifice also suggests that the two men are bound by their common adherence to the ideology expressed in Oswald's sentimental rhetoric.

The understanding between Oswald and Hermann fully revealed through the reading of the will confirms the existence of an underlying value system that permits those generally in charge of that system (in this case the men in Maria's life and the essentially male-dominated culture in which they act) to decide things for those in a subordinate position (in this case Maria, and by extension, the women of that culture); to in fact predetermine a course of events that secretly governs the lives of others and renders their individual ambitions and actions virtually ineffectual. The contents of the will constitute documentary proof of the working of such a system and a palpable example of how embedded the cultural values are, since both Oswald and Hermann have somehow taken the premises of the contract for granted and thus reveal their own subservience to the prevailing ideology and authoritarian value system.

Fassbinder's use of camera movement in the final sequence together with Maria's "suicidal gesture" in leaving the gas burner on prior to the will's revelation are typical strategies through which he undercuts the significance of the will as closure and emphasizes its actual significance to her as proof of something she has feared and resisted throughout the film. The erratically circling camera movement in which Maria's frantic last moments prior to the reading of the will are presented is a translation of her restless energy, using itself up in repetitive, aimless, and agitated movement around the house. In the final moment of recognition Maria clearly sees herself for the first time as an object of exchange between the two men.

If we reexamine Maria's role in the film, we can now clearly see the fatal contradictions on which her life is based and which she has worked so hard throughout the film to deny. We can also see that Fassbinder's characterization of Maria also involves some modifications of domestic melodrama's model of the female protagonist that make it easier for the audience to trace the psychological and ideological forces that have influenced

Maria's fate. In accordance with this model, Maria has always possessed the courage and independence usually associated with male characters. Because of her cleverness and initiative, the Braun family survives the war and flourishes during peacetime. Maria enjoys playing the active male role, not only by being the family provider, but by presenting Hermann with a gift of a checkbook while he sits in prison and by reversing social roles when she asks Bill if he would like to dance. She preserves an emotional control as well, refusing to commit herself fully to Bill or Oswald, and exercising her power over Oswald by establishing that the time he was with her depends entirely on her mood. Maria enjoys the prerogative which, outside melodrama, is usually allowed only to male protagonists, namely the separation of romantic love and sexual satisfaction. It is Maria who tells Oswald that she will sleep with him, but that her true love will always be Hermann, while Oswald must accept the traditionally feminine role of devotion and silent suffering.

However, Maria's pleasure in playing the male role and in succeeding in a man's world is gained by the compromising of her own identity. She has "made it" because she plays by society's rules, and in this society, the rules have been made by men. Maria must sometimes deny her own conscious and unconscious desires, those which are not approved for women in a bourgeois milieu; she must continually justify her ambition and desires with the rationale of "selfless love," openly declaring that whatever she does is for her husband's sake and their future life together. Her insistence on an artificial separation of romantic love and sexual pleasure is therefore a prerequisite to her fulfillment of her sexual needs.

In fact, the way Maria first gains entry into the man's world of money and power is by offering herself as a sexual object. In exchange for sex, Maria not only gets from Bill and the other American soldiers she serves in the bar cigarettes and nylon stockings, she also learns their language. It is her knowledge of English and the aggressive language of men that first impresses Oswald in Maria's handling of a drunken soldier on the train, and these are the very qualities, combined with her sex appeal, that lead to her success in the business world of men as Oswald's private secretary; it is her sex appeal, for instance, that succeeds where the men have failed when she proffers sexual favors to persuade an American businessman to make a crucial deal.

Maria's reward is an important position in Oswald's textile firm and a salary that assures economic security.

In the course of her rise, Maria gradually discovers that, quite beyond any "ideal" or "selfless" goal, she does derive pleasure and satisfaction from her relationship with Oswald and from her newfound authority. But because society does not endorse these as legitimate goals for women, she cannot consciously pursue these desires fully and freely, nor embrace their satisfactions as legitimate rewards. The double standard by which Maria lives eventually begins to take its toll. Her cherished myths – her confidence in her own autonomy and her ideal of selfless romantic love – begin to give way. The rift between her illusions and reality gradually widens under pressure from suppressed inner tensions and growing threats from the world outside. The effect on Maria as these pressures build can be seen in her growing dissatisfaction and frustration. She becomes increasingly irritable, hard to please, and distracted: alternating shouting at her secretary with outbursts of laughter, screaming at a furniture mover, arguing with her mother, absentmindedly putting her purse into a flower vase, then, fatally, leaving the gas burner on after lighting a cigarette.

While Maria clearly suffers from the contradiction and denial that dominate her life, she never confronts this on a conscious level. Nevertheless, Fassbinder has been confronting the audience with it all along through his distinctive adaptations of melodramatic devices and through his mise-en-scène. Fassbinder's goal in general is to make it easier for the audience to see the latent meanings that the prevailing ideology needs to hide. As the discrepancy between the ideal and the real becomes more and more difficult for Maria to reconcile, the audience becomes increasingly aware of the underlying significance not only of Fassbinder's melodramatic devices, but also of his bold camera movements and formal framing strategies, all of which converge in the ending – our sense of discovery coinciding with Maria's – to show how the unconscious mind deals with a contradiction the conscious mind cannot bear.

As the moving camera in the final sequence unmistakably implies, and the reading of the will subsequently confirms, it is not chance or coincidence, but the conflict between cultural and ideological constraints and Maria's unconscious defenses against them that bring about her downfall. In addition to the melodramatic contrivances Fassbinder uses to undermine Maria's sense of controlling her life and actions, the contrivances of Fassbinder's mise-en-scene have similarly prepared the way for Maria's unconscious suicidal gestures (leaving the gas on prior to the disclosure of the pact and, afterwards, going into the bathroom to run water over her wrist) and the explosive ending which results. Generally, Fassbinder's framing of characters in doorways, windows, stairwells, and mirrors is the trademark of his formal style. This detached perspective is manifested in a type of "point of view" shot that is not identified with any particular character, but presents Fassbinder's own insight into the predicament of his middle-class characters. The audience sees what the characters do not see: that they are confined by their everyday, middle-class surroundings, the unsuspecting victims of psychological and social forces that control and condition their behavior. Fassbinder's framing devices and distanced perspective permit the audience to momentarily look in on the action from outside the framework of the narrative, and herein lies the educative function of his mise-en-scène.

For example, though Maria asserts in her first visit to the doctor for a health certificate that she is going to sell beer and not herself, in her next visit to see if she is pregnant, she is conspicuously framed by a doorway that dominates the foreground. Even before this, Maria's figure is enclosed in the silhouetted entrance to a courtyard where she goes to meet the black market dealer, then is seen through the curtained entrance to Bronski's "office" in the bar while she waits to be interviewed by him. During her visits to Hermann, she is seen through prison bars. She is also seen surrounded by an unidentified frame-within-a-frame, which turns out to be the interior of Oswald's car as he watches her one day leaving her apartment to go to the prison. She is often seen tightly framed in the doorway of her own office. Just before the crucial final sequence, there is a shot of Maria with her head down on the kitchen table with a liquor bottle beside her. Prior to this shot, which Fassbinder films from the adjacent living room through the kitchen door, the audience's sympathy has been channelled toward Oswald, who has just died, a slave to his love for Maria. In conferring sympathy on Maria, the shot clearly hints at the reversal that is about to unfold when Oswald's will is read.

Though Fassbinder confirms the film's latent "message" in

the disclosure of the pact and Maria's reaction to it, he never makes it clear to the audience whether Maria's act of lighting the match that sets off the explosion is an accidental or deliberate one. This element of ambiguity was introduced by Fassbinder in the only major modification he made in the plot developed by his screenwriters. (In the screenplay, Maria's and Hermann's deaths are clearly the result of a deliberate act: she drives the car in which they are riding over an embankment.) It is important to Fassbinder that the ending remain ambiguous, not because it makes a difference in the plot or characterization, but because for Fassbinder an unconscious act is as much the result of a specific cause as a conscious one. Maria's act remains ambiguous in order to raise questions in the audience's mind: can it be that a woman would rather kill herself than live with the husband for whom she had waited so long? Is it possible that Maria is not really happy with her new home, her status, the inheritance, and now her beloved husband – the only thing that has been missing from this idyllic picture? Why would a woman do such a thing? These questions encourage the audience's active rethinking of everything that has gone before, a necessary step toward discovery of the message conveyed in Oswald's will: that Maria has been playing a role in someone else's scenario – one composed by the men.

The obvious parallel between Maria and German women of the wartime and postwar period extends this notion to the film's historical context. Fassbinder's comparison suggests that these women, too, were exploited and betrayed by a male conspiracy when, after beginning the reconstruction of Germany in the absence of men, they were put back in their places in the home or returned to unskilled or menial tasks on the soldiers' return. The culture born of the economic miracle is criticized throughout Fassbinder's work. Here, by showing the victories of Maria and the "women of the ruins" to be hollow, he also shows up the hollow victory of the economic miracle, which is parodied in sportscaster Zimmermann's voice hysterically screaming "*Deutschland ist Weltmeister!*" over the image of the smoldering ruins of Maria's new house.

This linking of past and present that is found in all of Fassbinder's historical films is perhaps most boldly and blatantly reasserted in the film's postscript: a montage of portraits, in negative, of the German postwar chancellors from Adenauer to

Helmut Schmidt (but excepting Willy Brandt, whom Fassbinder regarded as a progressive figure). The portrait of Schmidt – chancellor when the film was made – is the film's final image. As it fades from negative to positive, it corresponds to the portrait of Hitler (also nominally a German chancellor) that opens the film and is *followed* by an explosion. Through this circular structure, Fassbinder inscribes in the film the notion of a vicious cycle, thereby asserting another important connection – that between individual and national destiny and the real impact of ideology on individual lives.

12

Marianne Rosenbaum and the Aesthetics of *Angst*

gabriele weinberger

Marianne Rosenbaum's film Peppermint Peace *(completed in 1982, premiered 1983) also focuses on the end of the Second World War and its aftermath. Like many films by West German women filmmakers of the last fifteen years, it is autobiographical, as Gabriele Weinberger explains in her article on the film. Although Rosenbaum's film covers nearly the same history as Fassbinder's* Marriage of Maria Braun *or Sanders-Brahms's* Germany, Pale Mother, *the filmmaker rejects the "New German Cinema" as a model. According to Weinberger, Rosenbaum's work manifests other influences: the Czech "New Wave" and the theories of renegade psychoanalyst Wilhelm Reich. Weinberger also shows how Rosenbaum's feminist and pacifist agenda for the 1980s is clearly evident in her filmic reconstruction of the late 1940s and early 1950s.*
—The Editors

Gerard Samaan as Dr. Klug and Saskia Tyroller-Hauptmann as Marianne in Marianne Rosenbaum's *Peppermint Peace* (1983).
(Photo Courtesy of Nourfilm)

In 1982 Marianne Rosenbaum completed *Peppermint Peace,* her first film, which won five prestigious awards. This autobiographical work expresses the filmmaker's ideas about the destructive character of our socialization and the consequences for modern, patriarchal, Western societies of the limits set by this socialization. Rather than giving an interpretation or analysis of the film, I shall discuss the director's personal and professional background in regards to these ideas and the way in which they inform the work.

Peppermint Peace is the portrayal of a little girl's experience of war and peace. The time is World War II, and the opening scene shows her father's farewell on a train going to the Eastern front, leaving her behind with her mother and grandmother. After the war, the three women (re)join the father in Southern Germany. Using a stream-of-consciousness technique, the film represents the child's understanding of the world through her personal experience and the ways she internalizes the fear of war prevalent in West German society during the Cold War.

Since *Peppermint Peace* is an autobiographical work, many motifs in the film are drawn from important events in the director's life, starting with her family's move from her native Bohemia (in Czechoslovakia) to the Dresden area and later Southeastern Bavaria. As a child she experienced this odyssey as a "deportation" necessitated by the political situation that forced her parents to relocate. This impression, and her mother's consideration of the loss of her country as suffering caused by politics, shaped the reproach with which she countered the father's heroic and self-pitying stories of the war in the postwar years. They also inform the film scenes of the women's flight and the one scene in their postwar home that accentuates the fundamentally different way in which men and women existentially experienced the war and the way in which they came to terms with those experiences. In this regard, the grandmother plays a very important role, both in the filmmaker's life and in the work, as she adds the dimension of yet another generation that has already seen World War I and was not influenced by the fascist propaganda in her formative years. The grandmother in the film represents this kind of person who has wisdom, but chooses isolation over power:

> My Grandmother was different. I think she understood more; however, she was not a real feminist, but rather hated men. She felt that everything male was terrible, and that's why she didn't like the Führer and the army. She never went to church, and she fought hierarchies like crazy, because she regarded herself as the Pope.[1]

The most important person in her family, however, is the father, which is reflected in his crucial function in the film, almost unaltered from her real father, who as an artistically inclined teacher for the hearing-impaired retreated to his music and drawing when the political scene became unbearable. Brought up with his humanistic ideals and this tendency to escape into the ivory tower, the filmmaker followed in her father's footsteps and studied art at the Art Academy in Munich. After her graduation from the Academy, she received a stipend to spend two years at the Villa Massimo in Rome. This stay proved fruitful and decisive in various ways. Italian culture in general and the political climate in particular influenced her greatly. She was used to the deep-seated fears in German families – when she asked her father "what did you do against it?" he couldn't answer anything but: "We couldn't do anything against it. We were so alone. If I had done something my neighbor would have told the police."[2] Now Rosenbaum gained first hand insights into Italian versus German political courage:

> I lived in Italy for two years and was confronted with Italian reality, including the Resistenza. That was in the years 1965–67. For the Italians it's so natural! I lived in the house of an old woman who rented out rooms, lots of them; there were ten or twelve rooms like in Fellini's *Roma.* For this woman it was natural to take to the streets in 1944 when Mussolini was overthrown. They weren't so afraid.[3]

This experience of a different cultural and political atmosphere influenced Rosenbaum's painting – a medium which in the long run could not satisfy her:

---

1. Interview with Marianne Rosenbaum, conducted by Gabriele Weinberger in Munich, November 1985. "Meine Großmutter war anders. Ich glaub die hat schon mehr durchgeblickt, aber die war keine richtige Feministin, sondern die hat Männer gehaßt. Alles was mit Männern zu tun hat war für sie schlimm, und deswegen hat sie den Führer nicht mögen und die Armee nicht mögen, ist sie nie in die Kirche gegangen und hat Hierarchien wahnsinnig bekämpft, weil sie sich eigentlich als den Papst gesehen hat."

2. Ibid.

3. Ibid. "Dann hab ich in Italien zwei Jahre gelebt und bin auch mit der italienischen Realität konfrontiert worden, auch mit der Resistenza. Das war 1965–67. Diese Selbstverständlichkeit der Italiener! Ich hab da bei einer alten Frau gewohnt, die ganz viele Zimmer vermietet hat, eine 10 oder 12 Zimmerwohnung, so ähnlich wie bei Fellini in *Roma,* und für diese Frau war es selbstverständlich, daß sie beim Mussolini-Sturz, ich glaub 1944, alle auf die Straße gegangen sind. Und da gabs nicht diese Angst, während wenn ich meinen Vater gefragt hab 'was habt ihr dagegen gemacht?', dann konnte er immer nur sagen 'Wir haben nichts dagegen machen können. Wir waren alle so einsam. Hätte ich was gemacht, hätte mich mein Nachbar verraten.''

> I extracted the verbality out of my pictures and ran it through the typewriter, recorded texts on tape and analyzed the sounds of my environment and searched for the colors in the voices. I wrote poems and tried to put experiences into parables. When I wrote I wrote in pictures and I was longing for motives that could be visually captured.[4]

Most important for her artistic development was the inspiration that she received from the cinema. From her solitary retreat in the mountains (a chalet that belonged to the Villa Massimo) she returned to Rome, where she started to "watch films systematically."[5] It was at that time that a Czechoslovakian film delegation visited Rome. She got to know the filmmakers and their works. This encounter not only mobilized her cinematic ambitions but also took her back to her origin. In 1967, she was invited to Prague and went to study at the Prague Film Academy for five years with the "enemy." About these years she says:

> I went there, too, because I had to deal with a lot of things from my childhood. Also this "enemy in the east" and the different system were extremely important for me. Those five years were incredibly intensive. Partly because there were so many political events taking place there at the time. It was like three new lives, and I learned a lot.[6]

Upon graduation from the Prague Film Academy in 1972, she returned to Germany and started out with small productions. Later she made an award-winning children's program for German television together with her husband Gerard Samaan. They collaborated on other projects, and she taught at the Film Academy in Munich. Marianne started to work on the book *Peppermint Peace* following the birth of her daughter in 1975. After having missed a few deadlines for the annual Frankfurt Book Fair, she did not want to postpone the project any longer and started work on the film script for *Peppermint Peace* in 1978.

4. Ibid. "Ich holte Verbales aus meinen Bildern und ließ es durch die Schreibmaschine, sprach Texte auf Tonband und analysierte die Geräusche und Töne meiner Umgebung, suchte die Farben in den Stimmen. Ich schrieb Gedichte und versuchte Erlebnisse in Parabeln zu ordnen. Wenn ich schrieb, schrieb ich bildhaft und hatte Sehnsucht nach optisch erfaßbaren Motiven."

5. Ralph Schenk, "Zwischen Tag und Traum," *Film und Fernsehen* 13 (1985): 38.

6. Ibid. "Ich bin da auch hingegangen, weil ich da einiges aufzuarbeiten hatte aus meiner Kindheit. Auch dieser Feind im Osten und das andere System, das war unwahrscheinlich wichtig für mich. Das waren ungeheuer intensive fünf Jahre . . . Dann waren dort auch noch so viele politische Veränderungen in der Zeit. Das war wirklich wie drei neue Leben und ich hab sehr viel dort gelernt."

Unlike Helma Sanders-Brahms' *Germany, Pale Mother*, which focuses on the mother and questions of motherhood, the film *Peppermint Peace* presents history exclusively from the conceptual and visual perspective of a little girl. This choice of perspective and its particular realization is not necessitated by the autobiographical approach, as *Germany, Pale Mother* and Jutta Brückner's film *Years of Hunger* illustrate. Whereas Sanders-Brahms' film revolves around the notion of individual suffering, personified in the mother, Rosenbaum's film lacks this dimension. The reason for this is her specific concept of history: while her parents had accepted both the war and the suffering it brought about as fateful and fighting as an inherent part of a human nature not much different from animals, Rosenbaum refused to believe that wars just happen to nations and insisted on asking why they are started by people. Her later reading of Marx, Freud, and Reich confirmed her suspicions about social causes and provided her with a critical framework. Her views of society revolve mostly around the power structures in patriarchal society (the notion of "power over," i.e., the patriarchal impulse of domination, as opposed by the positive constructive energies of an individual, her subjective power to make things happen in a cooperative or solitary effort, but without gaining power over another being, dominating him/her) and the role that suffering plays in this system.

As a child Marianne Rosenbaum was confronted with fear: her own, which resulted from personal losses, and the fear of loss that was an integral part of the society around her (the purposely instilled political fear of a revengeful attack by the Russians, during the Cold War.) At a very young age she experienced the existential threat of *nonbeing*[7] as people whom she loved simply disappeared: first her tender, loving, nurturing father (who had taken the place of the sick mother), then others like the family doctor – in the film, Dr. Klug. As the director grew up, she had to deal with her partly irrational, partly empirically based fear that every time she loved someone this person would disappear or die.

Another source of fear was the threat to her own existence, i.e., the threat of war. This very real threat in her early childhood was perpetuated after the war by the hostile atmosphere

7. Rollo May, *The Meaning of Anxiety* (New York: Norton, 1977), 14. This threat is described by Paul Tillich as the cause of anxiety in religion.

of the Cold War and the effects that fear of military retaliation by the Russians produced in the German population. As a scene in *Peppermint Peace* demonstrates, the Catholic Church, in its explicitly political preaching, activated the people's fears and used them for its purposes.

In Bavaria irrational fears were supported by the predictions of Mühlhiasl, an early nineteenth-century Lower Bavarian soothsayer, whose prophecies had and still have a significant influence on the rural population.[8] When the film director was a little girl, ice had destroyed the bridge over the Danube. People remembered one of Mühlhiasl's prophecies and interpreted it: "When the bridge over the Danube is completed, the war begins."[9] When the new bridge was finished, people were intensely scared that the war would begin *because* the bridge was ready. When Rosenbaum returned recently to her home town, people referred to another one of the soothsayer's warnings: "When the roads have been built, the Russians will come and then World War III will start." Since the *Autobahn* was being built in this area during the early 1908s, those fears were very topical. At the time Rosenbaum worked on her film, a new edition of Mühlhiasl's prophecies was published. In 1985 the filmmaker commented:

> This "happened" to take place at a time when a new atmosphere of fear was being built up, when the communists and the east were again being affirmed as the enemy in the FRG. That had first been the case from 1946 to 1948 during the Cold War and now again, during the last few years, just before the deployment of the Pershing II missiles. The good American weapons arrived, which "protect" us. Otherwise they would not have been necessary. During the administration of the Social Democratic Party the communist scare was put into perspective. There were talks, negotiations, even commercial dealings. The new Christian Democratic administration and the necessity that the U.S.A. finance its weapons industry with our money made it necessary here to create the fear that we need missiles. Following that, irrational thinking was widely encouraged. Madame Teissier suddenly got TV coverage, Nostradamus was discussed, the apocalypse was anticipated for 1982, and everybody was

8. Mühlhiasl, Mathias Lang from Apoig, who worked at the nearby mill that was part of the Windberg monastery. He lived from 1758 to 1825.

9. Quoted in Wolfgang Johannes Bekh, *Das dritte Weltgeschehen: bayerische Hellseher schauen in die Zukunft* (Pfaffenhofen: Ludwig Verlag, 1980), 41 as: "'Wenn sie in Straubing über die Donau die große Brücke bauen, so wird sie fertig, aber nimmer ganz; dann geht's los.'" Die Donaubrücke in Straubing war im September 1939 fertig bis auf die Betondecke."

> shaking with fear. In the fall of 1982 the missile deployment was ratified. If one hears all this as separate facts, it would not look suspect . . . but it happened in 1948 and now again. There is a method behind this.[10]

An integral part of the prophecies of Mühlhiasl are male-chauvinistic scare tactics, implying that women who try to be like men would be to blame for the biggest war ever. From Mühlhiasl's days on this prediction has served as a perfect instrument to keep women in their traditional role. In *Peppermint Peace* the blind veteran uses it knowing that it is a powerful tool to regain control over women who during the war had experienced that they could hold their own, and who had in fact often been doing better without their men around. Fear and regression on the part of women are reactions to such scares. One such regression manifests itself in the film in Marianne's turn to the Virgin Mary as a role model. Marianne is so scared by the prophecy that she angrily tears off her tie (symbol of an attempt at emancipation) and prays to the Virgin Mary. The prophecies related by the veteran are followed by Marianne's fantasies prompted by fear and intimidation: the pure woman, first as the bridesmaid in white and then in the role of the Virgin Mary. The emancipation from patriarchal oppression is successfully blocked by patriarchal mechanisms implemented by the church.

Wilhelm Reich has pointed out the important role of the Virgin Mary cult in the church's attempt to suppress sexuality through the fetish of purity and sanctity.[11] The filmmaker not

10. Interview (by Gabriele Weinberger). "Das ist 'zufälligerweise' in der Zeit geschehen, wo in der BRD neue Atmosphäre der Angst aufgebaut wurde, die Kommunisten und der Osten als neues Feindbild aufgebaut wurden. Das war erst 1946 bis 48 im kalten Krieg und jetzt wieder in den letzten Jahren, kurz bevor stationiert wurde. Dann sind wieder die guten amerikanischen Raketen gekommen, die uns beschützen. Sonst wär ja keine Notwendigkeit für sie dagewesen. In der SPD Regierungszeit wurde das Feindbild Kommunist relativiert. Man sprach miteinander, verhandelte, machte Geschäfte. Mit der neuen CDU Regierung, mit der Notwendigkeit, daß die USA ihre Rüstungsindustrie mit unseren Geldern finanzieren muß, mußte hier wieder die Angst hergestellt werden: 'Wir brauchen die Raketen.' Darauf wurde wieder auf breiter Ebene Irrationales verbreitet. Madame Teissier trat plötzlich im Fernsehen auf, man hat über Nostradamus gesprochen, das Ende der Welt war für 1982 festgelegt und alle haben dahingezittert. Im Herbst 1982 wurden dann die Raketenstationierungen beschlossen. Wenn man das getrennt voneinander hört . . . aber es ist 1948 passiert und jetzt wieder. Es ist ein System dahinter."

11. Wilhelm Reich, *Mass Psychology of Fascism* (New York: Orgone Institute Press, 1946), 140–43.

only represents the impact of these patriarchal ideals and negative feminine role models on Marianne, but at the same time she has the little girl act out her own criticism of the patriarchal order: despite the threat of becoming like a man, Marianne's version of the Virgin Mary defies the image of the passive, suffering Mary invented by the Catholic Church. The seven sorrows (or dolors) of Catholic dogma, which are represented in religious images as knives thrust into Mary's heart, become in Marianne's imagination "seven swords" with which she can counter wrongdoing. Desperate in her fearful nightmares, she has the courage to fight the aggressions of the men's world – the atomic bomb dropped by the Americans, the patriarchal voice from the radio (*Volksempfänger*), etc. Instead of accepting Jesus' suffering, Marianne's Virgin Mary takes care of his wounds. In the representation on screen, Marianne's fantasy world and her actions are not two disparate entities but blend into each other, as is typical of children. The child Marianne rejects the most crucial element in the Catholic dogma: the concept of suffering. To the great dismay of the priest, she believes in the ideal of a strong, loving, and caring mother who takes Christ from the cross and soothes his pain. In her dreams, Marianne plays the role of the strong heroine who has the courage her to carry out her conviction that the suffering must end by dismantling the crucifixes in the cemetery.

Marianne's "activist" version of the Virgin shows the danger of accepting the traditional feminine role models dictated by patriarchal culture under the illusion of retrieving their original character. Marianne's belief in an idealized Virgin Mary nevertheless causes her to fall prey to the deception of the pure woman as a better being. The church's dogma of sexuality as the downfall of humanity has been completely internalized by her.

In Rosenbaum's film, sexuality, as perceived by children, is central, since the filmmaker, influenced by Reich's writings (especially *Mass Psychology of Fascism* and *The Function of the Orgasm*[12]), believes that the economy of the body plays the decisive role in patriarchal political power structures: "The core of the cultural politics of political reaction is the sexual question."[13] Reich's theory of the social function of sexual repres-

12. Wilhelm Reich, *Mass Psychology* and *The Function of the Orgasm* (New York: Orgone Institute Press, 1942).

13. Wilhelm Reich, *Mass Psychology*, 96.

sion and, moreover, his analysis of the anchoring of religion by means of sexual fear, provides a useful model for understanding the fear Rosenbaum experienced in her environment, given the particularly German patriarchal structure in which she grew up and the interest that the Catholic Church had in the nurturing of these fears. As Wilhelm Reich put it:

> The function which religion gradually assumes, that of maintaining renunciation and submission to authority, is secondary. It can build on a solid basis: the structure of the patriarchal individual as it is molded by sexual suppression. The source of religiosity and the core of any religious dogma formation is the negation of sexual pleasure.[14]

The protagonist's sexual repression in the film and the theme of the Virgin Mary cult are visual representations of Reich's insights. As an example of anchoring of religion through sexual fear, Reich quotes a case study of a little girl who replaces masturbation with an obsessive praying habit. The film puts into vivid images Reich's following claim:

> The prohibition of masturbation would remain ineffective were it not supported by the idea that God sees everything, that, consequently, one has to be "good" even when the parents are not around.[15]

This is represented in the film through an awe-inspiring demonstration (given as part of the children's religious instruction) of God's omnipresence and the "fact that He sees everything."

Marianne and her friends visually exhibit their initial innocent state of mind through nakedness and tender touching, which is associated with peace. The taboo of one's own body as the first primordial enemy is established in their lives. With Reich, Rosenbaum is saying that in order to establish the notion of outside enemies, the basic psychological structure has to be prepared by the notion of the enemy within yourself: your sexuality. The film very perceptively integrates the Church's openly dogmatic and restrictive strategies to keep the children in check and fearful of pleasure. It stresses dramatically in religious instruction that the sixth commandment is one of the mortal sins, which makes Marianne fear that Mr. Frieden (Mr. "Peace,"

14. Ibid., 130.
15. Ibid., 131.

the young American soldier in the film played by Peter Fonda) will be dead suddenly, imagining him as she had seen the victims of air raids. Her deduction becomes visible for seconds in the images of the victims and of the GI and his lover. *Peppermint Peace* also shows the very subtle ways in which the children are steered away from their sexuality: when Marianne is curious and delighted by Mr. Frieden's play with his lover Nilla down by the river, her mother tries to replace her interest in sex with food, offering her a sandwich. The family's inability to face its members' emotional needs, and its replacement of such needs with the fulfillment of other basic physical needs, like the need for food, were typical phenomena in the later postwar years in West Germany during the Adenauer era.[16]

The children's anxiety caused by repression is eventually reflected in their altered behavior: they do not dare to play naked anymore, their bodies do not move freely. Anything pleasurable, such as chewing gum, hopping on the sofa, or riding in Mr. Frieden's car and watching him kiss Nilla, is associated with guilt and causes the need for redeeming religious rituals: the worshipping of relics, staging of biblical scenes, and confession. Rather than being simply performed, these rites are, however, at the same time criticized in various ways: the children's worshipping the artificial limb of a veteran on one level indicates their lack of understanding and on another level criticizes the worshipping of relics as arbitrary and fake. At the same time it is a comment on the state's hypocrisy toward disabled veterans. In the staging of the biblical play, physical involvement and identification disturb their concentration while performing and indicate the interference of personal emotional factors in seemingly unrelated activities. The children's physical experiences overpower the spiritual experience that the priest hopes to convey. Finally, in one of Marianne's dream sequences, confession is depicted as an open lie. The priest is aware of politically opportunistic manipulations. In all these cases the director demonstrates that everyday reality and needs interfere and defeat the purpose and impact of the religious ritual.

The representation of anxiety through the body leads to the question of Marianne Rosenbaum's aesthetic. Whereas the New German Cinema impressed her as boring – she once compared

16. See Jutta Brückner's film *Years of Hunger.*

the new films to "slide lectures with sound recording"[17] – three or four films have left an exceedingly strong impression on her (one was Alain Resnais's film *Night and Fog*). Her own films, however, were most influenced by the films of the Czech new wave, for which she had a predilection, notably the films of Jan Nemec and Vera Chytilová. In its attempt to construct an artificial reality, Chytilová's film *Daisies* provided a significant model for Rosenbaum. *Daisies* utilizes sophisticated editing of motion filmed at an unreal speed, superimposition, and optical printing, frame tinting, and the combining of black and white and color. Rosenbaum uses such techniques in her dream and fantasy images. These aesthetic strategies and Rosenbaum's point-of-view technique (which almost always follows the perspective of the child) make for the particular visual quality of *Peppermint Peace* and give a kind of authenticity to the representation of the little girl's perception. Images that thematically follow the often surprising combinatory pattern of a child's mind are shot at camera angles that characterize the child's ability to see and comprehend, her "close-up perspective and her sharp focus" (camera angles mostly upward or downward from a child's height but usually not level with the perspective of a grown-up). The logic of this film is that of a child. The film director comments on this point:

> My film's logic is emotion, towards which you must open yourself. . . . Through emotional associations the meaning is carried on. . . . Dreams are as important as everyday reality . . . they transcend the present. That is the reason for their presentation in color.[18]

Much of the protagonist's insight and psychological reaction to events are expressed in her dreams and through the visualization of stream of consciousness. These "unreal" scenes, however, take on a much more important role in this film about a little girl than would be the case for an adult, because for children the dream world is not yet separated and relegated to a lower order. In fact, these "unreal" scenes represent a higher order

17. Interview by Bion Steinborn and Carola Hilmes, "'Frieden' hat für uns Deutsche einen amerikanischen Geschmack. Reihe: Der unbekannte deutsche Film." *Filmfaust* 39 (1984), 30.

18. Interview (by Gabriele Weinberger). "Die Logik in meinem Film ist das Gefühl, auf das man sich einlassen muß. . . . Über Assoziationen wird der Inhalt weitergetragen. . . Meine Träume sind ebenso wichtig wie die Realität des Tages . . . sie sind überzeitlich. Das ist der Grund für ihre farbliche Darstellung."

since they constitute to a great extent what Rosenbaum terms emblem, rather than the mere likeness of reality. For realism in film, according to Rosenbaum's definition,[19] all characters in the film have to be emblematic figures, i.e., figures made up of a plurality of impressions and facets on various levels, rather than one-dimensional representations of their function.

Having been brought up with the traditional humanistic ideal of art and politics being one, Marianne Rosenbaum's aesthetic cannot be separated from her political position. The film developed from her conviction that patriarchal structures are inherently fascist structures, according to Reich's definition and according to the new French theories of Fascism by Foucault et al., which Andre Glucksmann summarizes:

> Fascism is not brought about by a coup – because it doesn't spring into existence, it is already there; it is not launched into the present imperialist society; even if it does not govern totally, it is prevalent in certain areas, that prove that the ruling Bourgeoisie in our time has a constant fascist tendency. . . . Fascism is already in the state.[20]

In his article Glucksmann defines fascism as "power over all domains of the lives of the oppressed masses."[21] The filmmaker's own political utopia – the ideal of a nonhierarchical, nonfascist system – is implicit in her demand that we "make the world round":

> These centralisms are bad in East and West. They are very patriarchal and essentially out of date because the world is round and not a pyramid. Everywhere they build little pyramids and try to see whether they work. How can somebody far away know what I need here in Munich, what do they know in Bonn? What do they know in Moscow about what they need in Czechoslovakia? In order to preserve this world and in order to be able to respond immediately to certain conditions, one has to work decentralized. Decentralization

19. Interview (by Bion Steinborn and Carola Hilmes).

20. André Glucksmann, "Der alte und der neue Faschismus," in *Neuer Faschismus, Neue Demokratie*, ed. Michel Foucault (Berlin: Wagenbach Verlag, 1972), 7–68. This book is a German translation of the special issue no. 310 (1972) of the journal *Les temps modernes,* which is published by the editors of "Cause du peuple." It is not yet available in English. "Der Faschismus entsteht nicht durch einen Staatsstreich: weil er nicht 'entsteht', sondern bereits besteht; er wird nicht in die gegenwärtige imperialistische Gesellschaft 'katapultiert'; wenn er sie auch nicht ganz regiert, so herrscht er doch in begrenzten Bereichen, die davon zeugen, daß die herrschende Bourgeoisie in unserer Zeit eine ständige Tendenz zum Faschismus hat; . . . Der Faschismus ist bereits im Staat."

21. Ibid., 17.

is something more feminine. . . . We could handle energy differently and we would not have to be so destructive and have those huge projections of friend/foe. My neighbor would be a small-scale enemy, but I can handle him. . . . We meet at festivals all over the world and share a glass of champagne and at the same time we know: because you exist, we have bombs, and because I exist you have the bombs there. Such madness! These are the final stages of this strange patriarchal system.[22]

This quote demonstrates Rosenbaum's awareness and criticism of the absurdity of hierarchical power structures and her conviction that fundamental social and political changes will have to occur to break the vicious circle. The film focuses on the future – ending with the beginning of a new war, the Korean War – rather than dwelling on things gone wrong in the past, and the suffering and guilt connected with it. The ending stresses the fact that nothing has yet been learned from history and that the next war could start tomorrow, if only in other parts of the world.[23] Marianne Rosenbaum does not rewrite history from a woman's point of view, but rather creates in *Peppermint Peace* a powerful picture of a child's way of dealing with the threat of war. Whereas grown-ups have learned to compensate for their deep-seated fears and rationalize them away ("Seoul is much further away than Minsk and Smolensk"), Marianne's imagination is an ideal vehicle for the director to show fear, using a child's sometimes better, more direct understanding of her world and sometimes grotesque, but very revealing misunderstandings. The film also demonstrates how our natural

22. Interview (note 1 above). "Diese Zentralismen sind sowohl im Osten wie im Westen schädlich. Das ist etwas sehr Patriarchalisches, eigentlich schon überholt, denn die Erde ist rund und nicht eine Pyramide. Überall bauen sie so kleine hierarchische Pyramiden auf und meinen: versuchen wir ob's funktioniert. Wie kann einer weit weg wissen, was ich hier in München brauche, was wissen die in Bonn. Was wissen sie in Moskau was die in der Tschechoslowakei brauchen. Um die Erde zu erhalten und um auf bestimmte Verhältnisse sofort reagieren zu können kann man nur dezentral arbeiten. Das Dezentrale ist etwas eher Weibliches. . . . Wir könnten mit der Energie anders umgehen, wir müßten auch nicht so zerstörerisch umgehen und hätten auch nicht die riesigen Feind/Freund Bilder. Dann wäre mein Nachbar so ein kleiner Feind, aber mit dem kann ich noch umgehen. . . .Wir treffen uns bei Festivals aus der ganzen Welt, trinken miteinander Sekt und gleichzeitig wissen wir: weil es dich gibt, gibt es hier die Rakete und weil es mich gibt, gibt es drüben die Rakete. So ein Irrsinn. Das sind die Endphasen dieses seltsamen patriarchalischen Systems."

23. This is a device often used in postwar fiction by authors such as Ilse Aichinger, Günter Grass, etc.

potential for love and our sexual desire are replaced by fear and hatred of enemies as we grow up. Its achievement lies in the wit with which it plays off the adult world against the children's experience of it in order to produce its antiwar message.[24]

24. Editor's note: See also Gabriele Weinberger's more exhaustive discussion of *Peppermint Peace* in chapter 3 of her book *Nazi German and Its Aftermath in Women Directors' Autobiographical Films of the Late 1970s: In the Murderer's House* (San Francisco: Mellen Research University Press, 1992).

13

Representing Female Sexuality: On Jutta Brückner's Film *Years of Hunger*

barbara kosta

Jutta Brückner's Years of Hunger *(1979) is an autobiographical representation of girlhood in West Germany during the (politically and sexually) repressive 1950s. Barbara Kosta reads the film above all as an attempt by a woman director to represent female sexuality, an attempt to examine an area of obvious importance to all women, but one that has been depicted in the cinema in ways that cater primarily to male voyeurism, objectifying female sexuality for the delectation of the "male gaze," as so much feminist film criticism has demonstrated. The risks of such an attempt are obvious: how to explore female sexuality cinematically without reproducing the objectification so typical of conventional cinematic language? Kosta applauds Brückner's courage in attempting to expose those historical forces that have damaged women's relationships to their own bodies and images, and she demonstrates how this project is fused with a revisionist look at West German history.*
—THE EDITORS

The representation of women and female sexuality is a standard topos in most films, with classical narrative cinema often either localizing woman as spectacle (in which the female body becomes sexuality) or portraying women in their social roles as lover, mother, wife, and more recently as career woman. Yet, when these mainstream representations – almost exclusively produced by males – are matched against the new surplus of images by female filmmakers a disparity becomes apparent. For one, female sexuality, extensively displayed in male productions, is virtually absent from many female productions. With the long tradition of male perceptual domination that has pervaded the arts, women filmmakers, therefore, had first of all to face the fact that female sexuality has been defined primarily by male discourses. As Laura Mulvey and many other feminist critics have argued, the numerous images of woman that populate the screen have been fundamentally a construct of the male imagination.[1] Thus women's bodies have been inscribed by the ideological determinations of a male-dominated industry. Contained by the male glance that reproduces dichotomous strategies of perception, women have been seen traditionally in reference to men and men's pleasure. As a result, women confront the difficulty of establishing an unmediated relationship to their bodies and of expressing their sexuality in itself and for themselves. This may explain the frequent absence of female sexuality from many women's films.

When recent women filmmakers have broached the topic of female sexuality, how have they represented it? With this question we find ourselves treading on very sensitive ground. For as much of the literature and films of the last two decades have shown, these portraits often include women stricken by traditional gender-specific socialization processes that historically have turned women's bodies into objects. When women have set out to represent themselves, it has mostly been to depict the negative consequences of female socialization and to investigate the various forms of social and sexual oppression that pervade their lives. Marked by repression, absence, exclusion, and the traces of a culture that has objectified them, many women filmmakers still find themselves confronted with the necessity of breaking through barriers that have kept them in a position of deficiency and of exposing the forces that have damaged their relationship to their own bodies and images.[2] If women are to

1. Laura Mulvey discusses the projection of male "phantasies and obsessions" onto the "silent image of woman." Mulvey, "Visual Pleasure and Narrative Cinema," *Screen* 16, no. 3 (Autumn 1975). Since even a basic list of references that discusses the premise of the female image as a male construct would be too extensive, I will only cite a few: Claire Johnston, ed., *Notes on Women's Cinema* (London: SEFT, 1973); Julia Lesage, "Feminist Film Criticism: Theory and Practice," *Women and Film* 5/6 (1974); Annette Kuhn, *Women's Pictures* (London: Routledge and Keagan Paul, 1982); E. Ann Kaplan, *Women and Film: Both Sides of the Camera* (London and New York: Methuen, 1983) and Teresa de Lauretis, *Alice Doesn't: Feminism, Semiotics, Cinema.* (Bloomington: Indiana Univ. Press, 1984).

2. Jutta Brückner, "Hoffnung auf ein selbst-bewußtes Leben: Filme von Frauen auf Spurensuche," *Frankfurter Rundschau*, 26 August 1980; Jutta Brückner, interview, "Conversing together finally," with Marc Silberman, *Jump Cut* 27 (July 1982): 47.

discover and express who they are, they must begin by looking precisely at that which male discourses systematically tend to repress. This means that they must begin with their sexuality, and the female body, since historically it has been the source of their oppression and subordination. According to Jutta Brückner this process can be initiated through film:

> Film . . . offers the sole medium in which we can explore our collective labor of mourning for the cultural paralysis of our bodies, our eyes, and our space-time relations. The goal: recuperating the means to reconstruct symbolically . . . I mean recuperating our capacity to look.[3]

Women's biographies are a step in this direction.

In her autobiographical film *Years of Hunger* (*Hungerjahre - in einem reichen Land*, 1979), Jutta Brückner portrays an emotionally starved adolescent, Ursula Scheuner, growing up in the "golden Fifties" in the midst of plenty.[4] By reproducing the numerous voices that characterize both the private and public spheres, Brückner reconstructs a decade to review the experiences that shaped her identity. Her audio/visual montage of the years between 1953 and 1956 includes scenes of economic prosperity, suggested by the family's purchase of a car, political rehabilitation, represented by radio broadcasts of Adenauer's reinstatement of obligatory military service and Cold War policies; and social stabilization, initiated by the prohibition of Germany's Communist Party (KPD) (1956). These discourses are shown interacting with the private sphere, composed of the family whose constraints and expectations are an integral part of the historical backdrop. The black and white depiction heightens the intense political and moral polarization of the time. Thus the filmmaker supplies the historical context necessary to study the various textual coordinates that enmesh the public and private sphere and converge in a single body.[5] As Brückner explains, the body manifests these various tendencies:

3. Marc Silberman, Interview with Jutta Brückner, "Recognizing Collective Gestures," in *Jump Cut* 27 (1982), 46–7. Reprinted in this volume: pp. 253–58.

4. *Hungerjahre*, dir. Jutta Brückner, Basis Film, 1979.

5. For an overview of the 1950s, see Dieter Bänsch, ed. *Die fünfziger Jahre* (Tübingen: Günter Narr, 1985); in reference to women's imaging in the 1950s, see Barbara Sichtermann, "Über Schönheit, Demokratie und Tod," *Ästhetik und Kommunikation: Sex und Lust* 7 (1981): 13–25. In a discussion of *Years of Hunger* Brückner discusses her representation of history and memory: "Someone remembers experiences from the past but not in the linearity of a narrative sequence. The images are disparate and uncoordinated, juxtaposed just as

> The soul and body and the body and the world are therefore always the materialization of inside and outside, and the body, in its central position, is both at the same time. It is the place where the invisible soul can make itself visible and where the visible world can inscribe itself on the invisible.[6]

Through her autobiographical analysis, Jutta Brückner uncovers the cultural meaning attached to women's bodies and the "messages" a female adolescent receives in relation to her sexuality, her gender, hence her identity.[7] A voice-over at the beginning, the romantic description of a male's exotic adventure to the Ivory Coast ("As he went out into the world" – "Als er in die Welt hinausging"), contrasted with Ursula's asking what a veil is, implies the gender-specific framework for her socialization. As a girl, she is metaphorically veiled, concealed, and sequestered. This is particularly the case when growing up at a time in which birth control and abortion are unavailable, which means reducing women to their reproductive function. Thus, the constraints Ursula experiences are directly related to being female. For Ursula's mother, protecting her daughter from the possibility of an unwanted pregnancy entails rigorously guard-

---

memory progresses by leaps and associations. I don't like to reproduce reality as if history were simply a costume party. I am trying to suggest the complexity of a whole period, of the fifties, by letting it speak for itself." Brückner/Silberman, "Conversing together," 47.

6. "Nun sind Seele und Leib und Leib und Welt ja immer Materialisierung von inner und außen und der Leib in seiner Zentralstelle gleichzeitig beides: der Platz, wo sich die unsichtbare Seele sichtbar machen und die sichtbare Welt ins Unsichtbare einschreiben kann." Jutta Brückner, "Vom Pathos des Leibes oder: Der revolutionäre Exorcismus," in *Ästhetik und Kommunikation*, 57/58, "Intimität" (1985), 29–47.

7. Gudrun Lukasz and Christel Strobel, eds., *Der Frauenfilm* (Munich: Heyne Verlag, 1985), 148. Jutta Brückner describes *Years of Hunger*: "Was geschieht mit den Mädchen, wenn ihre Körper ihnen fremd werden, in Passivität erstarren, weil sie nicht wissen, wie sie werden müssen für die Augen aller anderen und deshalb auch für die eigenen Augen, denn wer wäre jemand, der sich anmaßen würde, ein Urteil zu haben, das aller anderer Urteil in Frage stellt und das mit 14 Jahren! Aufschwünge enden vor dem nächsten Spiegel, und der Weg durch ihn hindurch ist versperrt durch Mutters Körper, und es ist schwer, durch ihn hindurch zu etwas noch nicht Bekanntem, Undefiniertem zu kommen, zu etwas, das zu erforschen wäre." ("What happens to girls who become alienated from their own bodies that petrify through passivity, because they don't know how they are supposed to be in the eyes of others and therefore in their own eyes. For who would have been capable of passing a judgement that would place all other judgements in question at the age of fourteen!"). For other references, see Jutta Brückner, interview, "Frau zur Freiheit," *Abend*, Feb. 23, 1980; Heide Schlüppmann and Karola Gramann, *Hungerjahre, medienPraktisch*, ed. Gemeinschaftswerk der Evangelischen Publizistik (1983), 19–23.

ing her from possible moral "slip-ups." More specifically, though, it means ascribing an intrinsically negative value to the female body. The implication that women must tolerate their sexuality with resignation is conveyed by her mother, who says that *someone* must bear children. While washing herself after sleeping with her husband, she thinks: "It's not fair that we are made this way. We should be able to tear out our ovaries instead of always having to be afraid of becoming pregnant again."[8] Contempt for her own body predisposes her attitude towards her daughter's beginning sexuality. Thus Ursula's mother is a primary agent of her daughter's negative conditioning and the most powerful arbitrator in opposing her sexuality, through which process the sensual female body becomes effaced. She tucks her daughter into bed, tightly pulling the sheet over her, as though putting her into a straight jacket. As an afterthought, she takes Ursula's hands out from under the sheet to prevent her from touching herself. Denial, a severe mechanism of oppression, becomes one of the prevailing pedagogical measures in Ursula's upbringing. Not only is sexuality a taboo, but any other area of knowledge that tends to threaten a naive worldview also remains unaddressed. In fact, the title *Years of Hunger* appears for the first time when Ursula asks why the previous renters, an unmarried couple, were evicted. Her mother, at first refusing to answer, responds: "It is not always good to want to know everything." ("Man muß doch nicht alles wissen wollen.")

Her exclusion from certain spheres of knowledge, for which her mother is primarily responsible, leads to an increasing tension between the inner – her desires and needs to become a "normal girl" – and the outer – an oppressive bourgeois asceticism that her mother personifies. For Ursula the pictures of "normalcy" exist on the outside or in the imaginary. The school dance is portrayed by still photographs while she sits in her room, attempting to fill the inner deficit by eating. The incongruities that develop drive her into self-destructive isolation, visually portrayed at the outset with Ursula standing behind a window. This becomes a recurring motif throughout the film. The diffusion of her image at times also symbolizes the progres-

8. "Das ist eine Ungerechtigkeit, daß wir so gemacht sind. Man sollte sich die Eierstöcke raußreisen können. Ein Leben voller Angst, daß du wieder einen dicken Bauch kriegst."

sive dissolution of her identity. Thus *Years of Hunger* is the modern rendition of the *bürgerliches Trauerspiel* ("bourgeois tragedy") of the nineteenth century without the daughter's prescriptive moral transgression. Instead both the claustrophobic morality of the petite bourgeoisie and the mother's oppressive surveillance of her daughter generate a much subtler tragedy, the deformation of a young woman.

Years of Hunger, which Brückner describes as "a daughter's subjective work of mourning" ("subjektive Trauerarbeit einer Tochter"), belongs to the recent tradition of films in which daughters confront their mothers in an attempt to deal with their own identities. By reconstructing their pasts they analyze microscopically the gestures and attitudes they have internalized.[9] As much research on mother-daughter relationships in the past decade has shown, many of the attitudes women develop towards themselves as sexual and gendered beings are transmitted to daughters by mothers. Since most mothers have been traditionally complicit with patriarchal ideology, they too have programmed their daughters for psychological identification with the female role of passivity, submission, and silence. They too have been taught to subdue or inactivate a part of themselves. Yet, the proclivity for some generations to assume more readily this passive role is greater than others. Brückner contrasts two mother-daughter relationships: Ursula with her mother and Mrs. Scheuner with her mother. The uncritical symbiosis in the latter relationship is contrasted with the disharmony in the former, indicating that the 1950s marked a change in the possibilities available to women.[10] Ursula asserts a difference between herself and her mother when comparing their bodies in the mirror. In another scene, she complains to her grandmother: "She doesn't like me. She can't expect me to become just like her." ("Sie mag mich nicht. Sie kann doch nicht verlangen, daß ich genau so werde wie sie.") Yet, as author Barbara Frank shows in *Ich schau in den Spiegel und sehe meine Mutter* (*I Look into the Mirror and See My Mother*), a series of interviews with daughters, the lines demarcating mother and

9. A few other films that deal with this thematic are: *Deutschland, bleiche Mutter,* dir. Helma Sanders-Brahms, Basis Film, 1979; *Flügel und Fesseln,* dir. Helma Sanders-Brahms, Basis Film, 1984; *Malou,* dir. Jeanine Meerapfel, atlas film, 1981.

10. Ingrid Langer, "Die Mohrinnen hatten ihre Schuldigkeit getan: Staatlich-moralische Aufrüstung der Familien," *Die fünfziger Jahre,* ed. Dieter Bänsch (Tübingen: Günter Narr, 1985), 108–130.

daughter are often blurred, since women have lacked other models with which to identify.

The images of women outside of Ursula's immediate sphere equally reinforce traditional concepts of woman. For example, documentary footage of a fashion show, at which women parade on a stage in bathing suits, illustrates the pictures that served as models for female identification. The close-up of a line of women's buttocks visually dissects and fetishizes the female body for male visual pleasure, while a voice-over of a ribald song accompanied by laughter undercuts the visual panorama and pushes the scene into the direction of burlesque. "Woman" here is produced as spectacle, as an object to be looked at. She advertises herself as a product whose purpose is to arouse the consumer's desire. Such arsenals of female representations, of course, affect the way women construct themselves in a culture that teaches them to be attractive, to attract, but to shield themselves against being touched. In order to draw attention, they learn to package themselves. Ursula cultivates her own image when she sits in front of the mirror with crossed legs, a French beret, and a cigarette, pulling down her knee socks to study her legs. Her image is contained in two mirrors that visually fragment and dichotomize her body. One mirror reflects her head, and the other, much larger, her body. The emphasis of course is placed on the body. She reenacts this pose when a young man approaches her, signifying that she also constructs herself to be looked at. Though, when Ursula looks at herself for her *own* pleasure and curiosity, timidly pulling down her shirt to look at her breasts in the mirror, her inner voice, designated by a voice-over, repeats a sexually offensive rhyme. She resists the inclination to look and sticks out her tongue at the reflected image. The combination of her body and the rhyme signals the internalization of outer voices that negate and denigrate her own sexuality. At the same time, it is implied that the female body is solely reserved for the male glance.

The subtle messages that contribute to shaping a daughter's identity and to determining the relationship she develops to her gender become visible in Brückner's portrayal of the most intimate spheres of female experience. The rare cinematic presentation of menstruation is portrayed as a turning point in Ursula's life, not only because of its significance as a developmental stage, but also because of the meaning attached to it. At first Ursula naively interprets bleeding as a sign of illness, which immediately distresses her relationship to herself as having a healthy and normal female body. Her initial fear of a physical defect is reinforced by the conflicting fragments of information she receives. Her mother's assurance that "it is nice to be a woman" ("Es ist schön, eine Frau zu sein") is paradoxically accompanied by a number of disturbing restrictions. She can no longer play with boys, nor bathe when she has her period, nor change her underwear. At the same time, she is strapped into a sanitary napkin which completely impairs her freedom of movement. The shameful silence surrounding this event further demeans the natural function of the female body. Her father is told that Ursula has a stomach ache from eating too much cake, while she desperately hugs him in an attempt to seek refuge from womanhood. Women's own inability and discomfort in defining or verbalizing their sexuality is exemplified by Ursula's grandmother's advice. Her granddaughter should merely use the cryptic designation "d.u." to describe her condition, even though none of the women actually know what "d.u." means.[11] Hoping to divert any further questions, Mrs. Scheuner assures her daughter that all answers will be forthcoming in biology class. In many ways, the exemption of female realities from the public sphere and the absence of a language to describe women's experiences both contribute to the injured relationship many women have developed to their bodies. Even today the thematization of menstruation still seems to create great discomfort. Brückner herself faced problems when she attempted to challenge a cultural taboo by showing a used sanitary napkin. Her male camera operator refused to film the scene; when he finally conceded, he closed his eyes.[12]

Ursula's relationship to herself as a sexual being is primarily transmitted by the family. Their attitude towards sexuality, oftentimes merely conveyed through gestures, imprint themselves on the adolescent's self-awareness. Her mother's inhibition, for example, is demonstrated when she covers/conceals her breasts from Ursula, who enters the bathroom without

11. We are indebted to Robert Acker for informing us that "d.u." means "unfit for duty" (dienstuntauglich) –eds."

12. Renate Möhrmann, *Frau mit der Kamera* (Munich: Hanser, 1980), 223.

knocking, or when she struggles to put on her nightgown beneath her clothes in the dark – a gesture which Ursula repeats. Moreover, when Ursula's parents "make love" only her father's voice is audible, a sign of his gratification, while her mother, functionalized for male pleasure, remains silent. This scene of heterosexual coitus becomes a reference point for Ursula's own sexual development. In fact she associates heterosexual intercourse with violence as intimated in the recurring vision of her mother lying naked in the grass, signifying the victimization of the female body. The shadow of a man with a hat that hauntingly approaches her – a reminder of the murderer's shadow in Fritz Lang's film *M* – and the voice-over of a children's rhyme strengthen the allusion to sexual violation. Ursula's identification with this role of female sexuality becomes evident in the sequence portraying her first sexual experience, which ambiguously appears as rape.

A progressively widening rift between the inner and outer worlds of a female adolescent effects a disjunction which transposes itself onto Ursula's body. She cuts herself to destroy that which has been stunted by maternal direction. At the same time a voice-over representing her inner thoughts reveals the self-destructive rhythm driving her: "Mutilated – destroy the cold – shatter the shell." ("Verstümmelt – die Kälte zerstören – den Panzer zerbrechen.") The body is the outward manifestation of the invisible socializing processes that have slowly damaged the female Self. It becomes the object that Ursula wishes to destroy, which leads to her suicide attempt. The voice-over, the adult filmmaker speaking to the past, condemns the image of the young girl to a symbolic death: "In order to achieve something the ultimate sacrifice has to be made: sacrificing oneself." ("Wer was ausrichten will, muß was hinrichten - sich selbst.") At the end a portrait of the female self, which was assembled throughout the film, is seized in the form of a snap-shot and burned. This burning photograph of Ursula Scheuner evinces the autobiographer's exorcism of an image of herself, as well as a part of the past. Thus by releasing long repressed memories and restaging the key moments of her life in reference to a historical context, Brückner completes the first step toward a personal liberation by working through and destroying the old self-image. To do so she had "to work through the despondency, to call things by their name, to feel passion for myself, to be curious about myself, to communicate with myself."[13]

Yet, as Brückner suggests, initiating a personal liberation oftentimes depends on deprivatizing individual experience, which means seeing personal experience within a broad sociohistorical context. By including documentary footage of explosive historical moments of the 1950s, Brückner polemically counters the privatization of personal experience. Scenes of the workers' uprising in East Berlin on 17 June 1953, which became a battlefield of opposing ideological commentaries and interpretations, is but one example. Besides expanding the contextual meaning of oppression and spatially dispersing the narrative, documentary footage or allusions to other social revolutions (the Algerian revolution) function to activate a dialectical process between personal and sociopolitical circumstances. These sequences are strategically planted to spark the imagination and provide moments of identification, and so to politicize the personal realm. As Brückner argues in her article, "Vom Pathos des Leibes oder: Der revolutionäre Exorzismus" ("Regarding the Emotionalism of the Body or: Revolutionary Exorcism"), these scenes provide the possibility of linking personal oppression to periods of dissension against bourgeois ideology. Such ideology fragments the individual through its naturalization of dichotomies, for example, divisions along the axis of gender, public/private, etc.

In a voice-over the filmmaker questions: "How could one live both inside and outside?" ("Wie könnte man innen und außen gleichzeitig leben?"). The pro-filmic event, an explosion, presumably sparked by these conflicting tensions, appears to be the answer. Yet when individual despair is turned inward, the oppressed often become their own victims. The juxtaposition of the date 1789 (the French Revolution) written on the blackboard and Ursula cutting into her arm offers two images of eruptions. The personal in view of such an historical referential implies the misdirection of self-destruction. It seems as though the key is to channel violence against the oppressive forces, presuming they are identifiable. In "Vom Pathos des Leibes," Brückner draws an explicit parallel between the colonization of

13. "Den Kleinmut kaputtmachen, die Dinge beim Namen nennen, Leidenschaft für mich empfinden, auf mich neugierig sein, mich mit mir zu verständigen."

the female body by patriarchal thought and the social/political repression of nations and classes. Revolution against outer colonization, which in her article is exemplified by Algeria's struggle for independence, potentially provides a context for inner liberation through the introduction of alternatives and the possibility of changing the social structure. It initiates a consciousness-raising through its recognition and exposure of the mechanisms of oppression.

The feminist movement brought such a revolution by offering a new framework for analyzing female experience. It provided women with the possibility of coming out of their isolation to realize that personal oppression and discontent were not private problems. Women soon began to examine the multiple variables that determine their lives as a gender and, as Jutta Brückner suggests in her film, "to call things by their real name." ("Die Dinge beim Namen nennen.") "However," as Luce Irigaray notes, "in order for woman to arrive at the point where she can enjoy her pleasure as a woman, a long detour by the analysis of the various systems of oppression which affect her is certainly necessary."[14] Most of the films by women are still "detouring": they are still in the process of extricating female identities from phallocentric systems and structures and countering the cinematic apparatus, which has a long tradition of defining women and their sexuality. However, extricating does not preclude offering a new image, for it is still difficult for women to find a way to represent female sexuality and eroticism unmediated by the male glance, since it, just as the mother, has been internalized. Renate Möhrmann capsulizes the problem in the following way: "It is easier ideologically to require a clear separation between a genuine female and male eroticism than it is to visually produce it. Woman has literally lost sight of herself. She is all too often a mystery to herself."[15] *Years of Hunger* then is one answer to the question of how women represent their own sexuality, that is, their damaged sexuality. Films that

14. Luce Irigaray, "Demystifications" in *New French Feminisms,* eds. Elaine Marks and Isabella Courtivrons (New York: Schocken, 1980), pp. 99–110.

15. "Die säuberliche Trennung genuin weiblicher von männlicher Erotik ist ideologisch leichter zu fordern als bildlich zu gestalten. . . . Die Frau hat sich buchstäblich aus den Augen verloren. Sie ist sich selbst allzuoft 'ein blinder Fleck.'" Renate Möhrmann, "Ich sehe was, was du nicht siehst. Überlegungen zu den Darstellungs- und Wahrnehmungsformen weiblicher Kinofiguren im westdeutschen Frauenfilm," conference paper, Austin, Texas, May 1983.

stage a process of catharsis and deconstruct old images imply that women are striving to develop their own field of vision and that they are beginning to explore the possibilites for their own representations of female sexuality.[16]

16.For further articles by Jutta Brückner on film and female representation see: "Vom Erinnern, Vergessen, dem Leib und der Wut. Ein Kultur-Film-Projekt," *Frauen und Film* 35 (October 1983), 47; and Jutta Brückner, "Women Behind the Camera," in *Feminist Aesthetics*, ed. Gisela Ecker, trans. Harriet Anderson (Boston: Beacon, 1986), 120–24.

14

Interview with Jutta Brückner: Recognizing Collective Gestures

marc silberman

We reprint here Marc Silberman's interview with filmmaker Jutta Brückner, which first appeared in Jump Cut *27 (1982).*
—The Editors

I have been writing a long time, and I always find myself stumbling over the threshold of realism. When I point a camera out the window, I get a shot of the house across the way and a car. Yet if I try to describe a house or car verbally, I usually founder because the external world confuses, at times even threatens me. Film has saved me from this threshold of realism, for everything that could not be described verbally was simply in the film image. Thus, I can work with "pre-given" material. A disrupted relationship to the external world and to objects – which emerge so clearly in every female neurosis and latently in so many women's biographies – will not be displaced through description, nor simply by filming the external world. Yet the public production of space as is found in film opens up completely new opportunities to develop what has been maimed and to release what has been repressed. Film can integrate and release women's collective neuroses and maimings differently than literature, because film creates a public space for experience.

My films are all autobiographical. Autobiographical motivations counter the false generalizations into which we have been molded for years. These generalizations are false for men too; they simply don't realize it. We women tend to notice them more because our individuality simply cannot be contained within these generalizations. We must not just constitute images out of the small banalities of daily life, to do only that is false realism. Rather, we must find new forms to narrate private life, to recognize collective gestures in the most banal ones: for example, the way a wife hands her husband a cup of tea in the morning. To what extent does this collective gesture destroy me because it has nothing to do with me and makes me into a trained dog? I am trying to disrupt the habitual ways in which people see.

As to a particular relationship between feminism and film form: woman's historical and cultural oppression reveals itself not only in our familiar exclusion from the forms of exchange in a public sphere erected by men, but also especially in the deformation, renunciation, and incapacitation of our physical integrity and perception. This has most clearly affected sexuality but also looking. Through the look a person establishes space relations, and without space there is no time. Space-time-looking mean something else to women than to men: in film especially these three elements of perception come together. Moreover, film allows us women to represent our disrupted physical integrity, whereas literature restricts physical presence to the imagination. In filmic representation a vision of what undisrupted physical integrity might be emerges, and that vision presents itself not only to our imagination but also to our looking. Film for me offers the sole medium in which we can explore our collective labor of mourning for the cultural paralyzing of our bodies, our eyes, and our space-time relations. The goal: recuperating the means to reconstruct symbolically. This throws into question filming's own premises; film becomes filming's content not as the burden or joy of a tradition in which you are confined to sitting for hours in movie theaters; not as "real life," the way the French New Wave formulated it. I mean recuperating our capacity to look.

This has nothing to do with a specific style. There is no *one* feminist style. Nor can stylistic "innovations" be introduced like exotic commodities or clothes fashions. I am talking about new questions and new points of departure.

Do Right and Fear Nobody is a film about my mother, an historical film. I compiled photos by August Sander, from photo agencies, from history books and scrap books, with the intent of showing that this woman – Gerda Siepenbrink – is not a person in her own right. Rather she lives under the collective term "someone": "one should do this" or "one should do that." I did not choose photos of only Gerda Siepenbrink's family, which would have made only a fictional narrative in stills. I show a general image that a whole class devises for itself, and thus, I never come to the point of telling a story. Instead I focus on the damage caused to this woman by her class-bound upbringing. The film is done with much love.

You might wonder why I chose this specific form. August Sander's photographs first impelled me to make a film consisting of stills. If I want to depict history, I must demonstrate that people at that time had distinctive attitudes. For instance, look at this photo (a doctor with his wife in Monschau an der Eifel). Their pose expresses a very specific attitude, a certain stylization, an attempt to project an image of themselves. I feel Sander caught this petite-bourgeois comportment with its unmistakable traits so well that, were I to try to reproduce it with actors who used period gestures, it would become a matter of make-up and costumes. I want to show how the individual and his/her social class mutually condition one another and how consciousness is formed. This kind of film is really only possible with documentary material. At the same time, though, it was an attempt to tell an individual person's story with very disparate material, such as pictures of families and mothers.

A Fully Demoralized Girl was conceived as a fictionalized documentary – a personal story is interrupted by summary statements in which the young woman accounts for her development, particularly for the four central influences in her life: her attitude toward work, toward men, toward her parents, and toward her child. The woman (Rita Rischak, a personal friend of mine) plays her own life. It is not so important here that situations from her life are staged, but rather that she lives her life precisely this way. She acts out life as she acts in the film. In her life she acts as poorly as in the film. In this film she invents roles just as she does her identity in life. Her role-playing is interrupted, however, when she speaks her own commentaries directly into the camera, to the viewer, and she addresses the viewer as "you" (with the familiar form *du*). For that reason it is a documentary film which for long segments resorts to forms of the fiction film.

The narrative is once more interrupted, for the entire film is in black and white except for the last five minutes in color. Here, in images modelled after advertisements, with text bubbles as in cartoons, a life is told as she would fantasize it. It is the dream of a petite-bourgeois life and in each picture there is a man: Prince Charming or the savior places life at her feet without her lifting a finger. Nothing is offered as a counterbalance to this false utopia because I feel that its counterbalance must occur in the viewer: recognition of one's own situation. The film achieved that, even though some viewers became terribly aggressive. Many women viewers were sensitive to this young woman's inability to relate to others, to create meaningful bonds. They understood her fear of being hurt, which from the beginning led her to say, "Get lost!" That has nothing to do with social or legal conditions for emancipation, but rather with our conditioning to a certain kind of self-destruction. I show that we have to seek out the sources of these mistakes, not only in the social system (although that accounts for part of the problem) but also in what really lies in us. I show what has to be changed in us, and that elicited some viewers' aggression.

I conceive of my films unmistakably for women, not for men. The men don't get off very easily. But I also don't think we are obliged to be objective at this time. I think we should first figure out exactly where we are and learn, for example, to articulate hate. Most of us can't let anger out for fear of punishment, of being denied love because of our hate. If men too find an echo of their problems in my films, naturally I would be happy.

In my films I try to bewilder, disturb, and irritate. You can have seven murders in a film, you can show someone being chopped to pieces, but just don't show a sanitary napkin as I do in *Years of Hunger,* because then everyone will feel embarrassed. No one wants to see it, so everyone forgets it, pushes it from view. "You don't have to show everything; it's enough to suggest something." No, it is not sufficient to suggest; I want to show. We are confronted with images of women everywhere: mother, rosy lovers, or deceived wives. But a large part of female reality (which this napkin only represents) is not shown. Nor is the way in which we are trained to have an alienated relationship to our body, to ourself. In my new film *Years of Hunger* I try to show how a girl is forced to the brink of suicide. At the beginning she is bewildered because she is no longer permitted to like what she is. Gradually it leads to a more general bewilderment, expressed by her constant eating. She tries to consume everything, despite the title, until she is forced into silence and finally suicide.

This film is an attempt at a psychoanalytic cinematic form.

The problem concerning me is the relationship between the individual and society, a central issue of the women's movement that also implies the question of film content. As to the form, I try to work with newsreels and photos and with sound structures that introduce anonymous consciousness as anonymous voices. Someone remembers experiences from the past but not in the linearity of a narrative sequence. The images are disparate and uncoordinated, juxtaposed just as memory progresses by leaps and associations. I don't like to reproduce reality as if history were simply a costume party. I am trying to suggest the complexity of a whole period, of the fifties, by letting it speak for itself.

I discovered my own subjectivity by means of a long detour on a highly theoretical road through reading books about psychology, psychoanalysis, and social psychology, and, at the same time, in experiencing a deep, uncomprehended crisis. I experienced my subjectivity as alienation, as failure, as deficiency. For a long time I was unable to connect my intellectual schemes with the incomprehensibility of my lived process, although they influenced each other. The theoretical concepts helped me see more lucidly, and I did not let them swallow up my lived experience but corrected them through it. Because of this personal history I believe my understanding (not my concept!) of my own subjectivity may differ significantly from that developed by many others in the women's movement. Abstract, theoretical knowledge is very important to me. I don't consider scholarship and science a male conspiracy aimed at oppressing women.

My own subjectivity is also the result of a long cultural process – it is constituted by the history of the Western world. Women's turning point will not be found by starting at zero but by becoming conscious of this connection and emerging from unarticulated malaise. My subjectivity does not consist of negation – a position the student movement sometimes maintained. As a woman emerging from a male-dominated culture, the more I'd negate myself (as woman), the deeper I'd sink into the situation that women have known for centuries and that we, for the first time, have a chance to escape. Today negation serves men differently from women. Women cannot give up something which they have never possessed: access to a sphere of reality beyond the household. I also don't believe that my subjectivity can exhaust itself in political action. On the contrary, political action constitutes my subjectivity only insofar as it offers space to subjectivity and enters into that subjectivity. Political activities become "political" for me when they facilitate women's process of coming into subjectivity.

Reprinted from Jump Cut *27 (1982): 46–47.*

15

German History and Cinematic Convention Harmonized in Margarethe von Trotta's *Marianne and Juliane*

barton byg

Margarethe von Trotta, Jutta Lampe, and Barbara Sukowa on location for the filming of von Trotta's *Marianne and Juliane* (1981). (Lampe plays Juliane, Sukowa plays Marianne.) (Photo courtesy of New Yorker Films)

Margarethe von Trotta's film Marianne and Juliane *(1981) alludes to many of the same historical issues as does Sander's* The Subjective Factor *(see the next article in this volume), especially in its treatment of the legacy of the student movement and the women's movement in West Germany during the 1970s; it does so however in a more conventional (and more accessible) manner than does Sander's film, focusing on the story of two sisters in a way that encourages strong emotional identification on the part of viewers. Barton Byg examines the consequences of this cinematic strategy for the depiction of history, especially for the depiction of recent West German history. He echoes the concerns of much feminist film theory of the last twenty years in asking whether the use of the codes of conventional narrative cinema undo any feminist or emancipatory message the filmmaker might want to convey, since those codes themselves are the mainstay of a (patriarchal) "culture industry." Byg argues that such cinematic conventions ultimately co-opt the historical memory of those oppositional political tendencies von Trotta seems to want to rescue. He asserts that her film actually recuperates those tendencies for the harmonious restoration of a mythic national unity that shores up the West German state.*

(The two volumes of Gender and German Cinema *include a variety of positions on von Trotta. In this volume, Anna Kuhn's essay on* Rosa Luxemburg *(1986) evaluates von Trotta's filmmaking positively, in opposition to the stand Byg takes here. In Volume I, see Roswitha Mueller's essay on* Sisters *(1979) and Renate Möhrmann's essay on* The Second Awakening of Christa Klages *(1977) for other discussions of von Trotta's work.)**

—THE EDITORS

Margarethe von Trotta's film *Marianne und Juliane* (*Die bleierne Zeit,* 1981) depicts the relationship of two sisters against the background of West German terrorism. Although the film purports to have a progressive impulse, the functionalization of women's images in the film manipulates the audience according to conventions long under assault by feminist film theory. Equally suspect in the film are the conventionalized depictions of politics and history – particularly the politics and history of terrorism.

The cinematic means the film uses to fuse the women's narrative with the history of West German political violence are profoundly Oedipal. The feminist critique of the Oedipal narrative in film, as expressed by Laura Mulvey and others, has been that it reduces woman to a lifeless fetish that has nothing to do with the lives of real women. Instead, the projection of woman on the screen poses a threat to the male that has to be resolved by means of the cinematic narrative. The removal of such a threat becomes a source of pleasure in narrative film, but at the expense of women's place in visual representation. Von Trotta's film, as we shall see, uses highly effective and pleasurable cinematic means to remove the threat posed by both the "terrorist sister" as an image of woman and the metaphorical threat she poses to the stability of the German state.

Since the political threat identified with terrorism had already been put down by force in West Germany, its cinematic evocation in the 1980s served merely a representative function. In harmless, depoliticized, aesthetic form, the violent ruptures of the German past can now take the form of what Paul Piccone

*For a defense of *Marianne and Juliane,* see Susan E. Linville, "Retrieving History," *PMLA* 106.3 (1991): 446–58. –The Editors.

terms "artificial negativity." This serves as a non-threatening reminder of the dangers of instability and thus contributes to the legitimation of the existing order. In von Trotta's film, it is furthermore the image of woman that harmonizes the two sides of a violent, yet stable State. Since whatever feminist issues the film raises are subordinated to the imperatives of the film narrative, the impact of the film derives less from these issues than from its spectacular ability to evoke and incorporate them. The fascination with the cinema this film achieves thus works against any intervention in the history and politics of feminism or terrorism, raising and removing them to the level of legend. This combination of cinephilia and mystification, common to the international commercial cinema, promotes the stability and harmony required by commerce and, by means of a compelling metaphor, the West German state as well. Let us look at the two sides of this process, the manipulation of the image of women and the false harmonization of German history to which it leads.

The characters of *Marianne and Juliane* are based on Gudrun Ensslin, the accused terrorist and core member of the Red Army Faction, and her sister Christiane. Ensslin died of what was officially termed a suicide in Stammheim Prison in 1977.[1] The film uses flashbacks to depict their differing personalities as they grow up in postwar West Germany. Juliane (the fictional representation of Christiane) is a defiant beatnik in school; Marianne (the fictional representation of Gudrun) is a cello-playing, golden-haired, model daughter. In adulthood, Juliane's rather reformist feminism and political involvement (she writes for a feminist magazine and lives with a relatively enlightened architect named Wolfgang) are challenged by her sister's turn to political violence and imprisonment as a terrorist. After Marianne's death, the investigation of its actual circumstances and the care of Jan, Marianne's abandoned son, become Juliane's primary concerns.

The narrative conventions to which von Trotta subscribes in order to craft her film with so much audience appeal have in many ways dictated her interpretation of the historical raw materials. Thus the final "look" of *Marianne and Juliane* is quite

1. For more information on Stammheim and the trials of RAF members, see Stefen Aust, *Der Baader – Meinhof Komplex* (Hamburg: Hoffmann und Campe, 1986) and Pieter H. Bakker Schut, *Stammheim: Der Prozeß gegen die Rote Armee Fraktion* (Kiel: Neuer Malik Verlag, 1986).

close to the American films to which Thomas Elsaesser compared it,[2] and its narrative logic is dictated by the "exposé" theme of the thriller and the *film noir,* as Ellen Seiter and Sheila Johnston have pointed out.[3] Working within such conventions, von Trotta manipulates spectators' sympathy for victims on the basis of questionable historical connections, as the following examples illustrate.

Von Trotta depicts the developing social conscience of the two sisters by way of the films they see. First, in the 1950s, the "leaden times" of the film's German title, they are shown viewing the film *Night and Fog* by Alain Resnais (1955). The excerpt von Trotta chooses is of mounds of corpses at an extermination camp. Part of this sequence is shot over the heads of the sisters, so that von Trotta's audience joins them as spectators of Nazi violence. The sisters' father is seen apparently projecting the film. The sequence ends with the Nazis' well-known denials of guilt, and the sisters finally become literally nauseated.

To maintain this linkage of spectatorship and the victims of war, von Trotta repeats the arrangement of the *Night and Fog* sequence in a flashback showing Marianne, Juliane, and Wolfgang watching a film about Vietnam. The anachronism of having Vietnam – the television war – brought home to the sisters via film and the repeated emphasis on the burned, emaciated bodies of victims of war allows von Trotta to use film images to unite revulsion at the concentration camps with anti-Vietnam-war feeling. This connection sets the stage, then, for the "political" exhortation presented by the images within her own film. After Marianne's death, her son is badly burned by an anonymous attacker and is shown lying in a hospital, his young, charred body recalling the earlier images of victims.

Indirectly linked to the images of victims is Marianne's face. As Juliane observes after seeing Marianne's emaciated face in the coffin, "There will never be another face like that." A photograph of Marianne's face is seen at the beginning of the film, and near the end, Jan tears it up, prompting Juliane to begin to tell him what an extraordinary woman his mother was. A similar destruction of the dead woman's image in favor of the living has

2. Thomas Elsaesser, "Mother Courage and Divided Daughter," *Monthly Film Bulletin* 50 (July 1983): 177.

3. Ellen Seiter, "The Political is Personal: Margarethe von Trotta's *Marianne and Juliane,*" *Journal of Film and Video* 37 (Spring 1985): 43; Sheila Johnston, "The German Sisters," *Films & Filming* 334 (July 1982): 26.

already taken place in the last visit between Juliane and Marianne in prison. Here the glass between them functions as a projection screen on which the images of their faces merge for a moment until Juliane's moves to the side to emerge in clear focus, while Marianne's subsides into the shadows.

The overcoming of the threat posed by Marianne can be expressed in terms wholly consistent with the conventional narrative. Marianne has usurped the prerogatives of their father – a strict, fire-and-brimstone Protestant minister – by adopting the intransigent and vengeful stance of a terrorist. She has also usurped a male prerogative by becoming a guerilla warrior. The obsession with the discovery of the truth about Marianne's death eventually replaces her relationship with Wolfgang. Indeed, the surrealistic depiction of Juliane's receiving the news of her sister's death, skillfully juxtaposed with an Italian wedding in their vacation hotel, underscores the shift to a family commitment in place of a political one. Therefore it is necessary to the narrative that the media are not interested in the true story of Marianne (and Juliane seeks no other public sphere as an audience): the Oedipal narrative must be carried on by passing on the story to the son, restoring political and moral authority to its rightful place. By becoming a mother and storyteller, Juliane returns to her rightful place as well.

These examples presented von Trotta with an opportunity to explore the aesthetic and ethical implications of her artistic conditions. With the images of the two sisters, she could have explored the limitations of one person's understanding or even of seeing another person based on a photographic projection. She could have problematized the contradictions presented by the stereotypical images of both women and terrorists or investigated the sexist abuse suffered by Gudrun Ensslin in her relationship with Andreas Baader. With the images of victims, she could have interrogated the convention of depicting women, children, and victims of imperialistic wars as "stock" victims – icons of powerlessness offered up for the sympathy of the powerful. But von Trotta has chosen to subordinate these considerations to the demands of the narrative. She even goes so far as to construct a dubious progression of history in film, linking the viewing of sensational images from extermination camps with film images of Vietnamese victims. Having taken a step toward questioning the basis of representation, she opts in favor of cinematic convention.

If one grants that women spectators do derive pleasure from von Trotta's conventional drama, this fact in itself emphasizes the cinematic narrative at the expense of the women's realities it evokes. A positive reading of such a film from a feminist viewpoint would become an extension of the critical practice of reading the products of the patriarchal culture industry, for instance the "women's films" of the 1940s and 1950s. Using the tools of psychoanalytic or semiotic criticism, one can unearth in these cultural products evidence of the inscription of the feminine, locate gaps in patriarchy's erasure of women's experience, and follow the industry's ongoing activity of covering these gaps. But these attempts at finding signs of friction within the language system of cinema or of explaining how the system reproduces and represents itself are often predicated on the acceptance of mass culture as a language or sign-system into which neither the critic nor the artist can intervene from the outside. They accept the film industry as it is rather than propose a radical alternative.

This acceptance of patriarchal norms, even while criticizing them from within, is certainly understandable, given the realities of the 1980s, when no broad-based and radical social movement could offer women an alternative means for solidarity and cultural expression. In mass culture, conventions such as the Oedipal narrative and genre imperatives used in von Trotta's film, are inherently incapable of radical expression.

Therefore, working within the system as von Trotta does is inherently ambiguous, and it is pointless for E. Ann Kaplan to fault *Marianne and Juliane* for being open to various, contradictory readings.[4] This is a necessary result of its project. The problem is its easy accomodation of reactionary readings. In addition to her manipulation by way of conventional images, von Trotta's manipulation of history in the service of her narrative is also objectionable. Because she has chosen as her German sisters one terrorist and one feminist, and because the legacy of Nazi Germany is touched on at key points in the film, scrutiny of the treatment of these explosive issues is clearly justified. Charlotte Delorme goes somewhat too far in equating the film's aesthetics with the sensationalism of the West German right-

4. E. Ann Kaplan, "Discourses of Terrorism, Feminism, and the Family in von Trotta's *Marianne and Juliane*," *Persistence of Vision* 2 (Fall 1985).

wing press,[5] but such exaggerated clichés of terrorism are certainly employed as a powerful cinematic shorthand. But rather than criticize the hysteria of the reaction to terrorism, the film employs its emotive power. Conventionalized dualities are constantly stressed: as teenagers, one of the sisters was extremely good, the other extremely bad. One sister is blond, the other dark. The father is a stereotype of a strict fire-and-brimstone preacher. The mother is the long-suffering onlooker, complicitous through her passivity. The contradictions between Juliane's teenage rebelliousness and her later liberal conformism or between Marianne's early virtuousness and her later militancy are also rendered unproductive by the neatness of their reversal. Furthermore, Marianne's political motives are trivialized by the interpretation that it was merely the rigidity of her upbringing that led her to be both rigid and violent as an adult. As has often been noted,[6] the film avoids giving political explanations for Marianne's turn to violence and depicts it in either personal terms or in images already conventionalized by the mass media. Indeed, in this aspect it reflects a general trend in popular depictions of the 1960s twenty years later: political issues and social movements are trivialized to the level of "life-style" choices (cf. *The Big Chill, Men (Männer), thirtysomething*).

Politics does indeed enter the film in the form of a link between the narrative present (1977) and the Nazi and immediate postwar past. Until the last prison meeting between the sisters, suggestions of contemporary technology are scrupulously avoided. As with the anachronistic film screenings, the residences, institutions, prisons, and their personnel all have a nostalgic, old-fashioned aura. This look brings them closer in style to the flashbacks of the sisters' childhood than to the contradictory present (E. Ann Kaplan notes that *most* of the film's narrative is flashback[7]). But while this tonal consistency implies a political and contemporary continuity between the Nazi state and West German "persecution" of the terrorists, all political specificity is excluded from both phenomena. The film stresses

5. Charlotte Delorme, "On the Film *Marianne and Juliane* by Margarethe von Trotta," *Journal of Film and Video* 37 (Spring 1985): 48, 49.

6. Lisa DiCaprio, "*Marianne and Juliane / The German Sisters*: Baader-Meinhof Fictionalized," *Jump Cut* 29 (February 1984): 57; Seiter, "Political is Personal," 44; Lorenzo Codelli, "Die bleierne Zeit," *Positif* 248 (November 1981): 44.

7. Kaplan, "Discourses," 63.

the "personal" side in the equation, stating that the "personal is political" to the point of denying that the political is political.

This careful exclusion of the political context of the student and antiwar movements and the repressive methods used by the State to counteract them ignores one of the most important consequences of terrorism. As the editors of *New German Critique* noted in 1977, "There can be no doubt that terrorism has become a pretext for an attack, and this attack was already conceived as an attempt to discredit the entire tradition of social criticism and social thought that re-emerged in Germany in the 1960s."[8] The personalization of terrorism in the figure of Marianne precludes any connection to "a tradition of social criticism and social thought."

Given these problems, how is it, then, that critics such as Sklar and Harris could praise the film as "one of the major works in the West German cinema"?[9] *Marianne and Juliane* receives such acclaim because it rearticulates film conventions to help construct the narrative of a national myth. Although it refuses to provide a political analysis of developments from fascism to the present in West Germany, *Marianne and Juliane* constructs a powerful cinematic evocation of a land burdened by its past. An outstanding example of this construction revolves around the spaces within which von Trotta locates her flashbacks and the meetings between the sisters. The film's locations resonate with each other to leave the impression that "leaden times" prevail in a country composed almost entirely of interiors and courtyards, lit in somber tones stressing blues and grays. The stylistic consistency of these spaces also links them together as emotional locales within which the lives of the two women have been nurtured. Von Trotta interweaves present-day courtyards traversed by Juliane, the prison courtyard, the childhood courtyard Juliane remembers, and the rooms in which Marianne and Juliane meet for their symmetrically choreographed and edited dialogues. The museum yard, with its oversized stone sculptures and high walls, is a stylistic mingling between the shared spaces of the women's past and the close-ups of them within these spaces – the stone figures suggest many things about the ominous weight of history and Marianne's role in relation to her sis-

8. "Germany's Danse Macabre," *New German Critique* 12 (Fall 1977): 3.

9. Adrienne Harris and Robert Sklar, "Marianne and Juliane," *Cinéaste* 12, no. 3 (1983): 41.

ter: coldness, dominating stature, and intimidating perfection.

As noted above, part of the process of Juliane's "reconciliation" with her sister involves various forms of destruction of Marianne's image – Jan's tearing up the photo, the distorted face in the coffin, the face receding behind the prison's glass barrier. The courtyard motif, which links the sisters' childhood with the present, survives Marianne, however, and reappears near the end of the film as Jan and Juliane return home. For the first time, the courtyard again has children playing in it, as Marianne and Juliane had done.

Von Trotta's use of these carefully constructed, archaic interiors represents a visual coming-to-terms with Germany and its history. The reconciliation of Juliane with the memory of her dead sister has been seen as a process of growth and a decision leading to Juliane's "identification with the oppressed."[10] The merging of the two selves, on the other hand, can be read in quite the opposite way – as Juliane's emerging as "sole master of the discourse," having survived her sister's challenges and incorporated aspects of them into her own life (a similar reading is attributed to Miriam Hansen by Kaplan).[11]

The subtle interweaving of two sisters' images carries on a long German tradition which was prominent in Romantic literature as well as in Expressionist film: the image of the *Doppelgänger.* This adds another dimension to von Trotta's variation on "genres" – Marianne represents the forbidden other self of Juliane; her transgressions reveal Juliane's shallowness or point to her real (repressed) desires. This "Other" in literature as well as in film often possesses ideal traits that become evil when taken to an extreme, and in order to preserve the integrity of the narrative and the narrating subject, it must be destroyed or sacrificed so that its energies can be harnessed for good once more.

Ironically enough, even though literary tropes and the codes of popular culture promote insulation from political and historical reality, it is entirely plausible that the film plays a political role on a more abstract level, on the level of myth. This is why, despite the utmost artificiality, film and television consistently vampirize "true stories." Charlotte Delorme is justified in her irritation at von Trotta for teasing the audience with the per-

10. Kaplan, "Discourses," 63, 67.
11. Kaplan, "Discourses," 66n.

sonal dedication "for Christiane [Ensslin]" and the pseudo-documentary basis for her film, while its entire construction is one of mythologizing. But the myths of popular culture are not made out of nothing: their function is to address real concerns and fill real needs, but without disrupting the social system.

Marianne and Juliane's artistic rearticulation of genre formulas alone thus does not account for its popular impact. Rather, it is also deeply rooted in the ongoing search for a postwar German identity and a reunion of the Federal Republic with German history.[12] That is why the film is less controversial the farther one gets from West Germany. Seiter and Kaplan both contend that German history plays an insignificant role in the American reception of the film, while it accounts for negative reactions in the Federal Republic.[13] Elsaesser, on the other hand, asserts that von Trotta is an exceptional figure in New German Cinema for avoiding the theme of Nazis and guilt as well as the obsession with the United States found in the works of other West German directors.[14] To the contrary, I believe that the mythologizing potential of *Marianne and Juliane* – even in the United States – is intrinsically related to twentieth-century myths of German history. A major source of the film's interest is a metaphorical search for a German national identity that has long been mediated by the conventions of (American) popular culture. After all, in explaining the peculiar psychological identifications generated by the international reception of works of the New German Cinema, Elsaesser reminds us that they are "official representatives [of a] country that has had difficulty profiling itself either politically or culturally, except through a relatively recent, though intensive preoccupation with its internationally notorious past and its troubled ideological identity as a nation."[15]

12. In the context of the even more disturbing and recent "*Historikerstreit*" [Historians' Dispute], Hans Mommsen, among others, describes the promotion of West German national identity through the depoliticized "normalization of German history." Hans Mommsen, "Suche nach der 'verlorenen Geschichte'?" [The Search for a "Lost History"?] *Historikerstreit. Die Dokumentation der Kontroverse um die Einzigartigkeit der nationalsozialistischeng Judenvernichtun* [Historians' Dispute. Documentation of the Controversy Concerning the Uniqueness of the National Socialist Destruction of the Jews] (Munich: Piper, 1987), 168-69, 172-73. This phenomenon during the mid-1980s suggested an increased impulse toward suppression of political otherness in history of the sake of national self-representation.

13. Seiter, "Political is Personal," 43; Kaplan, "Discourses," 67.

14. Elsaesser, "Mother Courage," 177.

15. Elsaesser, "*Lili Marleen*: Fascism and the Film Industry," *October* 21 (Summer 1982): 117.

The German identity constituted with the help of international popular culture is given coherence and strength in part by its reference to and reconciliation with two central images of political violence and State repression in the twentieth century – National Socialism and the phenomenon of terrorism.[16] This phenomenon helps explain the narrative logic of *Marianne and Juliane* in the context of West German national identity. In Kaplan's view, the link between history and politics is made in Juliane's reconciliation with her sister. She believes that Juliane sees "the falsity of the established discourse about terrorism," but Juliane's is by no means a political critique of that discourse, but a totally private one. Conscious of this, Kaplan comes to the unsatisfactory conclusion (for her, too) that the film posits the family as the only solution to the political and social dilemmas it raises.[17] One could conclude, however, that Juliane's understanding and partial incorporation of her sister are neither a return to a particular family ideology nor a commitment to identify with the victims,[18] but a consolidation of a national identity that now can resume its violently interrupted narrative.

Another American reaction to the film similarly stresses the connection between the film and National Socialism, but with outdated assumptions which ignore the importance of international media images for West German culture. Lisa DiCaprio places von Trotta's film in the context of German guilt for the crimes of the Nazi regime, but pits it against purported West German apathy about or apologies for the Nazis. But such guilt feelings are no longer denied, they have merely been depoliticized. With the broadcast of *Holocaust* in West Germany in 1979, which DiCaprio wrongly assumes was consistently resisted by West Germans, international popular culture provided an outlet for feelings of guilt that divorced them from political consequences.[19] The catharsis of *Holocaust* in West Germany, which

16. Few filmmakers have considered rearmament and integration into NATO as a turning point for national identity. Exceptions would be Straub/Huillet's *Machorka-Muff* (1962), Fassbinder's *Die Ehe der Maria Braun* (1979) and *Lola* (1982), Brückner's *Hungerjahre* (1979), and Sanders-Brahms's *Deutschland, bleiche Mutter* (1979). On the contrary, the "leaden times" of von Trotta's film title have been misinterpreted to mean the 1970s, not the 1950s, as national reconciliation was proclaimed in the late 1980s. Cf. Mattias Horx and B. C. Möller, "Am Ende der bleiernen Zeit," *Zeitmagazin,* (1 July 1988).

17. Kaplan, "Discourses," 67.

18. Ibid.

19. DiCaprio, "Baader-Meinhof Fictionalized," 57.

achieved striking cultural consensus, allowed people to feel good about being German again, in large part by admitting their feelings of guilt. This was made possible by transforming the violence of German history from a politically open question into a spectacle that allowed all viewers finally to identify with the victims as well as the persecutors. In this context of pop-culture evocations of German guilt, it is not necessary for *Marianne and Juliane* to present an analytically sound link between Nazism and terrorism. Both are merely violent intrusions of political divisiveness upon the unity and harmony of the national family.

In this metaphorical, mythological interpretation of von Trotta's narrative, it is thoroughly conceivable that Juliane would sympathize with both the transgressions and the sufferings of her "other self." What cannot be permitted is for that other self to remain Other – hence destroying the national consensus necessary for such a pop-culture representation. What Kaplan calls "the danger" of such a conventionalized portrayal of complex issues is ultimately its essence: the fundamental victory of the culture industry lies in its ability to reconcile contradictory interpretations. Political opposition becomes impossible because a mediated version of it has been incorporated into the dominant culture itself. The prospect that von Trotta's film is part of such a totalizing cultural phenomenon is actually more horrifying than the suspicion that it might lend support to this or that reactionary political tendency. Neo-Nazis and Nazi ideology are obsolete and dysfunctional, too, except as mediated through the same system of totalizing representation – as pop-culture villains.

Two final examples will illustrate how *Marianne and Juliane* eradicates difference by incorporating it into a national myth. Much has already been written about the powerful pattern created by von Trotta in representing the bodies of victims – from Jesus to victims of Nazi death camps to Vietnamese to Jan, the son of the terrorist Marianne.[20] Because of the narrative and ideological necessities of this construction, we are expected, on the level of pop images, to see the suffering of this series of victims as equivalent – culminating in the burning of a German child. The issue, however, is not the real boy's suffering because of public reaction to terrorism. Instead it is the national feelings of both guilt and victimization which are aroused by identifica-

20. Johnston, "German Sisters," 26; Kaplan, "Discourses," 67.

tion with the suffering of a German boy. This lets us imagine that we identify also with the objectified sufferings of Third World children or the victims of the Nazis. The uncomfortable implications about this regarding race and representation would be obvious, I think, had the actors playing Jan been blond and blue-eyed. But von Trotta has made the issue more complicated by casting boys to play Ensslin's son who are not of typical northern-European appearance (Samir Jawad and Patrick Estrada-Pox). Although this may be intended as a gesture toward ethnic pluralism in West Germany, it seems more likely to affirm the legitimacy of the nationalistic consensus, since both terrorist violence and ethnic "otherness" are successfully incorporated.

Finally, the most obvious referent for the metaphor of Germany as a divided (female) character – Mari*anne* and Juli*ane* – is the division of Germany itself. The political and historical reality of the German Democratic Republic, however, has no place in von Trotta's fictionalized family narrative, nor in critics' interpretations of it, but remains an unconscious Other. Such a narrative raised to the level of a national myth performs the same function regarding left politics as it does regarding Nazism – distasteful or not, it appropriates them as the sole property of a West German national heritage, devoid of contemporary relevance. After years of equating "Deutschland" with the Federal Republic, unification of the two Germanys under the terms of the West German Basic Law completes this logic. West German cultural images helped to smooth and hide the contradiction and fragmentation of the national identity. Guilt and mourning, mediated by mass-produced images such as those of *Marianne and Juliane*, assist in the process.

16

Re-Presenting the Student Movement: Helke Sander's *The Subjective Factor*

richard w. mccormick

As male students demonstrate above, Annemarie (Johanna Sophia), Anni (Angelika Rommel), and Sonja (Karin Mumm) plan the first meeting of a new group dedicated to women's liberation. Helke Sander's *The Subjective Factor* (1981).
(Photo courtesy of Helke Sander)

The rejection of the historian's traditional pose of "objectivity" is clear already in the title of Helke Sander's film The Subjective Factor *(1981), a film that explores the origins of the West German women's movement within the student movement of the late 1960s. Sander's own position is foregrounded in the film, not only as one of the founders of the women's movement, and as an obvious model for the film's autobiographical protagonist, but also, as Richard McCormick argues, as a filmmaker who chose to retell the late 1960s in the early 1980s. The perspective of the 1980s is continually foregrounded in the film, and McCormick asserts that this is a key to understanding Sander's complex film, which is an experimental mix of autobiographical fiction, documentary footage, and voice-over narration.*

—The Editors

I ask myself, what kind of world are you bringing children into? We are by now at an age where we are responsible for what's happen-

> ing. And this is a realization that was made during the student movement. . . . For this is the decisive point: intervention, not refusal.[1]

Helke Sander, in a 1981 interview in connection with her film *The Subjective Factor* (*Der subjektive Faktor,* 1981), emphasized active intervention in historical struggles, a position that in many ways reflects the project of feminism as a whole: that women enter the political realm as active subjects, both making and writing their own history. It is also a position that motivates both Anni, the autobiographical protagonist of the film, and Sander herself, director of this film that chronicles the beginnings of the West German women's movement within the student movement of the late 1960s.

An interesting aspect of Sander's statement is the emphasis on the student movement as a *positive* tradition – this from the director of a film quite critical of that movement.[2] But *The Subjective Factor* depicts both the women's movement and the student movement as parts of a common oppositional struggle, which is shown as still necessary in the 1980s. The critique of the male-dominated student movement that informed the women's movement, and which is presented in the film, is itself a contribution to a common ongoing struggle. Sander made the film in order "that the lessons of our experiences not be lost,"[3] in order to counter conservative and/or primarily male-oriented histories of the student movement. The act of remembering is both "subjective" and "political," to combine two problematic terms so often used in opposition in discussions about West Germany since the 1960s; it can only occur from a specific

1. "Ich frage mich, in welche Welt setzt du die Kinder. Wir sind inzwischen in dem Alter, in dem wir Verantwortung haben für das, was geschieht. Und das ist ein Moment, was in der Studentenbewegung begriffen wurde. . . . Das ist aber das Entscheidende. Die Einmischung und nicht die Verweigerung." Helke Sander, in an interview with Gudula Lorez, "Einmischung statt Verweigerung," *die tageszeitung* (West Berlin), 20 July 1981, p. 9 (originally "aus der überregionalen Ausgabe des TIP").

2. Some critics used the film as another pretext to defame the student movement. For example: Manfred Delling, "Terror in Chile, Elend in der Küche," *Deutsches Allgemeines Sonntagsblatt,* 28 June 1981; and the review in the column "Ponkie sieht fern" in the *Abend- Zeitung* (Munich), 18/19 April 1981.

3. Sander, "Es gibt viel Falsches im Wahren," an interview with Karsten Witte, in "der subjektive faktor," a promotional program for film's opening in West Berlin at the Filmbühne am Steinplatz, 19 June 1981.

position within a specific set of attitudes toward what is being remembered. Hence the "subjective factor."[4]

I. The View from the Kitchen

In telling the story of the origins of the West German women's movement from the viewpoint of a woman who, like Sander herself, took part in those beginnings, Sander was motivated in part by her awareness that "official" histories had been mostly silent on the activities of earlier generations of women. When she became politically active in the 1960s, she herself had not been aware of these earlier efforts: "I didn't know at the time that there had already been a women's movement, and yet I had done well in history and was fairly educated. When I became aware of it, the unequivocal authority of the concepts I had learned crumbled. History was suddenly not at all 'objective' any more."[5]

The critical perspective that facilitated her loss of faith in the dominant version of German history resulted in part from her politicization in the student movement. But when the same crit-

4. Such a title is heavy with all sorts of associations within the discursive field of West Germany in the 1970s and the early 1980s; somewhat misleading are associations with the literary phenomenon "New Subjectivity" as commonly perceived in the media. In the latter perception, "subjective" is connected all too often to melancholy *Innerlichkeit* (inwardness) and to narcissistic self-absorption. Such an interpretation is debatable in any case, but it is especially inappropriate to make too many connections between Sander's film and the literary "New Subjectivity" of the mid-1970s. The film is, however, most certainly informed by the feminist principle that the personal sphere is an important locus of political struggle and development.

In my opinion, the "subjective factor" at work in the film has more to do with the conviction that in both art and politics discourse should not masquerade as "objective," but that the "subject of the enunciation," be it filmmaker or political theorist, be foregrounded. The film indeed hampers "subjectivity" in the sense of viewer identification through its complex use of montage and other distantiation devices. The film aligns itself with the modernist conviction that the process of constructing a story (or a political analysis) cannot be separated from the "end product," and that the temptation of simple, un-critical solutions must be resisted. "The longing for simple solutions creates new tragedies," says Sander, as the narrator, towards the end of her film ("Die Sehnsucht nach einfachen Lösungen schafft neue Tragödien"). She is as skeptical of such solutions in art as in politics.

5. "Ich wußte damals nicht, daß es schon mal eine Frauenbewegung gegeben hatte und doch war ich gut in Geschichte und durchschnittlich gebildet. Als mir das klar wurde, zerbröckelte auch die Eindeutigkeit der Begriffe für mich. Geschichte war da nichts 'Objektives' mehr." Sander, "Es gibt viel Falsches im Wahren."

ical outlook was applied to the social conventions governing her own role as a woman, she found most of her male comrades in the movement to be blind to the ideological nature of that positioning – as blind as the "official" history taught in schools had been to the political efforts of women in the past.

The male activists' insensitivity is depicted most effectively in the film when the character Anni waits patiently for a chance to speak to a small group of students holding a strategy meeting. Like Anni, the students belong to the primary political organization of the student movement in West Germany and West Berlin, the SDS (*Sozialistischer Deutscher Studentenbund*, the League of Socialist German Students).[6] Their discussion involves the SDS campaign against the Springer press.[7] Anni waits in order to make her point to the other activists that a good deal of the manipulation exerted in the Springer publications had to do with women, depicted as pin-ups or addressed as frugal housewives. She is finally told by one of the men to go to the kitchen, where she will find another woman, Annemarie, who is interested in such issues.[8] Anni is thus relegated to the kitchen, to the traditional realm of women, the "private" realm, apart from the discourse of politics and history that men control.

The subsequent scene, where Anni and Annemarie meet in the kitchen, represents a turning point in the film: this is the first scene in which there is any prolonged contact between women, without men around.[9] Anni and Annemarie decide to

6. The German SDS is to be distinguished from the SDS in the USA, i.e., the Students for a Democratic Society. The two groups did play analagous leadership roles in the student movements in each of the two countries, and both were also characterized by increasing radicalization in the course of the 1960s. The German SDS was initially affiliated with the West German Social Democratic Party, the SPD; but already in 1960, as the SPD moved towards reformism, it broke all ties with the SDS, which the party considered too radical.

7. The press empire built up by Axel Springer in Berlin and West Germany includes many publications, including the most widely read German daily newspaper, the *Bildzeitung*, a tabloid-style publication that is noted for its sensationalistic news coverage and its conservative political bias. During the late 1960s the Springer press was especially virulent in its attacks on the student movement.

8. See Sander's discussion of the actual incident that inspired this scene in "der subjektive faktor, vertrackt," a pamphlet on the film authored by Sander and published by Basis-Film-Verleih (West Berlin: 1981), 10–12. The man who told her to go to the kitchen was Peter Schneider, who within a few years would become a well-known author in West Germany. Sander says that actually Schneider was much more sympathetic – "einfühlsam" – than the average male activist, and that the suggestion to go to the kitchen was also meant to be sympathetic.

9. After this point in the film, Anni is seen ever more frequently with women; at the beginning, she is almost always with men (who are "enlightening" her).

call all the women they know to meet and discuss issues relevant to their role as women, the beginning thus of the "Action Committee for the Liberation of Women" ("*Aktionsrat zur Befreiung der Frau* "),[10] the focus of Anni's political activity throughout most of the rest of the film. It is in this kitchen where Anni and Annemarie begin their efforts at uniting and empowering the women for whom the kitchen had symbolized powerlessness and isolation, where they plan their intervention in the "public" discourse from which they have been excluded.

To do so, they must expose the contradictions in the ideological dichotomy between a public, male sphere and a private, female sphere, "ideological divisions," as Judith Mayne writes, "which mask profound links."[11] The dichotomy of the public and private is closely associated with the rise of capitalism, but it is also the basis for what Kaja Silverman calls the "continuity between the discourse of capitalism and the student left on the question of woman."[12] This is the first contradiction the women must expose – a contradiction so aptly symbolized in Sander's film by the men sending Anni to the kitchen.

That locale is central to the ideology of a private, female realm – central indeed within the traditional, three-part German definition of the limits of that realm: *Kinder, Küche und Kirche* ("children, kitchen, and church"). In the film, the kitchen becomes a motif used to depict various contradictions of the public/private dichotomy. It is the main locus of interaction within the collective household, the *Wohngemeinschaft,* on which the narrative is centered for that strand of the plot dealing with the years 1967 through 1970. Within the "private" space represented by the residence of the collective, the kitchen is obviously the most "public" place. It is here that disagreements about the sharing of household duties are most evident in the piles of dirty dishes that Anni finds a breach of collective policy, a conflict housemate Matthias personalizes by calling

10. This was the name of the actual group of women within the SDS who first banded together, and Sander was one of its founding members. For a discussion of the "Aktionsrat," see Renny Harrigan, "The German Women's Movement and Ours," *Jump Cut* 27 (1982): 43.

11. Judith Mayne, "Female Narration, Women's Cinema," *New German Critique* 24–25 (Fall/Winter 1981–82): 160.

12. Kaja Silverman, "Helke Sander and the Will to Change," *Discourse* 6 (1983): 20; cf. also Craig Owens on the "fundamentally patriarchal bias" of Marxism: Owens, "The Discourse of Others: Feminists and Postmodernism," in *The Anti-Aesthetic,* ed. Hal Foster (Port Townsend, WA: Bay, 1983), 62–63.

Anni "anally fixated" for her reaction. It is in the kitchen that a large meal prepared by Till and shared by the group represents the most harmonious moment in the collective living experiment. It is also here that Anni observes the contradiction between Matthias "the socialist," with his copy of Habermas's *Theory and Praxis*, and Matthias whose "praxis" includes mailing his laundry home to his mother.

Near the end of the film, the collective household (*Wohngemeinschaft*) – and the student movement – have been disintegrating. This is apparent in the final sequence set in the collective apartment. All harmony has disappeared: ex-household members Till and Annemarie, both now members of a terrorist cell, have reappeared in the apartment, and Till holds a gun. He orders Anni about, and when the doorbell rings, he commands that she go to the kitchen.

Kaja Silverman writes that "Till's relegation of Anni to the kitchen indicates that feminism has no more to gain from terrorism than orthodox Marxism."[13] Silverman bases this conclusion on one line by Till, a difficult line to hear (or rather an easy one to miss) in a short and rather puzzling scene, but in a film where the kitchen is such an important motif, its mention cannot be ignored. The significance – and irony – of Till's mention of the kitchen is all the greater when Till's own association with the kitchen is taken into account.

Till is a male who is associated with the preparation of food: when he is first mentioned, Annemarie tells Anni that he is moving into the apartment with her, adding that he makes breakfast – a boon to the collective (and somewhat of a rare catch as a boyfriend). In the group meal mentioned above, which he has prepared, he wears an apron; and when, after having moved out of the household, he returns to claim an item he has left behind, it is a large pot he is seeking. Beyond the association with work traditionally devalued as "women's work," he is also depicted as being concerned about the needs of Anni's son Andres. Andres keeps taking Till's reading pillow, but Till understands the child's need to cuddle with it, as well as his need for household duties that are interesting and give him a sense of participating in the collective on more of an equal basis with the adults. Whereas Matthias shows the child documentary footage from Vietnam as a way of encouraging him to do his

13. Silverman,"Helke Sander," 26.

chores with the correct amount of solidarity, Till teaches Andres to help in the kitchen with the preparation of food, which the child obviously enjoys.

II. Looking at the Men

That it is precisely Till who winds up on what Anni calls the "*Holzweg*," the "wrong track" – terrorism – is a contradiction typical of characters in the film, and an indication of their complexity.[14] An interesting comparison can be made between Till and Matthias, whose political theory is so often contradicted by his personal praxis, but in a manner almost the opposite from that of Till.

As a socialist, Matthias has a certain theoretical belief in the equality of women, and it motivates the experiment in group living which the film follows from 1967 through 1970: his concern for Anni as a single, working mother is cited by the narrator as the impulse for the founding of the collective household (*Wohngemeinschaft*). But in the practical matters of everyday household life, he is the most resistant to change and unable to see how the dialectical analysis of which he is so fond might be applied to his own attitudes. He calls Anni "anally fixated" for complaining about dirty dishes, he sends his dirty laundry home to mother, he is the one who laughs most defensively at the idea that a group of women have met together, separately from the men ("What? Only women?"). When he does extend his theoretical knowledge to the situation within the household, it is only to educate someone else, Andres, and in a manner most removed from the concrete situation at hand: he explains household responsibilities via the struggle in Vietnam.

Matthias's theoretical "enlightenment" (the association with Habermas, for instance) contrasts thus with his unenlightened praxis at the level of personal interactions and the "private" realm of reproduction (e.g., the dirty laundry). Till's sensitivity and constructive engagement in those latter areas are in turn contrasted with his political development. The film depicts his move into terrorism as a dead end, a mistake that indeed is a major factor in the disintegration of the collective household (*Wohngemeinschaft*) – as well as the student movement as a whole.

14. This also refutes those who accuse Sander of creating "two-dimensional" male characters. For example, see Uta Berg-Ganschow, "Geschichte eines Nebenwiderspruchs," *Filme* 9 (June 1981): 58.

It is precisely the parallel between the situation within the collective household (*Wohngemeinschaft*) and the movement as a whole through which Sander is able to make a statement that bridges the gap between the focus on the "private" sphere of household interactions and the "external" history of the movement, with its meetings, rallies, and demonstrations in the streets. The latter level of the narrative depends most on the documentary footage Sander incorporates into her film, providing a counterpoint to the fictional scenes, which focus mostly on the collective household (*Wohngemeinschaft*). Sander's critique in turn is not directed solely at the "personal politics" of the men in the student movement; the political strategies and attitudes that characterized the male activists in their attempts to influence the public sphere in West Germany are also the object of critical investigation. As mentioned above, Till is portrayed as personally sympathetic, but his move toward terrorism is shown as a mistake.

"Comrades, your public events are unbearable," write Anni and her two women colleagues as they compose a leaflet underneath the bleachers which (through clever montage) seem to be those upon which the cheering men sit shouting "Ho, Ho, Ho Chi Minh!" This chant is led by Rudi Dutschke and Peter Weiss, captured in a piece of documentary footage.[15] "It's as though we left our identities at home": the women are fed up with the mass ritual, the pseudo-revolutionary rhetoric and bravado that characterize many of the events the male activists organize.

What disturbs Anni and her friends is a certain male romance with such rhetoric and posturing. Immediately after the bleacher scene there is documentary footage of police using water cannons on student demonstrators.[16] The scene is defamiliarized by the use of a colored filter (a shade of orange) and fairly humorous tuba music on the soundtrack; this distantiation is increased by the commentary of the narrator (read by Sander

15. Rudi Dutschke was one of the main leaders of the SDS, probably the best known, and certainly the one most vilified in the Springer press. Peter Weiss, author of *Marat/Sade, The Investigation, Vietnam-Discourse,* and *The Aesthetics of Resistance,* was very sympathetic to the student movement and indeed functioned as a mentor of sorts to the protesters. The scene with Anni and her friends under the bleachers is depicted in the photo on p. 273, above).

16. The West Berlin police used water cannons against the protesters who came to demonstrate the opening of the government's trial against Fritz Teufel, a member of the *Kommune 1,* on 28 November 1967. See Wolfgang Kraushaar, "Notizen zu einer Chronologie der Studentenbewegung," in *Was wir wurden,*

herself), which presents Anni's sudden realization of a certain unity underlying the obvious polarization of the scene: "The thought occurred to me that I could view all of this under the aspect that these were all men. The idea that all of them were lovers."[17] The contradiction between masses of men in violent, public confrontation and individual males as lovers in private settings, as well as possible parallels between the two images, suggest a perspective that undermines the traditional dichotomy of "friend versus foe," which is the normal logic of male confrontation. The narrator implies that there may be in male socialization elements that are common to both police and demonstrators, elements that are not ultimately productive for the development of a new type of politics.

The next sequence, again a mix of documentary footage that interrupts a fictional scene, would seem to pursue the same logic. When Jörn, a household member, enters the apartment, drenching wet, there are chants on the soundtrack that seem to be the appropriate accompaniment for the (immediately preceding) water cannon sequence. A shot of the drenched Jörn is then followed by a medium shot of a young man laughing, a shot from documentary footage of a similar – perhaps even the same – demonstration. The young man is also wet, laughing defiantly at having been sprayed. The next shot returns to Jörn on his bed, below the poster of his pop idol, Humphrey Bogart, a poster with which Jörn has been associated since the beginning of the film. Soon thereafter is another quick cut to documentary footage of Rudi Dutschke. The implied association of a modern icon of masculinity, Bogart, with the laughing young men of the student movement, and with its hero, Dutschke, underscores the romantic nature of the male role models and male bonding in the movement. In spite of these activists' opposition to established authority, they are united with those who uphold its order through their socialization as males in similarly "heroic" games and role models (and these cultural images and rituals in turn mediate their relationships with women).

The reading of the protest scene from a new, non-male perspective provides a guideline for interpreting the subsequent developments in the film, both inside and outside the collective

17. Sander, as narrator: "Der Gedanke kam auf, dies alles mal unter dem Aspekt zu betrachten, daß es Männer sind. Die Vorstellung, daß alle Liebhaber sind."

household (*Wohngemeinschaft*). The attraction to romantic, pseudo-revolutionary bravado and rhetoric foreshadows the deterioration of the movement into terrorist cells on the one hand and dogmatic factions squabbling over the "correct" interpretations of Marx and Lenin on the other. The men's ability to bond in a mass ritual modeled on revolutionary movements of other times and places (Vietnam, the German Communist Party of the Weimar Republic)[18] is interpreted by the women as "leaving one's identity at home." This characterization can also elucidate the movement toward the fetishization of praxis – as terror – on the part of some and the fetishization of theory – as dogma – by others. These developments depend on forgetting – or repressing – one's own concrete situation and history (for example, as a student with a middle-class background). The women, on the other hand, organize their activities on the basis of their own situtation and needs: they establish their own child-care centers and then begin to attempt organizing women workers within state-run child-care centers. This model of activism – organizing around local, immediate issues – would prove the more successful model for the next decade.[19]

In terms of characters in the film, it is again Matthias who provides an early model for the tendency to enjoy the abstraction of socialist theory to the detriment of his skills in dealing with the immediate reality around him. But the tendency within the movement to drift toward dogmatism is better displayed by Uwe, the figure who laughs most loudly when Anni suggests that women might be a class. For it is Uwe who lectures Anni, at a later point when she is his lover (!),[20] on the merits of Lenin over Bakunin while strolling through West Berlin's Botanic Gardens. When Anni brings up specific points that contradict

18. *Die Kommunistische Partei Deutschlands*, the *KPD*, founded in 1918. In the wake of the failed revolution in Germany and the murder of founders Rosa Luxemburg and Karl Liebknecht, the *KPD* remained the bitter rival of the *SPD*, the Social Democrats, for working class votes throughout the Weimar Republic; in 1933, both of these parties on the left were outlawed, a fate that the KPD encountered again after the war in West Germany, where in 1956 it was banned.

19. A similar point is made by Heinz Kersten in his review of the film, "Erfahrungen weitergeben," *Frankfurter Rundschau*, 16 July 1981.

20. Anni's affair with Uwe shows that she too has some contradictions – she is not so perfect as some reviewers seem to think. See, e.g., Claudia Lenssen, "Die schwere Arbeit der Erinnerung," *Frauen und Film* (September 1981): 41–44. (Another reviewer, on the other hand, feels Anni is portrayed as too weak to be a co-founder of the *Aktionsrat* – see Berg-Ganschow, "Nebenwiderspruchs," 59.)

Uwe's abstract Marxist-Leninism, he accuses her of being too concrete: "Don't be so 'concretistic'!" ("Sei nicht so konkretistisch!") It is Uwe who feels more comfortable joining one of the new Maoist parties (the *K-Parteien*)[21] than continuing his relationship with Anni, who asks so many questions and is not trusted by party members.

Just after the scene in which Anni and Uwe presumably part, she comes upon Till playing pinball in a bar. Here she tells Till that she disagrees with his political choice, calling it a dead end, but Till says hardly a word to her. Dialogue with the faction moving toward terrorism has been cut off, too. The end of Anni's relationships with Till and Uwe reflects the generalized phenomenon of fragmentation in the student movement as it degenerated into dogmatic and/or terroristic rhetoric. The next sequence further illustrates this process: at home, Anni encounters two of her housemates practicing the Morse code. They tell her: "The real revolutionaries are now in jail." She then finds Andres with a young girl who calls Anni "bourgeois" for demanding she and Andres return some things she claimed they had stolen.[22] The narrator's voice is then heard over a shot of the apartment: "The longing for simple solutions creates new tragedies."[23]

From this point late in the film, the narrative strand following the collective household (*Wohngemeinschaft*) quickly comes to an end. Another piece of documentary footage is shown: a demonstration of childcare workers, one of the early organizing achievements of the new women's movement.[24] The budding women's movement gains strength as the student movement dissolves.

After this footage, the apartment is shown again, but as a meeting place for Anni's women's group. The next scene is that

21. The *K-Parteien* and *K-Gruppen* were the result of factional subdivisions among Maoist student activists in the late 1960s and early 1970s, each group claiming to be the true successor to the old *KPD* (*Kommunistische Partei Deutschlands*), the German Communist Party.

22. In an earlier sequence, Andres had already found a box of hand grenades in a closet, which his horrified mother had then removed from the apartment.

23. "Die Sehnsucht nach einfachen Lösungen schafft neue Tragödien."

24. On the soundtrack, as this footage of the women's demonstration is shown, the song "Honolulu" is heard, with its description of a utopian Honolulu (as opposed to the real one) in the "Land der Amazonen" ("land of the Amazons"). The song, by Valie Export and Ingrid Wiener, was composed some years later than the demonstration.

of the prostrate Jörn grieving for his deceased wife Sophie, with the noise of the household in obvious conflict with his mood. And the final scene in the *Wohngemeinschaft*, as mentioned above, is the one in which Till orders Anni to the kitchen.

The collective living experiment collapses as does the broader student movement. What is left is a fragmented movement, terrorist cells and dogmatic sects, as well as an emergent movement of women, which seems the only hopeful strand. What does this history mean to the filmmaker who chooses to return to it ten years later? What are the coordinates of that "constellation" that contains the events of the late 1960s and the perspective at the end of the next decade from which Sander constructs her vision of the earlier period? How does the filmmaker foreground her own position and interests with regard to those historical events she thematizes?

III. Ten Years After

Sander explicitly incorporates the perspective of 1980 – the year in which *The Subjective Factor* was made – into the film itself. The film opens in 1980, as Anni is joined in front of the television set by her son Andres. He brings her a collection of photographs documenting the student protests of the 1960s. For himself he has bought a book of photographs that documents the recent (as of 1980) occupation of the site of the proposed atomic reactor at Gorleben by antinuclear protestors.[25] The camera focuses on the books, one partially covering the other, as both Anni and Andres begin to page through them. This image concretizes the overlap of two historical positions: the late 1960s and the early 1980s. Anni starts to review her memory of the issues and events of the 1960s, while Andres looks at more current issues and events, the ones which engage him in 1980. Neither position can be seen as separate from its relation to the other.

It is Andres who makes possible Anni's act of remembrance, which opens up the narrative of the years 1967 through 1970. She pauses at a picture in the book he has given her; the picture then comes to life, as it were, through a cut to documentary footage of the car pictured in the photo. The transition to the representation of memory is underscored by Anni's voice-over: "That's your mother in that car." It is Andres who will provide

25. The book Anni receives is called *Ihr müßt diese Typen nur ins Gesicht sehen. Apo Berlin 1966–1969*. The book Andres holds is *Republik Freies Wendland*.

the major clue for the viewer as to whether a sequence in the film takes place in the later 1960s or in 1980, simply by his age (and of course the fact that two different actors play him). It is ultimately Andres who provides the link to the issues of the 1980s and thus indicates that the film is not merely a pessimistic treatise on the failures of the past, but a critique grounded in a concern that the struggle is still as necessary as ever.

Andres appears as an adolescent three times in the film. The first is at the beginning, where his age and Anni's hair length and style become associated with the 1980 strand of the film's narrative. After the documentary sequence initiated by Anni's paging through the book, a fictional sequence opens with a shot of a little blond boy calling to Anni; the transition to 1967 is thus completed, underscored by the ensuing voice-over narration.

The next sequence where Andres appears as an adolescent is one which could be called the "cockroach sequence," since it begins with an extreme close-up of a cockroach, seen from its underside as it climbs up a clear surface, presumably the transparent wall of some kind of encasement. The next shot shows seemingly gigantic cockroaches in what is actually a miniature kitchen; on a glass wall of the case that encloses this exhibit (in the aquarium at the Berlin Zoo)[26] one can see the reflection of the adolescent Andres. On the soundtrack one hears Anni's voice: "Do you know that we were here before, thirteen years ago?" She is thus presumably talking to Andres, as becomes clear in a subsequent shot. Then she mentions that NASA experiments with radioactivity have caused cockroaches to grow in size. This remark is followed immediately by Mick Jagger singing the words "Time is on my side" on the soundtrack, from the song of the same name. The next shot shows the same exhibit, and reflected on the glass are both Anni and Andres, now once again a small boy; the date is therefore thirteen years before, 1967.

Andres, filmically a sign of the 1980s, is thus once again associated thematically with nuclear issues. It is a relatively well known hypothesis among those concerned about the arms race that cockroaches may survive a nuclear war; time is on their side, so to speak, unless Andres's generation can prevent them from inheriting the planet. This is in any case the future that, from the standpoint of 1980, Andres faces.

26. According to Berg-Ganschow, "Nebenwiderspruch," 58.

The final sequence in which Andres appears as an adolescent is a montage of still photographs. It is a non-diegetic photo essay that begins after one of the many camera pans across the posters on the wall of the collective apartment.[27] The opening still depicts soldiers raping a woman. The camera then pans across a photo of Soviet leader Leonid Brezhnev with the Politburo, then across a photo of U.S. President Jimmy Carter with the leaders of the Western Alliance (all men, except for Prime Minister Margaret Thatcher of Great Britain); next one sees a photo of Carter and West German Chancellor Helmut Schmidt standing side by side, followed by one of Brezhnev and East German leader Erich Honecker kissing. Then there is a still of a jet behind rows of bombs in v-formation is followed by a photo of a pile of skulls, identified by Silverman as the skulls of Holocaust victims.[28] The sequence is concluded by the photo of the adolescent Andres.

There are various possible interpretations of this sequence of images primarily from about 1980. An obvious one would be that the world was still very much in danger long after America's involvement in Vietnam and the worldwide protest movement it spawned in the 1960s. Analyzing the montage of photos, one must not ignore another factor: gender. Two women are shown in the entire sequence, one being raped by soldiers, the other Prime Minister Thatcher, a woman who seems quite at home with her role as a member of one of the two dominant military blocs. She does not seem at all uncomfortable in the community of males about her, nor does she seem out of place in a montage unified thematically by images of soldiers, bombs, military alliances, and male bonding rites (best typified perhaps by Honecker and Brezhnev kissing). Her presence does not undermine a depiction of militarism as primarily masculine.[29]

Nonetheless, as Silverman asserts, the film does not settle for any easy "conflation of male subjectivity" with power and with

27. Two posters on which the camera lingers are movie posters for Louis Malle's *Viva Maria* and Godard's *La Chinoise.*

28. Silverman, "Helke Sander," 23.

29. The depiction of maleness and militarism as interrelated in this sequence is underscored both by the earlier narrative commentary on the maleness of both police and demonstrators and by the sequence that almost immediately precedes the photo montage: documentary footage of the defensive reactions of male SDS members to a satiric poem by women activists on the topic of penis envy, titled, appropriately enough, "Penisneid."

fascism.[30] For of course the last male in the photo montage is Andres, the child of the protagonist Anni, the child Anni declares more important to her than all the causes in the world. The association of Andres in the film with nuclear issues suggests an interpretation of his presence at the end of the photo montage: he represents the generation that will inherit – and have to confront – the world of soldiers, Cold War leaders, bombs, and the potential for mass genocide the photo sequence depicts. Silverman suggests that in Andres can be read the hope of a different kind of male, not aligned as much with "classic" male values.[31]

Sander avoids any kind of biological determinism. In the face of the situation threatening the planet, both men and women are needed, men who will resist the militaristic logic she indicates as having roots in male socialization (and certainly in patriarchy) and women who will refuse to accomodate to that pervasive logic. Just as Thatcher has little quarrel with the dominant logic, so too are women shown in the film who side with the male leadership against Anni. One of the most subversive aspects of the project of feminism is evident in Sander's film: the questioning of binarism and the traditional dichotomies so basic to dominant ideologies.[32] In seeing an underlying unity between police and students in terms of male socialization, in seeing the limitations of the traditional definitions of the split between "right" and "left,"[33] in seeing the danger to the world posed by both sides of the East/West power struggle, Sander undermines conventional dichotomies. Her film aligns itself both with feminism and the peace movement's search for peace and a world order that transcends the hegemony of the superpower blocs.[34]

She does not see the feminist project as requiring withdrawal

30. Silverman,"Helke Sander," 23.

31. Silverman,"Helke Sander," 23.

32. Cf. Craig Owens's remarks ("Discourse of Others," 61–62) on the "critique of binarism," as related to both the project of feminism and of postmodernism.

33. For example, the discussion with Uwe on concentration camps in China for not racial, but "class" enemies; the pictures of Brezhnev, Honecker, etc.

34. Now, in the aftermath of 1989, when the Soviet Union loosened its hegemonic hold on East Germany and Eastern Europe, one wonders whether in post-Cold-War Germany, the pacifist, "Green" tendencies with which Sander's film aligns itself will be able to play a role, or whether more conservative, nationalistic forces will remain dominant. After the early 1980s the peace move-

from other oppositional struggles, nor does she see the critique of the student movement which led to the formation of the women's movement as a denunciation of the former: "The women in the film write in their leaflet – an authentic one, by the way – for the Vietnam Congress: 'Comrades, your public events are unbearable'; but that didn't keep the women from participating in those events."[35] The women considered themselves part of a broader movement – as is clear from the wording of Sander's own speech to the SDS Congress in 1968.

That speech is cited in the film's most self-reflexive scene. Footage of Helke Sander's 1968 speech to the SDS is shown being projected onto a screen, at a point in the film when the fictional Anni is finally able to speak at the SDS congress. Then, as the documentary footage is being projected, Helke Sander herself appears, placing her body on the edge of the screen: the filmmaker in 1980 watches her own image from 1968, the newer image partially overlapping the older. This sequence foregrounds once again the overlap of perspectives and issues of the 1980s and 1960s which inform the film. Indeed, it foregrounds the historical and autobiographical project of the film itself: from the standpoint of 1980, the filmmaker reviews personal and collective history.[36]

In the speech to the SDS, Sander had appealed to the organi-

ment in Germany (and elsewhere) seemed stymied – until Gorbachev's ascension. Whether or not what E.P. Thompson calls "the forces of peace and freedom, of a greenish libertarian socialism" will ultimately prevail, I agree with him that one major factor influencing the changes in Eastern Europe has been precisely those nonaligned forces, through redefining "the political art of the possible" and playing a critical part in the "ideological moment" when the "ideological field of force" we call the Cold War became unstable. Thompson, "History Turns on A New Hinge," *The Nation,* 29 January 1990: 121.

35. "Wenn die Frauen in dem Film das–übrigens originale–Flugblatt zum Vietnamkongress schreiben: 'Genossen, eure Veranstaltungen sind unerträglich,' so hat sie das nicht davon abgehalten, an den Veranstaltungen teilzunehmen." Sander, interview with Lorez, "Einmischung," 9.

36. A similar sequence occurs earlier in the film, when the point is made that since the 1960s Central America has replaced Vietnam as the major site of U.S. intervention. The viewer sees a film projector being readied, and then documentary footage of demonstrations from the 1960s is projected onto the screen. The footage shows demonstrations in front of the corporate headquarters of the Springer Press, the so-called *Springer-Haus* in West Berlin. At the same time, a radio news report from 1980 is heard on the soundtrack, presenting the remarks of a conservative West German politician (Heiner Geissler) in support of the military junta then controlling El Salvador. Thus, while the filmmaker reviews historical footage from the 1960s, the radio reminds her of the state of events in 1980.

zation to take seriously the question of the role of women, warning of the waste of energy that would result should the men oppose women's attempts to include their concerns as part of the broader agenda of the movement.[37] The movement did instead fragment and dissipate; why that happened is one question Sander investigates in *The Subjective Factor.* Some possible answers are implied: the attraction of dogma and violence, for example, is depicted as a major cause. The filmmaker's interest in the demise of the movement from her perspective ten years later is in no small part to provide the oppositional movements she supports in the 1980s a chance to review the mistakes of the past and learn from them, and to arm a new generation with a history of the struggles that need to be continued.[38]

> To articulate the past historically does not mean to recognize it "the way it really was.". . . It means to seize hold of a memory as it flashes up at a moment of danger.
>
> — Walter Benjamin[39]

This article is a revised and abridged version of a section in Richard W. McCormick, The Politics of the Literature and Film, *Copyright © 1991 by Princeton University Press.*

37. Helke Sander's challenge to the male activists in September 1968 at the SDS's twenty-third "Delegiertenkonferenz" in Frankfurt: "If the SDS should not be capable of the leap forward to this realization, then we would be faced with a power struggle that would be a tremendous waste of energy. For we would win this struggle, because we are historically in the right!" ("Sollte dem SDS der Sprung nach vorn zu dieser Einsicht nicht gelingen, dann wären wir allerdings auf einen Machtkampf angewiesen, was eine ungeheure Energieverschwendung bedeuten würde, denn wir würden diesen Machtkampf gewinnen, weil wir historisch im Recht sind!" – quoted in the film.)

38. Sander in 1981 advised young women to intervene in the struggles of the 1980s, underscoring again the example of the women in the SDS: "They didn't perceive themselves as victims, but rather as autonomous human beings. What was most important was intervention, which is winning ground again today in the women's peace movement." ("Sie haben sich nicht als Opfer, sondern als eigenverantwortliche Menschen empfunden. Das Wichtige bestand in der Einmischung, die heute wieder Boden gewinnt mit der Frauen-Friedenbewegung.") Sander, interview with Lorez, 9.

39. Walter Benjamin, "Theses on the Philosophy of History," in *Illuminations,* ed. Hannah Arendt , trans. Harry Zohn (New York: Schocken, 1969), 255.

Appendix

History and Feminist Film Criticism

17

Frauen und Film and Feminist Film Culture in West Germany

miriam hansen

We reprint here an article by Miriam Hansen, in which, from the perspective of 1983, she traces the history of "the first and only European feminist film journal," Frauen und Film, *founded in 1974 by Helke Sander in West Berlin. This journal is now the oldest existing feminist journal on film anywhere. The development of the journal since the early 1980s is explored by Ramona Curry in the next article in our volume.*
—The Editors

German women filmmakers find themselves in a peculiar bind when it comes to modes of patriarchal cinema. Like all independent filmmakers, they are confronting Goliath – the hegemony of Hollywood and its Common Market subsidiaries. Beyond the domain of commercial control, however, in the precarious enclave of federal subsidies and TV co-productions, women filmmakers encounter the competition of a whole troop of Davids, already firmly entrenched in the field. It has become commonplace in discussions on contemporary German cinema to cite its unique legal and economic substructure as one of the keys to its artistic success and international visibility. It is equally common, though much less acknowledged, that women filmmakers are conspicuously absent from the pantheon of New German auteurs. The American-styled New German Cinema canonizes names like Werner Herzog, Rainer Werner Fassbinder, Wim Wenders, and Volker Schlöndorff, but rarely extends to Ula Stöckl, Helke Sander, Jutta Brückner, or Ulrike Ottinger. In New York the Museum of Modern Art's 1982–83 series of "Recent Films from West Germany," which prides itself on featuring lesser-known directors, did not include a single film directed by a woman – a glaring omission even if judged only by the enormous increase of women's productions in recent years.

Yet German women filmmakers are primarily involved in a struggle on the domestic front. Competing with both commercial cinema and the established male avant-garde, women filmmakers face tremendous problems financing their films and often incur considerable personal debts; only gradually have they succeeded in tapping the same system of federal grants and subsidies that advanced their male colleagues. Meanwhile, a large number of films directed by women are being co-produced by German television stations – a form of subsidy that guarantees access yet also tends to impose artistic and political restrictions via production guidelines and program committees.

The effect of not naming is censorship, whether caused by the imperialism of patriarchal language or the underdevelopment of a feminist language. We need to begin analyzing our own films, but first it is necessary to learn to speak in our own name.[1]

The search for a feminist language in film, a language that would transcend the patriarchal terms of sexual difference, is not exactly facilitated by the existence of a more or less established male avant garde. The peculiar history of German cinema complicates the oedipal scenario of avant-garde protest that feminist film theory and practice seek to displace. The Cinema of the Fathers, representing commercial interests, is one of the Stepfathers and Grandfathers at best; the Cinema of the Sons, at least in some of its representatives, is less concerned with conquering the international domain of Art than with applying its artistic efforts to the political transformation of the West German public sphere. As German women filmmakers are learning "to speak in [their] own name," they too are engaged in building an oppositional public sphere, linking the women's movement to female theatergoers and TV audiences across the country. Like their male colleagues, women filmmakers confront the key contradiction in store for all counterhegemonic film practice: how to develop an autonomous discourse while, at the same time, establishing, maintaining, and increasing rapport with an audience.

1. B. Ruby Rich, "In the Name of Feminist Film Criticism," *Heresies* 9 (1980): 78.

In both the work of "naming" and the construction of a public sphere essential to a feminist film culture, the journal *Frauen und Film (FuF – Women and Film)* has played and, I hope, will continue to play a crucial role. Founded by filmmaker Helke Sander (*REDUPERS; The Subjective Factor*) in 1974, *FuF* stands as the first and only European feminist film journal. Published by Rotbuch Verlag in Berlin as a quarterly (beginning with #7), the journal is into its 34th issue. Sander signed as *FuF*'s sole editor up to #27 (February 1981); with that issue, editorial responsibility shifted to collectives in Berlin, Frankfurt, Cologne, and Paris. In July 1982, the Berlin collective decided to discontinue the journal, thus causing the publisher to withdraw. Meanwhile, the Frankfurt collective formed a new editorial board and linked up with Verlag Roter Stern in Frankfurt, which will publish *FuF* on a biannual basis. I will not go into the Berlin/Frankfurt split, which bears only remote resemblance to the separation of the *Camera Obscura* collective from *Women and Film* in 1974. Suffice it to say that, with the continuation of *FuF*, feminist film culture has salvaged a centerpiece of its organizational substructure, a vital platform not only for issues of strategy, exchange of information, and critical discussion but also for the articulation and revision of feminist theories of film.

The program of *FuF*, as outlined in #6 (1975), lists two major objectives: (a) "to analyze the workings of patriarchal culture in cinema"; (b) "to recognize and name feminist starting points in film and develop them further." The first objective requires a critical analysis of existing cinema in all its aspects: film politics and economics, film theory and criticism, as well as the discourse of its products – in short, a comprehensive critique of patriarchal cinema. The second complex includes the relationship between women's cinema and the women's movement, the rediscovery of earlier women filmmakers, the current situation of women working in film and other media, textual analyses, and the question of a feminine/feminist aesthetics.

FuF's critique of patriarchal structures in New German Cinema can be traced on three different levels. On the level of the institutional framework, *FuF* calls attention to the inequities of the subsidy system that extends privileges to already successful directors rather than individual projects. Women are grossly underrepresented in the committees that decide on grants and awards – hence the political stress on the demand for equal representation. The standards of professionalism by which these committees tend to rationalize their decisions also discourage collective and nonhierarchic modes of production, thus pitting women filmmakers not only against male directors but also against each other. Financial support from TV stations, a primary source for women's films, is tied to production codes that restrict the critical treatment of issues crucial to a feminist film practice – abortion, female sexuality, marriage. The mechanism of public reception further ensures that patriarchal imbalance persists even in a protectionist film culture: festivals, press conferences, and reviews again and again confirm *FuF*'s contention that male arbiters still control the representation of women in German cinema. This control includes the token acclaim granted by male critics to some women filmmakers but not to others as well as the liberal endorsement of the new "woman's film."

On yet another level of critique, feminist analysis focuses on the notion of "indivisible labor." *FuF* programmatically devotes itself to the work of women in the media whose names disappear behind the name of the male auteur. A chief offender in this respect is undoubtedly Werner Herzog, who may give public credit to his cameraman but never to Beate Mainka-Jellinghaus, probably the best editor that German cinema has ever had.[2] *FuF*'s efforts to render invisible labor visible range from identifying editors and producers to scriptwriters and collaborators (see the interviews with M. von Trotta, Gisela Tuchtenhagen, and Danielle Huillet).

On a third – and actually the least conspicuous level – *FuF* criticizes patriarchal cinema's products. The analysis of male-directed films concentrates on the new wave of so-called "women's films" as the commercial response to the women's movement. In this context, we find reviews of Fassbinder's *Effi Briest* and Peter Handke's *The Left-Handed Woman* alongside reviews of foreign films featuring the alleged New Woman. The stars of New German Cinema, however, remain predictably marginal to *FuF*'s discussions: Herzog is represented only with a

2. Thanks to Ruby Rich for remembering an occasion on which, for once, he did: "My editor, Beate Mainka-Jellinghaus, is very important to me, and I would say that without her I would be only a shadow of myself. But there's always and enormous struggle going on between the two of us, and it's very strange how she behaves during this process. She's *very* rude with me, and she expresses her opinions in a manner that is like the *most* mediocre housewife" ("Images at the Horizon," workshop at Facet Multimedia Center, Chicago, 17 April 1979).

review of *Nosferatu*; Wenders, except for a recent interview concerning *Lightning over Water*, is featured with a single quote from *Kings of the Road*, "the story about the absence of women which is at the same time the story of the desire that wants them to be present." The photograph heading these lines shows the depopulated arena of the German Bundestag (parliament). The only male filmmaker given more extensive discussion space in *FuF* is Alexander Kluge, a director whose professed concern with "women's topics" has provoked feminist reactions ranging from severe polemics to measured ambivalence.

In the search for a feminist discourse in film, for modes of perception and production other than those circumscribed by patriarchal codes, *FuF* again and again encounters the difficulties of definition, of appropriating useful forms of resistance while asserting difference against cooptation. Consider, for example, the longstanding discussion on the principle of collectivity, starting with a special focus on collective production in #8 (1976). On the one hand, collectivity remains a utopian goal that fueled the women's movement, a weapon against the hierarchy, competition, and isolation imposed by patriarchal modes of production. On the other hand, the notion of collectivity may itself turn into an ideology when it is used to justify dilettantism, false harmony, and the exploitation of allegedly poorly qualified labor. Furthermore, the idea of collaborative films projects has been marketed by a group of male filmmakers (including Fassbinder, Kluge, and Schlöndorff), mostly to the exclusion of women directors. Together with a devastating review of *Germany in Autumn*, *FuF* prints an open letter signed by feminist film workers and activists, condemning the most saving claim of the film – its collective intervention at a time of political crisis – as an arrogant and hypocritical gesture that effectively denies similar efforts on the part of filmmakers of lesser means and reputations. In the same issue of *FuF* (#16), however, Sander, in an essay on "Film Politics as Politics of Production," refers to *Germany in Autumn* as a viable model for collaborative projects on a feminist basis.

When *FuF* advocates a "politics of production" or discusses "forms of production" from a feminist perspective, the term "production" has to be understood in the widest possible sense. As indicated, *FuF* has programmatically presented the work of women editors, cinematographers, and producers – each the focus of an individual issue. Similarly, it devoted a special issue to the "visible" woman – the actress. The work of naming – of making public – includes the creation of a countertradition of women directors, ranging from Leontine Sagan, Maya Deren, Marguerite Duras, and Vera Chytilova to filmmakers of a younger generation such as Valie Export, Elfi Mikesch, Margaret Raspé, and Pola Reuth. Beyond these traditional branches of film production, however, *FuF*'s discussion of forms of production encompasses the production of the very experience that requires a feminist film practice: the gender-specific mediation of all perception. In this vein, a special issue on women spectators bypasses psychoanalytic theories of reception in favor of documenting traces of authentic experience within and against the grain of patriarchal conditions of spectatorship.[3] Similarly, issues on lesbian cinema, pornography, and eroticism investigate the production of images that inscribe women's experience of their bodies and sexuality in a double structure of repression and subversion.

In its theoretical positions, articulated primarily by Helke Sander and Gertrud Koch, *FuF* shares the skepticism voiced in German feminist theory by Silvia Bovenschen and Ulrike Prokop[4] – adamantly opposed to feminine essentialism, yet more utopian and at the same time more iconoclastic than psychoanalytic-semiological directions of cinefeminism. While the "Parisian perspective," to use Ruby Rich's charming phrase, has made its way into *FuF* in the shape of translations and conference reports, its reception is counterbalanced by a notion of radical subjectivity that clearly betrays the influence of the Frankfurt School. Following this tradition, the theoretical search for the aesthetic dimension of feminist film practice inevitably entails a critical interaction with patriarchal film culture in its most complex instances – in the political and aesthetic avant-garde of male cinema.

This article appeared originally in Heresies *16 (vol. 4, no. 4, 1983): 30–31.*

3. The only essays translated so far are Sander's "Feminism and Film" and Koch's "Why Women Go to the Movies," *Jump Cut* 27 (1982): 49–53.

4. For Bovenschen, see, "Is There a Feminine Aesthetic?" *New German Critique* 10 (1977): 111–37, and "The Contemporary Witch, the Historical Witch and the Witch Myth," *NGC* 15 (1978): 83–119. *NGC* 13 (1978), an issue on the German women's movement, contains a translation from Prokop's book *Weiblicher Lebenszusammenhang* (Frankfurt/M.: Suhrkamp, 1976).

18

Frauen und Film — Then and Now

ramona curry

Ramona Curry, writing at the end of the 1980s, traces the history of Frauen und Film *with an emphasis on its shift during that decade. When founded in 1974 it was a praxis-oriented journal dedicated to agitating for women making films and creating a forum in which discussions of their films could take place. In the 1980s the journal has evolved into a more theoretically oriented journal, and it is now published in Frankfurt. But* Frauen und Film *has remained indispensable to those interested in feminist perspectives in (and on) German cinema, and Curry's history of the journal so far makes its significance even clearer, as well as contributing to a better understanding of the development of feminism and feminist film theory since the early 1970s.*
—THE EDITORS

This paper has a two-fold purpose: first, to inform about and motivate discussion of the German feminist film journal *Frauen and Film*, both in its earlier and current form, and second, using *Frauen and Film* as a model, to reflect on the importance and function of film publications in the context of film production and film studies.

With the term "film studies," I refer to a broad range of discussion about film – and increasingly also of video and television – that encompasses criticism and theory, history of film production and aesthetics, teaching and writing about media inside and outside academia. As this sentence indicates, I see a number of dichotomies within cinema studies, some more pronounced and explicit than others, which I believe have been set up and maintained by practitioners in the field for reasons other than convenience or even definition of interests. These dichotomies might be phrased succinctly, if somewhat simplistically, as oppositional pairs: film production / film theory, popular culture / esoteric art, political engagement / *de facto* analysis, in short, *Praxis* and *Theorie.* (I use these terms with the understanding that their referents are interdependent and the distinctions they specify are ultimately artificial, though operative.) I shall argue that these distinctions, as they might be used in describing the character of a given film journal, express a kind of political and professional "Weltanschauung" (worldview) – one perhaps ought to say "Filmweltanschauung" – which in fact itself has no small effect on the shape of that film world. That said, my ulterior purpose thus revealed, I wish to turn to the specific and significant case of *Frauen und Film.*

Film scholar Miriam Hansen's article "*Frauen und Film* and Feminist Film Culture in West Germany," published in 1983 in *Heresies,*[1] gives an excellent overview of the history and ideology of the film journal up to that point. In it, she notes the change in editorial board that had taken place shortly before but emphasizes the journal's continuity. Five years later, after the new editorial collective has brought out nine substantial issues, an updated evaluation of *Frauen und Film* might now more clearly indicate the shift in focus and policy changes that have occurred between the founding of the journal and its present form.

The feminist film journal *Frauen und Film* was brought out quarterly for almost eight years after its founding in 1974 by a group of women filmmakers and critics in West Berlin, with Helke Sander initially serving as its chief editor and publisher. Its primary objectives were an ongoing investigation and indictment of sexism in contemporary mass media, both in programming and production, and the concomitant demand for radically improved opportunities for women working in media in West Germany. Long-standing editors Claudia Lenssen and Uta Berg-Ganschow wrote in Issue No. 34, the last that collective would bring out:

> From the beginning, the texts in *Frauen und Film* were polemic, unfair, enraged, ironic and bitter. Helke Sander's intention was not to explain, rather, she wrote from her point of view as an unemployed filmmaker. . . . The case at issue was the lack of opportunities for work and expression for women in film.

Helke Sander (who had actually put out the first number single-handedly) was listed as publisher through Issue No. 27 (Feb-

1. Miriam Hansen, "*Frauen und Film* and Feminist Film Culture in West Germany," *Heresies* [Vl. 4, No. 4, Issue No. 16] (1983): 30–31 (also reprinted in this volume).

ruary 1981), but then turned all editorial responsibility over to colleagues on the journal who had been primary contributors and editors for a number of previous issues: Claudia Lenssen and Uta Berg-Ganschow in Berlin, Regine Halter in Cologne, Karola Gramann in Frankfurt, Heike Hurst in Paris, among a number of other regular contributors in those German cities and occasionally Munich. A politically leftist publishing house in Berlin, Rotbuch Verlag, had been won over to print the journal beginning with the seventh issue. Although that issue was twice reprinted and sold over 3000 copies, the publishing house generally had to subsidize the printing costs and was never able to pay contributors. Thus, the editors pointed out ironically, all labor was donated on a journal for which one of the primary principles was the elevation of work by women out of the realm of the unrecognized, unrewarded, unpaid.[2] The free-lance filmmakers and critics who regularly produced the journal, some among them mothers, had to meet other professional and personal demands on their time and, despite their dedication, over the years found bringing out a 55-page film journal every three months increasingly onerous.

Morale also sank, for the initial response to the journal appeared to wane. Subscriptions did not grow and sales in bookshops dropped, the magazine was no longer sold table to table in neighborhood bars, as initially, or actively promoted in women's centers. Advertising campaigns by the publishing company proved ineffective – the 1982 issues sold fewer than 100 copies each. The Berlin editors found the diminishing response particularly discouraging in light of their conscious attempt to unify film production, film criticism, and film theory, to address women working in all those fields and motivate them to cooperation.

On the other hand, the editors could point to the recognition *Frauen and Film* had attained among fellow (including male) film journalists and in some instances even a measure of influence on relevant decisions in media-related government agencies. (*Frauen and Film's* demand, concomitant with that of the Verband der Filmarbeiterinnen [organization of women working in film] that 50 percent of government positions making decisions about film subsidies go to women and for parity of women's involvement in other aspects of film work was never

2. The editorial board did receive a grant in 1980 from the Filmreferat of the Ministry of the Interior to support their work for six issues.

fully met, but the radicality of the demand forced attention to the issues and some policy adjustments, some even of substantial, rather than merely of a token nature.) Even this ostensible success of the journal did not seem to the editors to be without its cost, however. Lenssen and Berg-Ganschow wrote in their analysis in Issue No. 34:

> Professionalism seemed an ideal to us when nothing was expected of *Frauen und Film*; professionalism as praise became questionable to us as we moved into a position – marginal, yet still a position – of administered culture, as well-intentioned critics spoke of our filling an annoying gap. As film criticism could no longer ignore us and gave us friendly mention and respect, we could no longer ignore that we had achieved something we hadn't wanted.

These editors believed that the institutional recognition of the journal had co-opted its radical potential to call for new ways of creating, perceiving, and discussing images.

To those who knew of these internally discussed concerns, it came as no surprise when the Berlin editors decided to cease publication with Issue No. 34, which appeared in January 1983. Disagreeing that the journal had outlived its potential, three contributors and occasional editors associated with the University of Frankfurt decided to carry on with a new concept and format. The Frankfurt collective, consisting initially of Karola Gramann, Gertrud Koch, and Heide Schlüpmann,[3] has carried on the publication of *Frauen und Film* for five years, bringing out biannual issues devoted successively to German media and women's experience in the 1950's, psychoanalytic theory, the avant-garde, masquerade, masochism, the male as object of desire, early film history, and soap opera.

The format and contents of issues of the current *Frauen and Film* in comparison to those brought out under the previous editorial boards mark the journal as now serving a different audience and a different function. One should not ignore many similarities, however. Many of the contributors are identical, not only the editors, but many others including Noll Brinckmann, Jutta Brückner, Uta Berg-Ganschow, Claudia Hoff, and Monika

3. Frequent contributors include Annete Brauerhoch, Renate Lippert, Noll Brinkmann, Dagmar Ungureit, and Eva-Maria Warth. Karola Gramann, who became director of the West German Short Film Festival in Oberhausen in 1985, is no longer listed in every issue as copublisher with Koch and Schlüpmann.

Treut. Included among the contributors are filmmakers and critics as well as theorists and academics. As previously, each issue addresses a general theme, but contains additional, specifically topical information as well, including reviews or longer critical discussions of newly released films directed by European and American women, short annoucements of interest to women filmmakers and artists, and advertisements from some film distributors and other film journals.

The policy of discussing some unusual new films directed by men but particularly involving women appears to continue, as does the stance that women's films should not be exempt in principle from negative criticism by women critics. One sees the occasional specific (but previously not uncontroversial) contribution from a male. While twice as long as the quarterly, with about 120 pages of text, the revised journal resembles the earlier in its use of large black and white photographs and photo-essays interspersed in the text. The print is larger, but the paper quality not noticeably better. The look of the cover is somewhat slicker, however, and the graphic appearance overall less complex, particularly when compared to the first twenty or so issues of *Frauen und Film*, when the title was handwritten, no upper case letters were used, and a collage style was employed inside and out (with many cover-page collages contributed by Silke Grossmann.) These aspects of the material construction of the journal are not trivial or incidental, but comprise the syntax of a publication, much as do the choices of materials and formal techniques in a media production.

Given all these apparent similarities, what, then, are the contrasts between the previous and current forms of *Frauen und Film*, to which I've referred? The primary distinction is one of *emphasis*, which had in fact gradually shifted over the years, for reasons I shall further discuss below. It is only slightly overstating the case to assert that the shift in *Frauen und Film* has been toward the contrasting term in the oppositional pairs I've sketched: from political engagement with contemporary issues of film production and distribution to more theoretical concerns in film reception.

The earlier *Frauen and Film*, for example, would not, I believe, have devoted an issue to the 1950s (although individual articles on "our mothers' generation's film reception" did appear) nor to so thorough a discussion of psychoanalytic theory about viewer response or identification processes. The concern of the earlier *Frauen und Film* was instead with women's lived experience and the practical limitations on their making, viewing, and discussing images of themselves. There were issues on images of old women in the cinema, for example, and of mothers, on sexuality in film, on film politics, on the new "women's film" in Hollywood, on documentary film, on women cinematographers, etc. There was a predominance of interviews with filmmakers, mostly German women who theretofore had scarcely had opportunity to speak publicly of their work.

Specific topics and approaches taken to a general theme were quite eclectic within a single issue, with articles tending to be relatively short and to have the character of personal essays directed generally, but not exclusively, at an audience of feminist filmgoers. Reviews of newly completed films by women were given prominent place, as was distribution information about them and news about film festivals. One contributor founded a feminist film distribution company in Berlin, others coorganized women's film screenings and seminars.

The predominant interest of the earlier journal was thus clearly in contemporary film production and in sexual politics. That of *Frauen und Film* in its current form is in theoretical concerns, in particular with issues of reception theory. The journal now features long articles (including translations of theoretical essays originally published in English or French) of twenty-five pages or more in length, complete with footnotes referring to such luminaries as Adorno and Kant. The writing style is generally, although not exclusively, academic; the editorial standards seem high and largely consistent. Counter to expectation, the journal may in fact be *more* accessible, *easier* to read, in its current form, due to such stylistic consistency, than previously, when the style and layout were quite discursive and uneven, with some authors taking a rather poetic, fanciful tone, and others presenting a densely argued polemic. The old *Frauen und Film* was at once populist, pluralistic, and intellectual. *Frauen und Film* in its current form is distinctly aimed at a readership – male as well as female – specifically trained in film theory. Information about festivals and film and video distribution is clearly secondary, reviews of contemporary films are irregular; the interest in the practical business of filmmaking, distribution, and viewing seems quite limited.

How is this change to be understood? There is more to it, I believe, than the change in identity or even profession of the editors. (It might be noted that the new publisher, Stroemfeld/Roter Stern, is also unable to pay editors and contributors, but that the financing of the journal is otherwise conceived, Gertrud Koch has told me, so that a small readership will carry it. While yearly subscription rates did not initially rise, they have recently been increased slightly to DM 30 a year or DM 15 an issue.) The changes in *Frauen und Film* must be seen in the context of film politics and the women's movement in West Germany as well as in terms of international developments in film studies. The previous *Frauen und Film* had in fact already gradually begun to shift to a more standardized, theoretical direction, so that Issue No. 34 and those preceding it are pronouncedly removed from the journal's beginning, which was initially inspired by (and named after) *Women and Film*. That journal ceased publication after seven issues, whereas *Frauen und Film* was able to arrange for printing at a publishing house at that stage. In fact, one might see parallel to the shift in editorial policy and concerns between the earlier and current version of *Frauen und Film* and the founding of *Camera Obscura* in 1974 by some associate editors of *Women and Film*. Laura Mulvey discussed this development in 1979 in an article entitled "Feminism, Film and the Avant-Garde,"[4] citing the conviction of the *Camera Obscura* editors:

> It is important to know where to locate ideology and patriarchy within the mode of representation in order to intervene and transform society, to define a praxis for change.

This now seems a commonplace. However, the *definition* of a praxis for change is not yet its exercise. In speaking, as Mulvey does, of the need for investigation and theoretical reflection on the mechanisms by which meaning is produced in film, one may not neglect the economic, political, and social parameters of those mechanisms. One must not, that is, ignore the literal meaning of "production," since the actual production of *new* meanings by feminist filmmakers requires attention and support, as does feminist film *criticism* (using this term to contrast

4. Laura Mulvey, "Feminism, Film and the Avant-Garde," *Framework* 10 (Spring 1979). The citation from the *Camera Obscura* collective is from "Feminism and Film: Critical Approaches," *Camera Obscura* 1 (1974): 3.

to film theory, as is often done). B. Ruby Rich has made this point in speaking of the diminishing attention, never extensive, given by the mainstream press to feminist film. *Frauen und Film* early attempted a balance of concern with the *construction* and *propagation* as well as deconstruction of filmic texts. That particular balance may well have realized its full potential under different circumstances than now exist in West Germany or elsewhere. The current *Frauen und Film* has in any case struck a distinctly different balance.

A survey of the changes in editorial policies and contextual function of various other American, British, or French film journals would indicate a somewhat similar pattern, with the consistency in the politics and policies of the journal *Jump Cut* standing out as a unique exception. As film theory becomes more abstract and specialized, more widely recognized in the United States and Canada and in Europe as a legitimate academic pursuit, the remove from the technical processes that yield the images being analyzed becomes greater. (In fact, this distancing from conditions of production may be in part a prerequisite of such academic recognition.) The proliferation of film journals internationally and the curricula of film and media studies departments indicate this shift.

In the particular case of *Frauen und Film,* it must be noted that the "academization" of film is a rather recent phenomenon in contemporary West Germany,[5] where filmmaking can be learned at only two academies or a handful of art schools, none of which has university status. Only the universities in Cologne and Berlin have departments of film studies, with courses at other universities subsumed to Amerikanistik or Germanistik (American or German Studies, respectively), for example. *Frauen und Film* in its present form is not only the only European feminist film journal edited by women, it is the only film journal published in the Federal Republic of Germany of such high theoretical caliber, with such journals as *Filmkritik* and *Filmfaust* addressing quite different issues and audiences. (Briefly, *Filmkritik* is edited in Munich by a collective of leftist, poetic humanists/filmmakers, all male; *Filmfaust,* which is edited in

5. The interest of the German intelligentsia in film theory is, however, by no means recent. *Frauen und Film* copublishers and editors Gertrud Koch and Heide Schlüpmann have helped initiate and are actively pursuing research on early film theory written in German by such authors as Siegfried Kracauer, Georg Lukács, and Béla Balázs.

Frankfurt, deals with current Hollywood productions, national cinema, circumstances of production, etc., and features many glossy images of women but few women contributors. There are a few review guides, one each put out by the Catholic and the Lutheran church, but none of these deal with feminist film. Nor can the daily press be counted on to deal with feminist films or feminist perspective on films.)

The situation for women filmmakers in Germany also changed in the decade in which *Frauen und Film* was initially published. However, this was due in large part, I believe, to the efforts of the early *Frauen und Film* editors and contributors. When Helke Sander entered film school in Berlin in 1966, she was one of only two women students. (Although Ula Stöckl also learned filmmaking in a film program in Ulm initiated by Alexander Kluge, in the mid-1960s.) Now, over one half of the students learning filmmaking in West Germany are women. In the interim between then and now, German women filmmakers have been able to produce a number of films that have gained international recognition and have attracted attention to the work of German feminist filmmakers as a movement much admired by women working in media in other countries.

This is by no means to argue that it is easy for women to gain support to make films in West Germany, particularly since the conservative government has replaced the SPD (Social Democratic Party), strengthening a tendency toward a more conventional aesthetic that had already been observed. Newcomers working in critical or experimental styles have particular difficulty getting a start, despite the continuation – albeit with tighter restrictions – of a system of government subsidies to filmmaking and of television support that fostered the emergence and growth of "New German Cinema." But no consistent financial security or support has come to even such well-proven and widely recognized directors such as Sander, Stöckl, Mikesch, and Brückner. Even at its most generous, the West German film subsidy system privileged male filmmakers and many would argue that it continues to do so.[6]

6. See Helke Sander, "Sexism in den Massenmedien," *Frauen und Film* 1 (1974); Renate Holy in *Frauen und Film* 8 (1976): 48–50; and Helke Sander and Ula Stöckl, "Die Herren machen das selber, daß ihnen die arme Frau Feind wird: Ablehnungsgeschichten," *Frauen und Film* 23 (April 1980). See also the discussion among filmmakers Jutta Brückner, Christina Perincioli, and Helga Reidemeister, "Conversing Together Finally," in *Jump Cut* 27 (1982): 47–49; and for

It is understandable that German feminist filmmakers and critics, like many of the activists of the 1960s and 1970s, seem to have worn out fighting the big battles and to have retreated to a certain extent to their editing tables or desks, either to work on their own careers as best they can, in the world as it is, or to fight battles closer to home. The excitement about potential for change out of which *Frauen und Film* arose and to which it in very large part contributed had become institutionalized and stymied by the time the Frankfurt collective took over publication of the journal in 1983. As the remarks of Lenssen and Berg-Ganschow in the last Berlin issue indicate, *Frauen und Film* had itself become something of an institution, albeit a quite shaky one, which would have then been dissolved except for its continuation by the Frankfurt collective. In its present form *Frauen und Film* deals only peripherally with the crucial material foundations of alternative image-making and reception that were the primary concern of the original editors and contributors. But the journal carries on the banner of the conjunction of "women" and "film" in its title by addressing current concerns of feminist film analysis for an educated German-language audience. In the process, *Frauen und Film* has gained surer institutional footing as a respected theoretical journal and the concomitant recognition of its editors and contributors as feminist film scholars, editors, and critics.

Inquiries about orders for subscriptions or back issues of *Frauen und Film* should be directed to Stroemfeld/RoterStern, Postfach 180147, W-6000 Frankfurt, Germany.

---

more general mention of cases and issues of funding of women's films, see: Renate Möhrmann, *Die Frau mit der Kamera* (Munich: Carl Hanser Verlag, 1980), 18–21; Eric Rentschler, "American Friends and the New German Cinema," *New German Critique* 24–25 (Fall/Winter 1981–82): 21–24; and James Franklin, *New German Cinema* (Boston: Twayne, 1983), 33–34.

Chronology for Volume I and II

German Social and Political History	German Film History
A. The German Empire: 1871–1918	
1895	Two months before Lumiere's first public performance in France, the Skladanovsky brothers showed their "Bioscop" in the Berlin Wintergarten – "bits of scenes shot and projected with apparatus they had built," as Siegfried Kracauer writes in *From Caligari to Hitler* (Princeton Univ. Press, 1947), p. 15; but, as Kracauer also informs us, the nickelodeons and tent-theaters which sprung up in Germany around the turn of the century featured short films of French, Italian, and American origin; "until 1910 Germany had virtually no film industry of its own"
1913	Stellan Rye & Paul Wegener: *The Student of Prague*
1914 World War I begins	Henrik Galeen & Wegener: *The Golem*
1917 Russian Revolution	Wegener: *The Golem and the Dancer*
B. Weimar Republic: 1918–1933	
1918 Kaiser Wilhelm II abdicates; Social Democrats (SPD) asked to form government: Weimar Republic – Germany's first attempt at democracy – proclaimed; Germany surrenders	
1919 Versailles treaty: Germany given total blame for war, must pay heavy reparations to victorious powers	Robert Wiene: *The Cabinet of Dr. Caligari* Ernst Lubitsch: *Passion* (*Madame du Barry*) *The Doll* (*Die Puppe*) *The Oyster Princess*

1919–23	Revolution and Counterrevolution in Germany: left-wing Social Democrats (Spartakus) form Communist Party (KPD); mainstream Social Democrats in the gov't. use antidemocratic, right-wing military (and paramilitary) forces (*Freikorps*) to put down Spartakus uprising in Berlin, other uprisings in Munich, Hamburg, etc. Spartakus founders Karl Liebknecht and Rosa Luxemburg murdered by the *Freikorps* in Berlin on January 15, 1919. Right-wing groups also try to take over gov't.	
1920	Kapp putsch	Wegener & Carl Boese: *The Golem – How He Came into the World* Lubitsch: *Anne Boleyn*
1921		Fritz Lang: *Destiny* (*Der müde Tod*) Lubitsch: *Ph aroah's Wife*
1922	Assasination of Rathenau (gov't. minister, Jewish liberal) 1922	Friedrich Murnau: *Nosferatu* Lang: *Dr. Mabuse, the Gambler.*
1923	Hitler's "beer hall" putsch in Munich Germany falling behind on reparations, so French troops occupy Ruhr (German mining and industrial region); one result: German hyperinflation. At its worst, $1.00 U.S. = 4,000,000,000,000 German marks (*Reichsmark*)	Karl Grune: *The Street* Lubitsch to Hollywood, where he directed (among many other films): *Forbidden Paradise*, 1924 *The Student Prince*, 1927 *Design for Living*, 1933 *Ninotschka*, 1939, with Greta Garbo *To Be or Not to Be*, 1942 with Jack Benny & Carole Lombard *Heaven Can Wait*, 1943
1924	Dawes Plan ends inflation: American banks refinance reparations payments, make loans – and invest in Germany; beginning of "Stabilized Period," period of relative prosperity (for some) and (uneasy) social harmony	Murnau: *The Last Laugh* (*Der letzte Mann*)

1925		E. A. Dupont: *Variety* G. W. Pabst: *The Joyless Street* (with Greta Garbo)
1926	Paragraph 218, outlawing abortion, reformed, made slightly more lenient	Lang: *Metropolis* (which nearly bankrupts Ufa; it is only saved by being bought in 1921 by right-wing media czar Hugenberg) Murnau: *Faust*
1927		Bruno Rahn: *Tragedy of the Street* (*Dirnentragodie*: literally, "Tragedy of a Whore") Murnau to Hollywood (directs *Sunrise*, 1927)
1928		Pabst: *Pandora's Box* (with Louise Brooks)
1929	Stock Market crash: American banks fail, call in loans, so Germany is hit hard, too (first in Europe)	Piel Jutzi: *Mother Krause's Journey to Happiness*
1930	Elections: Nazis go from 12 to 107 seats in *Reichstag* (Parliament)	Pabst: *The 3-Penny Opera* (*without* Bertolt Brecht's approval) Josef von Sternberg: *The Blue Angel* (with Marlene Dietrich)
1931	Activists Dr. Else Kienle and Dr. Friedrich Wolf arrested for having performed abortions; protests lead to massive popular campaign for the legalization of abortion, which however does not succeed	Leontine Sagan: *Girls in Uniform* (*Mädchen in Uniform*) Lang: *M* (with Peter Lorre)
1932	Nazis win 230 seats; Social Democrats and Communists on left continue fighting each other rather than uniting against the Nazis on the right	Slatan Dudow: *Kuhle Wampe* (script: Bertolt Brecht) Leni Riefenstahl: *The Blue Light*
1933		Lang: *The Testament of Mabuse*, which the National Socialists do not like; Lang is nonetheless asked by Goebbels to direct films for the Nazis; Lang, not so thrilled about

1933 *(continued)*		this offer (and also part Jewish), flees first to Paris, later to Hollywood, where he directs (among other films): *Fury*, 1936 *Hangmen Also Die*, 1942 – (Brecht worked on an early version of screenplay) *Scarlet Street*, 1946 *The Big Heat*, 1954

C. The "Third Reich": 1933–45

1933	Hitler becomes Chancellor; *Reichstag* (Parliament) burns; "emergency laws" passed that ban leftist parties; first concentration camps; *Reichstag* building not repaired (nor is parliament re-called as a serious legislative body); books by ethnic and political "undesirables" (Freud, Marx, Thomas Mann, etc.) burned	Hans Steinhoff: *Hitler-Youth Quex.*
1935	First "racial" laws passed	Steinhoff: *The Old and the Young King* Leni Riefenstahl: *Triumph of the Will*
1936	Germany occupies Rhineland: breach of Versailles treaty	
1937		Ufa becomes a state-owned monopoly Gustav Ucicky: *The Broken Jug* Detlef Sierck: *To New Shores* *La Habanera.* Detlef Sierck began as a director in the German theater during the 1920s. A leftist, he turned more and more to filmmaking during the Third Reich, since the film industry was at first less politicized than the theater, to the extent it still attempted to market films internationally. In 1937, however, Sierck and his wife, the actor Hilde Jary (who was Jewish) fled Germany, and by 1940 they were living in the U.S., where he "americanized" his name. As Douglas Sirk, he made films in the U.S., including:

1937 *(continued)*		*Sleep My Love*, 1948 *Magnificent Obsession*, 1954 *All That Heaven Allows*, 1956 *Written on the Wind*, 1957 *Imitation of Life*, 1959
1938	*Anschluß*: Austria annexed; Munich agreement re Sudetenland; so-called "Kristallnacht" (night of the broken glass): Jews attacked, Jewish businesses, synagogues vandalized, burned	Riefenstahl: *Olympia* (Part II)
1939	Czechoslovakia under complete German control Hitler-Stalin Pact Invasion of Poland: World War II begins	
1940	Denmark, Norway, France, etc. fall to Germany	Hans Schweikart: *Fräulein von Barnhelm* Veit Harlan: *Jew Süß*
1941	Germany attacks the Soviet Union Pearl Harbor	
1942	Wannsee Conference: *Endlösung* ("final solution") i.e., genocide, decided upon	
1942–43	Battle of Stalingrad: turning point of war	
1943		Joseph von Baky: *Baron von Münchhausen*
1944	20 July plot to kill Hitler fails	
1945	Yalta Conference: Churchill, Stalin, Roosevelt agree on boundaries of postwar Europe Hitler's suicide, Apr. 30 Soviets take Berlin, May 2 German surrender, May 7	premiere of Veit Harlan's *Kolberg*

D. Allied Occupation: 1945–49

Year	Events	Film
1945	Potsdam Conference: division of Germany and Berlin into U.S., French, British, and Soviet Zones (Hiroshima 6 Aug.; Nagasaki 9 Aug.; Japan surrenders 14 Aug.)	In the three Western zones, under the initiative of the U.S., the state monopoly Ufa enjoyed under National Socialism is broken up; in the Soviet zone, Ufa is re-organized as "DEFA" (German Film Corporation), which would continue to control film production in the East German state (the German Democratic Republic, or the GDR) after its founding in 1949
1946	In Soviet Zone, Social Democrats and Communists (somewhat forcibly) united to form "Socialist Unity Party" (SED); Social Democrats in W. Berlin and Western Zones vote not to do so; Churchill coins term "Iron Curtain"	Wolfgang Staudte: *The Murderers are Among Us*, a DEFA-production
1947	U. S. announces Marshall Plan to rebuild (W.) Europe; Walter Lippmann coins term "Cold War"; "denazification" program in W. Zones gets de-emphasized	
1948	*Währungsreform*: currency of Western zones reorganized (basis of coming "*Wirtschaftswunder*" – "economic miracle"); in response to this, which they see as destabilization of the currency in their zone, Soviets blockade West Berlin; the U.S. responds with airlift ("*Luftbrücke*")	

E. The Two Postwar States: 1949–90

All films listed were made in FRG (West Germany) unless indicated as made in the GDR or Austria

Year	Events	Film
1949	Founding of two German states: Federal Republic of Germany, or the FRG (W. Germany) and German Democratic Republic, or	Staudte: *The Subject* (based on the novel by Heinrich Mann) – DEFA (GDR)

	GDR (E. Germany); Adenauer of Christian Democrats (CDU) first chancellor of FRG	
1951		Peter Lorre: *The Lost Man* (*Der Verlorene*)
1952	Stalin suggests united, neutral Germany; skeptical Western powers refuse; GDR fortifies (seals off) its border, gets an army	Veit Harlan: *The Blue Hour*
1953	Stalin dies "thaw" under Beria – opening to West on unifying Germany rejected by Dulles in U.S., then closed off by Soviet return to hard line under Malenkov June 17: workers' uprising in E. Berlin put down by Soviet tanks Ulbricht emerges as leader of party and government in GDR	
1954	FRG gets an army, joins NATO	Helmut Käutner: *The Devil's General*
1955	Soviets and E. Europe (incl. GDR) form Warsaw Pact Four powers – including Soviets – end occupation of Austria, leaving it united and neutral	Herbert Vesely: *Stop Running* (*nicht - mehr fliehen* – FRG) Staudte unable to make any more films with DEFA in the GDR
1956	Communist Party outlawed in FRG Soviets crush Hungarian uprising	
1957	Sputnik; Treaty of Rome: Common Market; Adenauer's Christian Democrats get absolute majority for his third term	Ottomar Dominick: *Jonas* Harlan: *The Third Sex*
1958	Debate in FRG over owning atomic weapons	

1959	Social Democrats approve "Godesberger Programm" – party distances itself from Marxism	Staudte: *Roses for the Prosecutor* Bernard Wicki: *The Bridge*
1960		Staudte: *Fairground* (*Kirmes*)
1961	August 13: after ever larger numbers of its citizens emigrate via W. Berlin, GDR erects Berlin Wall	At the Berlin Film Festival, the FRG's Minister of the Interior finds no German films worthy of the Federal Film Prize
1962	FRG: Spiegel-Affair: F.J. Strauß authorizes break-in, Adenauer stands behind him, causing new elections	26 young filmmakers, noted mostly for internationally recognized short films, sign the Oberhausen Manifesto: "The old film is dead. We believe in the new" usually considered birth of FRG's "New German. Cinema" Vesely: *The Bread of the Early Years*
1963	Kennedy in W. Berlin: "Ich bin ein Berliner" Adenauer resigns – precondition for Christian Democratic coalition with Free Democrats (FDP, the "Liberals") Erhard his successor	Konrad Wolf: *Divided Heaven* (*Der geteilte Himmel* – GDR)
1964	FRG already has more than one million "*Gastarbeiter*," or foreign workers after (dubious) "Gulf of Tonkin" incident, U. S. Congress gives Johnson free hand in Vietnam	
1965	Involvement of U. S. troops in Vietnam increases dramatically in FRG, end of "*Wirtschaftswunder*": two-year recession begins	"*Kuratorium junger deutscher Film*" founded in the FRG, making federally subsidized, interest-free loans to young filmmakers. Jean-Marie Straub & Danielle Huillet: *Not Reconciled*
1966	"*Große Koalition*" (Great Coalition) between Christian Democrats and Social Democrats; Christian Democrat – and ex-Nazi – Kiesinger becomes chancellor	Alexander Kluge: *Yesterday Girl* (*Abschied von gestern*) Volker Schlöndorff: *Young Törleß* *Yesterday Girl* wins the "Silver Lion" at the Venice Film Festival; *Not Reconciled* and *Young Törleß* win awards at the Cannes Festival

1967	Left-wing and student protesters in FRG form "*Außenparlamentarische Opposition*" (APO – extraparliamentary opposition) to oppose Kiesinger, the Social Democratic coalition with him, and FRG support for U. S. foreign policy, esp. in Vietnam; June 2: W. Berlin police shoot Benno Ohnesorg at student protest of visit of Shah of Iran – result: massive student demonstrations all over FRG	Werner Herzog: *Signs of Life* Konrad Wolf: *I Was 19* (GDR)
1968	High point of student movement in FRG (and internationally) – and beginning of decline: APO campaign against emergency laws (*Notstandsgesetze*) fails, factions begin to arise, e.g., "Rote Armee Faktion" (RAF, the "Red Army Faction," also called "Baader-Meinhof" gang); "Action Committee for the Liberation of Women" founded by feminists (including film maker Helke Sander) in FRG student movement Soviet tanks move into Czechoslovakia	Film Promotion Law ("*Filmforderungsgesetz*" or FFG) passed; in spite of the lobbying efforts of the young filmmakers, the new law subsidizes, not the new filmmakers, but the old commercial film industry in the FRG (the output of which consisted of approx. 50 percent sex films). Ula Stockl: *The Cat Has 9 Lives* May Spils: *Let's Get Down to Business, Darling* (*Zur Sache, Schätzchen*)
1969	FRG Elections: Social Democrats, in coalition w/ Free Democrats, form gov't .; Willi Brandt is chancellor	Rainer Werner Fassbinder: *Love is Colder Than Death* and *Katzelmacher* (the first 2 of 41 feature-length films he will make over the next 13 years) Werner Schroeter: *Eika Katappa*
1970	"Ostpolitik" (Eastern Policy): FRG regularizes relations w/ Soviets, Poland	Rosa von Praunheim: *Not the Homosexual is Perverse, but the Situation in which He Lives*
1971	GDR' s Ulbricht resigns, Honecker takes over Four-Power Agreement: Soviets guarantee status of and transit to, rom W. Berlin	13 young filmmakers, including Wim Wenders, form their own production and distribution company: the "*Filmverlag der Autoren*" (Film-Publishing-Co. of the Authors – or *auteurs*)

1971 *(continued)*

Brandt gets Nobel prize
inspired by French feminists, feminists in FRG start campaign against Paragraph 218, i.e., they campaign for legalization of abor-tion; movement becomes massive

Fassbinder's *The Merchant of the 4 Seasons* finally wins him critical acclaim in the FRG
Christian Ziewer: *Dear Mother, I'm OK*
Schroeter: *The Death of Maria Malibran*

1972 *Radikalenerlaß* ("Radicalism Decree") becomes law in the FRG; popularly known s the *Berufsverbot* ("career prohibition"), which led to a type of blacklisting; on the basis of this law, people with a record of having been involved in protest demonstrations were often denied civil service jobs (which in the FRG include almost all teaching jobs)
Palestinian "Black September" murders Israeli athletes at Munich Olympics

Herzog: *Aguirre the Wrath of God*
Schlöndorff: *A Free Woman* (*Strohfeuer*)
Fassbinder: *The Bitter Tears of Petra von Kant*
Wim Wenders: *The Scarlet Letter*
New York's Museum of Modern Art begins its yearly show featuring young German filmmakers

1973 "*Grundlagenvertrag*" (Basic Treaty) between FRG and GDR into effect; both states admitted to U.N.; beginning of international oil crisis

In West Berlin, Helke Sander and Claudia von Alemann organize first International Women's Film Seminar
Wenders: *Alice in the Cities*
Fassbinder: *Ali, or Fear Eats the Soul*

1974 Guillaume scandal: Brandt resigns; Schmidt (right-wing of Social Democrats) leads Social Democratic-Free Democratic coalition gov't

Helke Sander founds feminist film journal, *Frauen und Film.*
Film/Television Agreement: agreement between (public) television networks and Film Promotion Board in FRG turns networks into main funders of "New German Cinema"
Fassbinder's *Ali* wins the "Golden Palm" at Cannes
Fassbinder: *Effi Briest*
Wenders: *The Wrong Move* (*Falsche Bewegung*)
Herzog: *The Mystery of Kaspar Hauser* (*Jeder für sich und Gott gegen alle*)
Kluge: *Part-Time Work of a Domestic Slave* (*Gelegenheitsarbeit einer Sklavin*)

1975	U. S. withdraws from Vietnam RAF involved in bomb attack on FRG embassy in Stockholm Paragraph 218 liberalized somewhat, but FRG women's movement looks upon it as a defeat of their efforts to decriminalize abortion completely	Schlöndorff & Margarethe von Trotta: *The Lost Honor of Katharina Blum*; this politically controversial film, with Bernhard Sinkel's *Lina Braake*, become the first commercial successes of the "New German Cinema" Peter Lilienthal: *The Country is Calm* (*Es herrscht Ruhe im Land*)
1976	Brokdorf (FRG): demonstrations against proposed nuclear power plant U. Meinhof (RAF) dies in prison (suicide?)	*Newsweek* proclaims "German Film Boom" Wenders: *Kings of the Road* (*Im Lauf der Zeit*) Herzog: *Heart of Glass* Schlöndorff: *Coup de Grace* (*Der Fangschuß*) Stockl: *Erika's Passions* Frank Beyer: *Jacob the Liar* (GDR)
1977	RAF actions in FRG: Ponto, Buback murdered; then, "*Deutscher Herbst*," the "German Autumn": Schleyer kidnapped; Lufthansa jet highjacked, stormed by GS-9 unit; RAF old guard – Baader, Raspe, Ensslin – found dead in cells (suicide?); Schleyer found dead	Helke Sander: *The All-Around Reduced Personality* (or: *REDUPERS*) Valie Export: *Invisible Adversaries* (Austria) Ulrike Ottinger: *Madame X* Wenders: *The American Friend* Herzog: *Stroszek* Fassbinder: *Despair* Hans Jürgen Syberberg: *Our Hitler*
1978	FRG: Anti-Terrorism Law	*Time Magazine*: "The New German Cinema is the liveliest in Europe" Wenders, disgusted with the film scene in Germany, is lured to Hollywood by Francis Coppola to make *Hammett* Kluge, Fassbinder, Schlöndorff, Heinrich Böll, Edgar Reitz, et al.: *Germany in Autumn* von Trotta: *The 2nd Awakening of Christa Klages* Cristina Perincioli: *The Power of Men is the Patience of Women* (*Die Macht der Männer ist die Geduld der Frauen*) Fassbinder: *In a Year with 13 Moons* Reinhard Hauff: *Knife in the Head* Carow: *Till Death Do You Part* (GDR)

1979	Thatcher becomes Prime Minister in Britain NATO warns Soviets that if it does not remove SS-20 missiles, NATO will deploy Pershing missiles in W. Europe; in protest, new peace mvt. in W. Europe starts Soviet troops into Afghanistan	Manifesto of Women Film Workers; among its demands: 50 percent of ll film subsidies should be granted to women filmmakers Jutta Brückner: *Years of Hunger* Helma Sanders-Brahms: *Germany, Pale Mother* Ottinger: *Ticket of No Return* (*Bildnis einer Trinkerin* Helga Reidemeister: *Von wegen Schicksal* (*What do you mean, Fate?*) Heidi Genee: *1+1=3* von Trotta: *Sisters – or the Balance of Happiness* Fassbinder: *The Marriage of Maria Braun* Schlöndorff: *The Tin Drum* Kluge: *The Patriot* Lilienthal: *David* Schroeter: *The Kingdom of Naples*
1980	Reagan elected	*The Tin Drum* wins the Oscar for Best Foreign Film; it and *Maria Braun* are the first two German films to earn more than $1 million apiece in the US Fassbinder: *Berlin Alexanderplatz* Kluge, Schlöndorff, et al.: *The Candidate* von Praunheim: *Red Love* Lothar Lambert: *Nightmare Woman* Konrad Wolf: *Solo Sunny* (GDR)
1981	Squatter demonstrations in W. Berlin at high point: K.-J. Rattay killed	von Trotta: *Marianne & Juliane* (*Die bleierne Zeit*) Sander: *The Subjective Factor* Wolfgang Petersen: *The Boat* Lothar Warnecke: *Apprehension* (*Die Beunruhigung* – GDR)
1982	Free Democrats leave coalition w/Schmidt and Social Democrats, form gov't with Christian Democrats; Christian Democrat Kohl becomes chancellor	von Trotta: *Sheer Madness* (*Heller Wahn*) Wenders's *Hammett* finally appears, after four years in which various scriptwriters, as well as Wenders himself, had been fired (Wenders was rehired) Wenders: *The State of Things* (filmed in Portugal and the U.S.), in part a comment on his attempt at film making in Hollywood

		Herzog: *Fitzcarraldo* (filmed in South America) Fassbinder (born 1945) dies on 6 June 1982
1983	Kohl wins new elections, but Greens get into Bundestag more important house of FRG parliament) "*Heißer Herbst*" ("Hot Autumn"): in spite of massive protests, Free Democratic-Christian Democratic majority in Bundestag votes to accept deployment of Pershing missiles U.S. invades Grenada	Kluge, Schlöndorff, et al.: *War and Peace* Marianne Rosenbaum: *Peppermint Peace* Export: *Syntagma* (Austria) Lambert: *Paso Doble*; *Fräulein Berlin* Robert van Ackeren: *A Woman in Flames* (*Die flambierte Frau*) The "Achternbusch-Affair": at the end of 1982, a conservative coalition had come to power in the FRG; by mid-1983 the new Minister of the Interior, Zimmermann, gains notoriety by withdrawing financial support for filmmaker Herbert Achternbusch's *The Ghost* because it "offended religious values"; West German filmmakers join together in an ultimately unsuccessful attempt to stop this attack on their freedom of expression – and the subsidy system; end of "New German Cinema"? Petersen: *The Never-Ending Story* (filmed in Canada)
1984	Missile Deployment begins	Sander: *The Trouble with Love* (*Der Beginn aller Schrecken ist Liebe*) Ottinger: *The Mirror Image of Dorian Gray in the Yellow Press* (*Dorian Gray im Spiegel der Boulevard Presse*) Export: *The Practice of Love* (Austria) Stöckl: *Reason Asleep* Elfi Mikesch & Monika Treut: *Seduction: The Cruel Woman* Christa Mühl: *Pauline's Second Life* (GDR) Lambert: *Drama in Blonde* Straub/Huillet: *Class Relations* Edgar Reitz: *Heimat* Schlöndorff: *Swann in Love* (filmed in France) Herzog: *Where the Green Ants Dream* (filmed in Australia) Wenders: *Paris, Texas* (filmed in the US) wins at Cannes

1985	Gorbachev to power in USSR	Doris Dörrie: *Men* (breaks all German box office records since World War II) Kluge: *The Blind Director* (*Der Angriff der Gegenwart auf die übrige Zeit*) Percy Adlon: *Zuckerbaby*
1986	Reagan goes to Bitburg to honor German war dead – cemetery includes SS graves "Historian's Debate" in FRG over interpretation of the Holocaust nuclear accident at Chernobyl	Hauff: *Stammheim* Peter Timm: *Meier* von Trotta: *Rosa Luxemburg* Ottinger: *China* Ottinger, Export, Sander, et al.: *SevenWomen/Seven Sins*
1987		Wenders: *Wings of Desire* (*Himmel über Berlin*) Reidemeister: *Drehort Berlin* (*Shooting Location Berlin*) Adlon: *Bagdad Cafe* (*Out of Rosenheim*) von Praunheim: *Anita, Dances of Vice*
1988	Reagan and Gorbachev agree on INF treaty: Pershings & SS 20s, etc. to be removed from Europe	von Trotta: *3 Sisters* (filmed in Italy) Treut: *The Virgin Machine* Hark Bohm: *Jasmin* Thomas Brasch: *The Passenger* Sander: *The Germans and Their Men* (*Die Deutschen und ihre Männer*) Ottinger, *Johanna d'Arc of Mongolia* Dörrie: *Money* (*Geld*) Adlon *Rosalie Goes Shopping* Helke Misselwitz: *Winter Ade* (GDR) Heiner Carow: *Coming Out* (GDR)
1989	Christian Democrats lose elections in W. Berlin & Hessen by losing conservative voters to neo-fascist, anti-foreigner "Republican" party; leftist "redgreen" coalitions (Social Democrats & Greens) benefit from Christian Democratic losses and come to power	

Hungary cuts down its fences ("Iron Curtain"); GDR citizens escape from there to west, and then more try to flock to Hungary, then Prague; massive protests start in Leipzig, spread, led by dissidents who form umbrella group, New Forum

Gorbachev visits GDR; Honecker resigns

November 9: Berlin Wall opened

1990 Reunification on the fast track: in March elections in GDR, Christian Democrats beat Social Democrats, other parties, including New Forum, by promising quick reunification

1 July – yet another German currency reform: FRG and GDR merge monetary systems; FRG's D-Mark becomes currency in both states

Reunification official, October 3

Kohl and Christian Democrats win "all-German" elections in December

West German Greens lose representation in Bundestag; in East Greens in coalition w/New Forum do get enough votes to get into Bundestag

Michael Verhoeven's *The Nasty Girl* wins Silver Bear at Berlin Film Festival, wins acclaim at New York Film Festival

Filmography

Distribution information is provided for those films distributed in the U.S.[1] Addresses for the distributors are given after the filmography. Unless otherwise noted, films have English subtitles or, for silent films, English intertitles.

The Broken Jug. German title: *Der zerbrochene Krug.* Dir. Gustav Ucicky and Emil Jannings. 1937. 86 min. U.S. dist.: West Glen Films and Trans-World Films.

The Doll. German title: *Die Puppe.* Dir. Ernst Lubitsch. 1919. 80 min. U.S. dist.: West Glen Films. German intertitles.

Fräulein von Barnhelm. German title: *Das Fräulein von Barnhelm.* Dir. Hans Schweikart. 1940. 91 min. U.S. dist.: Trans-World Films.

Germany, Pale Mother. German title: *Deutschland bleiche Mutter.* Dir. Helma Sanders-Brahms. 1979. 123 min. U.S. dist.: New Yorker Films and West Glen Films.

Girls in Uniform. German title: *Mädchen in Uniform.* Dir. Leontine Sagan. 1931. 89 min. U.S. dist.: Films Inc.

The Joyless Street. German title: *Die freudlose Gasse.* Dir.: G.W. Pabst. 1925. U.S. dist.: MOMA (95 min.) and Budget (90 min.)

Jew Süss. German title: *Jud Süß.* Dir.: Veit Harlan. 1940. 97 min. U.S. dist.: International Films.

Marianne and Juliane (The German Sisters). German title: *Die Bleierne Zeit.* Dir. Margarethe von Trotta. 1981. 106 min. U.S. dist.: New Yorker Films.

1. For information about access to West German films not distributed in the U.S. contact the Goethe Haus in New York or one of the other Goethe Institutes in the U.S.: Boston, Chicago, Atlanta, Houston, Seattle, San Francisco, Los Angeles, etc. For information about distribution of films produced by DEFA ("Deutsche-Film-Aktiengesellschaft") in the former GDR (East Germany), contact the Bundesfilmarchiv, Fehrbellinerplatz 3, W-1000 Berlin 31.

The Marriage of Maria Braun. German title: *Die Ehe der Maria Braun.* Dir. Rainer Werner Fassbinder. 1979. 120 min. U.S. dist.: New Yorker Films.

The Old and the Young King. German title: *Der alte und der junge König.* Dir. Hans Steinhoff. 1935. 106 min. U.S. dist.: West Glen Films.

The Oyster Princess. German title: *Die Austernprinzessin.* Dir. Ernst Lubitsch. 1919. 48 min. U.S. dist.: West Glen Films.

Peppermint Peace. German title: *Peppermint Frieden.* Dir. Marianne S. W. Rosenbaum. 1983. 112 min. U.S. dist.: West Glen Films.

Rosa Luxemburg. Dir. Margarethe von Trotta. 1986. 112 min. U.S. dist.: New Yorker Films.

The Sinful Woman. German title: *Die Sünderin.* Dir. Willi Forst. 1950. 87 min. Deutsche Styria/Junge Film Union.

The Street. German title: *Die Straße.* Dir. Karl Grune. 1923. 87 min. U.S. dist.: MOMA.

The Subjective Factor. German title: *Der subjektive Faktor.* Dir. Helke Sander. 1981. 138 min. Basis Film (W. Berlin).

Years of Hunger. German title: *Hungerjahre.* Dir. Jutta Brückner. 1979. 114 min. Jutta Brückner/ZDF. (Former U.S. dist.: West Glen Films.)

U.S. Distributors

Budget Films, 4590 Santa Monica Blvd., Los Angeles, CA 90029. (213) 660-0187 or 0080.

Cinema Guild, 1697 Broadway, Suite 802, New York, NY 10019. (212) 246-5522.

Facets Multimedia, Inc., 1517 W. Fullerton Ave., Chicago, IL 60614. (800) 331-6197. Video sales and rental.

Films Incorporated / Central, South, West , and Alaska: 5547 N. Ravenswood, Chicago, IL 60640-1199. (800) 323-4222, ext. 42.

Films Incorporated / Northeast: 35 S. West St., Mt. Vernon, NY 10550. (800) 223-6246.

Foreign Images, 1213 Maple Ave., Evanston, Il 60202. (708) 869-0543.

International Films, Inc. Box 29035, Chicago, IL 60629. (312) 436-8051.

Krypton c/o Almi Productions, 1900 Broadway, New York, NY 10023. (212) 769-6400.

MOMA = Circulating Film Library, Museum of Modern Art, 11 W. 53 St., New York, NY 10019. (212) 708-9530.

New Yorker Films, 16 W. 61 St., New York, NY 10023. (212) 247-6110

Trans-World Films, Inc., 332 S. Michigan Ave., Chicago, IL 60604. (312) 922-1530.

West Glen Films, 1430 Broadway, New York, NY 10018-3396. (212) 921-2800.

Bibliography for Volume I and II

Albrecht, Gerd. *Nationalsozialistische Filmpolitik.* Stuttgart: Ferdinand Enke Verlag, 1969.

Albrecht, Gerd, ed. *Der Film im 3. Reich.* Karlsruhe: DOKU, 1979.

Alford, C. Fred. "Nature and Narcissim." *New German Critique* 36 (1985).

Alloula, Malek. *The Oriental Harem.* Trans. Myrna Godzich and Wlad Godzich. Introd. Barbara Harlow. Minneapolis: Univ. Minnesota, 1986.

Altbach, Edith Hoshino, Jeanette Clausen, Dagmar Schultz, and Naomi Stephan, eds. *German Feminism: Readings in Politics and Literature.* Albany, N.Y.: SUNY, 1984.

Althusser, Louis. "Idéologie et appareils idéologiques d'état." *La Pense* 151 (June 1970). Also later published in *Positions 1964–1975.* Paris: Éditions sociales, 1976.

Andrew, J. Dudley. *Concepts in Film Theory.* New York: Oxford Univ., 1984.

Anger, Kenneth. *Hollywood Babylon.* San Francisco: Straight Arrow, 1975.

Atwell, Lee. *G. W. Pabst.* Boston: Twayne, 1977.

Aust, Stefan. *Der Baader Meinhof Komplex.* Hamburg: Hoffmann und Campe, 1986.

Baaker Schut, Pieter H. *Stammheim: Der Prozeß gegen die Rote Armee Faktion.* Kiel: Neuer Malik Verlag, 1986.

Bachmann, Ingeborg. "Undine geht." *Das dreißigste Jahr.* Munich: R. Piper, 1961.

Bächlin, Peter. *Der Film als Ware.* Frankfurt/M.: Fischer, 1975.

Bänsch, Dieter, ed. *Die fünfziger Jahre.* Tübingen: Günter Narr, 1985.

Baer, Harry. *Schlafen kann ich, wenn ich tot bin.* Köln: Kiepenheuer & Witsch, 1982.

Bakhtin, Mikhail. *Rabelais and His World.* Trans. Helene Iswolsky. Cambridge: M.I.T., 1968.

Bammer, Angelika. "Through a Daughter's Eyes: Helma Sanders-Brahms's *Germany, Pale Mother.*" *New German Critique* 36 (1985).

Barck, Karlheinz et al., eds. *Künstlerische Avant-garde: Annäherungen an ein unabgeschlossenes Kapitel.* Berlin [DDR], 1979.

Barlow, John D. *Expressionist Film.* Boston: Twayne, 1982.

Bauer, Otto. *The Austrian Revolution.* Trans. H. J. Stenning. New York: Burt Franklin, 1970.

Becker, Gillian. *Hitler's Children.* Philadelphia and New York: Lippincott, 1977.

Bekh, Wolfgang Johannes. *Das dritte Weltgeschehen: bayerische Hellseher schauen in die Zukunft.* Pfaffenhofen: Ludwig, 1980.

Belotti, Elena Gianini. *Dalla Parte delle Bambine.* Milano: Gianciacomo Feltrinelli Editore, 1973.

Benjamin, Jessica. "Authority and the Family Revisited: Or, A World Without Fathers?" *New German Critique* 13 (Winter 1978).

Benjamin, Walter. "Theses on the Philosophy of History." In *Illuminations.*

________. *Illuminations.* Ed. Hannah Arendt. Trans. Harry Zohn. New York: Schocken, 1969 and 1978.

________. *Charles Baudelaire: A Lyric Poet in the Era of High Capitalism.* London: New Left, 1973.

Berens, E. M. *The Myths and Legends of Ancient Greece and Rome: Being a Popular Account of Greek and Roman Mythology.* London: Blackie and Son, 1880.

Berg-Ganschow, Uta. "Geschichte eines Nebenwiderspruchs." *Filme* 9 (June 1981).

________. "Die Puppe." In *Lubitsch,* ed. Hans Helmut Prinzler and Enno Patalas. Munich and Luzern: Stiftung Deutsche Kinemathek, 1984.

Bergman, Ingmar. *Persona* and *Shame.* Trans. K. Bradfield. London: Calder & Boyars, 1972.

Berning, Cornelia. *Vokabular des Nationalsozialismus.* Berlin: Walter de Gruyter, 1964.

Betancourt, Jeanne. *Women in Focus.* Dayton: Pflaum, 1974.

"Bischöfe fordern Jugendschutz–Gesetz." *Münchner Merkur.* (24 March 1950).

Bloch, Ernst. *Vom Hasard zur Katastrophe: Politische Aufsätze 1934–1939.* Frankfurt/M.: Suhrkamp, 1972.

Blum, Heiko R. "Gespräch mit Wim Wenders." *Filmkritik* (February 1972).

Boelcke, Willi A. *Kriegspropaganda 1939–1941.* Stuttgart: DVA, 1966.

Bond, Kirk. "Ernst Lubitsch." *Film Culture* 63/64 (1976).

Bovenschen, Silvia. "Is There a Feminine Aesthetic?" *New German Critique* 10 (1977).

________. "The Contemporary Witch, the Historical Witch and the Witch Myth." *New German Critique* 15 (1978).

________. *Die imaginierte Weiblichkeit. Exemplarische Untersuchungen zu kulturgeschichtlichen und literarischen Präsentationsformen des Weiblichen* Frankfurt/M.: Suhrkamp, 1978.

Brecht, Bertolt. *Der Dreigroschenprozeß. Versuche 1–12, Heft 3*. Berlin and Frankfurt: Suhrkamp, 1959.

Bridenthal, Renate, Atina Grossmann and Marion Kaplan, eds. *When Biology Became Destiny: Women in Weimar and Nazi Germany*. New York: Monthly Review, 1984.

Bridenthal, Renate, and Claudia Koonz. "Beyond *Kinder Küche Kirche*: Weimar Women in Politics and Work." In *When Biology Became Destiny: Women in Weimar and Nazi Germany*, ed. Renate Bridenthal, Atina Grossmann and Marion Kaplan. New York: Monthly Review, 1984.

Brinkmann, Richard. "Der angehaltene Moment. Requisiten – Genre – Tableau bei Fontane." *DVJS* 53 (1979).

Brooks, Louise. "On Making Pabst's *Lulu*." In *Women and the Cinema*, ed. Karyn Kay and Gerald Peary. New York: E. P. Dutton, 1977.

Brooks, Peter. *The Melodramatic Imagination*. New Haven: Yale Univ. Press, 1976.

Brunet, Rene. Appendix. *The New German Constitution*. Trans. Joseph Gollomb. New York: Alfred A. Knopf, 1922.

Brückner, Jutta. "Recognizing Collective Gestures." Interview with Jutta Brückner. *Jump Cut* 27 (1982).

________. "Sexualität als Arbeit im Pornofilm." *Argument* 141 (Sept./Oct. 1983).

________. "Vom Erinnern, Vergessen, dem Leib und der Wut. Ein Kultur-Film-Projekt." *Frauen und Film* 35 (Oct. 1983).

________. "Vom Pathos des Leibes oder: Der revolutionäre Exorzismus." *Ästhetik und Kommunikation: Intimität* 57/58 (1985).

________. "Women Behind the Camera." In *Feminist Aesthetics*, ed. Gisela Ecker, trans. Harriet Anderson. Boston: Beacon, 1986.

Brüne, Klaus. Review of *Die Sünderin*. Reprinted in *Zwischen Gestern und Morgen. Westdeutscher Nachkriegsfilm 1946–1962*. Frankfurt: Deutsches Filmmuseum, 1989. Originally in *Katholischer film–Dienst*. (2 February 1951)

Bürger, Peter. *Theorie der Avant-garde*. Frankfurt/M.: Suhrkamp, 1974. Available in English as: *Theory of the Avant-garde*. Trans. Michael Shaw. Minneapolis: Univ. of Minnesota Press, 1984.

Butler, Judith. *Gender Trouble: Feminism and the Subversion of Identity*. New York: Routledge, 1990.

Canby, Vincent. "The Decline and Fall of Effi Briest." *New York Times*, 17 June 1977.

Carow, Heiner. "Bis daß der Tod euch scheidet." Interview mit Heiner Carow. *Progress. Pressebulletin Kino der DDR* 5 (1979).

Ciment, Michel, and Hubert Niogret. "Entretien avec Wim Wenders." *Positif* (September 1984).

Cixous, Hélène. "The Laugh of the Medusa." Trans. Keith Cohen and Paula Cohen. In *New French Feminisms*. Ed. Elaine Marks and Isabelle de Courtivron. New York: Schocken, 1980. 245–264. Originally published in English in *Signs* (Summer 1976). 875–93. "Le rire de la méduse." *L'arc.* 61 (1975). 39–54.

Codelli, Lorenzo. "Die bleierne Zeit." *Positif* 248 (November 1981).

Cook, Blanche Wiesen. "'Women Alone Stir My Imagination': Lesbianism and the Cultural Tradition." *Signs* 4.4 (1979).

Corrigan, Timothy. *New German Film: The Displaced Image.* Austin: Univ of Texas, 1983.

Craig, Gordon. *Germany 1866–1945.* New York: Oxford Univ., 1978.

Curry, Ramona. "The Female Image as Critique in the Films of Valie Export." *Schatzkammer* 14.2 (Fall 1988)

Dawson, Jan. *Alexander Kluge and the Occasional Work of a Female Slave.* Perth: Perth Film Festival Publication, 1975.

Dawson, Jan. *Wim Wenders.* New York: Zoetrope, 1976.

DDR Handbuch, 2 vols. Cologne: Wissenschaft und Politik, 1985.

Debord, Guy. *Society of the Spectacle.* Detroit: Black and Red, 1972.

de Jonge, Alex. *The Weimar Chronicle: Prelude to Hitler.* London: Paddington, 1978.

de Lauretis, Teresa. *Alice Doesn't: Feminism, Semiotics, Cinema.* Bloomington: Indiana Univ. Press, 1984.

________. *Technologies of Gender: Essays on Theory, Film, and Fiction.* Bloomington: Indiana Univ. Press, 1987.

Deleuze, Gilles. *Présentation de Sacher-Masoch; le froid et le cruel.* Paris: UGE 10/18, 1976. Available in English as: *Sacher-Masoch. An Interpretation.* Trans. Jean McNeil. London: Faber and Faber, 1971.

Delorme, Charlotte. "On the Film *Marianne and Juliane* by Margarethe von Trotta." *Journal of Film and Video* 37 (Spring 1985). This is Ellen Seiter's translation of "Zum Film 'Die bleierne Zeit' von Margarethe von Trotta." *Frauen und Film* 31 (February 1982).

Derrida, Jacques. *Of Grammatology.* Trans. Gayatri Chakravorty Spivak. Baltimore: Johns Hopkins Univ. Press, 1976.

Diamond, Elin. "Brechtian Theory/Feminist Theory: Toward a Gestic Feminist Criticism." *TDR/The Drama Review* 32 (1988).

DiCaprio, Lisa. "*Marianne and Juliane/The German Sisters*: Baader-Meinhof Fictionalized." *Jump Cut* 29 (February 1984).

Dieckmann, Katherine. "Wim Wenders: an Interview." *Film Quarterly* 38.2 (Winter 1984–85).

Doane, Mary Ann. "The Voice in Cinema: The Articulation of Body and Space." *Yale French Studies* 60 (1980).

________. "Film and the Masquerade: Theorizing the Female Spectator." *Screen* 23.3–4 (Sept./Oct. 1982).

________. "The ' Woman's Film': Possession and Address." In *Re-Vision: Essays in Feminist Film Criticism..*

________, et al., eds. *Re-Vision. Essays in Feminist Film Criticism.* The American Film Institute Monograph Series. Frederick, MD: Univ. Publications of America, 1984.

Douglas, Carol Anne. "German Feminists and the Right: Can It Happen Here?" *off our backs* 10.11 (December 1980).
Dukes, Ashley. *Jew Süss: a tragic comedy in 5 acts* . London: Martin Secker, 1929.
Eco, Umberto. "The Frames of Comic 'Freedom.'" In *Carnival!*, ed. Thomas A. Sebeok. Berlin, New York, and Amsterdam: Mouton, 1984.
Eifler, Margret. "Valie Export: Feministische Filmautorin." In *Österreich in Amerikanischer Sicht*, ed. Luise Caputo-Mayr. New York: Austrian Institute, 1990.
Eisenführ, Juliane. *Die Sünderin. Geschichte und Analyse eines Kinoskandals.* Universität Osnabrück, 1982. Unpublished master's thesis.
Eisner, Lotte H. *The Haunted Screen.* Berkeley: Univ. of California, 1969.
Elsaesser, Thomas. "A Cinema of Vicious Circles." In *Fassbinder*, ed. Tony Rayns. London: British Film Institute, 1976.
________. "*Lili Marleen*: Fascism and the Film Industry." *October* 21 (Summer 1982).
________. "Social Mobility and the Fantastic: German Silent Cinema." *Wide Angle* 5.2 (1982).
________. "Mother Courage and Divided Daughter." *Monthly Film Bulletin* 50 (July 1983).
________. "Achternbusch and the German Avant-Garde." *Discourse* 6 (Fall 1983).
________. "Film History and Visual Pleasure: Weimar Cinema." In *Cinema Histories, Cinema Practices*, ed. Patricia Mellencamp and Philip Rosen. Frederick, MD: Univ. Publications of America, 1984.
________. "American Grafitti und Neuer Deutscher Film: Filmemacher zwischen Avantgarde und Postmoderne." In *Postmoderne. Zeichen eines kulturellen Wandels*, ed. Andreas Huyssen and Klaus R. Scherpe. Reinbek: Rowohlt, 1986.
________. "Tales of Sound and Fury: Observations on the Family Melodrama." In *Home is Where the Heart is: Studies in Melodrama and the Women's Film*, ed. Christine Gledhill. London: BFI, 1987.
________. *New German Cinema: A History.* New Brunswick: Rutgers Univ. Press, 1989.
Elwenspoek, Curt. *Joseph Süß Oppenheimer, der große Finanzier und galante Abenteurer des 18. Jahrhunderts.* Stuttgart: Süddeutsches Verlagshaus, 1926.
Ettinger, Elzbieta. *Rosa Luxemburg: A Life.* Boston: Beacon, 1981.
Evans, Richard. *The Feminist Movement in Germany 1894–1933.* Beverly Hills: Sage, 1976.
Export, Valie. *Zyklus Zur Zivilisation, Fotomappe.* Ed. Kurt Kalb. Vienna: Kurt Kalb, 1972.
________. "Women's Art Ein Manifest (1972)." *Neues Forum* (January 1973).
________. "Gertrude Stein/Virginia Woolf. Feminismus und Kunst I u. II." *Neues Forum* (1973)

________. "Zur Geschichte der Frau in der Kunstgeschichte." In *Magna,* ed. Valie Export. Vienna: Galerie nächst St. Stephan, 1975.

________. *Works from 1968–1975. A Comprehension.* Vienna: Valie Export,.1975.

________. "Gedichte." *Dimension* (1975).

________. "Überlegungen Zum Verhältnis Frau und Kreativität." In *Künstlerinnen International.* Berlin, 1977.

________. "Zeichnungen." In *Arsenikblüten,* ed. Danielle Sarréa. Munich: Matthes and Seitz, 1980.

________. "Feministischer Aktionismus," In *Frauen in der Kunst,* ed. Gislind Nabakowski, Helke Sander, Peter Gorsen. Frankfurt/M., 1980.

________. *Körpersplitter, Konfigurationen. Fotografien 1968–77.* Neue Texte. Vol 1. Linz, 1980.

________. *Kunst mit Eigen-Sinn: Aktuelle Kunst von Frauen, Texte und Dokumentation.* Vienna and Munich, 1985.

________. "The Real and Its Double: The Body." *Discourse* 11 (Fall/Winter 1988–89).

________. "Aspects of Feminist Actionism." *New German Critique* 47 (Spring/Summer 1989).

Faderman, Lillian. *Surpassing the Love of Men: Romantic Friendship and Love Between Women from the Renaissance to the Present.* New York: Morrow, 1981.

Faderman, Lillian, and Brigitte Eriksson. *Lesbian Feminism in Turn-of-the-Century Germany.* Tallahassee, FL: Naiad, 1979.

Fassbinder, Rainer Werner. "Six Films by Douglas Sirk." Trans. Thomas Elsaesser. In *Douglas Sirk,* ed. Laura Mulvey and John Halliday. Edinburgh: Edinburgh Film Festival, 1972.

________. *In a Year of 13 Moons.* Trans. Joyce Rheuban. *October* 21 (Summer 1982).

Fehrenbach, Heide. *Cinema in Democratizing Germany. The Reconstruction of Mass Culture and National Identity in the West, 1945–1960.* Rutgers University, 1990. Unpublished dissertation.

________. "The Fight for the Christian West: German Film Control, the Churches, and the Reconstruction of Civil Society in the Early Bonn Republic." *German Studies Review* 14.1 (February 1991).

Feuchtwanger, Lion. *Jud Süß. Schauspiel in drei Akten.* Munich: Georg Müller, 1918.

________. *Jud Süß.* Munich: Drei Masken Verlag, 1925.

"Film and Feminism in Germany Today." Special Section in *Jump Cut* 27 (1982)

Fischetti, Renate "Écriture Féminine in the New German Cinema: Ulrike Ottinger's *Portrait of a Woman Drinker.*" *Women in German Yearbook* 4 (1988).

________. *Das neue Kino – Filme von Frauen. Acht Porträts von Deutschen Regisseurinnen.* tende: Dülmen–Hiddingsel, 1992.

Fisk, Otis H. *Germany's Constitutions of 1871 and 1919.* Cincinnati: Court Index, 1924.

Fontane, Theodor. *Effi Briest.* Trans. Douglas Parmee. Middlesex: Penguin, 1967.

Foucault, Michel. *This is not a Pipe.* Trans. James Harkness. Berkeley: Univ. of California, 1983.

Franck, Barbara. *Ich schaue in den Spiegel und sehe meine Mutter.* Hamburg: Hoffmann und Campe, 1979.

Franklin, James. *New German Cinema.* Boston: Twayne, 1983.

Frenzel, Elisabeth, *Stoffe der Weltliteratur: ein Lexikon dichtungsgeschichtlicher Längsschnitte,* 2nd ed. Stuttgart: Kröner, 1963.

Freud, Sigmund. "The Psycho-Analytic View of Psychogenic Disturbance of Vision (1910)." In *The Standard Edition of the Complete Psychological Works of Sigmund Freud,* vol. XI, ed. James Strachey. London Hogarth, 1964.

Frevert, Ute. *Women in German History. From Bourgeois Emancipation to Sexual Liberation.* Providence/Oxford: Berg, 1989.

Frieden, Sandra. *Autobiography: Self Into Form. German Language Autobiographical Writings of the 1970s.* Frankfurt/M.: Lang, 1983.

Friedländer, Saul. *Reflections of Nazism: An Essay on Kitsch and Death.* New York: Harper and Row, 1985.

Friedman, Régine Mihal. *L'image et son juif.* Paris: Payot, 1983.

Fromm, Erich. *The Anatomy of Human Destructiveness.* New York: Holt, Rinehart and Winston, 1973.

"German Film Women." *Jump Cut* 29 (1984).

"Germany's Danse Macabre." *New German Critique* 12 (Fall 1977).

Giese, Fritz. *Girlkultur. Vergleiche zwischen amerikanischem und europäischem Lebensgefühl*. Munich: Delphin-Verlag, 1920.

Gleber, Anke. "Das Fräulein von Tellheim: Die ideologische Funktion der Frau in der nationalsozialistischen Lessing-Adaption." *German Quarterly* 59 (1986).

Gledhill, Christine. "The Melodramatic Field: An Investigation." In *Home is Where the Heart is: Studies in Melodrama and the Women's Film,* ed. Christine Gledhill. London: BFI, 1987.

Glucksmann, André. "Der alte und der neue Faschismus." In *Neuer Faschismus, Neue Demokratie,* ed. Michel Foucault. Berlin: Wagenbach Verlag, 1972.

Grafe, Frieda, and Enno Patalas. *Im Off. Filmartikel.* Munich: Hanser, 1977.

Gransow, Volker. *Kulturpolitik in der DDR.* Berlin: Volker Spiess, 1975.

Greer, Germaine. *Sex and Destiny: The Politics of Human Fertility.* New York: Harper and Row, 1984.

Grimm, Jacob, and Wilhelm Grimm. "The Twelve Brothers." In *Grimm's Tales for Young and Old,* trans. Ralph Manheim. New York: Doubleday, 1983.

Grunberger, Bela. *Narcissim: Psychoanalytic Essays.* Trans. Joyce S. Diamanti. New York: International Univ.Press, 1979.

H., F. "Die Männer dieser Generation." *Filmreport* 5–6 (1976).

Habermas, Jürgen. "Modernity: An Incomplete Project." In *The Anti-Aesthetic: Essays on Postmodern Culture,* ed. Hal Foster. Port Townsend, WA: Bay, 1983.

Hake, Sabine."Gold, Love, and Adventure: Postmodern Piracy of *Madame X.*" *Discourse* 11 (Winter 1988).

Hamilton, Edith. *Mythology.* Boston: Little, Brown, 1942.

Hamon, Philippe. "Pour un statut sémiotique du personnage." In *Poétique du récit.* Paris: Seuil, 1977.

Hansen, Miriam. "Cooperative Auteur Cinema and Oppositional Public Sphere." *New German Critique* 24–25 (Fall/Winter 1981–82).

________. "Silent Cinema: Whose Public Sphere?" *New German Critique* 29 (Spring/Summer 1983).

________. "Visual Pleasure, Fetishism, and the Problem of Feminine/Feminist Discourse: Ulrike Ottinger's *Ticket of No Return.*" *New German Critique* 31 (Winter 1984).

________. "Messages in a Bottle?" *Screen* 28.2 (1987).

Harlan, Veit. *Im Schatten meiner Filme. Autobiographie.* Gütersloh, 1966.

Harlan, Veit, and Werner Krauß. *Das Schauspiel meines Lebens, einem Freund erzählt.* Ed. Hans Weigel. Stuttgart, 1958.

Harrigan, Renny. "The German Women's Movement and Ours." *Jump Cut* 27 (1982).

Harris, Adrienne and Robert Sklar. "Marianne and Juliane." *Cinéaste* 12.3 (1983).

Haskell, Molly. *From Reverence to Rape.* New York: Penguin, 1974.

Hauff, Wilhelm. "Jud Süß." In *Gesammelte Werke.* Leipzig: Bonn Verlag, 1907.

Hausen, Karin. "Mother's Day in the Weimar Republic." Trans. Miriam Frank with Erika Busse Grossmann. Ed. Marion Kaplan with Ellen Weinstock. In *When Biology Became Destiny: Women in Weimar and Nazi Germany,* ed. Renate Bridenthal, Atina Grossmann, and Marion Kaplan. New York: Monthly Review, 1984.

Heath, Stephen. "Narrative Space." In *Questions of Cinema.* Bloomington: Univ. of Indiana Press, 1981. Also in *Narrative, Apparatus, Ideology,* ed. Philip Rosen. New York: Columbia Univ. Press, 1986.

Hiller, Eva. "mütter und töchter: zu 'deutschland, bleiche mutter,' (helma sanders-brahms), 'hungerjahre' (jutta brückner), 'daughter rite' (michelle citron)." *Frauen und Film* 24 (1980).

Hitler, Adolf. *Mein Kampf.* Munich: Zentralverlag der NSDAP, 1927.

Hippler, Fritz. *Betrachtungen zum Filmschaffen.* Berlin: Max Hesse Verlag, 1942.

________. *Die Verstrickung.* Düsseldorf: Verlag Mehrwissen, 1982.

Hirdina, Karin. "Der Kunstbegriff der Avant-garde." *Weimarer Beiträge* 32 (1986).

Hollstein, Dorothea. *"Jud Süß" und die Deutschen. Antisemitisches Vorurteil im nationalsozialistischen Spielfilm. Materialien.* Frankfurt/M. and Bern: Ullstein, 1983.

Horkheimer, Max, and Theodor W. Adorno. "Excursus II: Juliette or Enlightenment and Morality." In *Dialectic of Enlightenment* [1944], trans. John Cumming. New York: Continuum, 1987.

Huillet, Danièle. "Das Feuer im Innern des Berges." Interview with Helge Heberle and Monika Funke Stern. *Frauen und Film* 32 (June 1982).

Hull, David Stewart. *Film in the Third Reich,* Berkeley: Univ. of California Press, 1969. Also available in the more recent edition: New York: Simon and Schuster, 1973.

Hutcheon, Linda. *A Poetics of Postmodernism: History, Theory, Fiction.* London: Routledge, 1988.

Huyssen, Andreas. "Technology and Sexuality in Fritz Lang's Metropolis." *New German Critique* 24–25 (Fall/Winter 1981–82).

________. "Mass Culture as Woman: Modernism's Other." In *Studies in Entertainment. Critical Approaches to Mass Culture,* ed. Tania Modleski. Bloomington: Indiana University Press, 1989.

Hyams, Barbara. "Is the Apolitical Woman at Peace?: A Reading of the Fairy Tale in *Germany, Pale Mother.*" *Wide Angle* 10.3 (1988).

Irigaray, Luce. "Demystifications." In *New French Feminisms,* ed. Elaine Marks and Isabelle Courtivron. New York: Schocken, 1980.

Iser, Wolfgang. "Die Apellstruktur des Textes." In *Rezeptionsästhetik,* ed. Rainer Warning. Munich: Wilhelm Fink, 1975.

________. "Indeterminacy and the Reader's Response in Prose Fiction." In *Aspects of Narrative,* ed. J. Hillis Miller. New York: Columbia Univ. Press, 1971.

Jacobs, Monica. "Civil Rights and Women's Rights in the Federal Republic of Germany Today." *New German Critique* 13 (Winter 1978).

Jansen, Peter W. "Exil würde ich noch nicht sagen." *Cinema* (Zurich) 2 (1978).

Johnson, Catherine. "The Imaginary & *The Bitter Tears of Petra von Kant.*" *Wide Angle* 3 (1980).

Johnston, Claire. "Women's Cinema as Counter-Cinema," In *Notes on Women's Cinema..*

________, ed. *Notes on Women's Cinema.* London: Society for Education in Film and Television, 1973.

Johnston, Sheila. "The German Sisters." *Films & Filming* 334 (July 1982).

________. "A Star is Born: Fassbinder and the New German Cinema." *New German Critique* 24–25 (Fall/Winter 1981–82).

Jürschik, Rudolf. "Erkundungen. Filmbilder – Heldentypus – Alltag." *Film und Fernsehen* 4 (1981).

________. "Streitbare Spielfilme – sozialistisches Lebensgefühl," pt. 1. *Film und Fernsehen* 9 (1979); pt. 2. *Film und Fernsehen* 11 (1979).

Kaes, Anton. *From Hitler to Heimat: The Return of History as Film*. Cambridge: Harvard Univ. Press, 1989.

Kafka, Franz. *Amerika*. Frankfurt: Fischer, 1973.

________. "The Judgement." In *The Basic Kafka*. Intro. Erich Heller. New York: Washington Square, 1979.

________. *Tagebücher 1910–1923*. New York: Schocken, 1949.

Kann, Robert A. *A History of the Habsburg Empire 1526–1918*. Los Angeles: Univ. of California Press, 1974.

Kaplan, E. Ann. *Women and Film: Both Sides of the Camera*. London and New York: Methuen, 1983.

________. "Discourses of Terrorism, Feminism, and the Family in von Trotta's *Marianne and Juliane*." *Persistence of Vision* 2 (Fall 1985).

________. "The Search for the Mother/Land in Sanders-Brahms's *Germany, Pale Mother*." In *German Film and Literature: Adaptations and Transformations*, ed. Eric Rentschler. New York: Methuen, 1986.

Karesek, Helmuth. "Niemandsland Amerika." *Der Spiegel* 38 (27 Feb. 1984).

________. "In kitschigem Rosa," *Der Spiegel* 15 (7 April 1986).

Katz, Jonathan. *Gay American History*. New York: Avon, 1976.

Kay, Karyn. "Part-Time Work of a Domestic Slave, or Putting the Screws to Screwball Comedy." In *Women and the Cinema*, ed. Karyn Kay and Gerald Peary. New York: E.P. Dutton, 1978.

Kiernan, Joanna. "Films by Valie Export." *Millennium* 16, 17, 18 (Fall, Winter 1986–87).

Klein, Michael. "Peter Handke: *Die linkshändige Frau*: Fiktion eines Märchens." In *Studien zur Literatur des 19. und 20. Jahrhunderts in Österreich*. Ed. Johann Holzner, Michael Klein and Wolfgang Wiesmüller. Innsbruck: Kowatsch, 1981.

Koch, Gertrud. "Der höhere Befehl der Frau ist ihr niederer Instinkt. Frauenhaß und Männer-Mythos in Filmen über Preußen." In *Preussen im Film*, ed. Axel Marquardt and Heinz Rathsack. Reinbek: Rowohlt, 1981.

________. "Why Women Go to the Movies." *Jump Cut* 27 (1982).

________. "Die Internationale tanzt," *Konkret* 4 (1984).

________. "Exchanging the Gaze: Revisioning Feminist Film Theory." *New German Critique* 34 (Winter 1985).

Knode, Helen. "At long last, love: Wim Wenders." *East Village Eye* (November 1984).

Kokula, Ilse. "Die urnischen Damen treffen sich vielfach in Konditoreien." *Courage* 7 (July 1980).

Koonz, Claudia. *Mothers in the Fatherland: Women, the Family and Nazi Politics*. New York: St. Martin's, 1987.

Kosta, Barbara. "*Deutschland, bleiche Mutter*: An addendum to history." Berkeley, Univ. of California, 1983. Unpublished essay.

Kracauer, Siegfried. *Schriften*. Ed. Karsten Witte. Frankfurt/M.: Suhrkamp, 1971.

________. *From Caligari to Hitler.* Princeton: Princeton Univ. Press, 1947 and 1974.

Kraushaar, Wolfgang. "Notizen zu einer Chronologie der Studentenbewegung." In *Was wir wurden, was wir wollten,* by Peter Mosler. Reinbek: Rowohlt, 1977.

Kuhn, Anna K. "Rainer Werner Fassbinder: The Alienated Vision." In *New German Filmmakers: From Oberhausen Through the 1970s,* ed. Klaus Phillips. New York: Ungar, 1984.

Kuhn, Annette. *Women's Pictures.* London: Routledge and Keagan Paul, 1982.

________, ed. *Frauen in der deutschen Nachkriegszeit. Frauenarbeit. 1945–1949. Quellen und Materialien,* vol. 1. Düsseldorf: Pädagogischer Verlag Schwann–Bagel, 1984.

________, ed. *Frauen in der deutschen Nachkriegszeit. Frauenpolitik. 1945–1949. Quellen und Materialien,* vol. 2. Düsseldorf: Pädagogischer Verlag Schwann–Bagel, 1986.

Lacan, Jacques. *Le séminaire.* Paris: Seuil, 1973.

________. *Feminine Sexuality.* Ed. Juliet Mitchell and Jacqueline Rose. New York: Norton, 1982.

Lachman, Edward, Peter Lehman, and Robin Wood. "Wim Wenders: An Interview." *Wide Angle* 2 (1976).

Langer, Ingrid. "Die Mohrinnen hatten ihre Schuldigkeit getan: Staatlich-moralische Aufrüstung der Familien." In *Die fünfziger Jahre,* ed. Dieter Bänsch. Tübingen: Günter Narr, 1985.

Laplanche, Jean and J. B. Pontalis. *The Language of Psycho-Analysis.* Trans. Donald Nicholson-Smith. New York: Norton, 1973.

Leiser, Erwin. *Nazi Cinema.* New York: Macmillan, 1974.

Lemke, Christiane. "Social Change and Women's Issues in the GDR: Problems of Leadership Positions." In *Studies in GDR Culture and Society* 2. Washington, D.C.: Univ. Press of America, 1982.

Lennox, Sara. "Women in Brecht's Works." *New German Critique* 14 (1978).

Lenssen, Claudia. "When love goes right, nothing goes wrong. . . ." *Frauen und Film* 12 (1977).

________. "Mit glasigem Blick." *Frauen und Film* 22 (1979).

________. "Die schwere Arbeit der Erinnerung." *Frauen und Film* 29 (1981).

Lenssen, Claudia, Helen Fehervary and Judith Mayne. "From Hitler to Hepburn: A Discussion of Women's Film Production and Reception." *New German Critique* 24–25 (Fall/Winter 1981–82).

Lesage, Julia. "Feminist Film Criticism: Theory and Practice." *Women and Film* 5/6 (1974).

Lenz, Ilse. "Die öde Wildnis einer Schminkerin." *Frauen und Film* 22 (1979).

Limmer, Wolfgang. *Rainer Werner Fassbinder: Filmemacher.* Reinbek bei Hamburg: Rowohlt, 1981.

Linhart, Paula. "Zur Praxis des Filmjugendschutzes." In *Jugend–Film-Fernsehen* 3.4 (1959).

Longfellow, Brenda. "Sex/Textual Politics: Tracing the Imaginary in the Films of Valie Export." *Borderlines* (Winter 1985–1986).

Love, Myra. "Christa Wolf and Feminism: Breaking the Patriarchal Connection." *New German Critique* 16 (Winter 1979).

Luft, Herbert G. "G. W. Pabst: His Films and His Life Mirror the Tumult of 20th Century Europe." *Films in Review* 15.2 (February 1964).

Lukács, Georg. "The Marxism of Rosa Luxemburg." In *History and Class Consciousness*, trans. Rodney Livingston. Cambridge: MIT, 1972.

Lukasz, Gudrun, and Christel Strobel, eds. *Der Frauenfilm*. Munich: Heyne Verlag, 1985.

Luxemburg, Rosa. "The Russian Revolution." In *The Russian Revolution: Leninism or Marxism?*, trans. Bertram D. Wolfe. Ann Arbor: Univ. of Michigan Press, 1961.

________. *Selected Political Writings*. Ed. Dick Howard. New York: Monthly Review, 1971.

________. *Briefe an Leon Jogiches*. Trans. Mechthild Fricke Hochfield and Barbara Hoffmann. Frankfurt/M.: Europäische Verlagsanstalt, 1971.

________. *Comrade and Lover: Rosa Luxemburg's Letters to Leo Jogiches*. Translated and ed. Elzbieta Ettinger. Cambridge: MIT, 1981.

Maaß, Joachim. "Film *Die Beunruhigung*." *Neue Berliner Illustrierte* 7 (1982).

________. "Frauenrollen in DEFA-Filmen." *Neue Berliner Illustrierte* 37 (1982).

Maetzig, Kurt, Konrad Wolf, Lothar Warneke and Ruth Herlinghaus. "Discussion." *Film und Fernsehen* 7 (1980).

Mann, Erika and Klaus Mann. *Escape to Life*. Boston: Houghton Mifflin, 1939.

Manvell, Roger, and Heinrich Fraenkel. *The German Cinema*. New York: Praeger, 1971.

Marcuse, Herbert. *Eros and Civilization*. New York: Vintage, 1962.

Marks, Elaine. "Lesbian Intertextuality." In *Homosexualities and French Literature*, ed. George Stambolian and Elaine Marks. Ithaca, NY: Cornell Univ. Press, 1979.

Mason, Tim. "Women in Germany, 1925–1940: Family, Welfare and Work. Part II." *History Workshop* 2 (1976).

Masson, Alain, and Hubert Niogret. "Entretien avec Wim Wenders." *Positif* (October 1977).

May, Rollo. *The Meaning of Anxiety*. New York: Norton, 1977.

Mayne, Judith. "Fassbinder and Spectatorship." *New German Critique* 12 (Fall 1977).

________. "Female Narration, Women's Cinema: Helke Sander's *The*

All-Around Reduced Personality – REDUPERS." *New German Critique* 24–25 (Fall/Winter 1981–82).

McCormick, Richard W.. "The Politics of the Personal: West German Literature and Cinema in the Wake of the Student Movement" Ph.D. diss., Univ. of California, Berkeley, 1986.

________. *Politics of the Self: Feminism and the Postmodern in West German Literature and Film.* Princeton: Princeton Univ. Press, 1991.

McGarry, Eileen. "Documentary, Realism and Women's Cinema." *Women & Film* 2.7 (1975).

McRobbie, Angela. Introduction to "Interview with Ulrike Ottinger," by Erica Carter. Trans. Martin Chalmers. *Screen* 4 (Winter/Spring 1982).

Metz, Christian "The Imaginary Signifier." Trans. Ben Brewster, *Screen* 16.2 (Summer 1975).

________. *Le signifiant imaginaire.* Paris: 10/18 UGE, 1977.

________. *Psychoanalysis and the Cinema: The Imaginary Signifier.* Bloomington: Indiana Univ. Press, 1982.

________. "Story/Discourse: Notes on Two Kinds of Voyeurisms." In *Movies and Methods, Vol. II: An Anthology,* ed. Bill Nichols. Berkeley: Univ. of California Press, 1985.

Meyer, Sibylle and Eva Schulze. *Von Liebe sprach damals keiner. Familienalltag in der Nachkriegszeit.* Munich: C.H. Beck, 1985.

Mihan, Hans-Rainer. "Sabine, Sunny, Nina und der Zuschauer. Gedanken zum Gegenwartsspielfilm der DEFA." *Film und Fernsehen* 8 (1982).

Mittman, Elizabeth. "History and Subjectivity: Differences in German and French Feminisms." University of Minnesota, 1986. Unpublished essay.

Möhrmann, Renate. *Die Frau mit der Kamera: Filmemacherinnen in der Bundesrepublik Deutschland. Situation, Perspektiven. 10 exemplarische Lebensläufe.* Munich: Hanser, 1980.

________."Ich sehe was, was du nicht siehst . . . Überlegungen zu den Darstellungs- und Wahrnehmungsformen weiblicher Kinofiguren im westdeutschen Frauenfilm." Univ. of Texas, Austin. March, 1986. Unpublished essay.

Moeller, A.J.K. "The Woman as Survivor: The Development of the Female Figure in Heinrich Böll's Fiction." *DAI* 40A, no. 3 (1979).

Moeller, H-B. "West German Women's Cinema: The Case of Margarethe von Trotta." *Film Criticism* 9.2 (Winter 1984–85).

Moeller, Robert. "Protecting Mother's Work: From Production to Reproduction in Postwar West Germany." *Journal of Social History* 22.3 (Spring 1989).

Mommsen, Hans. "Suche nach der 'verlorenen Geschichte'?" *Historikerstreit. Die Dokumentation der Kontroverse um die Einzigartigkeit der nationalsozialistischen Judenvernichtung.* Munich: Piper, 1987.

Monaco, James. *How to Read a Film.* New York: Oxford, 1981.

Monaghan, Patricia. *The Book of Goddesses and Heroines.* New York: Dutton, 1984.

Moreck, Curt. *Sittengeschichte des Kinos.* Dresden: Paul Aretz, 1926.

Morgner, Irmtraud. *Amanda. Ein Hexenroman.* Darmstadt und Neuwied: Luchterhand, 1983.

Mosse, George L. *Nazi Culture.* New York: Schocken, 1981.

Mouton, Jan. "The Absent Mother Makes an Appearance in the Films of West German Women Directors." *Women in German Yearbook* 4 (1988).

Müller, André. "Das Kino könnte der Engel sein." *Der Spiegel* (19 October 1987).

Mueller, Roswitha. Interview with Ulrike Ottinger, *Discourse* 4 (1981/82).

________. "The Uncanny in the Eyes of a Woman: Valie Export's *Invisible Adversaries.*" *SubStance* 37/38 (1983).

________. "The Mirror and the Vamp." *New German Critique* 34 (Winter 1985).

Münzberg, Olav. "Schaudern vor der 'bleichen Mutter.'" *Medium* 10 (1980).

Mulvey, Laura. "Feminism, Film and the Avant-Garde." *Framework* 10 (Spring 1979).

________. "Visual Pleasure and Narrative Cinema." *Screen* 16.3 (Autumn 1975). Reprinted in *Women and the Cinema,* ed. Karyn Day and Gerald Peary. New York: Dutton, 1977; and also reprinted in *Film Theory and Criticism,* 3rd. ed., ed. Gerald Mast and Marshall Cohen, New York: Oxford Univ. Press, 1985.

Nettl, J.P. *Rosa Luxemburg.* London: Oxford Univ. Press, 1966.

Netzeband, Günter. Interview with Hans Dieter Mäde. *Film und Fernsehen* 5 (1978).

Neus, Chrisel. *Die Kopfgeburten der Arbeiterbewegung oder Die Genossin Luxemburg bringt alles durcheinander.* Hamburg/Zurich: Rasch und Rühring, 1985.

New German Critique 40 (Winter 1987). "Special Issue on Weimar Film Theory."

Newton, Judith. "History as Usual? Feminism and the 'New Historicism,'" in *The New Historicism,* ed. H. Aram Veeser. New York: Routledge, 1989.

Nichols, Bill. Introduction to "Visual Pleasure and Narrative Cinema," by Laura Mulvey. In *Movies and Methods: An Anthology,* vol.II, ed. Bill Nichols. Berkeley: Univ. of California, 1985.

Owens, Craig. "The Discourse of Others: Feminists and Postmodernism." In *The Anti- Aesthetic,* ed. Hal Foster. Port Townsend, WA: Bay, 1983.

Ottinger, Ulrike. *Madame X – eine absolute Herrscherin. Drehbuch.* Berlin/ Basel: Stroemfeld/ Roter Stern, 1979.

________. "Der Zwang zum Genrekino. Von der Gefährdung des Autoren-Kinos." *Courage* 4 (1983).

Pardo, Herbert, and Siegfried Schiffner. *"Jud Süß:" Historisches und juristisches Material zum Fall Veit Harlan.* Hamburg: Auerbach, 1949.

Penley, Constance. *The Future of an Illusion: Film, Feminism, and Psychoanalysis.* Minneapolis: Univ. of Minnesota Press, 1989.

Perlmutter, Ruth. "Visible Narrative, Visible Woman: A Study of Under-narratives." *Millenium Film Journal* (Spring 1980).

Petro, Patrice. *Joyless Streets: Women and Melodramatic Representation in Weimar Germany.* Princeton: Princeton Univ. Press, 1989.

Pflaum, Hans Günther and Hans Helmut Prinzler. *Cinema in the Federal Republic of Germany.* Bonn: Internationes, 1983.

Phillips, Klaus, ed. *New German Filmmakers. From Oberhausen Through the 1970s.* New York: Ungar, 1984.

Piccone, Paul. "The Crisis of One-Dimensionality." *Telos* 35 (Spring 1978).

Pipolo, Tony. "Bewitched by the Holy Whore." *October* 21 (Summer 1982).

Plat, Wolfgang. *Die Familie in der DDR.* Frankfurt/M: S. Fischer, 1972.

Plummer, Thomas G., ed. *Film and Politics in the Weimar Republic.* Minneapolis: Univ. of Minnesota Press, 1982.

Pore, Renate. *A Conflict of Interest: Women in German Social Democracy, 1919–1933.* Westport, CT: Greenwood, 1981.

Potamkin, Harry Alan. "Pabst and the Social Film." *Hound and Horn* 6.2 (Jan.-Mar. 1933).

Prammer, Anita. *Valie Export. Eine Multi-mediale Künstlerin.* Frauenforschung, vol. 7. Vienna: Wiener Frauenverlag, 1988.

Prokop, Ulrike. *Weiblicher Lebenszusammenhang.* Frankfurt/M.: Suhrkamp, 1976.

Ramm, Klaus. *Reduktion als Erzählprinzip bei Kafka.* Frankfurt/M.: Athenaum, 1971.

Rawlinson, Arthur-Richard. *Scenario and dialogues of "Jew Süß" from the novel by L. Feuchtwanger.* London: Methuen, 1935.

Regel, Helmut. "Historische Stoffe als Propagandaträger." In *Der Spielfilm im III. Reich.* Oberhausen, 1966.

Reich, Wilhelm. *The Function of the Orgasm.* New York: Orgone Institute, 1942.

Reich, Wilhelm. *Mass Psychology of Fascism.* New York: Orgone Institute, 1946.

Reichwaldau, Franz. "Das ideale Kino." *Die Weltbühne.* 16.19 (1920).

Reitlinger, Gerald. *The Final Solution.* London, 1971.

Rentmeister, Cillie. "Frauen, Körper, Kunst: Mikrophysik der patriarchalischen Macht." *Ästhetik und Kommunikation* 37 (1979).

Rentschler, Eric. "American Friends and the New German Cinema." *New German Critique* 24–25 (Fall/Winter 1981–82).

________. *West German Film in the Course of Time.* Bedford Hills, NY: Redgrave, 1984.

________, ed. *West German Filmmakers on Film: Visions and Voices.* New York: Holmes and Meier, 1988.

Reschke, Karin. "Frau Ottingers (Kunst)gewerbe." *Frauen und Film* 22 (1979).

Rheuban, Joyce, ed. *The Marriage of Maria Braun.* New Brunswick, NJ: Rutgers Univ. Press, 1986.

Rich, Adrienne. *On Lies, Secrets and Silence.* New York: Norton, 1979.

Rich, B. Ruby. "The Crisis Of Naming in Feminist Film Criticism." *Jump Cut* 19 (December 1978)

_______. "In the Name of Feminist Film Criticism." *Heresies* 9 (Spring 1980). Also reprinted in *Movies and Methods,* ed. Bill Nichols. Berkeley: Univ. of California Press, 1985.

_______. "*Mädchen in Uniform*: From Repressive Tolerance to Erotic Liberation." *Jump Cut* 24–25 (1981).

_______. "She Says, He Says: The Power of the Narrator in Modernist Film Politics." *Discourse* 6 (1983).

Rotha, Paul. *The Film Till Now.* 2d ed. New York: Funk and Wagnalls, 1951.

Rother, Hans-Jörg. "Kino neuer Ideen im Meinungsstreit. Gedanken zu DEFA-Filmen aus den Jahren 1979/80." *Prisma. Kino- und Fernseh-Almanach* 12 (1981).

Rubin, Gayle. "The Traffic in Women: Notes On the 'Political Economy' of Sex." In *Toward Anthropology of Women,* ed. Rayna R. Reiter. New York: Monthly Review, 1975.

Ruhl, Klaus-Jörg, ed. *Frauen in der Nachkriegszeit, 1945–1963. Dokumente.* Munich: Deutscher Taschenbuch Verlag, 1988.

Ruppelt, Georg. *Schiller im nationalsozialistischen Deutschland: Der Versuch einer Gleichschaltung.* Stuttgart: Metzler, 1979.

Russo, Vito. *The Celluloid Closet: Homosexuality in the Movies.* New York: Harper and Row/Colophon, 1981.

Said, Edward. *Orientalism.* New York: Random House, 1979.

Sander, Helke. "Sexism in den Massenmedien." *Frauen und Film* 1 (1974).

_______. "Feminism and Film." Trans. Ramona Curry. *Jump Cut* 27 (1982).

Sander, Helke, and Ula Stöckl. "Die Herren machen das selber, daß ihnen die arme Frau Feind wird: Ablehnungsgeschichten." *Frauen und Film* 23 (April 1980).

Sanders, Marion K. *Dorothy Thompson: A Legend in Her Time.* Boston: Houghton Mifflin, 1973.

Sanders-Brahms, Helma. *Deutschland, bleiche Mutter. Film-Erzählung.* Reinbek bei Hamburg: Rowohlt, 1980.

Sandford, John. *The New German Cinema.* New York: DeCapo, 1980.

Schanze, Helmut. "*Fontane Effi Briest*: Bemerkungen zu einem Drehbuch von Rainer Werner Fassbinder." In *Literatur in den Massenmedien – Demontage von Dichtung?,* ed. Friedrich Knilli, Knut Hickethier, and Wolf Dieter Lützen. Munich and Vienna: Carl Hanser Verlag, 1976.

Schenk, Ralph. "Zwischen Tag und Traum." *Film und Fernsehen* 13 (1985).

Schlüpmann, Heide, and Karola Gramann. "Momente erotischer Utopie – ästhetisierte Verdrängung: Zu *Mädchen in Uniform* and *Anna und Elisabeth*." *Frauen und Film* 28 (1981).

Schlüpmann, Heide, and Karola Gramann. *Hungerjahre, medienpraktisch.* Ed. Gemeinschaftswerk der Evangelischen Publizistik, 1983.

Schlungbaum, Barbara, and Claudia Hoff. "Eindruck – Ausdruck. Tabea talks." *Frauen und Film* 26 (1980).

Schneider, Michael. "Väter und Söhne, posthum. Das beschädigte Verhältnis zweier Generationen." In *Den Kopf verkehrt aufgesetzt* . Darmstadt: Luchterhand, 1981.

_______. "Fathers and Sons Retrospectively: The Damaged Relationship between Two Generations." Trans. Jamie Owen Daniel. *New German Critique* 31 (1984).

Scholar, Nancy. "*Mädchen in Uniform.*" In *Sexual Stratagems: The World of Women in Film,* ed. Patricia Erens. New York: Horizon, 1979.

Scholar, Nancy and Sharon Smith. *Women Who Make Movies.* New York: Hopkinson and Blake, 1975.

Schröder-Krassnow, Sabine. "The Changing View of Abortion: A Study of Friedrich Wolf's *Cyankali* and Arnold Zweig's *Junge Frau von 1914.*" *Studies in Twentieth Century Literature* 1 (1981).

Schütte, Wolfram. "Arbeit, Gerechtigkeit, Liebe." *Frankfurter Rundschau* (24 Feb. 1984).

Schulte-Sasse, Linda. "The Never Was as History." Ph. D. diss., Univ. of Minnesota, 1985.

Schuster, Peter-Klaus. *Theodor Fontane: Effi Briest—Ein Leben nach christlichen Bildern.* Studien zur deutschen Literatur, vol. 55. Tübingen: Max Niemeyer, 1979.

Seiter, Ellen. "The Political is Personal: Margarethe von Trotta's *Marianne and Juliane.*" *Journal of Film and Video* 37 (Spring 1985).

_______ "Women's History, Women's Melodrama: *Deutschland, bleiche Mutter.*" *German Quarterly* 59 (1986).

Seldon, Caroline. "Lesbians and Film: Some Thoughts." In *Gays and Film,* ed. Richard Dyer. London: British Film Institute, 1977.

Shaffer, Harry G. *Women in the Two Germanies.* New York: Pergamon, 1981.

Sichtermann, Barbara. "Über Schönheit, Demokratie und Tod." *Ästhetik und Kommunikation : Sex und Lust* 7 (1981).

Silberman, Marc. "Cine-Feminists in West Berlin." *Quarterly Review of Film Studies* 5.2 (Spring 1981).

_______. An interview with Jutta Brückner, Cristina Perincioli and Helga Reidemeister, "Conversing together finally." *Jump Cut* 27 (July 1982).

_______. "The Ideology of Re-Presenting the Classics: Filming *Der Zer-*

brochene Krug in the Third Reich." *German Quarterly* 57 (1984).

________. "Ula Stöckl: How Women See Themselves." In *New German Filmmakers From Oberhausen Through the 1970s*, ed. Klaus Phillips. New York: Ungar, 1984.

Silverman, Kaja. *The Subject of Semiotics* . New York: Oxford Univ. Press, 1983.

________. "Helke Sander and the Will to Change." *Discourse* 6 (1983).

________. "Dis-Embodying the Female Voice." In *Re-Vision. Essays in Feminist Film Criticism*, ed. Mary Ann Doane et al. Frederick, MD: Univ. Publications of America, 1984.

Sontag, Susan. "Notes on 'Camp.'" In *Against Interpretation*. New York: Farrar, Strauss and Giroux, 1967.

Snitow, Ann Barr. "The Front Line: Notes on Sex in Novels by Women, 1969–1979." In *Women: Sex and Sexuality*, ed. Catherine R. Stimpson and Ethel Spector Person. Chicago: Univ. of Chicago Press, 1980.

"*Solo Sunny*: Kritische Diskussion." *Film und Fernsehen* 6 (1980).

Sparrow, Norbert. "'*I let the Audience Feel and Think'* – An Interview with Rainer Werner Fassbinder." *Cineaste* 8 (1977).

Steakley, James D. *The Homosexual Emancipation Movement in Germany*. New York: Arno, 1975.

Steinborn, Bion and Carola Hilmes. "'Frieden' hat für uns Deutsche einen amerikanischen Geschmack." Reihe: Der unbekannte deutsche Film. *Filmfaust* 39 (1984).

Stephan, Cora. "Der widerspenstigen Zähmung." *Der Spiegel* 15 (7 April1986).

Stern, Selma. *Jud Süß, ein Beitrag zur deutschen und zur jüdischen Geschichte*. Berlin: Akademie Verlag, 1929.

Stöckl, Ula. "Die herren machen das selber, daß ihnen die arme frau feind wird ablehnungsgeschichten." *Frauen und Film* 23 (1980).

________. "The Medea Myth in Contemporary Cinema." *Film Criticism* 10.1 (Fall 1985).

Strempel, Gesine. "Nicht einfach nur klauen mit einem Tonband und einem Fotoapparat. Gespräch mit der Filmemacherin Ulrike Ottinger." *Courage* 3 (1979).

Studlar, Gaylyn. "Visual Pleasure and the Masochistic Aesthetic." *Journal of Film and Video* 37 (Spring 1985).

Taubin, Amy. "Von Trotta, Wanting it All," *The Voice* (12 May 1987).

Thalmann, Rita. *Frausein im dritten Reich*. Karlsruhe: DOKU, 1979.

Theweleit, Klaus. *Männerphantasien*. 2 vols. Frankfurt/M.: Roter Stern, 1977–78.

Theweleit, Klaus. *Male Fantasies. Vol. 1. Women, Floods, Bodies, History*. Trans. Erica Carter and Chris Turner in collaboration with Stephen Conway. Theory of History and Literature. Vol. 22. Minneapolis: Univ. of Minnesota, 1987.

________. *Male Fantasies. Vol. 2. Male bodies: Psychoanalyzing the White Terroe.* Trans. Erica Carter and Chris Turner in collaboration with

StephenConway. Theory of History and Literature. Vol. 23. Minneapolis: University of Minnesota Press, 1989.

Thomas, Paul. "Fassbinder: The Poetry of the Inarticulate." *Film Quarterly* 30 (Winter 1976).

Thompson, E. P. "History Turns on A New Hinge." *The Nation* 29 (January 1990).

Thomsen, Christian Braad. "Interview with Fassbinder (Berlin, 1974)." In *Fassbinder*, ed. Tony Rayns. London: British Film Institute, 1976.

Thomsen, Christian Braad. "Five Interviews with Fassbinder." In *Fassbinder*, ed. Tony Rayns. London: British Film Institute, 1980.

Thurm, Brigitte. "Rückhaltlos und verletzbar." *Film und Fernsehen* 2 (1980).

Treut, Monika. "Ein Nachtrag zu Ulrike Ottinger's Film *Madame X*." *Frauen und Film* 28 (1981).

Truffaut, Francois. *Hitchcock*. London: Granada, 1978. Also available from New York: Simon and Schuster, 1984.

Todorov, Tzvetan. *The Fantastic. A Structural Approach to a Literary Genre*. Cleveland and London: Press of Case Western Reserve Univ., 1973.

Tröger, Annemarie. "Between Rape and Prostitution. Survival Strategies and Chances of Emancipation for Berlin Women after World War II," trans. Joan Reutershan. In *Women in Culture and Politics: A Century of Change*, ed. J. Friedlander, B. Wiesen Cook, et al. Bloomington: Indiana University Press, 1986.

Trotta, Margarethe von. *Die bleierne Zeit: ein Film von Margarethe von Trotta*. Ed. Hans Jürgen Weber and Ingeborg Weber. Frankfurt/M.: Fischer Taschenbuch, 1981.

Tyler, Parker. *Screening the Sexes*. New York: Holt, Rinehart and Winston, 1972.

Viertel, Salka. *The Kindness of Strangers*. New York: Holt, 1969.

Virmaux, Alain and Odette Virmaux, eds. *Colette au cinéma*. Paris: Librairie Ernest Flammarion, 1975.

Vogel, Angela. "Familie." In *Die Bundesrepublik Deutschland. Band 2: Gesellschaft*, ed. Wolfgang Benz. Frankfurt/M.: Fischer, 1985.

Waniek, Erdmann. "Beim zweiten Lesen: der Beginn von Fontanes *Effi Briest* als verdinglichtes *tableau vivant*." *German Quarterly* 55 (March 1982).

Warneke, Lothar. Interview. *Progress. Pressebulletin Kino der DDR* 2 (1982).

Weber-Kellermann, Ingeborg. *Die deutsche Familie: Versuch einer Sozialgeschichte*. Frankfurt/M.: Hanser, 1984.

Weibel, Peter and Valie Export. *Wien. Bildkompendium Wiener Aktionismus und Film*. Frankfurt/M.: Kohlkunstverlag, 1970.

Weinberg, Herman G. *The Lubitsch Touch*. New York: Dover, 1977.

Weinstock, Jane. "Sexual Difference and the Moving Image." In *Difference: On Representation and Sexuality*. New York: New Museum of Contemporary Art, 1984.

Welch, David. *Propaganda and the German Cinema, 1933–1945*. Oxford: Clarendon, 1983.

Whalen, Robert Weldon. *Bitter Wounds. German Victims of the Great War, 1914–1939.* Ithaca: Cornell University Press, 1984.

Wiegand, Wilfried. "Interview with Rainer Werner Fassbinder." In *Fassbinder,* Trans. Ruth McCormick. New York: Tanam, 1981.

Wiggerhaus, Renate. *Frauen unterm Nationalsozialismus.* Wuppertal: Hammer, 1984.

Wilde, Oscar. "Preface," *The Picture of Dorian Gray.* New York: Ward Lock, 1891.

Wilson, Elizabeth. "Psychoanalysis: Psychic Law and Order." *Feminist Review* 8 (1981).

Windmöller, Eva, and Thomas Höpker. *Leben in der DDR.* Hamburg: Gruner + Jahr, n.d.

Winsloe, Christa. *Das Mädchen Manuela: Der Roman von "Mädchen in Uniform."* Leipzig: E.P. Tal, 1933.

________. *Gestern und Heute (Ritter Nérestan): Schauspiel in 3 Akten.* Vienna: Georg Marton Verlag, 1930.

________. *Girls in Uniform: A Play in Three Acts.* Trans. Barbara Burnham. Boston: Little, Brown, 1933.

________. *The Child Manuela: The Novel of "Mädchen in Uniform."* Trans. Agnes Niel Scott. London: Chapman and Hall , 1934.

Wischnewski, Klaus et al. "Gespräch zwischen Klaus Wischnewski, Konrad Wolf und Wolfgang Kohlhaase." *Film und Fernsehen* 1 (1980).

Witte, Karsten. "Die Filmkomödie im Dritten Reich." In *Die deutsche Literatur im Dritten Reich,* ed. Horst Denkler and Karl Prümm. Stuttgart: Reclam, 1976.

________. "Dame and Dandy. Ulrike Ottinger's Filme." In *Im Kino. Texte von Sehen & Hören.* Frankfurt/M.: Fischer, 1985.

________. "How Nazi Cinema Mobilizes the Classics: Schweikart's *Das Fräulein von Barnhelm* (1940)." In *German Film and Literature: Adaptations and Transformations,* ed. Eric Rentschler. New York: Methuen, 1986.

Wolf, Christa. *The Quest for Christa T.* Trans. Christopher Middleton. New York: Delta, 1970.

________. "The Reader and the Writer." In *The Reader and the Writer: Essays, Sketches, Memories,* trans. Joan Becker. New York: International Publishers, 1977.

________. *Kein Ort Nirgends.* Darmstadt/Neuwied: Luchterhand, 1979. (English version, *No Place on Earth.* Trans. Jan van Heurck. New York: Farrar Straus Giroux, 1982.)

________. *Cassandra.* Trans. Jan van Heurck. New York: Farrar Straus Giroux, 1984.

Wolf, Dieter. "Die Kunst, miteinander zu reden. 'Bis daß der Tod euch scheidet' im Gespräch." *Film und Fernsehen* 11 (1979).

Wolf, Konrad. "Es ist etwas im Gange. Spiegel-Interview mit dem DDR-Filmregisseur Konrad Wolf." *Der Spiegel* 15 (1980).
Wolf, Renate. "Tabea Blumenschein und Ulrike Ottinger." *Zeitmagazin* 14 (25 Mar. 1977).
Wollen, Peter. "The Two Avant-gardes." *Edinburgh Magazine* 7 (1976).
Wulf, Joseph. *Theater und Film im Dritten Reich.* Gütersloh, 1964.
Zimmermann, Manfred. *Joseph Süß Oppenheimer: ein Finanzmann des 18. Jahrhunderts.* Stuttgart: Riegersche Verlagsbuchhandlung, 1874.

Notes on Contributors

Barton Byg teaches German and film at the University of Massachusetts, Amherst. He pursued graduate study at Washington University (St. Louis) and at the Free University of Berlin. In addition to writing a general survey of GDR film history, he is presently completing a book on the cinema of Danièle Huillet and Jean-Marie Straub.

Ramona Curry teaches media studies in the Department of English at the University of Illinois at Urbana-Champaign. Between earning academic degrees, she worked as program coordinator of the Goethe Institute in Chicago and made independent films. She is presently completing a book-length feminist analysis of the star image of Mae West.

Heide Fehrenbach is Assistant Professor of History at Colgate University in Hamilton, NY. She is currently engaged in research on cultural reconstruction in postwar West Germany. Her article, "A Fight for the Christian West," which examines church intervention in German film production and control during the early Adenauer period, recently appeared in *German Studies Review* (1991). That article, in conjunction with the essay in this collection, are part of a larger project entitled *Cinema in Democratizing Germany: The Reconstruction of Mass Culture and National Identity in the West, 1945-62* (University of North Carolina Press, forthcoming).

Sandra Frieden is the author of *Autobiography: Self into Form. German Language Autobiographical Writings of the 1970s* (Frankfurt: Lang, 1983), and has published articles on contemporary German literature, film, and film pedagogy. She has taught German film at the University of Houston since 1982.

Régine-Mihal Friedman was born and educated in France. She is Lecturer in the Department of Film and Television at the University of Tel-Aviv. She is the author of "L'image et son Juif: le Juif dans le Cinema Nazi," several articles on the representation of women and Jews in film, and contributions to the German feminist film journal *Frauen und Film.*

Anke Gleber is Assistant Professor of German at Princeton University, where she teaches German literature and Film Studies. She has published on Nazi cinema, Weimar culture, Heinrich Heine, and travel literature.

Sabine Hake is Associate Professor of German at the University of Pittsburgh. She is the author of *Passions and Deceptions: The Early Films of Ernst Lubitsch* (Princeton: Princeton Univ. Press, 1992). Her other work on Weimar culture includes articles on Lang, Chaplin, Sander, von Unruh, and Kracauer, and a book-length study of early German film theory.

Miriam Hansen is Professor of English and Director of the Film Studies Center at the University of Chicago as well as co-editor of *New German Critique.* Her most recent book is *Babel and Babylon: Spectatorship in American Silent Film* (Cambridge: Harvard Univ. Press, 1991). She has published on a wide variety of topics in German film history and film theory, from female moviegoing in the silent era to Alexander Kluge, and is currently writing a book on the Frankfurt School's debates on film and mass culture.

Barbara Kosta is Assistant Professor of German at the University of Arizona where she teaches courses on film and literature. She is currently working on a book on autobiographical writing and filming by contemporary women and has co-authored a first year German language textbook with Helga Kraft entitled *Auf Deutsch.*

Anna K. Kuhn is Professor of German at the University of California, Davis. Her main fields of interest are twentieth-century literature and culture, women's studies and film studies. She has published on modern German drama, GDR literature and Christa Wolf. Her work on film includes articles on Max Ophuls, Rainer Werner Fassbinder and Margarethe von Trotta.

Richard McCormick is the author of *Politics of the Self: Feminism and the Postmodern in West German Literature and Film* (Princeton: Princeton Univ. Press, 1991). He is Associate Professor in the Department of German at the University of Minnesota, where he teaches courses on German film and literature. He has published articles on West German cinema and on Weimar cinema.

Bruce Murray is Assistant Professor of German at the University of Illinois at Chicago. He is the author of *Film and the German Left in the Weimar Republic,* coauthor of *Film and Politics in the Weimar Republic,* and co-editor of *Framing the Past: The Historiography of German Cinema and Television.* His other published work includes articles on Weimar cinema, postwar German cinema, and Bertolt Brecht.

Tracy Myers received her Master's degree in Art History from Hunter College (CUNY) and is a doctoral fellow at the University of Delaware. Her areas of concentration are American art from Reconstruction to the inter-war period and German culture of the Weimar Republic. This is her first publication.

Lisa Ohm received her Ph.D from University of California Santa Barbara and is Assistant Professor at the College of St. Benedict. She has published articles on both German language and film, among them "The Filmic Adaptation of the Novel *Das Kind Manuela*" for *Neue Germanistik.*

Vibeke Rützou Petersen is Associate Professor of German and Director of Women's Studies at Drake University where she teaches film, German, and Women's Studies. She has published on sociopolitical and literary issues of West Germany, Doris Dörrie, Anna Seghers, and is currently writing a booklength study on Vicki Baum, women, and Weimar consciousness.

Joyce Rheuban is Associate Professor of Cinema Studies at LaGuardia Community College and the Graduate School of the City University of New York. She is the author of *Harry Langdon: The Comedian as Metteur-en-Scène,* editor of *The Marriage of Maria Braun: Rainer Werner Fassbinder, director* and author of essays on German and American cinema. She has translated works by R.W. Fassbinder, Alexander Kluge, and German critics on cinema and photography.

B. Ruby Rich is a cultural critic who contributes regularly to *The Village Voice, Mirabella, Sight and Sound,* and numerous other popular and scholarly journals. An Adjunct Visiting Professor (spring semesters) at the University of California, Berkeley, she recently was honored with a residency as Distinguished Visitor at the John D. and Catherine T. MacArthur Foundation in Chicago. For a decade, she served as Executive Director of the Film Program at the New York State Council on the Arts. She is currently preparing a volume of her collected essays.

Marc Silberman teaches at the University of Wisconsin-Madison in the German Department and the Communication Arts Department. He has published on twentieth-century Germany literature and on German Cinema. He is the editor of the Brecht Yearbook and is completing a manuscript on history and the German cinema.

Laurie Melissa Vogelsang is completing a dissertation on German canon formation in the eighteenth century at Yale University, where she has also worked to incorporate film into the second-year language program.

Gabriele Weinberger teaches German, Film and Women's Studies at Lenoir-Rhyne College in Hickory, North Carolina. She has taught Film and German Studies at Cornell University and does research in Film and Women's Studies.

Index